W0010521

THE FATHERS
OF THE CHURCH

A NEW TRANSLATION

THE FATHERS
OF THE CHURCH

A NEW TRANSLATION

VOLUME 72

ST. JOHN CHRYSOSTOM

ON THE INCOMPREHENSIBLE NATURE OF GOD

Translated by

PAUL W. HARKINS
Professor Emeritus
Xavier University
Cincinnati, Ohio

THE CATHOLIC UNIVERSITY OF AMERICA PRESS
Washington, D.C.

Nihil Obstat:

REVEREND HERMIGILD DRESSLER, O.F.M.
Censor Deputatus

Imprimatur:

REV. MSGR. JOHN F. DONOGHUE
Vicar General for the Archdiocese of Washington

September 2, 1982

The *nihil obstat* and *imprimatur* are official declarations that a book or pamphlet is free of doctrinal or moral error. No implication is contained therein that those who have granted the *nihil obstat* and the *imprimatur* agree with content, opinions, or statements expressed.

Library of Congress Cataloging in Publication Data

John Chrysostom, Saint, d. 407.
　On the incomprehensible nature of God.

　(Fathers of the Church; v. 72)
　Translation of: Peri akataleptou.
　September 2, 1982.
　Bibliography: p. vii-xii
　Includes indexes.
　1. God—Knowableness—Sermons.　2. Eunomianism—Sermons.
3. Sermons, Greek—Translations into English.
4. Sermons, English—Translations from Greek.
I. Harkins, Paul W. (Paul William), 1911-
II. Title.　III. Series.
BR60.F3C42　　[BR65.C43]　　270s [231]　　83-1984
ISBN 0-8132-1027-5 (pbk.)
ISBN-13: 978-0-8132-1027-8 (pbk.)

CONTENTS

SELECT BIBLIOGRAPHY

Texts and Translations

Duc, Fronton du (Fronto Ducaeus). *Ad populum Antiochenum adv. Iudaeos, De incomprehensibili Dei natura, De sanctis deque diversis eiusmodi argumentis homiliae 77* (Paris 1602 and 1609).

Savile, Henry. *S. Iohannis Chrysostomi opera omnia* 8 vols. (Eton 1612). Title actually in Greek only.

Duc, Fronton du (Fronto Ducaeus). *S. Iohannis Chrysostomi opera omnia* 12 vols. (Paris 1636–42).

Maucroix, Mr. de, trans. *Homélies ou sermons de saint Jean Chrysostome au peuple d'Antioche, augmentez en cette seconde édition des homélies sur l'incompréhensibilité de Dieu contre les Anoméens.* (Paris 1689).

Montfaucon, Bernard de. *S. Iohannis Chrysostomi opera omnia* 13 vols. (Paris 1718–38 and Venice 1734–41). Second edition by T. Fix (Paris 1834–39; reprinted by J.-P. Migne in PG 47–61; Paris 1863 [earlier printings of vol. 48: 1859]]).

Jeannin, M., trans. *Saint Jean Chrysostome Oeuvres complètes* 11 vols. (Bar-le-Duc 1863–67).

Bareille, J. *Oeuvres complètes de S. Jean Chrysostome* 12 vols. (Paris 1865–73). Montfaucon's text with French translation.

Daniélou, J. (Introduction), Malingrey, A.-M. (Texte critique et notes), Flacelière, R. (Traduction). *Jean Chrysostome sur l'incompréhensibilité de Dieu*, Vol. 1: *Homélies I–V,* SC 28 bis (Paris 1970).

Other Patristic Texts and Translations

Augustine, St. *Confessions,* trans. V. Bourke, FOTC 21 (New York 1953).

Basil, St. *Adversus Eunomium libri 5,* PG 29.498–774 (Paris n.d.).

Cyril of Jerusalem, St. *The Works of Saint Cyril of Jerusalem,* Vol. 1, trans. L.P. McCauley and A.A. Stevenson, FOTC 61 (Washington, D.C. 1969).

———— *Catecheses mystagogicae* 5, PG 33.1066–1128 (n.d.).

Epiphanius, St. *Panarion* or *Adversus haereses,* PG 41.174–1200 and PG 42.9–832 (Paris 1863).

Eunomius. *Apologia,* PG 30.835–68 (Paris 1888).

Eusebius. *Ecclesiastical History,* 2 vols. trans. K. Lake and J.E. Oulton, The Loeb Classical Library (Cambridge, Mass. 1926–32).

———— *Histoire ecclésiastique,* trans. G. Bardy, SC 31, 41, 55, 73 (Paris 1952–60).

Gregory of Nyssa, St. *Contra Eunomium,* vol. 1, ed. W. Jaeger (Leiden 1960).

———— *In Canticum Canticorum,* vol. 6, ed. W. Jaeger (Leiden 1960).

———— *In Ecclesiasten,* vol. 5, ed. W. Jaeger (Leiden 1962).

———— *The Lord's Prayer and The Beatitudes,* trans. H. Graef, ACW 18 (Westminister, Md. 1954).

Hilary of Poitiers, St. *The Trinity,* trans. S. McKenna, FOTC 25 (New York 1954).

Ignatius of Antioch, St. *The Epistles of St. Clement of Rome and St. Ignatius of Antioch*, trans. J. Kleist, ACW 1 (Westminster, Md. 1946).

Irenaeus, St. *Proof of the Apostolic Preaching*, trans. J.P. Smith, ACW 16 (Westminster, Md. 1952).

———— *Adversus haereses libri 5*, PG 7 (pars prior) 433–1118; PG 7 (pars secunda) 1119–1224 (Paris 1857).

John Chrysostom, St. *Baptismal Instructions*, trans. P.W. Harkins, ACW 31 (Westminster, Md. 1963).

———— *Discourses against Judaizing Christians*, trans. P.W. Harkins, FOTC 68 (Washington 1979).

———— *Homilies on the Gospel of St. John*, trans. Sr. Thomas Aquinas Goggin, FOTC 33 and 41 (New York 1957 and 1960).

———— *Sur la providence de Dieu*, trans. A.-M. Malingrey, SC 79 (Paris 1961).

———— *Sur l'incompréhensibilité de Dieu [De incomp. 1–5]*, introd. J. Daniélou; text and notes A.-M. Malingrey; trans. R. Flacelière, SC 28 bis (Paris 1951).

Justin Martyr, St. *The Writings of Justin Martyr*, trans. T. Falls, FOTC 6 (New York 1948).

Marius Victorinus. *Theological Treatises on the Trinity*, trans. Sr. Mary Clark, FOTC 69 (Washington, D.C. 1981).

Novatian. *Novatian Presbyter: De trinitate*, trans. R.J. Simone, FOTC 67 (Washington, D.C. 1974).

Origen. *Homilies on Genesis and Exodus*, trans. R.E. Heine, FOTC 71 (Washington, D.C. 1982).

Socrates. *Historia ecclesiastica libri 7*, PG 67.30–842 (Paris 1864).

Sozomen. *Historia ecclesiastica libri 9*, PG 67.854–1630 (Paris 1864).

Tertullian. *Apologetical Works*, trans. R. Arbesmann et al., FOTC 10 (New York 1950).

———— *Treatises on Penance*, trans. W.P. LeSaint, ACW 28 (Westminster, Md. 1959).

Theodore of Mopsuestia. *Les Homélies catéchetiques de Théodore de Mopsueste*, ed. R. Tonneau and R. Devreesse, *Studi e Testi* 145 (Vatican City 1949).

Theodoret. *Haereticarum fabularum compendium*, PG 83.335–556 (Paris 1864).

Bible

The Septuagint Version of the Old Testament and Apochrypha with an English Translation (London n.d.).

Septuaginta, ed. A. Rahlfs, 2 vols. (Stuttgart 1935).

The Jerusalem Bible, ed. A. Jones (Garden City, New York 1966).

The New American Bible, trans. Members of the Catholic Biblical Association of America, sponsored by the Bishop's Committee of the Confraternity of Christian Doctrine (Paterson, New Jersey 1970).

Biblia sacra juxta vulgatae exemplaria, ed. A.C. Fillion, 8th ed. (Paris 1921).

Novum testamentum graece et latine, ed. A. Merk, 7th ed. (Rome 1951).

Novum testamentum graece, ed. K. Aland, M. Black, C. Martini, B. Metzger, A. Wilkgren, 26th ed (Stuttgart 1979).

Brown, R.E., Fitzmyer, J.A., Murphy, R.E., ed. *The Jerome Biblical Commentary* (Englewood Cliffs, N.J., 1968).

Fuller, R.E., Johnson, L., Kearns, C., ed. *A New Catholic Commentary on Holy Scripture* (London 1969).

McKenzie, J.L. *Dictionary of the Bible* (Milwaukee 1965).
Orchard, B., Sutcliffe, E., ed. *A Catholic Commentary on Holy Scripture* (London 1953).

Other Works
Acta sanctorum, vol. 4 (Venice 1748).
Albert, P. S. *Jean Chrysostome considéré comme orateur populaire* (Paris 1858).
Amann, E. "Mélèce d'Antioche," DTC 10.1 520–31.
Ammianus Marcellinus. *Rerum gestarum libri 29*, 3 vols. trans. J. Rolfe, Loeb Classical Library (Cambridge, Mass. 1939).
Arendzen, J.P. "Docetae," CE 5 70–72.
——— "Ebionites," CE 5 242–44.
——— "Gnosticism," CE 6 592–602.
——— "Manichaeism" CE 9 591–97.
——— "Marcionites," CE 9 645–49.
Arndt, W. and Gingrich, F.W. *A Greek-English Lexicon of the New Testament and Other Early Christian Literature*, 4th ed. (Chicago 1952).
Attwater, D. *St. John Chrysostom* (Milwaukee 1939).
Aubineau, M. "Un nouveau 'Panegyricon Chrysostomien' pour les fêtes fixes de l'année liturgique," *Analecta bollandiana* 92 (1974) 79–96.
Balducelli, R. "The Apostolic Origins of Clerical Continence: A Critical Appraisal of a New Book," *Theological Studies* 43 (1982) 693–705.
Bardy, G. "St. Jean Chrysostome," DTC 8.1 660–90.
——— "Justin (Saint)," DTC 8.2 2254–56.
——— "Manichéisme," DTC 9.2 1841–95.
——— "Monarchianisme," DTC 10.2 2193–2209.
——— "Montanisme," DTC 10.2 2355–70.
——— "Paul de Samosate," DTC 12.1 46–51.
——— *Paul de Samosate* (Louvain-Paris 1923).
——— "Valentine," DTC 15.2 2497–2519.
Bareille, G. "Docètes," DTC 4.2 1480–84.
——— "Docètisme," DTC 4.2 1484–1501.
——— "Eusèbe de Nicomédie," DTC 5.2 1539–52.
Barry, W. "Arianism," CE 1 707–10.
——— "Arius," CE 1 718–19.
Baur, C. "John Chrysostom," CE 8 452–57.
——— *John Chrysostom and His Time:* Vol. 1 *Antioch*, Vol. 2 *Constantinople*, trans. Sister M. Gonzaga (Westminster, Md., 1960–61).
——— *S. Jean Chrysostome et ses oeuvres dans l'histoire littéraire* (Louvain 1907).
Bertrans, F. *Mystique de Jesus chez Origène* (Paris 1951).
Besse, J. "Basile (Saint)," DTC 2.1 441–59.
Bois, J. "Constantinople (Ier Concile de)," DTC 3.1 1227–31.
Boularand, E. "Les Debuts d'Arius," *Bulletin de littérature ecclésiastique* 65 (1974) 175–203.
Brightman, F.E., ed. *Liturgies Eastern and Western*, Vol. 1 (Oxford 1967).
Brown, R.E. "Does the New Testament Call Jesus God?" *Theological Studies* 26 (1965) 545–73.
——— "The Pater Noster as an Eschatological Prayer," *Theological Studies* 22 (1961) 175–208.
Burger, D.C. *A Complete Bibliography of the Scholarship on the Life and Works of St. John Chrysostom* (Evanston 1964).

Butler, A. *The Lives of the Saints,* vol. 12, ed. H. Thurston and D. Attwater (London 1938).

Campenhausen, H. von. *The Fathers of the Greek Church,* trans. S. Godman (New York 1955).

Carnivet, P. "Meletian Schism," NCE 9 631.

Carter, R.E. "The Chronology of St. John Chrysostom's Early Life," *Traditio* 18 (1962) 357–64.

Cavallera, F. *Le schisme d'Antioche* (Paris 1905).

Cayré, F. *Manual of Patrology and History of Theology,* vol. 1, trans. H. Howitt (Paris 1935).

Chadwick, H. "Justin Martyr, St." NCE 8 94–95.

Chapman, J. "Monarchians," CE 10 448–51.

——— "Montanists," CE 10 521–24.

——— "Paul of Samosata," CE 11 589–90.

——— "Tertullian," CE 14 520–25.

Clifford, C. "Acacius, Bishop of Caesarea," CE 1 81–82.

——— "Athanasius, St.," NCE 1 996–99.

Cochini, C. *Origines apostoliques du célibat sacerdotal* (Paris 1981).

Cross, F.L. *The Early Christian Fathers* (London 1960).

Crouzel, H. "Origen and Origenism," NCE 767–74.

——— *Théologie de l'image de Dieu chez Origène* (Paris 1955).

Cummings, J.T. "Gregory of Nazianzus, Saint," NCE 6 791–94.

Daniélou, J. "L'incompréhensibilité de Dieu d'après S. Jean Chrysostome," *Recherches de science religieuse* 37 (1950) 176–94.

——— *Origène* (Paris 1948).

De Clercq, V.C. "Acacius of Caesarea," NCE 1 62.

——— "Arianism," NCE 1 791–94.

——— "Arius," NCE 1 814–15.

——— "Eunomius of Constantinople," NCE 5 631.

Delehaye, H. "Martyr et Confesseur," *Analecta bollandiana* 39 (1921) 20–49.

——— *Synaxarium ecclesiae Constantinopolitanae* (Brussels 1902).

Delehaye, H., ed. *Acta sanctorum novum propylaeum* (Brussels 1902).

Delehaye, H. et al. *Propylaeum ad acta sanctorum decembris* (Brussels 1940).

Devreesse, R. *L'patriarchat d'Antioche* (Paris 1945).

Dodd, C.H. *The Interpretation of the Fourth Gospel* (Cambridge, Eng. 1960).

Dölger, F.J. "Das Segnen der Sinne mit der Eucharistie," *Antike und Christentum* 3 (1932) 231–44.

Downey, G. *A History of Antioch in Syria* (Princeton 1961).

——— *Antioch in the Age of Theodosius the Great* (Norman, Okla. 1962).

Dressler, H. "Irenaeus, St.," NCE 7 631–32.

Duling, D.C. *Jesus Christ Through History* (New York 1979).

Evans, E. *Tertullian's Treatise against Praxeas* (London 1948).

Finegan, J. *Light from the Ancient Past* 2nd ed. (Princeton N.J. 1959).

Fritz, G. "Nicée (1er Concile de)," DTC 11.1 399–417.

Galtier, P. "St. Jean Chrysostome et la confession," *Recherches de science religieuse* 1 (1910) 209–40, 315–50.

Godet, P. "Gregoire de Nazianze (Saint)," DTC 6.2 1839–44.

——— "Gregoire de Nysse (Saint)," DTC 6.2 1847–52.

Grant, R.M. *Gnosticism and Early Christianity* (New York 1959).

Greenslade, S.L., ed. "General Introduction to Tertullian," in *Early Latin Theology,* Library of Christian Classics, vol. 5 (Philadelphia 1956).

Gribomont, J. "Basil, Saint," NCE 2 143–46.

Gwatkin, G. *Studies of Arianism* (Cambridge, Eng. 1900).
Hammell, P.J. "Modalism," NCE 9 998.
_____ "Monarchianism," NCE 9 1019–20.
Harkins, P.W. "John Chrysostom, St.," NCE 7 1041–44.
Harvanek, R.F. "Gregory of Nyssa, Saint," NCE 6 791–96.
Healy, P.J. "Valentinus and Valentinians," CE 15 256.
Hefele, C.J. *Histoire des conciles* (Paris 1907).
Humbert, A. "Docetism," NCE 4 934–35.
Hunter-Blair, D.O. "Gregory of Nazianzus, Saint," CE 7 10–15.
Jacobs, L. "Rosh Ha-Shanah," *Encyclopedia Judaica* 14 (1972) 309–10.
Jonas, H. *The Gnostic Religion* (Boston 1963).
Jones, A.H.M. "Chrysostom's Parentage and Education," *The Harvard Theological Review* 46 (1953) 171–73.
Jurgens, W.A. "A Letter of Meletius of Antioch," *The Harvard Theological Review* 53 (1960) 251–60.
Keane, H. "The Sacrament of Penance in St. John Chrysostom," *Irish Theological Quarterly* 14 (1919) 305–17.
Kelly, J.N.D. *Early Christian Creeds* 2nd ed. (London 1964).
Kreilkamp, H.D. "Constantinople I, Council of," NCE 4 237–38.
Lagrange, M.J. *Saint Justin* (Paris 1914).
Lampe, G. *A Patristic Greek Lexicon* (Oxford 1961).
Lebreton, J. "Justin Martyr," CE 8 580–86.
LeBachelet, X. "Acace le Borgne ou de Cesarée," DTC 1.1 290.
_____ "Acaciens," DTC 1.1 290–91.
_____ "Aetius," DTC 1.1 516–17.
_____ "Arianisme," DTC 1.2 1779–1863.
_____ "Athanase (Saint)," DTC 1.2 2143–78.
_____ "Basile d'Ancyre," DTC 2.1 461–63.
_____ "Eunomius," DTC 5.2 1501–14.
Lebeau, P. "Patripassianism," NCE 10 1103.
_____ "Paul of Samosata," NCE 11 26.
_____ "Sabellianism," NCE 12 783.
Leclercq, H. "Gregory of Nyssa, Saint," CE 7 16–18.
_____ "Meletius of Antioch," CE 10 161–64.
_____ "Nicaea, Council of," CE 11 44–46.
LeSaint, W.P. "Montanism," NCE 9 1078–79.
_____ "Tertullian," NCE 13 1009–22.
Lieske, A. *Die Theologie der Logosmystik bei Origines* (Münster 1938).
Lubac, H. de. *Histoire et esprit: L'intelligence de l'écriture d'après Origène* (Paris 1950).
MacRae, G.W. "Gnosticism," NCE 6 523–28.
_____ "Valentinus," NCE 14 518–19.
Martain, P. "Saint Jean Chrysostome et la confession," *Revue augustinienne* 6 (1907) 460–62.
Murphy, F.X. "Ebionites," NCE 5 29.
Musurillo, H. "Basil of Ancyra," NCE 2 147.
Myers, E. "Eunomianism," CE 5 605–06.
Newman, J.H. *Arians of the Fourth Century* 4th ed. (London 1876).
Ortiz de Urbina, I. "Nicaea I, Council of," NCE 10 432–34.
Ott, M. "Eustathius, Saint," CE 5 627–28.
Otten, J.B. *Manual of the History of Dogma*, vol. 1 (St. Louis 1922).
Oulton, J.E. and Chadwick, H. *Alexandrian Christianity* (Philadelphia 1954).

Peterson, J.B. "Basil the Great, Saint," CE 2 330–34.

Plato. *The Dialogues of Plato*, 2 vols., trans. B. Jowett (New York 1937).

Poncelet, A. "Irenaeus, St.," CE 8 130–31.

Prat, F. "Origen and Origenism," CE 11 306–12.

Quasten, J. *Patrology*, 3 vols. (Westminster, Md. 1950–60).

———— *Patrología*, 3 vols., Spanish edition (Madrid 1977).

Quispel, J. "The Original Doctrine of Valentine," *Vigiliae christianae* 1 (1947) 43–73.

Ramsey, B. "Almsgiving in the Latin Church," *Theological Studies* 43 (1982) 226–59.

Ries, J. "Manichaeism," NCE 9 153–60.

Salaville, S. "Eustathiens d'Antioche," DTC 5.2 1574–76.

Schoeps, H.-J. *Jewish Christianity*, trans. D. Hare (Philadelphia 1969).

Sellars, R.V. *Eustathius of Antioch and His Place in the Early History of Christian Doctrine* (Cambridge, Eng. 1928).

Shahan, T.J. "Constantinople, Councils of," CE 4 308.

Simon, M. *Verus Israel* (Paris 1948).

Spanneut, M. "Eustathius of Antioch," NCE 5 638.

Stephenson, A.A. "Marcion," NCE 9 193–94.

Thurston, H. "Celibacy of the Clergy," CE 3 481–88.

Vernet, F. "Irenée (Saint)," DTC 7.2 2394–2533.

Vogt, A. "Le Théatre à Byzance," *Revue des questions historiques* 115 (1931) 257–96.

Wolfson, H.A. *The Philosophy of the Church Fathers*, vol. 1 (Cambridge, Mass. 1956).

ABBREVIATIONS

Abbreviations of Works of Chrysostom

Ad vid. iun. *Ad viduam iuniorem,* PG 48.599–610. Paris 1862.

De Anna. *De Anna sermones 1–5,* PG 54.631–676. Paris 1862.

De anath. *De non anathematizandis vivis atque defunctis,* PG 48.945–52; Paris 1862.

De bap. Christi. *De baptismo Christi homilia,* PG 49.363–72. Paris 1862.

De incomp. *De incomprehensibili Dei natura homilae 1–12,* PG 48.701–812. Paris 1862. Homilies 1–5 also SC 28 bis.

De Laz. *De Lazaro conciones 1–7,* PG 48.963–1044. Paris 1862.

Demonstratio. *Contra Iudaeos et gentiles demonstratio quod Christus sit Deus,* PG 48.813–38. Paris 1862.

De poenit. *De poenitentia homiliae 1–9,* PG 49.277–350 Paris 1862.

De sac. *De sacerdotio libri 1–6,* PG 48.623–92. Paris 1862.

De stat. *Ad populum Antiochenum de statuis homiliae 1–21,* PG 49.15–222. Paris 1862.

In act. apos. *In acta apostolorum homiliae 55,* PG 60.13–584. Paris 1862.

In 2 Cor. *In epistolam 2 ad Corinthios homiliae 1–30,* PG 61.381–610. Paris 1862.

In Eph. *In epistolam ad Ephesios homiliae 1–24,* PG 62.9–176. Paris 1862.

In kal. *In kalendas sermo,* PG 48.953–962. Paris 1862.

In Matt. *In s. Matthaei evangelium homiliae 1–91,* PG 57.21–472. Paris 1862.

In Philip. *In epistolam ad Philippenses homiliae 1–15,* PG 62.177–198. Paris 1862.

In Rom. 12.20. *In illud: Si esurierit inimicus,* PG 51.171–86.

In s. Lucianum. *In sanctum Lucianum martyrem,* PG 50.519–26. Paris 1862.

Vidi Dom. *In illud: vidi Dominum homiliae 1–6,* PG 56.97–142. Paris 1862.

Other Abbreviations

ACW	*Ancient Christian Writers.* Westminster, Md.–London (later New York, N.Y./Ramsey, N.J.) 1946–.
ACW 31	Harkins, P.W. *St. John Chrysostom: Baptismal Instructions.* Westminster, Md., 1963.
Baur	Baur, C. *John Chrysostom and His Time:* Vol. 1, *Antioch,* Vol. 2, *Constantinople,* trans. Sister M. Gonzaga, Westminster, Md. 1960–61.
Brightman	Brightman, F.E. ed., *Liturgies Eastern and Western,* Vol. 1. Oxford 1967.
Cayré	Cayré, F. *Manual of Patrology and History of Theology,* trans. H. Howitt. Paris 1935.
CCHS	Orchard B., Sutcliffe, E. eds. *A Catholic Commentary on Holy Scripture.* London 1953.

CE   *The Catholic Encyclopedia.* New York 1907–14.

DACL   *Dictionnaire d'archéologie chrétienne et de liturgie.* Paris 1907–53.

DB   McKenzie, J.L. *Dictionary of the Bible.* Milwaukee 1965.

Demonstration   John Chrysostom. *Demonstration against Jews and Pagans on the Divinity of Christ,* PG 48.813–38. Paris 1862.

Downey, *History*   Downey, G. *A History of Antioch.* Princeton 1961.

DTC   *Dictionnaire de théologie catholique.* Paris 1903–50.

Duling   Duling, D.C. *Jesus Christ through History.* New York 1979.

FOTC   *The Fathers of the Church: A New Translation.* New York (later Washington, D.C.) 1947–.

FOTC 33   Goggin, Sister Thomas Aquinas, trans. *St. John Chrysostom: Homilies on the Gospel of St. John.* New York 1957.

FOTC 68   Harkins, P.W. *St. John Chrysostom: Discourses Against Judaizing Christians.* Washington, D.C. 1979.

JB   Jones, A., ed. *The Jerusalem Bible.* Garden City, New York 1966.

JBC   Brown, R.E., Fitzmyer, J.A., Murphy, R.E., eds. *The Jerome Biblical Commentary.* Englewood Cliffs, New Jersey 1968.

LXX   Rahlfs, A. *Septuaginta.* 2 vols. Stuttgart 1935.

NAB   Members of the Catholic Biblical Association of America, trans. *The New American Bible.* New York 1970.

NCE   *New Catholic Encyclopedia.* New York 1967.

NT   New Testament.

OT   Old Testament.

PG   Migne, J.-P., ed. *Patrologiae cursus completus: Series graeca.* Paris 1857–66.

PL   Migne, J.-P., ed. *Patrologia cursus completus: Series latina.* Paris 1844–55.

Quasten   Quasten, J. *Patrology,* 3 vols., Westminster, Md. 1950–60.

SC   *Sources chrétiennes.* Paris 1942–.

SC 28 bis   Daniélou, J. (introd.), Malingrey, A.-M. (text and notes), Flacelière, R. (trans.) *Sur l'incompréhensibilité de Dieu (De incomp. 1–5).* Paris 1951.

JOHN CHRYSOSTOM

INTRODUCTION

Pre-Arian Christology

WO PREVIOUS VOLUMES in this series have dealt with the Trinitarian and Christological errors of Arianism. *St. Hilary of Poitiers: The Trinity*, translated by Stephen McKenna, C.SS.R.,[1] appeared in 1954 and offers in English the saint's Latin treatise, *De Trinitate*. Hilary became bishop of Poitiers about A.D. 354 but was exiled to Phrygia some two years later because he refused the Emperor Constantius' demand that he repudiate the orthodox teaching of St. Athanasius against the Arians on the divinity of Christ. During his exile he completed the twelve books of his *De Trinitate*; in this work his chief targets are the Arians and the Anomoeans (as the strictest Arians were also called),[2] although he mentions Arius by name only twice and his followers only once. The Trinitarian doctrine of Hilary is both orthodox and precise: there is one God in three divine Persons—the Father, the Son, and the Holy Spirit. In his Christology he was more interested in proving that the divine nature of Christ was consubstantial with that of his heavenly Father than in showing that his human nature was consubstantial with ours.

(2) The second anti-Arian volume in this series is *Marius Victorinus: Theological Treatises on the Trinity*, translated by Sister

---

1 FOTC 25 (New York 1954).
2 The Greek word for Anomoean means "unlike" or "dissimilar," and, as a sect, taught that the Son not only was not one in substance with the Father but not even of a like or similar substance. Hence the Son could neither be divine nor one in being with the Father.

Mary T. Clark, R.S.C.J.[3] Victorinus was born in Africa toward the end of the third century. Later he came to Rome and became famous as a teacher of rhetoric. He also steeped himself in Neoplatonism. After his conversion to Christianity (ca. A.D. 356), he turned his Neoplatonic philosophy and rhetoric against Arianism to refute it in his *Theological Treatises on the Trinity*. St. Jerome[4] calls the treatises very obscure and says that only the learned can understand them. But Victorinus emerged from several traditions: that of classical Rome, the new trends in the philosophic thought of Plotinus and Porphyry, and the developing positions of Christianity in East and West which still needed an adequate vocabulary to become clear. Writing in Latin but systematizing Christian beliefs in a Neoplatonic structure made it necessary for Victorinus to introduce many neologisms and to give extended meanings to existing terms. This contributes to his obscurity but cannot disguise the profundity of his insight into one God in three divine Persons. He is the first Latin writer to compose a systematic metaphysical treatise on the Trinity and stands out as the precursor of the medieval theologians. Sister Clark's translation is at once simple and elegant.

(3) But these books were written in Latin and for those born to this language. In the present volume, Chrysostom's homilies, which were delivered in Greek to congregations of eastern Christians in Antioch and Constantinople, are presented to English readers whose knowledge of the Arian turmoil may well be limited. It may be profitable, then, to give a sketch of

---

3 FOTC 69 (Washington, D.C. 1981). Another volume in the same series which is most deserving of mention is the translation of the *De Trinitate* by Russell J. DeSimone, O.S.A., in his *Novatian the Presbyter*, FOTC 67 (Washington, D.C. 1974). Since this Trinitarian treatise was written before A.D. 250, some seventy years before Arianism tore the Church asunder by denying the divinity of Christ, it does not attack that heresiarch's doctrine as such. But it does set forth a picture of Christ, the Word, as both God and man, as one with the Father although posterior in origin. This led to accusations of subordinationism although Novatian may only have been defending the distinction in person of the Father and the Son.

4 Cf. *De viris illustribus* 101 (PL 23.701–702). Cited by F. Cayré. *Manual of Patrology and History of Theology*, Vol. 1, trans. H. Howitt 331 (Paris 1935) (hereafter cited as Cayré).

the antecedents of Arianism and early Christology before turning to Chrysostom's answer to the Arian Anomoeans, who presented so grave a problem to the purity of the faith in the fourth century.

(4) How did the Christians of the first three centuries look on Christ? One day Jesus asked his disciples: "Who do people say that I am?"[5] They answered: "Some say John the Baptizer, others Elijah, still others Jeremiah or one of the prophets."[6] Then Jesus said: "Who do you say that I am?"[7] Peter answered him and said: "You are the Christ, the Son of the living God."[8] Jesus replied to this confession of faith with the words: "No mere man revealed this to you, but my heavenly Father."[9] By this Jesus was showing that his messianic identity and divinity cannot be truly known from human reason but only from God's revelation.[10]

(5) "Since he was in the form of God, Christ did not consider it robbery to be equal to God but he did empty himself and take the form of a servant; he was born in the likeness of men. Since he was found in human estate, he humbled himself and became obedient to the point of death, even the death of the cross. Because of this, God highly exalted him and bestowed on him the name above every other name, so that at Jesus' name every knee must bend in the heavens, on the earth, and under the earth, and every tongue proclaim that Jesus Christ is Lord to the glory of God the Father."[11] In other words, Christ is true

---

5 Mk 8.27. Cf. Mt 16.13.
6 Mt 16.14. Cf. Mk 8.28.
7 Mt 16.15. Cf. Mk 8.29.
8 Mt 16.16. Cf. Mk ibid.
9 Mt 16.17.
10 Cf. 1 Cor 12.3.
11 Cf. Phil 2.6–11 and NAB note ad loc. This Pauline passage certainly qualifies as one of the Christological hymns which are found in the NT and which can be isolated by their style and content. D.C. Duling, *Jesus Christ Through History* (New York 1979) 43–52 (hereafter cited as Duling), points out that these hymns seem to have been a common part of early Christian worship (cf. 1 Cor 14.26) and picture Jesus as preexistent in heaven as a divine being who came down to earth, became human and ascended to heaven—even though not every stage of this pattern is explicit in every hymn. Other Christological hymns are found, e.g., in Jn 1.1–18, 1 Tm 3.16, 1 Pt 3.18–19, 22, Eph 2.14–16, and Col 1.15–20.

God, equal to the Father, and true man. He redeemed us by his death on the cross and was raised up from the dead and took his place at the right hand of God, sharing the Father's glory and the name of Lord.

(6) Perhaps, the earliest Christians were quite satisfied with a concept of Christ such as was revealed in the hymns, prayers, and actions found in their worship and daily life. In their religious life it sufficed that their concept of Christ rest on what God had revealed of him. They did not probe philosophically into this concept but were satisfied with the confession and creeds which enriched their liturgies. But the vast influx of converts from varied backgrounds made it necessary that revealed truths be defined with greater precision. The new Christians and their instructors both wanted a reasonable explanation for the faith which they had embraced. This search for a philosophical basis for belief gave rise to conflicts between the orthodoxy of revelation and the reason of philosophy. All too often the attempts to reconcile revelation and reason led to heresies, especially in the positions adopted by various sects in explaining the divinity and humanity of Christ.

(7) Since Jesus was a Jew and exercised his ministry among his countrymen, it is not surprising that so many early converts became Jewish Christians, who held on to many of their Jewish practices and caused problems for the apostles, especially Paul.[12] One of the strictest sects was known as the Ebionites.[13] The Ebionites were led by their strong Jewish monotheism to hold to an heretical Christology. Jesus was the prophet like Moses,[14] indeed, the last and greatest prophet. Because he completely fulfilled the Jewish Law, God "adopted" him as his son when John baptized him in the Jordan.[15] But it was a man

---

12 Cf. Gal 2 (where in v. 4 Paul calls them "false claimants to the title of brother"); Acts 21.15–25.
13 Cf. Duling, 67 for the origin of this name. For the whole question of Jewish Christianity see H.-J. Schoeps, *Jewish Christianity*, trans. Douglas Hare (Philadelphia 1969). For shorter accounts cf. J.P. Arendzen, "Ebionites," CE 5.242–44, especially for their drifting into heresy, and also F.X. Murphy, "Ebionites," NCE 5.29.
14 Cf. Acts 3.22 and NAB note ad loc.
15 Cf. Ps 2.7 and Mk 1.11.

whom God "adopted" and who died, rose, and became a supernatural angel. In heaven he also became Lord of all creation and, as Lord, would come again. Since Jesus was a man, he could never be considered as a second God, much less as consubstantial and equal to the Father. This strongly offended the basic monotheism of the Ebionites.

(8) The Gnostics,[16] on the other hand, whose origins are lost in a syncretism of Greek philosophy and eastern religions, saw God as an infinitely remote deity whom they called the Silence or the Depth. Such a perfect God, one so far removed from essentially evil matter, could not have created the material world. Although quite separate from material beings, God is capable of expansion which reveals itself by successive series of emanations called aeons. These aeons are like God inasmuch as they are eternal. They serve as intermediaries between God and matter. As they recede from God, they become less perfect, and when one of the aeons strays from the others, it is cast into a lower world. This world is then peopled by a new but evil series of aeons of an inferior nature. The rejected aeon becomes the God of the Jews who creates man and the material world.[17]

(9) When some Gnostics embraced Christianity, they attempted to transform Christianity into a religious philosophy. But they still saw this created world of darkness as the work of a lower god who opposed the true God of light. The process of redemption involves the deliverance of the divine spark, lost in matter. This was not accomplished by the merits of Christ but through the *gnōsis* (knowledge) manifested in him when one of the higher aeons was united to him from the time of his baptism until his passion.[18]

---

16 See Hans Jonas, *The Gnostic Religion* (Boston 1963); Robert M. Grant, *Gnosticism and Early Christianity* (New York 1959); J.P. Arendzen, "Gnosticism," CE 6.592–602; G.W. Mac Rae, "Gnosticism," NCE 6.523–28; J. Quasten, 3 vols. *Patrology* (Utrecht/Antwerp 1950–60) 1.154–77; H.A. Wolfson, *The Philosophy of the Church Fathers*, vol. 1, 3rd ed. (Cambridge, Mass. 1970) 495–574.
17 This paragraph is a summary of a summary of Gnosticism given by Cayré, vol. 1, 100–102.
18 Cayré, ibid.

(10) Since the Redeemer was from the world of light, the gnostic Christians could not think of him as true man. Indeed, when he took the form of sinful, bodily flesh, he was only a phantom or an appearance of a man who seemed to be human. This denial of Christ's humanity is known as the heresy of Docetism.[19]

(11) Hence, the Ebionites show us a Christ who became divine by adoption, while the gnostics show us a Christ who was a divine being (of a lower order) who assumed only the appearance of a man. This dichotomy found some resolution in the philosophical concept of Christ as Logos, the Word and Wisdom of the Father. Although he was not the first to use the term, it was Justin Martyr (ca. A.D. 100–65) who was the first to develop the Logos idea by bringing together God's Wisdom, the Stoic notion of rational order in the universe, and the Son of God.[20] In Justin's teaching on God some see no more than philosophical speculation while others find in it a truly Christian faith. Following a Platonic trend, God is without origin and, therefore, nameless. As creator of all things he may best be called Father. Substantially, the Father is not omnipresent because he cannot leave his dwelling in the regions above the sky and is unable to appear in the world.

(12) But if God's transcendence puts him beyond all human beings, the abyss is bridged by the Logos, who is numerically distinct from the Father but born of the Father's very substance. The Word proceeds from the Father with no division of

---

19 Cf. J.P. Arendzen, "Docetae," CE 5.70–72; A. Humbert, "Docetism," NCE 4.934–35; G. Bareille, "Docètes," DTC 4.2 1480–84; id., ""Docétisme," ibid. 1484–1501; Irenaeus, *Contra haereses* (usually called *Adversus haereses*) 5.1.2 (PG 7.1119–28); John Chrysostom, *Homilies on the Gospel of St. John,* trans. Sister Thomas Aquinas Goggin, FOTC 33 (New York 1957) 107 and note.

20 C.H.Dodd gives a rather technical discussion of the Logos and its background in *The Interpretation of the Fourth Gospel* (Cambridge, Eng. 1960) 263–85. For Justin see Quasten 1, 196–219; Cayré, vol. 1, 114–29; Jules Lebreton, "Justin Martyr, Saint," CE 8.580–86; H. Chadwick, "Justin Martyr, St." NCE 8.94–5; H. von Campenhausen, *The Fathers of the Greek Church,* trans. S. Godman (New York 1955) 12–20 (hereafter cited as von Campenhausen); T. Falls, trans., *The Writings of Justin Martyr,* FOTC 6 (New York 1948).

substance but as one fire passes to another from which it is lit. The Word is truly Son and, as the only begotten, he alone may properly be called Son. But the divinity of the Logos appears to be subordinate to the Father's since the Father engendered him by a voluntary act at the beginning of all his works. He also used his Word as an instrumental cause in creation, in appearing to the patriarchs, and in inspiring the prophets. It is the Word who became incarnate and is Jesus Christ. Justin owes to revelation his concept of the distinct personality of the Word, his divinity, and incarnation. Philosophical speculation is responsible for his unfortunate ideas on the temporal and voluntary generation of the Logos and for the subordination of the Son to the Father.[21]

(13) Irenaeus,[22] born in Asia Minor but later a priest and bishop of Lyons, is first heard of in A.D. 177 and may have died a martyr about A.D. 203. His primary work, *Adversus Haereses*, chiefly refutes the gnostics. He does this by posing a dilemma. If the gnostics separate God from the world, they limit the Divine Being and circumscribe the sphere of his activity—which is to deny God. If they suppose the creation to be in God, all the imperfections of creatures fall back on God because his substance has become theirs. In this confusion of the finite with the Infinite, it is the divine nature which falls and degenerates.

(14) In Christology, he teaches that the one Christ is called by many names but is identical with the Son of God, with the Logos, with the God-man Jesus, with our Savior and Lord. He sees in Christ a recapitulation in which all things are made new. God restores through Christ the first plan for the salvation of mankind which the fall of Adam had interrupted; the Father

---

21 Cayré, vol. 1, 125–27, excuses Justin on all these lapses, citing M.J. Lagrange, *Saint Justin* (Paris 1914) 155, and G. Bardy, DTC 8.2.2254–56.

22 For St.Irenaeus see A. Poncelet, "Irenaeus, St.," CE 8.130–31; H. Dressler, "Irenaeus, St.," NCE 7.631–32; Quasten 1.287–313; Cayré 1.141–53; Von Campenhausen, 21–18; J.P. Smith, trans. *St. Irenaeus: Proof of the Apostolic Preaching*, ACW 16 (Westminster, Md. 1952) particularly the introduction (pp. 3–43); F. Vernet, "Irenée (Saint)," DTC 7.2.2394–2533, esp. 2400–2403 and 2442–51.

gathers up his entire work from the beginning to renew, restore, and reorganize it in his incarnate Son, who thus becomes for us a second Adam. The whole human race had been lost by the fall of the first Adam. Hence, the Son of God had to become man in order that he, as the second Adam, could effect the re-creation of mankind and reconcile it to the Father.[23]

(15) In Irenaeus we also find that the Logos was preexistent with God before creation. After he took flesh, he truly suffered and, therefore, was true man. He did not come to be after God as his highest emanation. The Logos was always with God, identical with God in substance but yet a distinct person. Both Justin and Irenaeus tried to make it possible to have a Logos doctrine where strict monotheism was protected and in which the Logos possessed both a divine and human nature. Irenaeus sought to find a reconciliation which would present a Logos who was identical with God because he was always with God. The Logos was divine and became true man rather than the human phantom of Docetism. Neither was he a true man who became divine because the Father adopted him.

(16) As the third century advanced, a strong challenge against the Logos concept of Christ arose. The Modalist Monarchians (also called Patripassians or Sabellians) feared that the Logos doctrine led to a notion of two Gods, although it was trying to protect monotheism. These Modalists thought of the one God as appearing in three separate and successive modes, as Father, Son, and Holy Spirit. Hence, Christ is the Father;[24] therefore it is the Father himself who was born, suffered, and died (Patripassianism). Since God is one, simple, and indivisible, he is called the Word inasmuch as he is Creator; Father, as the Lawgiver of the Old Testament; Son, because he is the

---

23 See Quasten 1.295–96. Cf. also Rom 5.12–21 and NAB note ad loc; J. Fitzmyer, JBC 53:52–60.

24 Cf. Epiphanius, *Panarion* (or *Adversus Haereses*) 62.1 (PG 41.1051); for Modalism, P.J. Hammell, "Modalism," NCE 9. 988; for Monarchianism, cf. J. Chapman, "Monarchians," CE 10.448–51; P.J. Hammell, "Monarchianism," NCE 9.1019–20; G. Bardy, "Monarchianisme," DTC 10.2.2193–2209; for Patripassianism see P. Lebeau, "Patripassianism," NCE 10.1103.

Redeemer; and Holy Spirit inasmuch as he is the Sanctifier. But it is one and the same person who underlies all these aspects or modes. Or, as Sabellius said: "Father, Son, and Holy Spirit are one and the same being."[25]

(17) The great champion of the Logos concept was Tertullian,[26] born of pagan parents at Carthage in North Africa about A.D. 160. He became a Christian about A.D. 195, and a priest some five years later. His iron will, intemperate zeal, and lack of empathy for the weakness of others soon led him to embrace the harsh tenets of the heretical Montanists which made no allowances for the weakness of the flesh.[27]

(18) It was after A.D. 213 and as a Montanist that he wrote his *Adversus Praxean*[28] against Monarchianism. In this work he defends the unity of God but does away with the successive modes by using his legal background. In Latin, property and possessions are called *substantia* (substance). Just as several people could own one piece of property, so one *substantia* could be jointly shared by three persons. So the one substance of God is found in the Father, Son, and Holy Spirit.

(19) Thus, Father and Son are different persons. For Tertullian, Christ the Logos is also God's Reason, his Power, his Word. He is the same substance as the Father but the Logos does not possess the same amount of deity as the Father.

(20) One of the most prolific writers of the third century was Origen (A.D. 185–255). His influence was great both in the East

---

25 For Sabellianism cf. Cayré, vol. 1, 174, 295–96; P. Lebeau, "Sabellianism," NCE 12.783; H.A. Wolfson, *The Philosophy of the Church Fathers*, vol. 1 (Cambridge, Mass. 1956) 570–608.

26 For Tertullian see S.L. Greenslade, ed., "General Introduction to Tertullian," in *Early Latin Theology*, Library of Christian Classics, vol. 5 (Philadelphia 1956) 21–24; J. Chapman, "Tertullian," CE 14.520–25; W.P. LeSaint, "Tertullian," NCE 13.1019–22; Quasten 2.246–340; Cayré, vol. 1, 229–49; Duling 69–71; R. Arbesmann et al., *Tertullian: Apologetical Works*, FOTC 10 (New York 1950).

27 For Tertullian's positions on receiving pardon for sins committed after baptism see *Tertullian: Treatises on Penance*, trans. W.P. LeSaint, ACW 28 (Westminster, Md. 1959).

28 See E. Evans, *Tertullian's Treatise Against Praxeas* (London 1948). For Montanism see G. Bardy, "Montanisme," DTC 10.2 (Paris 1929) 2355–70, esp. 2363–70; J. Chapman, "Montanists," CE 10.521–24; W. LeSaint, "Montanism," NCE 9.1078–79.

and the West. He headed the famous school of Alexandria until after his austere asceticism led him to self-mutilation. For this rash act his bishop refused to ordain him a priest. During a trip to Palestine about A.D. 230, he was ordained without the knowledge or permission of his own bishop. His ordination was declared illicit on his return to Alexandria, and he was soon after forced into exile. At Caesarea he opened a new theological school and taught there for twenty years with some of the most brilliant minds of the time as his students.[29]

(21) Origen's theological thinking was shaped largely by his allegorical interpretation of Scripture and by his Stoic and Neoplatonic concept of the nature of the universe. The pre-existent Logos seems to be subordinate to the one, transcendent, invisible, incomprehensible God, but superior to all external spirits, angels, demons, and souls imprisoned in human bodies. The Logos is the image of God, while the other "deities" are copies of that image. The Logos existed from eternity since there never was a time when the Logos was not. He is unique, he is the only begotten, and never existed as a being separate from God. He is *a* God but not *the* God, since *the* God is not subordinate to God, but the Logos is superior to and mediator of all other beings.[30]

(22) Origen's theology of the Word seems clearly to teach that the Logos is subordinate to the Father. Although Athanasius defended the orthodoxy of Origen on the Trinity, and Basil and Gregory of Nazianzus maintained that he was misunderstood by the heretics who claimed his support for

---

29 Eusebius of Caesarea devotes almost the entire sixth book of his *Ecclesiastical History* to Origen and his works. For texts and translations of Eusebius see *Ecclesiastical History*, trans. K. Lake and J.E.L. Oulton, 2 vols., The Loeb Classical Library (Cambridge, Mass. 1926–32); *Histoire ecclésiastique*, trans. G. Bardy, 4 vols. in SC 31,41, 55, 73 (Paris 1952–60). See also Cayré, vol. 1, 191–220; Duling, 71–74; F. Prat, "Origen and Origenism," CE 11. 306–12; H. Crouzel, "Origen and Origenism," NCE 11.767–74; Quasten 2. 37–101; J.E. Oulton and H. Chadwick, *Alexandrian Christianity* (Philadelphia 1954) 171–79 and bibliography, 456–58. For the debatable reliability of Eusebius' story about Origen's self-mutilation, as well as for an account on Eusebius's life of Origen, see Ronald E. Heine, trans. *Origen: Homilies on Genesis and Exodus* FOTC 71 (Washington, D.C. 1982) 2–11.

30 Cf. Duling, 74 for this doctrinal summary.

their teachings, it was not until recently that Origen's doctrine found further defenders.[31]

(23) Origen does affirm that the Word is essentially God, although the title of *the* God is reserved to the Father, who is not engendered. The Word is the same substance as the Father, engendered in a spiritual manner, as an act of will is produced by the soul. The Word is eternal because there never was a time when he was not. The language of theology was not yet fixed, and Origen's use, e.g., of *hypostasis* sometimes for "nature" and sometimes for "person" can be extremely confusing.

(24) Origen also attempted to develop a systematic doctrine on Jesus, the Christ. He tended to separate the divine and the human in Christ and to see the soul of Christ as the soul of the Logos. This led to a conclusion that the soul of Christ was not totally human and, therefore, Christ was not true man but a mere appearance of man. And this is Docetism.[32]

(25) If the Alexandrians tended to Docetism and Subordinationism in the third century, about the same time the School of Antioch tended to Adoptionism. Antioch was an active Jewish center and held strongly to monotheism. The Christian thinkers of Antioch were not strongly influenced by gnosticism or the speculations of Greek philosophy. Since they, too, were staunch monotheists, their speculations centered on the humanity of Jesus. In fact, in the latter half of the third century, Paul of Samosata, bishop of Antioch, was excommunicated for his modalistic Sabellianism.[33] He maintained that the Logos was a power of God and was so unified with God as to acquire a distinct existence from God only

---

31 See A. Lieske, *Die Theologie der Logosmystik bei Origines* (Münster 1938); H. De Lubac, *Histoire et Esprit; l'intelligence de l'écriture d'après Origène* (Paris 1950) especially chaps. 2–4; J. Daniélou, *Origène* (Paris 1948); F. Bertrans, *Mystique de Jesus chez Origène* (Paris 1951); H. Crouzel, *Théologie de l'image de Dieu chez Origène* (Paris 1955). For further literature see Quasten 2.100–101.

32 See above, paragraph 10 and note 19.

33 Cf. J. Chapman, "Paul of Samosata," CE 11.589–90; P. Lebeau, "Paul of Samosata," NCE 11.26; Quasten 2.140–42; G. Bardy, "Paul de Samosate," DTC 12.1.46–51.

periodically, by being uttered. Therefore the divine Logos was never fully a man but from time to time dwelt in individual prophets and, finally, in Jesus. So Christ was not the Logos become flesh but a mere man united to God through God's Logos for the good of humanity.[34] In this way Paul denied the divinity of Christ while, at the same time, weakening the unity of God because of the transient separations of the Logos from the Godhead. This Modalism and Adoptionism lasted well into and beyond the fourth century.

Arianism and Nicaea

(26) In A.D. 313 the Emperor Constantine recognized the Church throughout the Roman Empire. Although politically this may have been a triumph, that triumph was not to be enjoyed by a Church which was united in doctrine and free from theological disputes. Most serious was the continuing debate on the relationship of Christ to God. Arius (ca. A.D. 250–ca. 336) was the prime mover in this discord.[35] Nonetheless he was ordained a priest at Alexandria in 313 but eight years later was excommunicated at a synod of Egyptian and Libyan bishops.

(27) The teaching of Arius on the nature of the Son and Logos showed him a lineal descendant of the gnostics. He described the Son as a second or inferior God, standing midway between the First Cause and creatures; indeed, the Son was himself created out of nothing although he created all other creatures. He existed before the world but was not eternal; there was a time when he was not. Unlike the Father, who alone was without beginning, the Son was originated and

---

34 Cf. Duling, 74.
35 The monumental work of John Henry Newman, *Arians of the Fourth Century*, 4th ed. (London 1876) is the richest source of information on Arianism. However much I owe to it for my discussion of Arianism, I rarely cite it because it is not too generally available and is difficult to use. It lacks a general index, which is partially counterbalanced by a detailed table of contents. For Arius himself cf. W. Barry, "Arius," CE 1.718–19; V.C. DeClercq, "Arius," NCE 1.814–15; E. Boularand, "Les Debuts d'Arius," *Bulletin de littérature ecclésiastique* 75 (1964) 175–201.

once had not existed, for whatever has origin must begin to be. As a creature, he was changeable. As the Logos he dwelled in Jesus, so that Jesus could not have had a human soul. So for Arius, Jesus was neither truly God nor truly man.[36]

(28) Arius' denial of the eternal generation of the Son was more than his bishop, Alexander, could tolerate, and he summoned the synod which deposed Arius and exiled him. Arius fled to Palestine to Eusebius, his old friend and fellow student at the school of Antioch. Eusebius[37] at that time was bishop of Nicomedia and he interceded with Alexander in behalf of Arius. His argument was the old standard of the Antioch school: a coeternal, uncreated Son would destroy monotheism. Alexander replied that only the Father was the Unbegotten, the Word is not created, he is eternal, and he is God's only begotten Son, uniquely generated in the Father's own image. He is inferior to the Father only in that he is engendered but he derives his divine being from the very being of the Father.[38]

(29) Political and party motives embittered the strife. Many bishops of Asia Minor and Syria defended Arius, and synods in Palestine and Bithynia opposed synods in Egypt. The Emperor Constantine had just defeated Licinius (A.D. 312) and, as sole emperor, had restored civil order. He was also anxious to reestablish religious peace and, with Pope Silvester I, (pontificate A.D. 314–35), called the first ecumenical council to meet in A.D. 325 at Nicaea in Bithynia.[39]

---

36 Cf. Duling, 79; W. Barry, "Arianism," CE 1.707–710; V.C. DeClercq, "Arianism," NCE 1.791–94; X. Le Bachelet, "Arianisme," DTC 1.2. 1779–1863; G. Gwatkin, *Studies of Arianism* (Cambridge, Eng. 1900); J.N.D. Kelly, *Early Christian Creeds*, 2nd ed. (London 1964) 231–34; J.H. Newman, *Arians of the Fourth Century*, 4th ed. (London 1876) 201–211; G. Bareille, "Eusèbe de Nicomédie," DTC 5.2.1539–52.

37 For Eusebius of Nicomedia cf. Cayré, vol. 1, 314; Quasten 3.190–93. He is not to be confused with the great Church historian, Eusebius of Caesarea (Cayré, vol. 1, 319–27), another old friend of Arius and also a fellow student at Antioch. It was Eusebius of Nicomedia who, after Arius' death, took over the Arian leadership with the result that the Arians were also called Eusebians.

38 For Alexander's reply see Cayré, vol. 1, 328.

39 For the Council of Nicaea see H. Leclercq, "Nicaea, Council of," CE 11.44–46; I. Ortiz de Urbina, "Nicaea I, Council of," NCE 10.432–34; Newman, *Arians of the Fourth Century* 237–58; G. Fritz, "Nicée (1er Concile de)," DTC 11.1 399–417.

(30) Arius was often summoned before the assembly. His opinions were seriously discussed and the opposing arguments attentively considered. All but two bishops agreed to a symbol or creed which stated the orthodox relationship of Jesus to the Father and anathematized the teachings of Arius. The creed adopted at Nicaea reads as follows:

> We believe in one God the Father Almighty, creator of all things visible and invisible; and in one Lord Jesus Christ, begotten from the Father, only begotten, that is, from the substance of the Father, God from God, light from light, true God from true God, begotten not made, of one substance with the Father, through whom all things came into being, things in heaven and things on earth; who because of us men and because of our salvation came down and became incarnate, becoming man, suffered and rose again the third day, ascended to heaven and will come to judge the living and the dead. And in the Holy Spirit. But as for those who say: There was a time when He was not, and, before being born He was not, and that He came into existence out of nothing, or who assert that the Son of God is of a different hypostasis or substance, or is created, or is subject to alteration or change—these the Catholic Church anathematizes.[40]

(31) The key words in this creed are "of the same substance with the Father," which in Greek reads *homoousion tōi patri,* and in Latin, *consubstantialem patri. Homoousion*[41] became a watchword of the orthodox, just as the strictest Arians were called *Anomoeans* (those who held that Christ was of a substance in no way similar to the Father's), and the semi-Arians were called *Homoeousians* (because they believed that Christ was of a substance similar or like to the Father's). Today, in the Roman Catholic Church, the consubstantiality of Christ and the Father is less accurately and more simply expressed as "one in Being with the Father."

---

40 J.N.D. Kelly, *Early Christian Creeds* (London 1960) 215–16 (hereafter cited as Kelly); cf. ibid. 231–34 for the Arian theology and 234–42 for the Nicene reply.
41 See Kelly, 242–54.

(32) The first results of the adoption of the Nicene Creed were that Arius and his writings were anathematized, his books were burned, and he himself was exiled to Illyria. Yet Arianism did not die; in fact it grew for four decades and was still a disturbing factor at the end of the fourth century. Indeed, it might have been reestablished after Nicaea were it not for Athanasius of Alexandria.

Athanasius and the Decline of Arianism

(33) Athanasius (298–373)[42] was still a young deacon when he attended the Council of Nicaea as secretary to his bishop, Alexander. Less than a year later (326) Alexander died, and Athanasius was chosen to succeed him as bishop of Alexandria. He held this post until his death although his tenure was interrupted by five banishments brought about by the political influence of his Arian foes. The first two exiles were engineered by Eusebius, bishop of Nicomedia, a master of intrigue, and an out-and-out Arian. Eusebius sought to have Arius restored to fellowship with the Church of Alexandria and the Arians readmitted to the fold. Constantine, on the urging of Eusebius, even ordered Athanasius to do so, but Athanasius firmly declined.

(34) In 335 two councils, one at Tyre and the other at Jerusalem, absolved Arius, and he returned in triumph to Alexandria. The night before his official reconciliation was to take place, the heresiarch died of a sudden disorder, which the orthodox regarded as a judgment from heaven. But the influence of successive emperors continued to affect theology either by embracing Arianism, tending to favor it, or in allowing a freedom in religion with little or no eye to orthodoxy.[43]

(35) For example, Constantius, son of Constantine and sole

---

42 For Athanasius see Duling 76–78; "The Life of St. Athanasius" in *St. Athanasius on the Incarnation*, trans. and ed. A Religious of C.S.M.V. (London 1944); C. Clifford, "Athanasius, St.," CE 2.35–40; Quasten 3.20–79; X. LeBachelet, "Athanase (Saint)," DTC 1.2. 2143–78.

43 See J.B. Otten, *Manual of the History of Dogma*, vol. 1, (St. Louis 1922) 241 (hereafter cited as Otten).

emperor from 353 to 361, favored the Eusebian Arians. Soon the anti-Athanasians were openly attacking the Nicene faith.[44] A strong left-wing party revived the heretical ideas of Arius, restated them in radical terms, and came into prominence under the leadership of extremists like Aetius (d. ca. 370) and his secretary, Eunomius (d. after 390), who succeeded to the leadership. These Arians maintained that God is essentially simple and one; unbegotten and not produced. Therefore no being begotten or produced can be God, nor can it be either of the same substance (*homoousios*), or of a similar substance (*homoiousios*), or like (*homoios*) God, but must be dissimilar and unlike (*anomoios*) God. Since the Son is produced, he is physically unlike (*anomoios*) the Father. The followers of this Arian revivalism are known in history as Anomoeans or New Arians,[45] and they are the targets of Chrysostom's homilies contained in the present volume.

(36) The extreme right, led by Basil of Ancyra, consisted of the majority of churchmen who opposed Athanasius and the wording of the creed of Nicaea. When they saw the menace involved in the virulent doctrine of the Anomoeans, they met at Ancyra and issued a synodal letter to announce their position. Their watchword was *homoiousios* since they held the Son to be like or similar in substance to the Father, and Basil succeeded in winning the emperor over to the Homoeousian or semi-Arian position.[46]

(37) The center party leaned to both extremes. Led by Eusebius' successor, Acacius[47] of Caesarea in Palestine, they were actuated by political motives as much as by theological conviction. Their motto was *homoios* or "like." The Son, they maintained, was simply like the Father, according to the Scrip-

---

44 See Kelly, 238–95.

45 Otten, 244.

46 Ibid. Cf. H. Musurillo, "Basil of Ancyra," NCE 2.147; X. LeBachelet, "Basile d'Ancyre," DTC 2.1.461–63; Quasten 3.201–203.

47 Cf. C. Clifford, "Acacius, Bishop of Caesarea," CE 1.81–82; V.C. DeClercq, "Acacius of Caesarea," NCE 1.62; Quasten 3.345–46; X. LeBachelet, "Acace le Borgne ou de Cesarée," DTC 1.1.290; id., "Acaciens," ibid. 290–91; Socrates, HE 2.39–41 (PG 67.331–50); Sozomen, HE 4.23 (PG 67.1186–87).

ture, without any reference to substance or essence. What the Homoeans or Acacians (as they were also called) were trying to do was to compromise and find a middle road between the irreconcilable positions of the Anomoeans on the one hand, and of the orthodox Homoousians and the heterodox Homoeousians on the other.[48] This compromise was formulated into a creed and circulated by Constantius among all the bishops of Christendom together with an imperial letter commanding them either to sign it or take the consequences.[49] The very triumph of the Arians was beginning to lead to their disintegration.

(38) With the death of Constantius in 361, the agitation against the creed of Nicaea, which had made such effective use of his support, began to lose its force. Under Julian the Apostate (361–63) and his Catholic successor Jovian (363–64), a reaction towards orthodoxy began to set in. This was somewhat checked during the reign of the Arian Valens (364–67) but won out under Theodosius, who convened the Second Ecumenical Council held at Constantinople in 381.[50] So, it would seem, imperial support was the telling force in subduing the divided Arians and in bringing victory to Athanasius and the *homoousion* creed of Nicaea. But the victory was not an utter rout.

Chrysostom and the Anomoeans

(39) St. Eustathius,[51] who had been bishop of Antioch from 324–30, was one of the most energetic opponents of Arianism

48 Otten, 245.
49 Socrates, HE 2.43 (PG 67.353); Sozomen, HE 4.26 (PG 67.1197). This incident, reported by both Church historians, is cited by Kelly, 295.
50 Cf. T.J. Shahan, "Constantinople, Councils of," CE 4.308; H.D. Kreilkamp, "Constantinople I, Council of," NCE 4.237–38; J. Bois, "Constantinople (Ier Concile de)," DTC 3.1.1227–31.
51 Cf. Cayré, vol. 1, 328–29; M. Ott, "Eustathius, Saint," CE 5.627–28; M. Spanneut, "Eustathius of Antioch," NCE 5.638; R.V. Sellars, *Eustathius of Antioch and His Place in the Early History of Christian Doctrine* (Cambridge, Eng. 1928); Socrates, *Historia ecclesiastica* 2.43 (PG 67.351–54); Quasten 3.302–306; S. Salaville, "Eustathiens d'Antioche," DTC 5.2.1574–76.

when its fortunes were on the rise in the east even after its condemnation at Nicaea in 325. He adopted strong measures against the heresy in all its forms both in his own diocese and throughout Syria. For this the Arian Eusebians had him deposed at a synod held at Antioch in 329 or 330. After he was deposed, a part of the Church at Antioch remained faithful to him and formed what has been called the Eustathian party.

(40) For the next thirty years Arian bishops held the see of Antioch. The Eustathians stood steadfast in their orthodoxy until they were outraged by their countryman, Aetius,[52] who became a bishop without a see under Julian the Apostate. Aetius revived the purest Arianism in its most virulent form, Anomoeanism, and gathered around himself the most ardent Antiochene Arians. Among these was Eunomius,[53] who became bishop of Cyzicus in 360. Even from distant Cappadocia Eunomius kept up a steady stream of correspondence to Antioch. In his letters he constantly repeated the same Anomoean sophistries. These succeeded in impressing the less learned and more ignorant Antiochenes since his arguments were presented with some semblance of rigorous logic. When Aetius died, Eunomius became the acknowledged leader of the Anomoeans. Indeed, they were often called Eunomians.

(41) In 360 Meletius was elected bishop of Antioch with the support of Acacius, a Homoean Arian.[54] Since Meletius had made promises to both Arians and orthodox and since each group thought he was on its side, the choice of Meletius was generally satisfactory. The new bishop was regarded alternately as an Anomoean, a Homoeousian, a Homoean, or a Neo-Nicene. Probably he was neither a thorough Nicene nor a

---

52 Cf. X. LeBachelet, "Aetius," DTC 1.1.516–17; Gregory of Nyssa, *Contra Eunomium*, vol. 1, ed. Werner Jaeger (Leiden 1960) Book 1.34–55, pp. 33–41 (PG 45.259–66); Socrates, HE 2.35 (PG 67.298–99); Kelly, 283–295.
53 See E. Myers, "Eunomianism," CE 5.605–06; V.C. DeClercq, "Eunomius of Constantinople," NCE 5.631; X. LeBachelet, "Eunomius," DTC 5.2.1501–14; Quasten 3.306–309; Kelly, 283, 287–88.
54 Cf. H. Leclercq, "Meletius of Antioch," CE 10.161–64; P. Canivet, "Meletian Schism," NCE 9.631; W.A. Jurgens, "A Letter of Meletius of Antioch," *The Harvard Theological Review* 53 (1960) 251–260; E. Amann, "Mélèce d'Antioche," DTC 10.1.520–31; Socrates, HE 2.44 (PG 67.355–57).

decided Arian. But his gentle temper promised a much desired peace for his subjects who were weary of endless debate.
But he proved himself ultimately orthodox and the emperor
Constans banished him almost immediately after he had occupied his see. During a second exile (under Valens) a certain
Paulinus, who had been irregularly nominated, was recognized as bishop of Antioch by Pope Damasus. This caused a
split among orthodox Antiochenes and a schism with Rome.[55]
This schism lasted almost to the end of the century.

(42) It was after Meletius returned from his second exile
that John Chrysostom, at the age of nineteen, was baptized
(368).[56] By 371 he was serving Meletius as a lector but left
Antioch the following year to adopt the monastic life. His
imprudent austerities broke his health and forced him to
return to Antioch in 378, where he resumed his services as
lector. In 380 or 381 Meletius ordained him to the diaconate.
Since he had earlier received an excellent rhetorical training in
the school of Libanius,[57] he turned his gifted pen to the com-

55 Cayré vol. 1, 329–30; See F. Cavallera, *Le schisme d'Antioche* (Paris 1905); R.
Devreesse, *Le patriarchat d'Antioche* (Paris 1945) 39–47.
56 See R.E. Carter, "The Chronology of St. John Chrysostom's Early Life,"
Traditio 18 (1962) 357–64. (hereafter cited as Carter). Others date Chrysostom's baptism in 370. The present volume has no need to offer any
lengthy biographical notice on St. John Chrysostom. Two previous volumes of this series have already given information on his life and works. See
Sister Thomas Aquinas Goggin, S.C.H., trans., *St. John Chrysostom: Homilies
on the Gospel of St. John*, FOTC 33 (New York 1957) and P.W. Harkins,
trans., *St. John Chrysostom: Discourses against Judaizing Christians*, FOTC 68
(Washington, D.C. 1979). For biographies see, e.g., D. Attwater, *St. John
Chrysostom* (Milwaukee 1939) and C. Baur, *John Chrysostom and His Time:*
Vol. 1, *Antioch;* Vol. 2, *Constantinople*, trans. Sister M. Gonzaga, R.S.M.
(Westminster, Md. 1960–61). For shorter accounts see C. Baur, "John
Chrysostom," CE 8.452–57; P.W. Harkins, "Chrysostom (John), " *Ency-
clopaedia Brittanica* (1961) 665–66; "John Chrysostom, St.," NCE
7.1041–44. For bibliographies on Chrysostom and his works up to 1959 see
Quasten 3.424–82. The bibliographies are extended to 1977 in Quasten's
Spanish edition, *Patrología*, vol. 2 (Madrid 1977) 471–537; see also D.C.
Burger, *A Complete Bibliography of the Scholarship on the Life and Works of St.
John Chrysostom* (Evanston, Ill. 1964).
57 G. Downey, *Antioch in the Age of Theodosius the Great* (Norman, Okla. 1962)
85–102 gives an excellent account of Libanius and his school. See also A.H.
M. Jones, "Chrysostom's Parentage and Education," *The Harvard Theo
logical Review* 46 (1953) 171–73.

position of several instructive and apologetic treatises such as his treatise *On the Priesthood* (381–85), *On St. Babylas against Julian and the Pagans* (ca. 382), and *Against Jews and Pagans on the Divinity of Christ* (386), and many others.

(43) On February 28, in the year 380, the emperor Theodosius issued his famous edict *Cunctos populos* which established orthodoxy as the religion of the empire[58] and, in 381, another edict which deprived the heretics of the right to meet in the churches they had previously occupied.[59] The same year (381) Meletius died, and Flavian was chosen to succeed him. It was Flavian who ordained Chrysostom to the priesthood (Feb. 26, 386)[60] and entrusted to him the task of preaching to the Christians of Antioch, instructing them in the faith, and winning back the Arian Anomoeans to orthodoxy.

(44) At this time Antioch, like most cosmopolitan centers, had a decidedly pluralistic population. This pluralism showed itself especially in matters of religion. Pagans, Jews, and Christians (both heterodox and orthodox) all claimed the attention of Chrysostom. First, he wrote his treatises *On St. Babylas against Julian and the Pagans* while still a deacon and, shortly after his priesthood, *Against Jews and Pagans on the Divinity of Christ*. He next turned to the heterodox Anomoeans but had to interrupt his attack on them at least twice to take up the gauntlet *Against Judaizing Christians*, who were observing the feasts and fasts of the Jews.[61]

(45) The homilies *Against the Anomoeans* (twelve in number) fall into two series both in theme as well as in time and place. The first five homilies have been published in two editions in

---

58 *Codex Theodosianus* 16.1.2. Cited by G. Downey, *A History of Antioch in Syria* (Princeton 1961) 416 (hereafter cited as Downey, *History*). See C. Pharr, *The Theodosian Code and Novels and the Sirmondian Constitutions* (Princeton 1952) 440.

59 Ibid. 16.5.6. Cited by Downey, *History* 416.

60 For the date of his ordination see H. Delehaye, ed., *Synaxarium ecclesiae Constantinopolitanae* (Brussels 1902) col. 492 (under Feb. 26); cf. also M. Aubineau, "Un nouveau 'panegyricon chrysostomien' pour les fêtes fixes de l'année liturgique: Athos Panteleimon 58" *Analecta bollandiana* 92 (1974) 87. Carter, 364 sets the date as 385/86.

61 Cf. P.W. Harkins, trans., FOTC 68.1–5, 47.

the series *Sources chrétiennes.*[62] The first edition uses Bernard de Montfaucon's (1655–1741) text found in PG 48.701–48, while the second presents a new critical edition of Mlle. Anne-Marie Malingrey. I have used the second edition as the basis of my English translation of Homilies I–V.

(46) These first five homilies were delivered at Antioch in the first year of Chrysostom's priesthood and deal with the theme of the incomprehensible nature of God. The setting was unique because not only were the heretic Anomoeans present to hear him but they had even challenged him to do battle with them (cf. Hom I.39). Here was an opportunity both to refute and root out the errors of the heterodox and also to instruct the orthodox in the tenets of the true faith. In this way Chrysostom could work for the conversion of the Anomoeans, and, at the same time, he could protect his own flock from the enticing simplicity and appeal of Anomoean logic.

(47) Although Arianism had suffered severe blows under Constantius, its heretical beliefs were still strongly rampant at Antioch. There the Anomoeans had revived all the main tenets of Arius. What seems to have earned for them the name of Neo-Arians at this time is that they stressed in their heretical beliefs a theory of knowledge of God's nature. For them man can and does know God as God knows himself.

(48) This was not a new tenet in Arianism. Some twenty years before, Eunomius, who had succeeded Aetius as leader of the Anomoeans, had taught that God has no more knowledge of his own substance than we do; his being is no more clearly understood by him than by us. All we know of him he knows equally well, and all that he knows, the same also we will find without any difference in ourselves.[63] God can be defined in his nature: he is *agennētos* or "unengendered."[64]

---

62 J. Daniélou (Introd.) and R. Flacelière, trans., *Jean Chrysostome: Sur l'incompréhensibilité de Dieu,* vol. 1, SC 28 (Paris 1951); J. Daniélou (Introd.), A.-M. Malingrey (text and notes), and R. Flacelière, trans., vol. 1, SC 28 bis (Paris 1970). The reprint of Montfaucon's edition of all twelve homilies is found in PG 48.701–812.
63 Cf. Socrates, HE 4.7 (PG 67.473).
64 Cf. Cayré, vol. 1, 314.

(49) God's first creative act was to beget the Word, who must, therefore be less than God and can be called his Son only by adoption. To the Son the Father communicates a lesser divinity and power because the Father wishes the Word to serve as his instrument and to produce other creatures according to the Father's intention and command. The highest in rank of these creatures is the Holy Spirit who will collaborate with the Son in creating the world. But both Son and Spirit are creatures and, hence, are *anomoioi*, that is, in no way like the substance and being of the Father.[65]

(50) The first five homilies are aimed at the Anomoeans' pretension of a perfect knowledge of God, and Chrysostom's arguments will rest chiefly on explanations of texts from Scripture which show that God's nature is beyond the comprehension of all creatures.

(51) The first homily, delivered on a Sunday,[66] a short while before the Jewish feast of Rosh Hashanah,[67] clearly points out how meager and mediocre human knowledge is and what madness it is for men to pretend they possess the fullness of knowledge of God since God is incomprehensible to both men and angels. Chrysostom closes his homily with a plea for gentleness, kindness, and moderation toward all men, even enemies of the faith.

(52) The second homily followed the first only after the first discourse of the series against Judaizing Christians, after he had entertained a throng of "spiritual fathers," and after the celebration of many martyrs' feasts had occupied him.[68] Now he is back in the arena and he shows that the Anomoeans are meddlesome, inquisitive, and cannot accept what God says in Scripture because they lack confidence in God. Yet they have the boldness to say that they know God as God himself knows himself. They see the vastness of his works and the in-

---

65 Cf. Theodoret, *Haereticarum fabularum compendium* 4.3 (PG 83.419).
66 Cf. Harkins, FOTC 68.I.1 (p.1) and nn. 1 and 2.
67 This feast (the Jewish New Year) falls on the first day of the month Tishri (Sept.–Oct.). See J. McKenzie, DB 613–15 and L. Jacobs, "Rosh Ha-Shanah," *Encyclopedia Judaica* 14 (New York 1972) 309–10. Cf. Harkins, FOTC 68 I.5 (p. 3) and ibid., introduction liii, paragraph 10.
68 See below Hom. II.3–4.

significance of man, yet they fail to see the great distance between God and man. Man can see the sky but he does not know its essence. Can the Anomoeans know perfectly the essence of a God whom they cannot see? Still, they must be treated gently because they are sick. We must pray that God may lead them back to the light of true knowledge.

(53) In the third homily Chrysostom first points out that nothing can add to or detract from the intrinsic glory of God. Hence, God is not hurt by the blasphemous pretense of the Anomoeans that they know God in his essence. The heretics are only hurting themselves. No man or angel can know God in his essence since this is known only by the Son and the Spirit. Even though the Scripture says that a man or an angel sees God, this does not mean that God is seen as he really is but that he appears to men or angels by a condescension accommodated to their natures. In fact, a man may see an angel only by a similar condescension. Yet, the Anomoeans pretend to know the very essence of the Lord of angels. Still we must pray that the Anomoeans may be restored to health. Chrysostom closes the homily with an exhortation to those who come to the church only for the homily but then leave immediately after, without remaining for the Mysteries.

(54) The opening paragraph of the third discourse *Against Judaizing Christians* clearly points out that it follows a second interruption in the series against the Anomoeans,[69] which may have occurred after the second, third, or fourth homily. The third seems to be the most likely place because Hom. IV opens with a rather lengthy recapitulation (paragraphs 1-10) of what was said in Hom. III.

(55) Chrysostom then goes on to explain that when John the Evangelist said: "No one has ever seen God" (Jn 1.18), he was speaking not of condescension and accommodation but of a clear knowledge and perfect comprehension. In the same way God had said to Moses: "No one shall see my face and live" (cf. Ex 33.20). And in these texts sight means knowledge. But only the Son, who dwells in the bosom of the Father, i.e., who is of the same essence as the Father, and the Spirit know God with

---

69 FOTC 68.III.1.1 (p. 47) and n.1.

full and perfect knowledge. They are one in being with the Father. Chrysostom then ends his homily with an exhortation to keep a proper attitude in church and advises the congregation to leave their purses at home for fear that robbers may pick their pockets.

(56) In the fifth homily Chrysostom picks up on the theme that only the Son and the Spirit know the Father and then answers the Anomoeans' objections that the Son is not equal to the Father. Paul had said (cf. 1 Cor 8.6): "One God, the Father, from whom are all things, and one Lord, Jesus Christ, through whom are all things." This, explains Chrysostom, does not exclude the Father from being Lord nor the Son from being God. Both names, God and Lord, are common to Father and Son and show that the essence is exactly the same. The names *Father* and *Son* show what is proper to their realities as distinct divine Persons, although one in essence.

(57) But how can man know perfectly this one essence of God? Although God made man only a little less than the angels, man cannot know or understand the essence of an angel. Indeed, man cannot know or understand the essence of his own soul. When one does not know the essence itself—not that it is but what it is—it would be the height of folly to give that essence a name. Still the Anomoeans have given a name to the essence of God when they define him as *agennētos*, "unengendered." Not even a pagan ever dared to set down a definition of the divine essence or to encompass it with a name.

(58) The Anomoeans have a further objection. They say: "If you do not know God's essence, you do not know what you are adoring." Chrysostom replies that being ignorant of God's essence is not the same thing as not knowing him. We need only know that he is; we need not know what he is. To contend obstinately that one does know his essence is really not to know him. All we are required to know is that he exists; we are not expected to be inquisitive about his essence.

(59) Lastly, they tell us that, as St. John says (Jn 4.24): "God is spirit." If they draw a definition of God from the Scriptures, they will also have to call him a consuming fire and a fountain of living water. Furthermore, the word *spirit* had many meanings such as a soul, a wind, a human mind, even anger.

According to the Anomoeans, then, God will be all these things and compounded of as many elements as these things are.

(60) At this point he puts an end to discussion with the Anomoeans on the incomprehensible nature of God and turns to an encomium of prayer, an exhortation to true humility, the need to confess our faults and surrender ourselves to Christ.

(61) These first five homilies, which were delivered at Antioch in the first year of Chrysostom's priesthood (386), deal with the theme of the incomprehensible nature of God. Hom. VI is an interruption in the series which falls between the first and second themes and was occasioned by the feast of St. Philogonius on Dec. 20, 386. Chrysostom preached a panegyric on this blessed bishop who held the episcopal see of Antioch about the year 320 when Arianism was beginning to flourish.

(62) That Hom. VI was an interruption in the series is made quite clear in the very first sentence. There Chrysostom says: "Today I was preparing to strip for the struggles against the heretical Anomoeans and to pay off the balance of my debt to you. But the feast of the Blessed Philogonius, which we are celebrating today, has summoned my voice to recount his virtuous deeds." Nor was Chrysostom the only panegyrist to voice the praises of Philogonius on that day. In Hom. VI. 22 he tells us that Bishop Flavian will complete the panegyric because Flavian has a more exact knowledge of those earlier days when Philogonius was bishop of Antioch. Chrysostom completes this sixth homily by speaking on another feast, the feast of Christ's Nativity, which will come in five days. This is what enables us to date the homily as delivered on Dec 20, 386.[70]

(63) If we look for a single theme in Homilies VII–XII, it

---

70 Montfaucon discusses these points in his *Notice* on Homilies VI, VII, and VIII (PG 48.747–48). He admits that Hom. VI is foreign to the argument of the sermons which precede and follow it but he still retains it in this place because Chrysostom states that it is an interruption of the series against the Anomoeans and because several of the older MSS keep the same numerical order for Homilies I–VIII. These eight are found in the same sequence in the edition of Fronton du Duc (Fronto Ducaeus [1558-1624] (Paris 1636–39). I shall add translations of all Montfaucon's *Notices* (preliminary remarks) to the end of my introduction.

would be that the Son is one in substance with the Father, the *homoousios* of Nicaea. But in Chrysostom we must not look for the theological depth of the treatises of Basil the Great or Gregory of Nyssa or Gregory of Nazianzus.[71] They were writing for theologians. Chrysostom was addressing himself to Christian people both orthodox and heterodox. The orthodox he instructs and edifies; the heterodox he tries to turn from their error by exposing the fallacies on which their arguments rest.

(64) In Homilies I–V we see the Anomoeans obstinately claiming for themselves that they know God as perfectly as God knows himself. But therein they claim what belongs alone to the only begotten and to the Spirit.[72] In the following homilies (VII–X) Chrysostom's argument moves to a second stage where he will show the glory of the only begotten. Why does the Son possess this glory? Because he has the same power and might as does the Father, because Father and Son have the same nature and essence, because the Son is *homoousios* or one in substance with the Father.

(65) Therefore, in these homilies Chrysostom is proving and explaining the consubstantialty of the Son with the Father. But in answering the objections of the Anomoeans he is also explaining the Incarnation and Christ's consubstantiality with mankind. He is not only true God; he is also true man. Whatever the Son says or does in a lowly spirit, whenever he prays to his heavenly Father, he does so as man. This in no way is done because of any inferiority in Godhead but because his divine nature and equality with the Father is condescending to and

---

71 For the three Cappadocians see J.B. Peterson, "Basil the Great, Saint," CE 2.330–34; J. Gribomont, "Basil, Saint," NCE 2.143–46; P. Allard, "Basile (Saint)," DTC 2.1.441–59, especially 448–50; J. Lebon, "Le Sort du 'Consubstantiel' Nicéen," *Revue d'histoire ecclésiastique* 48 (1953) 632–82. For Gregory of Nazianzus see D.O. Hunter-Blair, "Gregory of Nazianzus, Saint," CE 7.10–15; J.T. Cummings, "Gregory of Nazianzus, Saint," NCE 6.791–94; P. Godet, "Grégoire de Nazianze (Saint)," DTC 6.2.1839–44. For Gregory of Nyssa see H. Leclercq, "Gregory of Nyssa, Saint," CE 7.16–18; R.F. Harvanek, "Gregory of Nyssa, Saint," NCE 6.791–96; P. Godet, "Grégoire de Nysse (Saint)," DTC 6.2.1847–52.
72 See below Hom. IV.24–25; 31; V.5–8; 9–17.

accommodating itself to the weakness of those to whom he speaks and for whom he acts.

(66) Since Hom. VI was delivered so near the close of the year 386, we will not be far wrong in conjecturing that Hom. VII was delivered early in 387, very possibly on January 5. In the very first sentence he laments that the congregation has shrunk because of the chariot races, and these were run on that day according to Montfaucon.[73] Furthermore, January 5 fell on a Sunday in 387.[74] Chrysostom also points out (Hom. VII.7) that he has just recently proved that God's nature is beyond the comprehension of every creature and is clearly understood by the only begotten and the Spirit alone. This is a clear reference to Homilies I–V. Therefore, Hom. VII (as well as VIII–X) seem to be joined to the first five by proximity of time and place.

(67) Hom. VIII was delivered the day after Hom. VII. This Chrysostom himself states clearly at the very opening of Hom. VIII.[75] In fact, he chides those who missed yesterday's discourse (presumably to attend the chariot races), refuses to recapitulate his arguments, and urges those who were absent then to find out from those who had been present the arguments with which he had routed the Anomoeans. Chrysostom then continues to answer the heretics' objections that the Son is inferior to the Father especially in the matter of the request of the mother of the sons of Zebedee that James and John be given the highest places in the Kingdom.

(68) The ninth and tenth homilies are widely separated in the earlier editions as if they had no relation to the first eight. Indeed, Hales, an English scholar who aided Savile in textual criticism and wrote notes for the Eton edition of 1612,[76] considered Hom. IX of doubtful authenticity. He admitted the style was not much different but did not consider that the method of treatment and manner of invention sounded much like Chrysostom.

---

73 *Notice* 2.5 below (PG 48.748).
74 Ibid.
75 Hom.VIII.1–2.
76 C. Baur, *S. Jean Chrysostome et ses oeuvres dans l'histoire littéraire* (Louvain 1907) 84.

(69) Montfaucon refutes this because he finds the genuineness of Hom. IX (*On Lazarus Four Days Dead*) confirmed by Chrysostom himself in Hom. X (*On the Prayers of Christ*). In Hom. X he refers at least three times to his discourse *On Lazarus Four Days Dead* and in each place Chrysostom makes it clear that Christ is praying to his Father in a spirit of condescension and accommodation to the weakness of those nearby.[77]

(70) No one questions the validity of Hom. X, which gives a triple guarantee that Hom. IX is also genuine. However, Montfaucon does offer for consideration the possibility that the ninth discourse was delivered extemporaneously. As we see from the first paragraph, the story of the raising of Lazarus was read at that day's liturgy to those assembled in the church. The Anomoeans and the Jews (probably Judaizing Christians) saw in the reading an argument for their belief that the Son was not like the Father but inferior to him. Hence, Christ had need to pray to the Father to raise Lazarus back to life. Chrysostom refutes this by demonstrating that Christ prayed out of condescension and accommodation, even if his argument is impromptu and somewhat hurried.[78]

(71) Therefore, Homilies IX and X belong together even though several days intervened between the times they were delivered.[79] It is also reasonably certain that these two discourses are properly joined to Homilies VII and VIII in theme because all strongly stress the glory of the only begotten, consubstantiality, and his equality in power with the Father. Whatever the Son said or did in a lowly fashion was done out of condescension and accommodation and to teach the humility proper to human nature. In the plan of redemption, the Incarnation did not take away Christ's glory. That glory was truly and genuinely his by nature.

(72) We have already seen that Homilies VII and VIII are closely related in time to Homilies I–V. Hom. X makes it clear

---

77 Cf. Hom. X.7, 17, 18.
78 See Montfaucon, *Notice* III.7 (PG 48.777). All of Montfaucon's *Notices* on the homilies contained in this volume appear in translation at the end of this introduction.
79 Cf. Hom.X.1.

that both it and the discourse which precedes it are not far
separated from all those which go before.[80] Hence, it seems
quite safe to date Homilies I–X as belonging to 386–87 and as
delivered in Antioch.

(73) At this point, it may be that Chrysostom felt that the
Anomoeans were thoroughly vanquished. In the first paragraph of Hom. X he says that it is time to finish repaying his
debt to his congregation. The debt was the refutation of the
Anomoeans and the instruction of the orthodox to keep them
from falling into the Arian errors. At the end of the discourse
he gives an exhortation to reconciliation with the enemy. His
arguments have reset the dislocated limbs of the Anomoeans.
Now is the time for friendship and love for all the members of
Christ's body. Harmony will win a crown of peace, for love is
the beginning and end of every virtue.

(74) One might wonder how it was that the heretics would
come to the church to hear their convictions refuted. We must
recall, first, that Theodosius' decree *Cunctos populos* had established orthodox Christianity as the official religion of the
empire in 380. Second, in 381, another Theodosian edict had
deprived the Arian heretics of the right to meet in the churches
they had occupied and turned all these churches over to the
orthodox Christians. Finally, with no other place to worship,
the Anomoeans came to hear and applaud Chrysostom, who
was already famous as an orator.

(75) Chrysostom saw them in church but, for a time, did not
bring forward his arguments to refute their heresy. As he
himself said: "I hesitated and held back when I saw that many
who were sick with this disease were listening to my words and
finding pleasure in what I said. Since I did not wish to frighten
off my prey, for a time I restrained my tongue from engaging
in these contests with them. I wished to have them in perfect
check before I stripped myself to face them in combat.

(76) "But when I heard, thanks be to God, that they were
clamoring and challenging me to enter the arena, it was then

---

80 Cf. Hom.X.1 and X.7. The latter, which stresses reasons given in recent
discourses, is a very clear reference to Hom.VII.17–22, 23–30 and to
many other places.

that I felt confident in my courage, readied myself for action, and took up the weapons 'to destroy their sophistries and every proud pretension which raises itself against the knowledge of God (cf. 2 Cor 10.4–5).' I did not take up these weapons to strike my adversaries down but to lift them up as they lie prostrate. For these weapons have the power to strike the obstinate and to give zealous care to those who have the prudence to listen. These weapons do not inflict wounds; rather they cure those who are sick."[81]

(77) Here we see Chrysostom's eagerness to reclaim the heretics and his pastoral care for the flock which has wandered. Neither in his discussion of the incomprehensibility of God's nature nor in his arguments for the Son's consubstantiality with the Father do we find the rancor with which he speaks of the Jews in his *Discourses against Judaizing Christians.*

(78) Perhaps there is good reason for believing that the Antioch series with its two themes and two stages was successful. At least no further series against the Anomoeans is found in Chrysostom's works except for the final two discourses in this volume (XI–XII), which were delivered some eleven years later at Constantinople in the year 398, almost immediately after Chrysostom became bishop of that imperial metropolis.

(79) Although these two are far removed from the first series in time and place, Montfaucon has put them as a second series in sequence with the earlier homilies because of the nature of the argument they use. Neither homily touches on the incomprehensibility of God, but both do discuss the consubstantiality of the Son with the Father, and Chrysostom frequently refers to this relationship in his favorite phrase: "the glory of the only begotten."

(80) Perhaps the Anomoeans of Constantinople were not making the idle boast that they knew God as God knows himself, that God could be defined as *agennētos* or unbegotten, but they certainly rejected the divinity of Christ. Neither of the

---

81 Hom.I.38–39.

series of two homilies (XI–XII) offers internal evidence that Arian Anomoeans were present in the church. Hence, Chrysostom's main purpose may have been less one of refutation of the heretics and more one of instructing the orthodox and deepening their faith in the glory of the only begotten.

(81) Nonetheless, Constantinople must have had a large Anomoean population which might well have constituted a threat to the faithful. In Hom. XI.3, Chrysostom says: "On every side wolves surround you ... The fires of heresy threaten with their encircling flames ...." Indeed, the church itself—probably once a seat of Arian worship—stood in an Anomoean section of the city. For Chrysostom goes on to say: "To see it here is like seeing an olive tree in bloom, weighted down with fruit, yet standing in the middle of a furnace."

(82) Hom. XI is only the second he preached after his arrival in Constantinople. This is made clear in the very first sentence of the discourse. Unfortunately, the first homily he delivered in his see has not come down to us, but it is quite possible that it, too, dealt with Anomoeanism and, perhaps, with the incomprehensibility of God's nature.

(83) The lost discourse and Hom. XI certainly had some connection because in XI.4, Chrysostom says: " ... come now, and let me, with all love, make payment on the promise I made to you yesterday when I discussed with you the weapons of David and Goliath." Goliath was in full panoply while David was armed with a sling and the spiritual stone of faith.

(84) Then, in Hom XI.6, Chrysostom goes on to add: "This is why, at that time, I promised that I would say nothing based on reasoned arguments. 'The weapons of our warfare are not merely human but spiritual. They demolish sophistries and reasoning and every proud pretension that raises itself against the knowledge of God.' ... [82] Since reasoned arguments are so weak, come, let us join battle with our opponents with arguments from the Scriptures as our weapons."

(85) Chrysostom alludes to this text from 2 Corinthians in two other places. The first is in Hom. I.39 when he had heard

---

82 Cf. 2 Cor 10.4–5.

the Anomoeans were challenging him and he took up his weapons "to destroy their sophistries and every proud pretension which raises itself against the knowledge of God." There he is using his weapons of the spirit to combat the madness of those who pretend to possess the fullness of knowledge whereby they make God's very essence subject to their powers and processes of reasoning. If Chrysostom used this text in that same connection in the lost first homily, his discourse might well have dealt with the fact that God is incomprehensible to men.

(86) The second place we find the text from 2 Corinthians used is in the opening paragraph of Hom. VIII. There Chrysostom is referring back to his combat with the Anomoeans the previous day in Hom. VII. But Hom. VII dealt with his second theme—the glory of the only begotten, the consubstantiality of the Son with the Father. When he spoke in a lowly and humble fashion, he spoke as God made flesh and in a spirit of condescension and accommodation because the understanding of his hearers was weak.

(87) It is most unfortunate that Chrysostom's first discourse given at Constantinople has been lost. We can be quite sure that it was aimed against the Anomoeans but we can only guess at what aspect of the heresy it attacked. But we can be grateful that we have the two discourses which have survived. They continue to establish "the glory of the only begotten" and his equality in power with the Father for a new congregation in a different time and place.

(88) We have seen that there can be no doubt about the connection of Hom. XI with the lost discourse. We can be equally certain that Hom. XII followed Hom. XI after a short interval. In the first paragraph of Hom. XII, Chrysostom thanks God for the increase in the congregation after he had closed his preceding discourse with a plea that entire families—husbands, wives and children—attend the assemblies in church together and be supportive of each other by worshipping together. He then says: "Even if we count how few were the days since we sowed this seed, look how rich a crop has sprouted up because of your obedience." Hence, the two could not have been far separated in time.

(89) Also, in Hom. XII.5, he says: "In my earlier discourse, I mentioned that Christ had said: 'If you believed Moses, you would believe me.'" This is a clear reference to Hom. XI.11 where we find the same text quoted.[83] And again in Hom. XII.4, Chrysostom states: "I have come to provide you with the conclusion of what I said earlier. At that time, I wove my discourse on the glory of the only begotten Son of God from Old Testament texts. Now I shall continue to do the same thing and will again take my start from the same Testament." And he does exactly that.

(90) Chrysostom's statement about providing a conclusion gives some hint that this twelfth homily may be the conclusion of this series. After a stirring account of Christ's cure of the paralytic on the Sabbath, Chrysostom goes on to show that this was no violation of the Sabbath because Christ is divine, equal to the Father, and master of the Law. The work he does on the Sabbath is work he does with the Father in the divine providence and care for the world. If that providential care should cease, every creature would waste away, perish and be gone.

(91) So it is that the twelve sermons against the Neo-Arian Anomoeans treat of two themes, the incomprehensibility of God (I–V) and the consubstantiality of Christ with the Father (VII–XII); they fall into two series separated by time and place. Homilies I–X were delivered at Antioch in the years 386–87; Homilies XI and XII belong to 398 and were preached in Constantinople. The fact that they are numbered sequentially is due to Montfaucon, but not without good reason.

(92) It would be remiss on my part if I were to fail to mention how much I have benefitted from the sound and splendid scholarship which characterizes the edition of the first five homilies found in SC 28 bis. The introduction by J. Daniélou is excellent and treats of several important matters which seemed to lie beyond the scope of my own introductory remarks.[84] His treatment of the holy dread a Christian must

---

83 Cf. Jn 5.46.
84 His introduction (SC 28 bis 9–61) goes far beyond his excellent article, "L'incompréhensibilité de Dieu d'après s. Jean Chrysostome," in *Recherches de science religieuse* 37 (1950) 176–94.

feel as a reaction to the divine transcendence is indeed most penetrating and rich in inspiration. The same must be said of his section on angelology, which also throws much light on this subject which does not seem to receive the attention it deserves in the catechesis of the Western Church. Daniélou has also noted in Homilies I–V many liturgical data which, again, enlighten the Western Christian on matters of Eastern worship.

(93) Mlle. Malingrey has established herself as a world-known figure in the editing of Chrysostomica.[85] Her careful work has given us a long-needed critical text of Homilies I–V, the value of which she has enhanced with annotations which throw much light on the meaning of the text. R. Flacelière has also been helpful with his translations of several thorny passages which I might have otherwise misconstrued. Much of what I say in my own commentary may well stem from Daniélou's introduction and Malingrey's annotations, and for this I am most grateful to them. Where my information is drawn solely or entirely from either of these sources, I have marked my notes either with a (D) for Daniélou's introduction or an (M) for Malingrey's commentary on Homilies I–V.

(94) I have used Malingrey's Greek text for my translation of Homilies I–V and Montfaucon's 2nd Benedictine edition (ed. T. Fix, Paris 1834) as reprinted in Migne's *Patrologia Graeca* (Paris 1862) as the basis for my translation of Homilies VI–XII. The Migne reprint has Latin translations printed on pages facing the Greek text. Montfaucon prepared the translations for Homilies I–V, Erasmus, for VI, and Fronton du Duc did the translations for Homilies VII–X. The translator of Hom. XI is someone whose identity is not sure, and the translation of the final homily (XII) is by the Italian humanist Flaminio Nobili (Flaminius Nobilius).

(95) As already mentioned, R. Flacelière has translated Homilies I–V into French for SC 28 bis. J. Bareille prints all twelve discourses in his *Oeuvres Complètes de Saint Jean Chry-*

---

85 She has provided critical texts for at least six volumes in SC, the latest (SC 272, 1980) contains Chrysostom's homily on the day of his ordination and his treatise on the priesthood.

sostome (Paris 1865) with his own French translation accompanying the Greek text (a reprint of Montfaucon). There is also a slightly older rendering in the complete French Chrysostom produced largely under the direction of M. Jeannin: Arras and Bar-le-Duc 1863–69. My own version presented in the present volume is, to the best of my knowledge, the first published translation of the homilies into English.

(96) Biblical texts have been translated directly from Chrysostom's Greek. I have found it useful to compare Chrysostom's citations from the Old Testament with the readings of the Septuagint as given in A. Rahlfs' sixth edition (2 vols. Stuttgart 1935), which is herein designated by the abbreviation LXX. In my renderings from both Testaments I have consulted *The Jerusalem Bible* (JB) and *The New American Bible* (NAB). Wherever "cf." precedes a Scriptural citation in my notes, it means either that the reader is referred to the text for confirmation of Chrysostom's argument, or that Chrysostom has quoted the text in a partial or an abridged form, or that his quotation varies from Rahlfs' LXX.

(97) Biblical proper names generally appear in the form used in NAB, from which I have drawn also the abbreviations for the books of Scripture. Where a given book of the Bible is differently designated in NAB and the Septuagint (Vulgate), both forms are given, that from NAB first. Thus I give, e.g., 2 Kgs (4 Kgs), 1 Chr (1 Par), Sir (Ecclus), Rv (Apoc). In the enumeration of the Psalms (or of verses thereof), however, the Septuagint (Vulgate) number is given first; e.g., Ps 138 (139).14. I have made extensive use of *The Jerome Biblical Commentary* (JBC), edited by R. Brown, J. Fitzmyer, and R. Murphy (Englewood Cliffs, N.J. 1968) and my references to it follow the form employed in the book itself, i.e., by article and section numbers.

(98) The paragraphing of the homilies is my own, and I have numbered each paragraph for convenience of cross-reference. These references are given by the number of the homily in Roman numerals and the number of my paragraph in Arabic numerals, e.g., VIII.16.

(99) To close this introduction, I am adding my translations of Montfaucon's four *Monita*, notices or preliminary remarks

to the twelve Homilies. His first *Notice* covers Homilies I–V (PG 48.699–700); the second, Homilies VI–VIII (PG 48.747–48); the third, Homilies IX–X (PG 48.777–78); the last, Homilies XI–XII (PG 48.795–96).

NOTICE I
On Homilies I–V

(1) We put these sermons *De Incomprehensibili [On the Incomprehensible Nature of God]* among Chrysostom's first, namely, those which he delivered to the people of Antioch in the year 386. Chrysostom himself gives us indications of this time, although, in his usual way, these signs are perplexing and not carefully stated. The first indication is found in Homily III.38–39 *De incomprehensibili*, where we read: "Ten years ago some men were arrested for trying to seize supreme power, as you know. One of them—a man in a position of power—was found guilty of the charge. He was gagged and was being led to execution. Then the whole city ran to the hippodrome even bringing workmen from their shops. All the people came together from every side and rescued the condemned man from the imperial wrath, even though he deserved no pardon."

(2) It is surely obvious that here it is a question of the conspiracy of Theodore who at the very latest suffered capital punishment in the year 374. Passing over the difficulties which arise from this story which Chrysostom tells but which must be explained in his *Life*, it surely seems clear that Theodore's death cannot be dated after 374. After this reckoning has been set down and established, Chrysostom was not going to say, "ten years ago," or, "twelve years ago," so that the calculation might stand. This sermon was delivered after some months had elapsed since his ordination to the priesthood in 386.

(3) We borrow another indication from one of the homilies *Contra Judaeos* which was delivered in 387, where Chrysostom says: "But what I am going to tell you is clear and obvious even to the very young. For it did not happen in the time of Hadrian or Constantine, but during our own lifetime, in the reign of the

emperor of twenty years ago. Julian, who surpassed all the emperors in irreligion, invited the Jews to sacrifice to idols, etc.," where we notice a similar anachronism. For Julian died in 363, and if the calculation were to start with this year, Chrysostom would have delivered these sermons in 383.

(4) But he was then a deacon and he delivered no sermons to the people before he was ordained a priest, as he, himself, testifies in his first homily (PG 48.693–700). But he was ordained in 386, as we have often said and will be proved by many arguments in the *Life* which is to be provided at the end of the *Works*.

(5) And so we assign these homilies to 386. But we do not think that these debates *Against the Anomoeans* were completed in that same year. As we shall say about the homilies *Contra Judaeos (Against Judaizing Christians)*, the series of sermons which he began in 386 he completed at the beginning of the following year. The reason for this chronology will become clear from what we shall say in our *Notice* to the homilies *Contra Judaeos*.

(6) The first homily was delivered to the people during the absence of Bishop Flavian. From this fact he skillfully seized an opportunity to praise his pastor. Afterwards he enters the battle against the Anomoeans as he had long since resolved to do. So he mentions that he had undertaken this battle rather late because he saw that many Anomoeans were present at his sermons and were listening to him with pleasure. Therefore, so as not to drive away his prey, he says, so that he might catch their souls in his snare, he curbed his tongue from struggles and contests of this sort. Finally, when the heretics themselves were urging him to come down into the arena, he began to attack the errors of the Anomoeans, but with a friendly spirit and not so much to strike enemies as to lift up those who were lying prostrate.

(7) After an interval of many days he gave the second homily *Against the Anomoeans*. Many things interrupted Chrysostom from the course on which he had resolved. There was the struggle against the Jews which was very necessary. Also there was the arrival of several spiritual fathers, as he says. Furthermore, these were neighboring bishops as the man who

prepared the title of the homily says. But more about this in the *Life* of Chrysostom. Finally, after these bishops had gone back to their own lands, the throngs took him as the holy herald of the memorial of the martyrs. After these feasts were celebrated, he took up the interrupted struggle.

(8) In the third homily he pursues the same argument on the incomprehensibility of God against the Anomoeans. At the end he inveighs against his hearers because, after the sermon (to which they paid eager attention) was finished, they immediately slipped out of church and were not present for the mysteries which were celebrated immediately after.

(9) In the fourth homily, after his usual skirmishes against the heretics, he congratulates the throng because they had gone along with his warnings and rid themselves of the practice of retiring before the mysteries. Still he is pained because purse snatchers were disturbing the sermon and he warns the people not to carry gold or silver in their purses if they wish to drive away such a curse.

(10) Finally, in the fifth homily, after a brief review of what he had said before, he brings forward new arguments against the Anomoeans. In these sermons not only Chrysostom's eloquence shines forth but also his forceful argumentation. Nonetheless his replies to the heretics' objections must be eyed with some suspicion. But not with so much suspicion that a man would not be far from the truth if he counted these homilies among the most outstanding works of the saintly doctor.

(11) Furthermore, we have published a new translation and rejected that of Theodore of Gaza[86] because his was adorned with roundabout language and was redundant in words and sometimes in thought.

---

86 On this little known scholar, who died in 1478, see L. Stein, "Der Humanist Theodor Gaza als Philosoph," *Archiv für Geschichte der Philosophie* 2 (1889) 426–58.

NOTICE II
On Homilies VI, VII, and VIII

(1) Here we are following the order of the older MSS, which that famous man, Fronton du Duc, also followed. It is true that several MSS, after the five discourses *Against the Anomoeans*, add as the sixth the sermon *On Saint Philogonius*, as the seventh *On the Consubstantiality*, and as the eighth the one *On the Petition of the Sons of Zebedee*. The seventh and eighth fit in with the first five in both time and argument. Even if the sixth was delivered after the fifth with no other intervening, it would appear altogether foreign to the argument if Chrysostom were not to state at the beginning that the feast of Saint Philogonius was interrupting the usual struggle against the Anomoeans which he had undertaken by his own choice. Hence, it became usual to keep the same order found in the older MSS, and we, following the example of Fronton du Duc, did not wish to disturb this.

(2) Furthermore, this homily *On Saint Philogonius* was delivered on Dec. 20, 386, five days before Christmas, as is said in Hom. VI.26 and 30. For at that time the feast of the birth of Christ, just as it is today in the West, was already being celebrated at Antioch on December 25, and this was the case for a few years, as will be recounted in the *Notice* to the homily on the same feast of the Nativity, which is found among the panegyrics.

(3) Chrysostom did not complete the panegyric on Saint Philogonius. He left the greatest portion of the encomium for Bishop Flavian who was going to preach on the same day. So Chrysostom broke off the panegyric in the middle of the sermon so as to exhort the people to celebrate properly the birthday of Christ. After he traced out the way for sinners to do penance and reform, he closed his sermon.

(4) In his *Epistola ad episcopos Aegypti et Libyae*, Athanasius mentions this Philogonius who, after practicing law was bishop of Antioch about the year 320 when Arianism was at its beginning. Athanasius numbers him among the orthodox and apostolic men. He was the twenty-first bishop of Antioch; he followed Vitalis in the see and was succeeded by Paulinus

who was followed by Eustathius. We have published the translation of Erasmus, corrected in many places from the Greek text.

(5) He delivered the following homily *On the Consubstantiality* (VII) against the Anomoeans, as he himself points out in VII.7, a few days after he had preached on the same argument, namely, at the beginning of 387 and, as far as we may conjecture, on Jan. 5, when the games in the circus were held. Furthermore, that day fell on a Sunday in 387.

(6) On the following day he delivered a homily which, for the reasons mentioned, is put down as Number VIII to refute the Anomoeans who were taking an opportunity for opposing him from the petition of the sons of Zebedee, and from Christ's answer to them: "But to sit at my right hand or my left is not mine to give to you." Fronton du Duc translated both VII and VIII into Latin and we have published his translations with very few changes.

NOTICE III
On Homilies IX–X

(1) Both the reason of time and argument urge us to put together and join to the other homilies *Against the Anomoeans* the two following sermons on the prayers of Christ although they were widely separated in the earlier editions. Both of them treat of Christ's prayers offered to the Father. From these prayers the heretical Anomoeans and the Jews drew the conclusion that Christ's power was not equal to the Father's and also that he was not the same in substance but different. This argument belongs to the series of polemics which he delivered against the Anomoeans at the end of 386 and the beginning of 387.

(2) Chrysostom clearly indicates in the second (X.7), that they were delivered about the same time where he hints that at that time the controversies regarding the glory of the only begotten were flourishing, and that was a name by which he was in the habit of calling his disputations against the Anomoeans.

(3) Furthermore, in the same sermon (X) he more than once mentions the first of these two (IX), on Lazarus four days dead or *On the Prayers of Christ over Lazarus Who Was Four Days Dead*, as if it had been delivered not long before. But regarding the first (IX), in [Henry] Savile's [1549–1622] notes, [John] Hales [1584–1656] raises a question which we must not overlook. In the notes we read: "We have corrected a MS of this sermon from the Royal Library in Paris by a MS from the Augsburg library." Hales does not think it is genuine. He says, to be sure, that the style is not much different. But the method of treatment and at the same time the manner of invention do not sound like our John. "The reason which he gives why Christ addressed Lazarus by name, his turning to address Hell, and its personification sound like the rather youthful boldness of the stamp of some more recent talent but not like John's solid arguments. Certainly the sermon must be put among the doubtful works or those considered spurious. But somehow or other it came about that, while we were busy with something else, it crept into the number of the genuine and unadulterated works."

(4) This is what Hales said, but if he had noticed that this sermon is eloquently mentioned in the sermon which is entitled *On the Prayers of Christ* (X) on which no suspicion of spuriousness can fall, perhaps he would have refrained from such a heavy judgment. But because in Savile's edition, this first on Lazarus (IX) lies separated by a great distance from the second (X) on the prayers of Christ, Hales did not notice that Chrysostom himself confirms the genuiness of the first (IX) on Lazarus in this second sermon (X).

(5) This is what he has in X.7: "You know and recall that in my recent discourses on the glory of the only begotten . . . at that time we discussed those reasons at sufficient length when we recalled to your mind the prayer he offered at the raising of Lazarus and the prayer he offered on the cross itself. I clearly proved that he offered the one of these prayers as a guarantee of the plan of redemption and the other to correct the weakness of those who heard him, even though he had no need of help himself. And listen to this as a proof that he did many things while he was teaching them to be humble in their

thoughts. He poured water into a basin, etc." All of these items are clearly related in the sermon on Lazarus four days dead.

(6) And in X.17–18: "You must know that he prayed so as to condescend and accommodate himself to us. I have already proved this especially in what I said about the events which occurred in the raising of Lazarus . . . as we said in our earlier discourse, the reason was that he was correcting the weakness of those who were there. And he, himself, gave this as the reason when he clearly stated: 'I spoke because of the people standing nearby.' In that discourse we gave sufficient proof that it was not the prayer but his word which raised the dead man to life."

(7) Furthermore compare these things with what he says about the homily *On Lazarus* in Hom. X.18 and you will see that this very homily is mentioned by Chrysostom as recently delivered. To meet the rest of the arguments raised by Hales, I would like you to consider that the sermon of Chrysostom *On Lazarus Four Days Dead* is an impromptu work done offhand, extemporaneously and hurriedly. For when, from the Gospel passage on Lazarus four days dead which was at that time read at the assembly in the church, the Anomoeans and the Jews, as Chrysostom says at the beginning, were taking the opportunity to contradict him and say that the Son was not equal to the Father because he prayed to the Father, Chrysostom delivered this sermon extempore. In it, with his marvellous and usual force of reasoning, he refutes the arguments of his opponents. Although the sermon does not boast his usual adornments of rhetorical figures, surely because the state of affairs did not demand them, still the style, all in all, sounds like Chrysostom even as Hales himself does not completely deny.

(8) But Hales continues: "The reason which he gives why Christ addressed Lazarus by name, his turning to address Hell, and the personification of Hell sound like the rather youthful boldness of the stamp of some more recent talent but not like John's solid arguments." But that reason which Chrysostom gives why Christ addressed Lazarus by name, "Lazarus, come out," is this: "If he were to have extended a general command to the dead, he would have raised all those in the tomb." That is, if he were only to have said: "Come out here," since this

command would not summon forth Lazarus more than any other dead person, all the dead would certainly have arisen—such is the power of Christ.

(9) I will not argue about the exactness of this reasoning, but I will gladly say this. If a decision has to be made from the spuriousness of reasoning of this sort, a great number of other homilies of Chrysostom which it is certainly clear that he published, would have to be removed from the series of genuine works.

(10) And you could say this with equally good reason about his address to Hell and the personification which goes like this: "When Christ prayed, the dead man did not arise. He arose when Christ said: 'Lazarus, come forth!' O the tyranny of death! O the tyranny of the power which took possession of that soul! O Hell, the prayer was uttered, and do you refuse to let his soul go?" "I do refuse," Hell says. But why? "Because I was not commanded to do so, etc." (Hom. IX.20)

(11) How many apostrophes and personifications of this sort are there in Chrysostom's works? If Hales had noticed that this homily was clearly mentioned in the other (X), which nobody can doubt is Chrysostom's, I am sure Hales would not have brought forward either the apostrophe or the personification as an argument that the sermon was spurious.

(12) Therefore, following the example of Fronton du Duc, we felt no hesitation about publishing it among Chrysostom's genuine works and, as we said above, we joined to it the other sermon on the prayers of Christ. We did this not only because the reason of the argument and of time demand it but also because the second (X) confirms and affirms the genuineness of the first (IX).

(13) We have published Fronton du Duc's translation of both homilies.

NOTICE IV
On Homilies XI–XII

(1) Chrysostom delivered these homilies at Constantinople *Against the Anomoeans* about eleven years after he completed

the other homilies against the Anomoeans at Antioch. Nonetheless we were influenced by the nature of the argument to
place them in a sequence with those earlier ones.

(2) Fronton du Duc does not do this. He edited the first (XI)
in a place far from the others against the Anomoeans although
he gives to this one (XI) the title *Contra Anomoeos VI*. He
failed to notice that the second one (XII) was delivered a few
days after *Against the Anomoeans* and put it in his fifth
volume.

(3) However both were delivered in the year 398. The first
(XI) was his second sermon to the people of Constantinople as
he himself testifies at its beginning. But the sermon which
preceded it seems to have perished.

(4) If we trust two old MSS, Chrysostom delivered the first
(XI) in the New Church. But it is likely that the copyists put this
in the title because they were influenced by that statement of
Chrysostom, which, shortly after the beginning, reads: "It is
wonderful and unexpected to see that this church has been
planted in this section of the city. To see it here is like seeing an
olive tree in bloom, rich with foliage, and weighted down with
fruit, standing in the middle of a furnace" (Hom. XI.3).

(5) But he speaks in this way, as is clear from what precedes
it, because that part of the city was for the most part inhabited
by heretics. But he nowhere states that the church was recently
built. Therefore, until some surer evidence is found, I do not
think we should put our trust in this title of the two MSS.

(6) As we said, influenced by reason of the time and by the
nature of the argument, we join to this first (XI) the homily
(XII) *On the Paralytic, and On the Divinity of Christ and His
Equality with the Father*, which he delivered a few days after
the one entitled *Contra Anomoeos* at Constantinople.

(7) He clearly indicates this when he says: "At that time (i.e.,
recently as is clear from what goes before) I wove my discourse
on the glory of the only begotten Son of God from Old
Testament texts. Now I shall do the same thing from the same
Testament.

(8) "In my earlier discourse I mentioned that Christ had
said: 'If you believed Moses, you would believe me.' Now I am
telling you that what Moses said was this: 'The Lord God shall

raise up for you a prophet from among your brethren as he raised up me; to him shall you listen etc.' "

(9) But that text is explained at length in the preceding homily (XI.11–13). Furthermore, from the words of Chrysostom already cited, it is clear that he delivered this sermon (XII) so as to pursue there an argument set forth in the preceding homily (XI) which he also did.

(10) For even though he has many things to say about the paralytic, still all of them look to this purpose, namely, that from Christ's works of this kind he may prove that Christ is God and equal to the Father.

(11) To complete that proof, after the account of the paralytic, he hurries on to explain these words of the gospel: "My Father works even until now, and I work," and, as is his fashion, he gives an outstanding defense of the divinity of Christ. It was a bad thing that this sermon on the paralytic (XII) had been separated from the preceding one (XI) in all the earlier editions. The place, the time, and the argument, and Chrysostom himself show that both must be put together and are not to be separated.

(12) The Latin translation of the first homily (XI) is that of someone whose identity is not sure. The translation of the second homily is that of Flaminio Nobili. We give both translations with many corrections based on the Greek text.

ON THE INCOMPREHENSIBLE NATURE OF GOD

(Peri akataleptou)

HOMILY I

HAT IS THIS I SEE? The shepherd[1] is not here and still his sheep show a well-disciplined attitude. And this marks the pastoral success and virtue of the shepherd when, whether he is present or away, his flocks display complete earnestness and attention. Dumb sheep must remain in their pens when no one is there to lead them to pasture. If they put their heads out of the fold when no one is tending them, there must be a risk that they may roam far away. Here, however, we have no dumb sheep. Even if your shepherd is away, because of your well–disciplined attitude, you have met together in your usual pastures.[2]

(2) But your shepherd is here. If he is not here in the flesh, he is here in mind and spirit; if he is not bodily among you, his presence is felt in the orderly discipline shown by you, his flock. And this is why I am struck with greater admiration for him and I count him the more blessed because he had the power to instill in you such earnestness and attention. Surely we admire a general most when his troops maintain discipline even in his absence. This is what Paul was looking for in his disciples when he said: "So that, my dearly beloved, you are obedient as always, not only when I happen to be with you, but all the more now that I am absent . . . . "[3]

---

1 The bishop is Flavian, successor to Meletius and shepherd of the Christian flock of Antioch. See F. Cavallera, *Le schisme d'Antioche* (Paris 1905) 254–55. In Chrysostom's discourse on the day of his ordination (PG 48.696) he mentions the many trips Flavian made to preserve peace and order in the Church. It must have been during one such journey that Chrysostom delivered the present homily. Cf. *In kal.* I (PG 48.953) where we find an exordium quite similar to this one (M).

2 The pastures are, of course, the church where the flock will be nourished by the word of God. See below, e.g., III.35.

3 Cf. Phil 2.12. Chrysostom stresses the presence–absence portion of the text because Flavian is away. What is omitted from the citation is Paul's urging that the Philippians work with anxious concern to achieve their salvation, but that is implied by the orderly discipline of Flavian's flock. Cf. J. Fitzmyer, JBC 50.20.

(3) Why "all the more in my absence?" Because even if a wolf[4] comes upon the flock, he is easily driven off from the sheep when the shepherd is present. If he is away, the flock must face a greater risk because there is no one to protect them. And furthermore, when the shepherd is on hand, he shares with his sheep the reward for earnestness and zeal; when he is away, he lets their virtuous action be seen by itself and as their own.

(4) And yet it is your teacher[5] who, even in his absence, speaks these words of Paul to you; wherever he may be at this moment, he has you and your assembly before his mind's eye; wherever he may now be, people are with him and talking to him, but he does not see them in the same way as, at this moment, he sees you, even if you are not before his eyes.

(5) I know your teacher's love. It seethes and burns with ungovernable warmth. He keeps it rooted in the depths of his heart and cherishes it with abundant zeal. For he clearly understands that this love is the chief blessing of them all. In it all blessings have their root and source and mother. If there is no love, other blessings profit us nothing. Love is the mark of the Lord's disciples, it stamps the servants of God, by it we recognize his apostles.[6] Christ said: "This is how all will know you for my disciples."[7] By what? Tell me. Was it by raising the dead or by cleansing lepers or by driving out demons? No. Christ passed over all these signs and wonders when he said:

---

4 The image of the shepherd and his flock naturally brings to mind the image of marauding wolves who are the enemies of Christ's flock. See below II.5, where the wolves were the converts from Judaism who were insisting on circumcision for gentile Christians, and IV.37 where the wolves are the demons inhabiting the souls of the possessed. Here the reference is most likely to the Anomoeans, as it most certainly is in XI.3, delivered in Constantinople.

5 Bishop Flavian is not only shepherd but teacher as well. This function of both bishops and priests is emphasized in De sac. IV.3 and 4 (PG 48.665), especially to combat heresies such as Arian Anomoeanism.

6 Flavian's love in the midst of the struggles which were tearing to pieces the Church of Antioch are stressed in De anath. (PG 48.943–52).

7 Cf. Jn 13.35.

"This is how all will know you for my disciples: your love for one another."[8]

(6) For the power to perform those other wonders is a gift which comes only through a grace from on high. This gift of love must also be achieved through man's own earnestness and zeal. A man's nobility does not usually stamp the gifts which are given from above in the same way as it marks the achievements which come from a man's own efforts. Therefore, Christ said that his disciples are recognized not by miracles but by love.[9] For when love is present, the one who possesses it lacks no portion of wisdom but has the fullness of complete and perfect virtue. In the same way, when love is not there, man is bereft of every blessing. This is why Paul exalts love and lifts it on high in what he writes. Still, for all he may say about love, he never fully explains its true worth.

(7) For what could equal this love which embraces all the prophets and the whole Law? Without it nothing will be able to save a man even if he possess faith, understanding, knowledge of mysteries, martyrdom itself, or any other gift. For Paul says: "If I hand over my body to be burned but have not love, I gain nothing."[10] And again in another place, where he is showing that love is greater than all things and the crown of all blessings, he said: "But prophecies will cease, and tongues will be silent, and knowledge will pass away.[11] There are in the end three things that last: faith, hope, and love, and the greatest of these is love."[12]

(8) But surely my discourse on love has led us to another question which is no ordinary one. For the disappearance of prophecy and the silencing of tongues raises no difficult prob-

---

8 Ibid. Fraternal charity is a sign of the true Church as it waits for Christ to come again. Cf. B. Vawter, JBC 63.142.
9 Man must respond to God's gift of love by cooperating by his own earnestness and zeal, and these require man's own efforts. The gift of miracles is purely gratuitous. Hence charity is the greater gift, indeed the greatest. Cf. 1 Cor 13.13.
10 Cf. 1 Cor 13.3.
11 Cf. ibid. 8.
12 Ibid. 13.

lem. These charismatic gifts[13] served us preachers for a time and now have ceased. But their passing can do no harm to the word we preach. See how now, at least, there is no prophecy nor gift of tongues. Still this did not hinder or thwart the preaching of piety. But the passing away of knowledge does raise a question. For after Paul said: "Whereas prophecies will cease and tongues will be silent," he went on to say: "Knowledge will pass away."[14] If indeed, then, knowledge should be going to pass away, our situation will not improve but will grow worse; without knowledge we shall destroy what makes us completely men.

(9) The prophet said: "Fear God and keep his commandments, for this is man's all."[15] However, if this is man, namely, to fear God, and if fear of God comes from knowledge, but knowledge is going to pass away, as Paul says, then we shall be completely destroyed when there is no knowledge; all that we are will be gone, and we shall be in a state no better but much worse than irrational beings. For in knowledge we have the advantage over them, whereas in all other things pertaining to the body they surpass us by far.

---

13 The charismatic gifts are particular types of spiritual gifts which enable those who receive them to perform some office or function in the Church. Among these offices or functions Rm 12.6–8 lists prophecy, ministry, teaching, exhortation, almsgiving, ruling, the works of mercy. In 1 Cor 12.8–11 we find wisdom, knowledge, faith, healing, miraculous powers, prophecy, the distinction of spirits, tongues, and the interpretation of tongues. To Paul all of these are inferior to love (1 Cor 13.1–3). These gifts were not irrelevant in the primitive development of Christianity. Such external manifestations were a visible sign that a new force, a new spirit was at work. But it is evident from the NT and the literature of the postapostolic age that these phenomena were elements of the early Church which did not endure once it was securely established in the various communities. Cf. J. McKenzie, DB 326.

14 Cf. 1 Cor 13.8. In quoting this verse Chrysostom seems to understand knowledge as the natural knowledge which leads men by their use of reason to be completely human.

15 Cf. Eccl 12.13 and NAB note ad loc. This quotation seems strange at first until Chrysostom connects the fear of God with knowledge. By doing so, he can now pass from the natural order to the supernatural in his argument. He may also be thinking of Ps 110 (111).10: "The fear of the Lord is the beginning of wisdom."

(10) What is this that Paul says, then, and about what is he talking when he says: "Knowledge will pass away?"[16] He does not say this about complete and perfect knowledge but about partial knowledge. He speaks of passing away as an advance to something better where, by passing away, the partial knowledge is no longer partial but complete and perfect.

(11) The age of a child passes away but the child's essence does not disappear nor does it cease to exist. The child's age increases and turns him into a complete and perfect man. Such is the case with knowledge. Paul is saying that this little knowledge would no longer be little when it has become great through continuous growth. This is the meaning of "passes away," and he made it clear to us in the words which follow. After you heard him say that "it passes away", he did not wish you to think of this as complete dissolution but as an increase and advancement to something better.

(12) So after he had said, "It passes away," he went on to add: "Our knowledge is imperfect and our prophesying is imperfect. When the perfect comes, then the imperfect will pass away."[17] So the imperfect no longer exists, but the perfect does. The result is that imperfect knowledge passes away and no longer exists, but the perfect remains. This is because the passing away is a fulfillment and advancement to something better.[18]

(13) Please consider Paul's sagacity. He did not say: "We know a part," but: "Our knowledge is imperfect."[19] We grasp the part of a part. Perhaps you are anxious to hear how great a part we grasp and how great a part we have failed to grasp, whether we grasp the greater part or a part that is smaller. That you may learn, then, that you grasp the smaller, and not

---

16 Cf. 1 Cor 13.8.
17 Ibid. 9–10.
18 Paul distinguishes between imperfect and perfect knowledge only to show the superiority of love over all the charismatic gifts. Chrysostom, however, makes the distinction of primary importance because he is preparing to refute the pretentious boast of the Anomoeans that they have the fulness of knowledge.
19 Cf. 1 Cor 13.9.

simply the smaller but the hundredth or the ten thousandth part, listen to the words Paul goes on to say.

(14) Rather, before reading[20] the Apostle's words to you, I will give you an example which can set before your minds, as an example can, how much we have failed to grasp and how great is the part we do grasp. How great is the distance between the knowledge which is going to be given to us and the knowledge which we now have? How great is the distance between a complete and perfect man and an infant at the breast? For that is the degree of superiority of the knowledge to come in comparison to our present knowledge.

(15) That this is true and that future knowledge is so much greater than the present, let Paul himself again tell you. For after he said: "Our knowledge is imperfect" and because he wished to show how much we understand and that we grasp only the smallest part, he went on to say: "When I was a child, I used to talk like a child, think like a child, reason like a child. When I became a man, I put childish ways aside."[21] He was comparing present knowledge to the condition of a child, and future knowledge to the state of complete and perfect manhood.

(16) And Paul did not say: "When I was a lad" (for a twelve-year-old is called a lad), but: "When I was a child," showing us that by this term he means an infant who is still nursing, still being nourished by milk, still at the breast. So that you may know that Scripture calls such a one a child, listen to the Psalm which says: "O Lord, our Lord, how glorious is your name over all the earth, for you have exalted your majesty above the heavens. Out of the mouths of children and sucklings you have fashioned praise."[22] Do you see that everywhere Scripture speaks of the infant at the breast as a child?

---

20 Chrysostom often says "read" when he must mean "recite."

21 1 Cor 13.11. Paul, no doubt, compares the man with the child to show that charity is eternal but the charismatic gifts are transitory and temporal. There will be no need or use for them in heaven, just as the man has no use for the ways of his childhood. Cf. R. Kugelman, JBC 51:78. However, Chrysostom's different understanding of the comparison is quite apt for his argument.

22 Ps 8.2–3.

(17) Then, because he foresaw by the power of the Spirit the shamelessness of men of future times,[23] Paul was not satisfied with this one example but he made the matter certain by a second and a third. When Moses was sent to the Jews, he received the proof of three signs.[24] If the Jews failed to believe in the first, they might still listen to the second; and if they also disdained the second, out of respect for the third, they might at last heed the prophet.

(18) In this same way Paul sets down three examples. He gives one, that of the infant, when he says: "When I was a child, I used to reason like a child."[25] The second example was that of the mirror, and the third, that of the indistinct image. For after he said: "When I was a child," he went on: "Now we see as in a mirror by an indistinct image."[26] You see the second example of our present weakness and how our knowledge is incomplete and imperfect. See, too, the third example when he adds: "by an indistinct image." Surely, the young child sees and hears many things and utters many a sound. But nothing he sees or hears or utters is clear and distinct. He thinks, but his thoughts are not articulate.

(19) I, too, know many things but I do not know how to explain them. I know that God is everywhere and I know that

---

23 Chrysostom speaks as if 1 Cor 13 were directed against the Anomoeans and their shameless pretension of knowing God as God knows himself.

24 Cf. Ex 4.1–9. The first sign God gave to Moses was the staff which, when thrown on the ground, turned into a serpent; when picked up, it again became a staff. The second sign was Moses' hand covered with leprosy; the leprosy disappeared when he took his hand from under his cloak. The third sign was the drawing of water from the river and pouring it on dry land; the poured out water then turned to blood.

25 Cf. 1 Cor 13.11, where the child's knowledge is far inferior to that of a grown man.

26 Cf. 1 Cor 13.12. Paul (and Chrysostom) are comparing the knowledge we have of God in this world ("now") with that hoped for in the world to come ("then"). Paul uses two metaphors: one borrowed from the OT, "by an indistinct image" or "in riddles" (cf. Nm 12.8), the other from the popular Cynic-Stoic philosophy, "in a mirror." The first contrasts the privileged revelations given to Moses with those given to the other prophets. Not even Moses could see God "face to face" in this world (Ex 32.20). The second refers to the indirect vision of an object seen in a mirror; one sees not the object itself, but its reflection. Never, in this life, is our knowledge complete and perfect, as the Anomoeans maintained. Cf. R. Kugelman, JBC 51.78.

he is everywhere in his whole being. But I do not know how he is everywhere. I know that he is eternal and has no beginning. But I do not know how. My reason fails to grasp how it is possible for an essence to exist when that essence has received its existence neither from itself nor from another. I know that he begot a Son. But I do not know how. I know that the Spirit is from him. But I do not know how the Spirit is from him.[27] [I eat food but I do not know how it is separated into phlegm, into blood, into juice, into bile. We do not even understand the foods which we see and eat every day. Will we be inquisitive, then, and meddle with the essence of God?][28]

(20) Where are those who say they have attained and possess the fullness of knowledge? The fact is that they have really fallen into the deepest ignorance. For people who say that they have attained the totality of knowledge in the present life are only depriving themselves of perfect knowledge for the life hereafter. As for me, I say that my knowledge is imperfect and incomplete. And if I say that this knowledge will pass away, I am advancing on the road to a better and more perfect state. There, the partial knowledge becomes a more perfect knowledge once what was partial and imperfect has passed away.

(21) They are the ones who say that their knowledge is entire, perfect, and complete. If they then go on to admit that this knowledge of theirs in the future will pass away, they are proving that they will be bereft of all knowledge. Why? Because this knowledge of theirs passes away, and no other more

---

27 Here we have an application of the distinction between perfect and imperfect knowledge to the doctrines of the Anomoeans: the omnipresence of God in his whole being, the generation of the Son from eternity, the procession of the Holy Spirit—all of which orthodox theology held, while Anomoeanism denied. On earth, our imperfect natural knowledge knows what the true doctrine is but cannot know how the doctrine is true. That will come hereafter when we progress to perfect knowledge.

28 The lines in brackets could be a gloss, but a comparison with Hom.II.49–50 makes this far from sure. Furthermore, inquisitiveness and meddlesomeness are watchwords by which Chrysostom describes the pretensions to knowledge of the Anomoeans. See below, e.g., I.36; II.8, 16, 19, 31, 32, 39; IV.3; V.29.

perfect knowledge comes to take its place—if, as they say, the knowledge they now have is the very perfection of knowledge.

(22) They are obstinately set on having the fullness of knowledge here on earth. If they will have perfect knowledge here, they will not have the partial and imperfect knowledge proper to this life. And, at the same time, they will lose for themselves the full and more perfect knowledge which comes in the life hereafter.[29] You see that, do you not? Such is the great evil of failing to stay within the bounds which God fixed for us from the beginning. This is why Adam, in his hope for higher honor, fell from the honor which he had.[30] And the same thing happens in the case of men who have an avaricious love for money. Many of them, many a time, have lost what they had because they wanted more than they had. So also those who think they have the fullness of knowledge here will even lose the partial knowledge proper to this world.

(23) I urge you, then, to flee from the madness of these men. They are obstinately striving to know what God is in his essence. And I tell you that this is the ultimate madness. Do you wish to know why this is the very height of folly? I shall prove it to you from the prophets.[31] Not only is it clear that the prophets do not know what his essence is but they do not even know how vast his wisdom is. Yet his essence does not come from his wisdom, but his wisdom comes from his essence. When the prophets cannot perfectly comprehend his wisdom, how mad and foolish would the Anomoeans be to think that they could

---

29 Chrysostom gives to his argument a moral perspective. Those who make a pretense of knowing God in his entirety here on earth will be punished by excluding themselves from the knowledge of God they could have had in the hereafter (M).

30 The reference is to Gn 2.16–17 where Adam is forbidden to eat from the tree of the knowledge of good and evil; also to Gn 3.4–5 where the serpent tempts Eve to disobey God's command. Their disobedience led to loss. So, too, a man's avarice for greater wealth or knowledge can lead him to lose all—both here and hereafter.

31 Every prophet speaks through the action of the Spirit (cf. Hom.III.14). It is with this in mind that Chrysostom will quote the texts from the Psalms, Isaiah, and Paul.

make his very essence subject to their powers and processes of reasoning?[32]

(24) Therefore, let us listen to what the prophet says about this: "Your knowledge is too wonderful for me."[33] But let us see what he says further on: "I will give you thanks for you are fearfully wondrous."[34] Why "fearfully?" We wonder at the beauty of columns, mural art, the physical bloom of youth. Again, we wonder at the open sea and its limitless depth; but we wonder fearfully when we stoop down and see how deep it is. It was in this way that the prophet stooped down and looked at the limitless and yawning sea of God's wisdom. And he was struck with shuddering. He was deeply frightened, he drew back, and he said in a loud voice: "I will give you thanks for you are fearfully wondrous; wondrous are your works."[35] And again: "Your knowledge is too wondrous for me; it is too lofty and I cannot attain to it."[36]

(25) Do you see how prudent the servant is and how grateful is his heart? What he is saying is this: "I thank you that I have a Master whom I cannot comprehend."[37] And he is not now speaking of God's essence. He passes over the incomprehensibility of his essence as if it is something on which

---

32 Chrysostom here contrasts the clear grasp of the mystery of God, which the Anomoeans boast that they accurately understand, to the knowledge of conjecture which is necessarily imperfect since it depends solely on human reasoning. In fact, Eunomius, successor to Arius, says that he relies entirely on his own reasoning, but thanks to a theory of language which he draws from the text "Let there be light (Gn 1.3)," he attributes to God the origin of the name which exactly defines God himself. Cf. Eunomius, *Apologia* 7 (PG 30.841).

33 Cf. Ps 138(139).6 (LXX). Wisdom and knowledge are linked in Rom 11.33.

34 Cf. ibid. 14 (LXX). NAB reads ". . . that I am fearfully, wonderfully made . . . ." "Fearfully wondrous" evokes the image of a man gripped by a reverential fear in God's presence, standing before the infinite ocean of God's wisdom.

35 Ps 138(139).14 (LXX).

36 Ibid. 6 (LXX).

37 Here, for the first time in these homilies, we find the word "incomprehensible." Originally a philosophical term, it is not found in the NT but became quite usual in the language of Christian theology in the fourth century. It is used to denote God himself considered as being beyond our powers to grasp (M).

everybody is agreed. What he is speaking of here is God's omnipresence; and he is showing that this is the very thing that he does not understand, namely, how God is present everywhere. To prove to you that he is speaking of God's omnipresence, listen to what follows: "If I go up to heaven, you are there; if I go down to hell, you are present."[38] Do you see how God is everywhere present? The prophet did not know how this was true but he shudders,[39] he is upset, he is at a loss when he so much as thinks about it.

(26) How, then, can it fail to be the ultimate insanity for men who are so far below the prophet in grace to meddle and be inquisitive[40] about the very essence of God? And yet this is the same prophet who says: "You have manifested to me the secret and hidden things of your wisdom."[41] But still, after he has

---

38 Ps 138(139).8. R. Murphy finds it difficult to classify this Psalm as a hymn, or a sapiential consideration of God's active presence, or the prayer of an accused man. Murphy seems to favor the third classification since, in commenting on v. 8, he links the psalmist with the rebels Korah and Dathan (JBC 35.155). Chrysostom obviously understands the verse as a proof of God's omnipresence.

39 Shuddering is a part of the dizziness which characterizes the "holy dread" which Daniélou describes in his introduction to SC 28 bis (pp. 30–39). He cites a passage from Gregory of Nyssa (In eccl. hom. VII [PG 44.729D–732A]) which describes the vertigo which grips a man before the abyss of the divinity as follows: "He finds himself, as it were, on a steep cliff. In fact, let us imagine a smooth and precipitous rock whose bulk sinks down into the sea to a limitless depth and raises up its ridge on high, whose summit plunges down from its brink into a yawning abyss. Then, what generally happens to a man whose toes touch the brink which overhangs the abyss but find no support for his foot nor grip for his hand, this same sensation usually comes to a soul which has gone beyond any place where it had a footing as it searched for the nature which is before time and cannot be measured by space. Since this soul no longer has anything on which to take hold—neither place, nor time, nor measure, nor anything else—it no longer finds any point of support for its thoughts. As it feels that what is incomprehensible is slipping away on all sides, the soul is gripped by dizziness and it has no way to get out of its difficulty" (Daniélou, SC 28 bis, 34–35).

40 "Meddlesome inquisitiveness" is an accusation Chrysostom often levels against the Anomoeans (see above n.28) and indicates an activity which leads a person to be busy about many things—especially things which do not concern him (M).

41 Ps 50(51).8.

learned the secret and hidden things of God's wisdom, he says
that this very wisdom is inaccessible and incomprehensible.
"Great is our Lord, and mighty in power: to his wisdom there is
no limit,"[42] that is, there is no way to comprehend it. So what is
it you heretics are saying? Is his wisdom beyond the prophet's
grasp, and do we comprehend his essence? Is this not obvious
madness? His greatness has no limit, and do you put his
essence within the limits of a definition?

(27) Isaiah was pondering on these matters when he said:
"Who shall declare his generation?"[43] He did not say: "Who
declares," but; "Who shall declare," and in this way he shuts
out any future declaration. David on the one hand says: "Your
knowledge is too wonderful for me;"[44] on the other hand,
Isaiah says that this declaration has been shut off not only from
himself but also from all human nature. However, let us see if
Paul, inasmuch as he had enjoyed greater grace, did not know
his generation. But Paul is the one who said: "Our knowledge
is imperfect and our prophesying is imperfect."[45] Still, Paul is
not discussing God's essence in this place but, both here and
elsewhere, he does speak of the wisdom made manifest in
God's providence.

---

42 Ps 146(147).5. See below III.11–13; IV.8.

43 Cf. Is 53.8 (LXX). See FOTC 68, p.1 n.3, which points out that the Hebrew
text of this verse has been variously emended and translated. NAB reads:
". . . and who would have thought any more of his destiny?" JB gives:
". . . would anyone plead his cause?" and adds a note that the words "who
will explain his generation (or descent)?" of the Greek and Latin translations have been taken by Christian tradition to refer to the mysterious
origin of Christ. E. Power (CCHS 568) points out that the Hebrew noun dôr
(the reading probably basic to LXX) usually means "generation" in the
sense of lifetime or contemporaries, but that it cannot indicate the act of
generating, the eternal or temporal generation of Christ. Chrysostom takes
the Greek word *genea* in its literal meaning of descent or generation. Here
he is obviously more interested in the future tense of the verb which
excludes any future declaration or explanation. Hence the Anomoean
heretics can never define the substance of God.

44 Cf. Ps 138(139).6 and see above I.24.

45 Cf. 1 Cor 13.9 and see above I.13, 15, 20. In 1 Cor 13 Paul is speaking of the
primacy of love but not of the wisdom made manifest in God's providence.
It is true that Paul's "imperfect knowledge" fell far short of grasping not
only God's essence but also his wisdom and providence of which he will
speak in Rom 11.

(28) Nor does he speak of God's complete providence, which includes his benevolent care for the angels, archangels, and the powers above. What Paul is here examining is that portion of God's providence by which his benevolent care provides for men on earth. Furthermore, his scrutiny touches only a portion of that part. For he does not fully and completely examine that part of God's providence by which he makes the sun to rise, by which he breathes souls into men, by which he fashions their bodies and nourishes them on earth, by which he controls the world and gives annual crops to nurture it. Paul passed over all these things and examined only the small portion of God's providence by which he rejected the Jews and accepted the gentiles.[46]

(29) As he looked at this small part by itself, it was as if he were shuddering at a limitless sea and were peering into its yawning depth.[47] And immediately he drew back and, with a loud shout he exclaimed: "How deep are the riches and the wisdom and the knowledge of God! How inscrutable are his judgments!"[48] Paul did not say: "incomprehensible," but: "inscrutable." But if his judgments cannot be searched out, it is much less possible that they can be comprehended. "How unsearchable are his ways!"[49] Are his ways unsearchable while he himself is comprehensible? Tell me that.

(30) And why do I just speak about his ways? The rewards which he has stored for us are also incomprehensible. "Eye has not seen them, ear has not heard, nor has it entered into the

---

46 In Rom 9 Paul makes it clear that Israel's infidelity is not contrary to God's direction of history; but in Rom 10 he points out that Israel's failure to accept Christ is derived from its own culpable refusal; however this failure (Rom 11) is partial and temporary. See J. Fitzmyer's commentary on these three chapters in JBC 53:95–115.

47 Here Chrysostom attributes to Paul the same shuddering and "holy dread" with which he characterized the reaction of the psalmist in I.24 above (see n.39). Fitzmyer (JBC 53:115), however, says that Paul's exclamation is not made in awe and fear, but in admiration and gratitude at the boundless wonder of God's providence in arranging for the mutual assistance of Jews and gentiles in attaining their salvation. Israel's role in the divine plan of salvation would never have been suspected otherwise.

48 Cf. Rom 11.33 and NAB note ad loc.

49 Cf. ibid.

heart of man what God has prepared for those who love him."[50] His gift is beyond all description. For Paul says: "Thanks be to God for his indescribable gift,"[51] and: "His peace surpasses all understanding."[52] What are you heretics saying? His judgments are inscrutable, his ways are unsearchable, his peace surpasses all understanding, his gift is indescribable, what God has prepared for those who love him has not entered into the heart of man, his greatness has no bound, his understanding is infinite. Are all these incomprehensible while only God himself can be comprehended? What excessive madness would it be to say that?

(31) Stop the heretic; do not let him get away. Tell me. What does Paul say? "Our knowledge is imperfect."[53] The heretic answers that Paul is not talking about God's essence but about his governance of the universe. Very good, then.[54] If he is talking about the governance of the universe, our victory is all the more complete. For if his governance of the universe is incomprehensible, then all the more so is God himself beyond our powers of comprehension. But so that you may know that Paul is not talking here about God's governance of the universe but about God himself, listen to what follows.

(32) After Paul said: "Our knowledge is imperfect and our prophesying is imperfect," he went on to say: "My knowledge

---

50 Cf. 1 Cor 2.9.

51 2 Cor 9.15. The text actually has to do with the generosity of the Church of Corinth toward the needs of the Church of Jerusalem and the rewards God bestows on generous giving. The generosity of the Corinthian community and the resultant attitude of the Jerusalem community is an outward sign of the unity of the Church; this unity in the Spirit is so great a reality that its meaning cannot be fully explained in human language. Moreover, this unity and all that it implies is a gift from God. See J. O'Rourke, JBC 52:31.

52 Cf. Phil 4.7. God's peace surpasses all understanding either because the ordinary mind of man cannot comprehend it or because such a state of serenity surpasses all human efforts to attain it. Cf. J. Fitzmyer, JBC 50:25. Either reason is consonant with Chrysostom's argument.

53 Cf. 1 Cor 13.9.

54 This does not mean that Chrysostom agrees with the heretic's reply. Rather it looks to a new point which Chrysostom will win as he again resumes his argument a fortiori in the following lines (M).

is imperfect now; then I shall know even as I was known."[55] By whom, then, was he known? Was it by God or by the governance of the universe? Clearly, it was by God. Therefore, he is saying that his present knowledge of God is imperfect and in part. Paul did not say "imperfect" because he knows one part of God's essence and does not know another part—for God is simple and has no parts.

(33) Paul said this because on the one hand he knows that God exists, whereas, on the other, he does not know what God is in his essence. He knows that God is wise but he does not know how great his wisdom is. He knows that God is great but he does not know how or what his greatness is. He also knows that God is everywhere present but he does not know how this is so. He knows that God provides for all things and that he preserves and governs them to perfection. But he does not know the way in which God does all these things. Therefore, he said: "Our knowledge is imperfect and our prophesying is imperfect."[56]

(34) Suppose—and it seems a good idea to do so—suppose we forget Paul and the prophets for the moment. Let us now mount up to the heavens and see if there are those on high who know what God is in his essence. But even if there are in heaven beings possessed of this knowledge, we must realize that they will have nothing in common with us. For the distance which separates men from angels is a great one, and this gives us the best of reasons for trying to find out if the angels do have such knowledge. Let us, therefore, listen to the angels so that you may know—and know abundantly—that, not even in heaven, does any created power know God in his essence.[57]

---

55 Cf. 1 Cor 13.12. R. Kugelman explains this difficult text in JBC 51:78 as follows: "Then I shall know" implies a relationship between the perfect vision or knowledge of God and the charity by which we love God even in this life. "As I have been known" refers to the prevenient and merciful love of God shown in Paul's election to the faith and apostolate.

56 Cf. 1 Cor 13.9. This paragraph echoes I.19 above and n.27.

57 Chrysostom will discuss this at length in Homilies III and IV. For angelology in Homilies I–V see Daniélou's introduction in SC 28 bis, pp. 40–50. Cf. also the series of six homilies Vidi Dom. (PG 56.97–142).

(35) What, then, do you think? Do you think that the angels in heaven talk over and ask each other questions about the divine essence? By no means! What are the angels doing? They give glory to God, they adore him, they chant without ceasing their triumphal and mystical hymns with a deep feeling of religious awe. Some sing: "Glory to God in the highest;"[58] the seraphim chant: "Holy, holy, holy,"[59] and they turn away their eyes because they cannot endure God's presence as he comes down to adapt himself to them in condescension.[60] And the cherubim sing: "Blessed be his glory from this place,"[61] not that God is surrounded by a place—heaven forbid!—but they are speaking after the fashion of men, just as if they were to say: "wherever he is," or, "in whatever way he is,"—if, indeed, it is safe to speak in this way about God. For our tongues speak with the words of men.

(36) Did you see how great is the holy dread in heaven and how great the arrogant presumption here below? The angels in heaven give him glory; these heretics on earth carry on meddlesome investigations. In heaven they honor and praise him; on earth we find curious busybodies. In heaven they veil their eyes; on earth the busybodies are obstinate and shamelessly try to hold their eyes fixed on his ineffable glory. Who would not groan, who would not weep for them because of this ultimate madness and folly of theirs?

(37) I did wish to develop this argument at greater length. However, since this is the first time I have come down to meet my adversaries in the arena, I think it is to your advantage to be satisfied for now with what I have already said. In this way, the

---

58 Cf. Lk 2.14.

59 Cf. Is 6.3.

60 "Accommodation" and "condescension" are the key words by which Chrysostom explains how creatures may see God; he uses them constantly in the course of these homilies and defines them in III.15. There he says: "God condescends whenever he is not seen as he is, but in the way one incapable of beholding him is able to look upon him. In this way God reveals himself by accommodating what he reveals to the weakness of vision of those who behold him." See R.C. Hill, "On Looking again at *Sunkatabasis*," *Prudentia* 13 (1981) 3–11.

61 Cf. Ez 3.12 (LXX).

multitude of arguments which I will be advancing will not come upon you with a rush and sweep away your recollection of the arguments I have just given.

(38) At any rate, if God permits, we shall treat this topic at length in the future. For a long time before now, like a mother in labor, I felt anguish in my desire to bring forth these arguments and present them to you. But I hesitated and held back when I saw that many who were sick with this disease were listening to my words and finding pleasure in what I said. Since I did not wish to frighten off my prey, for a time I restrained my tongue from engaging in these contests with them. I wished to have them in perfect check before I stripped myself to face them in combat.

(39) But when I heard, thanks be to God, that they were clamoring and challenging me to enter the arena, it was then that I felt confident in my courage, readied myself for action, and took up the weapons "to destroy their sophistries and every proud pretension which raises itself against the knowledge of God."[62] I did not take up these weapons to strike my adversaries down but to lift them up as they lie prostrate. For these weapons have the power both to strike the obstinate and to give zealous care to those who have the prudence to listen. These weapons do not inflict wounds; rather they cure those who are sick.[63]

(40) Therefore, let us not be provoked with these men, let us not use anger as an excuse, but let us talk with them gently and with kindness. Nothing is more forceful and effective than treatment which is gentle and kind. This is why Paul told us to

---

62 Cf. 2 Cor 10.4–5. See also below VIII.1; XI.6.

63 See above Introduction 46, 74–77. Christian preaching in the fourth century was addressed to a large and very mixed audience. True worshippers were mingled with the curious who attended church as they would the oratorical declamations. Eloquence had its passionate partisans. Orators were held in high honor both by those who were orthodox Christians and by those who were not (M). Even many Christians came to church only for the homily and left immediately afterwards, as we learn from III.32–44. In FOTC 68 Chrysostom refers to the Judaizing Christians as being sick with the Judaizing disease and in need of what cure his words may bring. See ibid., passim and especially pp. 3, 4, 15, 33, 36.

hold fast to such conduct with all the earnestness of our hearts when he said: "The servant of the Lord must not be quarrelsome but must be kindly toward all."[64] He did not say "only to your brothers," but "toward all." And again, when he said: "Let your gentleness be known,"[65] he did not say "to your brothers," but "to all men." What good does it do you, he means, if you love those who love you?

(41) But if their love injures you and drags you down to share their godlessness, even if they are your parents, you must run away from them. If it be your eye, gouge it out. For Matthew tells us: "If your right eye leads you to sin, gouge it out."[66] But Matthew was not here talking of the body. How do we know this? If he were talking about the body's nature, the charge and the reproach would go right back against the author of nature.

(42) Besides, there would be no use in gouging out one eye. If the left eye will still be there, it leads the man whose eye it is into sin—just as his right eye did. But so that you may know that he is not talking about an eye, Matthew added the word "right." By this he is showing that if you have a friend as dear as your right eye, and if he causes you to sin, you must cast him out and cut him off from his friendship for you. What good would it do you to have an eye if it destroys the rest of your body?

(43) If, as I said, friendships do us harm, let us flee from them and run away. But if people do no harm to us in the matter of godliness, let us win them over and draw them to ourselves as our friends. However, if you are of no help to a person, and he does harm to you, cut off such an association and draw profit from the fact that you remain unhurt. If people do you harm, avoid having them as friends. Just run away, do not fight, do not start a battle. This is what Paul recommends when he says: "If possible, as far as in you lies, live peaceably with all men."[67]

---

64 2 Tm 2.24.
65 Cf. Phil 4.5.
66 Cf. Mt 5.29. See below II.53.
67 Cf. Rom 12.18.

(44) You are the servant of the God of peace. He it is who cast out demons and wrought countless good deeds. Even when they called him a demon,[68] he did not hurl a thunderbolt at them, he did not grind to dust those who were blaspheming him, he did not sear their shameless and arrogant tongues. He could have done all these things but he merely struck aside their accusation by saying: "I am not possessed by a demon but I honor the one who sent me."[69]

(45) And when the servant of the high priest struck him, what did he say? "If I said anything wrong, produce the evidence; but if I spoke the truth, why hit me?"[70] It is the Lord of angels who is defending himself and giving an accounting to a servant. There is no need for a longer explanation. Just turn these words over in your mind, ponder them continuously, and say: "If I said anything wrong, produce the evidence; but if I spoke the truth, why hit me?"[71] And think of the one who spoke them, to whom he spoke them, and for what purpose. You will have a sort of divine and never-ceasing incantation in these words; they will be able to soothe and reduce every swelling and inflammation of your soul.

(46) Consider the dignity of the one who is outraged, the worthlessness of him who commits the outrage, and the enormity of the outrage itself. Not only was Christ treated with indignity, but the servant also struck him; he did not merely hit him but he struck him in the face. And nothing dishonors a person more than slapping him in the face. But still Christ endured it all so that you may learn from his superior self-control to control yourself.[72]

(47) Let us ponder these things now and, when a time of need arises, let us recall them to mind. You showed your approval of what I said. Now show me your approval by your

---

68 The allusion is to Mt 9.34 and Jn 8.48.
69 Cf. Jn 8.49.
70 Jn 18.23.
71 Ibid.
72 See SC 28 bis 137, n.3 (M) on the theme of Christ as the model of all virtue.

deeds.[73] The athlete trains in the wrestling school so that he may show in the matches what benefit he got from his training there. Whenever anger comes upon you, show the profit you gained from listening to me here. Keep saying those words over and over again: "If I said anything wrong, produce the evidence; but if I spoke the truth, why hit me?"[74]

(48) Write this in your hearts. This is why I am constantly reminding you of these words. I do it so that everything I have said may be fixed in your souls and the memory of these words may remain indelible—as well as the profit you will derive from remembering them.[75] If we keep these words engraved over the whole breadth of our understanding, no one of us will be so rocklike, so senseless, so devoid of feeling as ever to be carried away by anger. Better than any rein or bridle these words will be able to restrain our tongues when they are being swept beyond proper moderation. They will be able to reduce the swelling of the mind and keep it constantly calm and unruffled. They can make perfect peace dwell within us.[76]

(49) May we enjoy this peace through the grace and loving-kindness of our Lord Jesus Christ, with whom be glory to the Father together with the Holy Spirit now and forever, world without end. Amen.

---

73 As often, Chrysostom urges that the fruit of his words be proved in deeds. See, e.g., *In act. apos.*30.4 (PG 60.225): "Why be puffed up with pride? Because you are teaching by word? But it is easy to be wise in words. Teach me by your life; that is the best instruction (M)."

74 Jn 18.23.

75 See below VII.56.

76 This exhortation to peace was particularly urgent at Antioch where the Church was split into factions, each with its own bishop. For the scandal raised by this division and the sorrow it caused Chrysostom see *In epist. ad Eph.*11.4 (PG 62.86) (M).

HOMILY II

OME NOW, LET US AGAIN[1] GIRD OURSELVES against the unbe-
lieving and infidel Anomoeans.[2] If they are vexed
because I call them infidels, let them flee the fact, and I
will hide the name; let them lay aside their heretical ideas, and
I will put aside this title of reproach. However, if they do not
hide away these thoughts but continue to dishonor the faith
and disgrace themselves by their actions, why are they vexed
with me because my words indict them on charges which they
themselves prove by their deeds?

(2) As you recall, a short time ago I did go down into the
arena to debate with them, I did come to grips with them in this
same contest. But immediately after that, the struggles with the
Jews took my attention, and it was not safe to neglect the
members of our own body who were sick.[3] Yet there is no time

---

1 Chrysostom explains in II.2–3 why there was a short delay between Homilies I and II; first, the problem of Judaizing Christians had to be faced and
their illness treated because the Jewish feasts and fasts were at hand (FOTC
68, pp.3–4); second, he was involved in attending to the needs of several
bishops visiting Antioch; finally, he was the preacher on the feast days of
several martyrs whose memorials called for panegyrics.
2 Chrysostom will explain why he calls the Anomoeans unbelievers and
infidels below in II.6. Their heretical ideas are the results of their meddlesome inquisitiveness into the essence of God and their denial of the Son's
consubstantiality with the Father, which destroyed the orthodox tenets of
the Trinity and the divinity of Christ.
3 In FOTC 68, pp. 3–4 Chrysostom says: "Yet some of these [Judaizing
Christians] will watch the festivals and others will join the Jews in keeping
their feasts and observing their fasts. I wish to drive this perverse custom
from the Church right now. My discourses against the Anomoeans can be
put off to another time . . ." In the preceding paragraph he had said: "We
must first root this ailment out and then take thought for matters outside;
we must first cure our own and then be concerned for others who are
strangers." Although this is a generalization, Chrysostom implies that the
Anomoeans are strangers outside the fold. On Judaizing Christians in the
fourth century see M. Simon, *Verus Israel* (Paris 1948) 256.

which is not a proper one to speak against the Anomoeans. However, if we had failed to anticipate on the spot the weakness of our brothers who were sick with the Jewish disease, if we had failed to snatch them, on that occasion, from the funeral pyre of this illness, there would have been no use to exhort them at a later time. The sin of participating in the Jewish fast would have already succeeded in destroying them.

(3) Then, after my struggles against the Jews, many spiritual fathers[4] who had come to our city from many places again took up my attention. And that would not have been a very suitable time to extend my debate with the Anomoeans because, as I might put it, all those rivers were emptying their waters into this spiritual sea. And after these spiritual fathers left for home, there came upon us, one after the other, an unbroken succession of martyrs' anniversaries.[5] Surely we could not rightly neglect preaching the praises of these athletes. I mention and enumerate these events to prevent you from thinking that I postponed my contests with the Anomoeans because of any cowardice or sluggishness on my part.

(4) Now we are rid of our battles against the Jews. Now the fathers have gone off to their own homelands. Now we have had the pleasure of praising the martyrs. Come now and let me set you free from the long-lasting pangs of your yearning to hear me. I know well that each of you feels the birth pains of your desire to hear what I shall say about the Arian Anomoeans no less than I feel the pangs of my desire to tell you. The reason for this is that our city has loved Christ from the beginning.[6] You have received as your patrimony the desire

---

4 Antioch was an important city as a center of the imperial administration; it was also the metropolitan see of the Eastern dioceses. See *In Sanctum Meletium* (PG 50.518): "Drawn by the greatness of the city and the service of the emperor, a great number of people from all parts of the world came to Antioch at that time; bishops of the Churches were convened there by order of the emperor (M)." We do not know what events occasioned the visits of the "spiritual fathers" alluded to here.

5 We might hazard the guess that two of the panegyrics referred to have been preserved for us: the one delivered on October 9, the feast of St. Pelagius (PG 50.579–84) and the other on October 17, the feast of St. Ignatius (PG 50.587–96).

6 It was at Antioch that the followers of Christ were first called Christians. Cf. Acts 11.26.

never to allow the teachings of our faith to degenerate into heresy.

(5) What makes this clear? In the time of your ancestors, men came here from Judea who were muddying the clear waters of the doctrine taught by the apostles. They were exhorting your ancestors to practice circumcision and to observe the Mosaic Law.[7] Those who then lived in your city did not remain silent nor did they put up with this innovation. They were like courageous hounds who saw wolves attacking and destroying the entire flock. They sprang after the wolves and did not let up chasing them and driving them away. They saw to it that the apostles from every corner of the world sent them their decision in the form of a letter which would protect them from any attack launched against the faithful by those innovators and all such as might come thereafter.[8]

(6) How, then, am I to begin my discourses against those Anomoeans? How else than with the accusation that they are infidels? Everything they do, all their meddlesome inquisitiveness is aimed at driving the faith from the hearts of those who hear them. And what charge of impiety and godlessness could be more serious than this? When God reveals something, we must accept his words on faith; we must not be arrogant and busy ourselves making investigations into what he has said.

(7) If any Anomoean wishes to do so, let him say that I am the one who does not believe. This neither vexes me nor displeases me. Why? Because my actions show whether the name fits. Let him call me an infidel. Let him also call me a fool for Christ. I rejoice in the names they call me as I would rejoice in a crown of victory. Why? Because I share this accusation with Paul. For he said: "We are fools on Christ's account."[9] This foolishness is more prudent than any wisdom. This foolishness on Christ's account succeeded in finding what the wisdom of the world could not find. This foolishness drove the darkness

---

7 The incident is recounted in Acts 15.1–12.

8 The letter is given in Acts 15.23–29.

9 1 Cor 4.10. To be a fool for Christ is to be wise, but not with the wisdom of the world. In 1 Cor 1 and 2 Paul contrasts the wisdom of the world with the wisdom given by God through revelation and grace.

from the world and brought back the light of knowledge.

(8) What is the foolishness of Christ? It is the foolishness we show when we hold in check our own thoughts and importunate ravings, when we free our minds and keep them emptied of this world's teaching. Then, when we should be accepting the teachings of Christ, we will present a mind which is swept clean and is free to hear God's words. Surely, whenever God reveals something with which it is not our place to meddle, we must accept it on faith. When God makes such revelations, only an insolent and reckless soul is so meddlesome as to seek causes, as to call for an explanation and accounting, as to search out how God's revelations can be true.[10] And again I shall try to prove this from the Scriptures themselves.

(9) There was a great and wonderful man named Zechariah. He had received the honor of the high priesthood.[11] He had been entrusted with the leadership of all the people. This man Zechariah came into the Holy of Holies, to the innermost sanctuary, upon which he alone of all men had the right to look. Consider how he was equal in importance to all the people. When he offered prayers for the whole people, when he was making the Master propitious to his servants, he was serving as a mediator between God and men.[12] This man

---

10 The Anomoeans' meddlesome curiosity makes them so reckless as to question what God reveals. If their worldly wisdom cannot find an explanation of what is revealed, they insolently reject the wisdom of God and refuse to accept it on faith.

11 Zechariah was not the high priest, and it is strange that Chrysostom gives this title and some of its functions to the husband of Elizabeth, the future father of John the Baptist. Lk 1.8–9 make it clear that Zechariah was a priest of the class of Abijah and was chosen by lot to exercise the privilege of offering incense in the Holy Place, the first (and outer) two rooms constituting the temple's Tabernacle (cf. Ex 30.1–9). See C. Stuhlmueller, JBC 44:28. The inner room was the Holy of Holies (cf. J. McKenzie, DB 862) which could be entered only by the high priest and by him only once a year, on the Day of Atonement. Cf. FOTC 68, pp. 172–3 n. 78.

12 Jewish priests had three functions: they gave oracles (Dt 33.7–11; Jgs 18.5; 1 Sm [1 Kgs] 14.41; 28.6); they instructed in the law (Dt 33.10); they offered sacrifice (Dt 33.10). "They are the indisputable mediators for entrance into the sphere of the divine," since they were the custodians of the sacred traditions of cult and of the knowledge of God. Cf. J. McKenzie, DB 691 and J. Castelot, JBC 76:3–10. Chrysostom also sees Zechariah as a mediator between God and men because Christ, the High Priest, is such a mediator. Cf. 1 Tm 2.5 and Heb 8.6.

Zechariah saw an angel standing inside the sanctuary. And the sight deeply disturbed him. But the angel said to him: "Do not be frightened, Zechariah; your prayer has been heard and behold you shall beget a son."[13]

(10) And what was the result of this? He used to pray for the people, to beg mercy for their sins, to ask pardon for his fellow servants. And the angel said to him: "Do not be frightened, Zechariah, your prayer has been heard."[14] As proof that Zechariah's prayer had been heard, the angel promised that a son, John, would be born to him. And this was very reasonable. Since Zechariah used to pray for the people because of their sins, he was going to beget a son who would cry out: "Look! There is the Lamb of God who takes away the sin of the world."[15] So it was reasonable that the angel said: "Your prayer has been heard and you will beget a son."[16]

(11) What did Zechariah do? For this is the subject under investigation, namely, that it is an unpardonable thing to be so curious as to question how God's revelations can be true. Rather it is our duty to accept on faith whatever God says. Zechariah looked at his age, his gray hair, his body which had lost its strength. He looked at his wife's sterility, and he refused to accept on faith what the angel revealed would come to pass.

(12) He questioned how this could be true and said: "How am I to know this?"[17] How, he said, will this be? Look! I have grown old and I have turned gray. My wife is sterile and advanced in years. My time of life lacks the freshness of youth; my nature is no longer useful for begetting children. How can what you have promised be reasonable? I lack the strength to beget; my wife's womb is no longer fruitful. Some of you may

---

13 Cf. Lk 1.13. NT actually reads: "Your wife Elizabeth will bear a son to you."
14 Cf. ibid.
15 Jn 1.29 and NAB note ad loc.
16 Cf. Lk 1.13. See n. 13 above.
17 Lk 1.18. Zechariah's question is similar to Abraham's in Gn 15.3–5. That Zechariah is punished is rather surprising since it was not unusual biblical practice to ask for a sign as Abraham did (Gn 15.8), as Gideon did (Jgs 6.36–40), and also Hezekiah (2 Kgs [4 Kgs] 20.8–11). God himself volunteered a sign to Moses (Ex 3.12) and Ahaz (Is 7.11–16). However, Zechariah's affliction was not permanent. But Chrysostom takes Zechariah's question as owing to a lack of faith in what God has revealed.

think he should be pardoned for probing into the predicted sequence of events. Should he not be excused for thinking that his question was reasonable?

(13) But God did not think that he deserved pardon. And this was very reasonable. For whenever God makes a revelation, there is no need to stir up the workings of one's reason nor to propose to oneself either a sequence of events, or a necessity rooted in nature, or any other such thing. The power of God's revealed word is above all these things, and no hindrance has ever checked its course. So what are you, a mere human, doing? When God makes you a promise, do you reject it and seek refuge in your old age? Do you argue that God cannot do what he promises because you are too old? Old age is not stronger than God's promise, is it? Nature is not more powerful than the creator of nature, is it?

(14) Do you now know, Zechariah, that the works which come from his words are strong and mighty? His word set up the heavens; his words produced creation, his word made the angels. Do you doubt that his word can produce a child? This is why the angel was angry and why he did not pardon Zechariah, for all the fact that he was a priest. Because of his priesthood Zechariah was subjected to greater punishment. For the man who has a higher title of honor should surpass others in accepting God's revelations on faith.

(15) How was Zechariah punished? "Look, you will be mute and unable to speak."[18] Your tongue, said the angel, which served you in disbelieving my words, will itself receive the punishment for your disbelief. "Look, you will be mute and unable to speak, until these things shall take place."[19] Think of the loving-kindness of the Master. You do not have faith in me, he says; now take your punishment. When I shall furnish proof through my deeds that my words are true, then will my anger cease. When you learn that you have been punished justly, then will I release you from your chastisement.

(16) Let the Anomoeans hear how vexed God is when he is the subject of curious inquiry. If Zechariah was punished

18 Cf. Lk 1.20.
19 Cf. ibid.

because he refused to believe in the birth of a mortal, how will you Anomoeans escape punishment for your meddlesome inquiries into the ineffable generation from above?[20] Tell me this. Zechariah did not flatly deny the possibility but he wanted to learn how this could be done. Nonetheless, he met with punishment. But what defense will you Anomoeans have when you arrogantly affirm that you know what no man can see or comprehend? What punishment will you not draw down on yourselves?

(17) But let our discussion of the generation of the Word await a suitable time.[21] Meanwhile, let us retrace our path to the former topic which we recently left unfinished. Let us try to tear out by the roots this destructive force because in it we have the mother of all evils, the source from which those teachings of the Anomoeans grew. What is the root of all these evils? Believe me, a holy trembling[22] lays hold of me as I am about to speak of it. I tremble to let my tongue utter the thought they are constantly pondering in their minds. What, then, is the root of these evils? A mere human has the boldness to say: "I know God as God himself knows himself."[23]

---

20 Again we have the a fortiori argument. The ineffable generation of the only begotten is beyond all created ken and must be taken on faith. Those who are meddlesome and inquire into it deserve a much stronger punishment than Zechariah receives for questioning how God can grant a son to an aged man and his sterile wife.

21 It would seem that no suitable time presents itself in any of these homilies. The generation of the Son remains ineffable since, as seen in Hom. I.27, any future declaration of this generation has been ruled out. However, Chrysostom will speak often of the glory of the Only Begotten and his equality with the Father. See, e.g., below Hom. IV.28–31; V. 1–28; VII-XII passim. None of these places explains the mysterious generation, but all prove the consubstantiality of the Son with the Father.

22 J. Daniélou, in SC 28 bis, Introduction pp. 36–37, has pointed out the importance of the terms holy trembling or dread. At the very thought of stating precisely the blasphemy of the Anomoeans, a shiver of fright grips Chrysostom.

23 We find the whole account of the Anomoeans' theories on their knowledge of God as God himself knows himself in the Apologia of Eunomius, (PG 30.837–68). See Hom. I.23 and n.32. These have been refuted by St. Basil, Adversus Eunomium (PG 29.497–773) and St. Gregory of Nyssa, Contra Eunomium (ed. W. Jaeger, vols. I and II; PG 45.248–1121). Notice the similarity of arguments which are given here with those found in Hom. I. 23–36. Both homilies, as do the rest, show Chrysostom's fondness for the argument a fortiori.

(18) Does this require refutation? Must I prove it wrong? Is not the mere utterance of the words enough to prove all the godlessness of the Anomoeans? In these words we have an obvious folly, an unpardonable madness, a new kind of impiety and godlessness. No one ever had dared to let such a thought enter his mind or to utter it with his tongue. You poor, miserable Anomoeans! Think of who you are and in what things you are meddling. Even though you are only a man, are you such a busybody as to be inquisitive about God?

(19) You are only a man, and the bare names we call a man are enough to prove how excessive your madness is. A man is dust and ashes,[24] flesh and blood,[25] grass and the flower of grass,[26] a shadow[27] and smoke[28] and vanity,[29] and whatever is weaker and more worthless than these. And do not think that what I am saying is an accusation against nature. I am not the one who says this, but it is the prophets who are expressing their thoughts on the lowliness of man. Nor are they seeking to heap dishonor on humankind but they are trying to check the conceits of the foolish.[30] Their aim is not to disparage our nature but to discourage the folly of those who are mad with pride.

---

24 Cf. Gn 18.27. This verse occurs where Abraham is interceding with God not to destroy Sodom and Gomorrah. The text is particularly apt because it comes just after the Lord has promised Abraham (as he promised Zechariah) that he will beget a son despite his age and Sarah's sterility and while Abraham is striving to soften God's wrath against the sinful cities. In both cases Abraham is humbly admitting his inadequacies and nothingness in God's sight.

25 Cf. Sir (Ecclus) 10.9 and 17.27. Cf. NAB note on 10.9. Cf. also Mt 16.17 where the Greek text reads: "Flesh and blood did not reveal this to you," which NAB translates: "No mere man has revealed this to you," equating "flesh and blood" with "mere man."

26 Cf. Is 40.6. See W. Hill, NCE 7.666–71. In vv. 6–7 the prophet heightens the all-powerful care of God by enunciating the helplessness of the people. Cf. C. Stuhlmueller, JBC 22:10. Cf. also Ps 102 (103) 15–16.

27 Cf. Chr 29.15; Ps 101 (102).12.

28 Cf. Ps 101 (102).4.

29 Cf. Eccl 1.2.

30 Chrysostom and the prophets are not disparaging human nature as such. Compared to the divine, it is indeed lowly, but all men have been created by God and in his own image; they are redeemed by his blood and are heirs to his kingdom. However, when man uses his reason to make himself equal to God by claiming to know God as God knows himself, this abuse of reason leads to a diabolical pride which will destroy him.

(20) Even though the prophets used so many and such harsh words, we still find some men who surpass the devil himself with their boasting. If the prophets had said none of these things, to what excess of madness would these Anomoeans not have rushed? Tell me that! These men have at hand the medicine to cure themselves and still they are swollen with festering sores. How puffed up would they have become with their arrogance and folly if the prophets had not used so many and such strong terms to describe human nature?

(21) At least listen to what the just patriarch says about himself: "I am dust and ashes."[31] He was talking to God, yet his confidence to approach God and speak freely to him did not exalt him to pride. In fact, it was this very freedom which kept urging him to speak with moderation. These men, who are not worth as much as the prophet's shadow, think they are greater than the angels. This proves that they have gone to the ultimate bounds of madness.

(22) Tell me. Are you meddling with God, who has no beginning, who cannot change, who has no body, who cannot corrupt, who is everywhere present, who surpasses all things, and who is above the whole of creation? Listen to what the prophets thought about God and then shudder with fear.[32] "He who looks upon the earth and makes it tremble."[33] He only looked at it and he shook the earth for all its immense size. "He touches the mountains and they smoke[34] . . . he shakes the earth under heaven from its foundations, and its pillars totter".[35] "He threatens the sea and makes it dry."[36] "He says to the

---

31 Gn 18.27 and n. 24 above.
32 Again we have the motif of shuddering and holy dread—here at even the thought of the Almighty. Not only the Father but also the Son are without beginning, incapable of corruption, and everlasting. The Anomoeans would deny these qualities to the Son, who for them is a creature. Cf. Basil, *Adversus Eunomium* I.7 (PG 29.525).
33 Ps 103 (104).32 (LXX).
34 Cf. ibid. The psalmist is fully aware of the mysterious and majestic aspect of God whose mere glance or touch is cataclysmic. Cf. R. Murphy, JBC 35:120.
35 Cf. Jb 9.6 (LXX).
36 Cf. Is 51.10. Chrysostom's reading of this text may be a conflation of some sort. It differs from Rahlfs' text and any variants given in his critical apparatus. The notion of threatening appears in none of the pertinent texts. The reference to drying up the waters seems to relate to the crossing of the Red Sea.

deep: 'You shall be dried up.' "[37] "The sea saw and fled: Jordan was turned back; the mountains skipped like rams, and the hills like lambs."[38] All creation is shaken, is afraid, and quakes. Only the Anomoeans look on with scorn, take no notice of their own salvation and disparage it. For I would not say that they scorn, disdain, and disparage the Master of all things.

(23) The other day we were admonishing and correcting them by using the example of the powers on high, the angels, the archangels, the Cherubim, and the Seraphim.[39] Today our example is drawn from inanimate creation, but they still feel no shame nor are they moved by fear of it. Do you not see how beautiful and vast these heavens are, how they are crowned and bedecked with a dancing troop of stars? How long a time have they lasted? They have stood five thousand years and more,[40] and this great length of time did not bring old age upon them. Just as a young body in full health keeps the prime of its youth flourishing and in bloom, so, too, the heavens have kept the beauty which was given to them from the beginning, and this beauty has in no way been marred by time. These great, beautiful, shining, starry heavens, which have lasted and stood for so long a time, were made by God with the same ease with which a man would set up a tent for sport.

(24) This is the God with whom you are meddling and whom you are bringing down to fit the limits of your own processes of thought. Isaiah made this clear when he said: "It is he who set up the heaven as a vaulted chamber and stretched it out as a tent over the earth."[41] Do you wish to turn your gaze to the earth? He also made this as if it were nothing. When he spoke of the heavens, Isaiah said: "It is he who set up the heaven as a vaulted chamber and stretched it out as a tent over the earth."[42] And he said of the earth: "It is he that com-

---

37 Is 44.27 (LXX).
38 Cf. Ps 113 (114).3–4. This entire Psalm commemorates Israel's deliverance from Egypt.
39 Cf. Hom. I.34–36 and see below II.29–30.
40 Chrysostom is, of course, using the old method of dating from creation.
41 Cf. Is 40.22.
42 Cf. ibid.

prehends the circle of the earth and made the earth as if it were nothing,"[43] even though the earth is so great and vast.

(25) Think how mighty are the masses of mountains, how numerous the nations of people, how tall and countless the trees, how huge the size of buildings, how many kinds of four-footed animals, of wild beasts, of reptiles of every sort which the earth carries on its back. Despite the fact that the earth is so great and so vast, God made it with such ease that the prophet could find no fitting example. So he said that God made the earth "as if it were nothing." Yet the vastness and beauty of the visible creation did not adequately serve to set before our minds the power of the creator. They fell far short of the greatness and fullness of strength of him who made these things. So the prophets discovered another way by which, with what strength and power were given to them, they could better reveal to us the power of God. And what was that way?

(26) They not only put before us the magnitude of the created universe but they also spoke of the manner in which it was created. They did this so that, from both sides—from the magnitude of what was brought into being and from the ease with which God created—we might be able, as far as was in our power, to get a proper idea of the power of God. Therefore, you must not only examine the magnitude of what was created but you must also look at the ease with which God made these things.

(27) This is shown to us not only in the case of the earth but also in the case of the nature of man. In one place Scripture says: "It is he that comprehends the circle of the earth and those dwelling on it like grasshoppers;"[44] and in another: "All

---

43 Cf. ibid. 22–23. These verses, in the context of Is 40, show the power of the Creator to save his people. As Chrysostom uses them, they show not only God's creative power but his ability to accomplish easily and in a moment what is eternally enduring. Cf. C. Stuhlmueller, JBC 22:12.

44 Cf. Is 40.22 (LXX). C. Stuhlmueller, JBC 22:12 comments that "grasshoppers" is used in an endearing rather than a demeaning sense. Chrysostom is showing God's great power in creating the inhabitants of earth and the vast numbers of humans dwelling on it.

the nations are like a drop from a bucket before him."[45] Do not simply skim over the passage but read and examine carefully what is well said.

(28) Count up all the nations; Syrians, Cilicians, Cappadocians, Bithynians, those dwelling by the Black Sea, in Thrace, in Macedonia, in the whole of Greece, on the islands, in Italy, those living beyond the inhabited world as we know it, those in the British Isles, the Sarmatians, the Indians, those dwelling in the land of the Persians, and the other countless nations and tribes whose names we do not even know. All these nations, Scripture says, are "like a drop from a bucket before him."[46] Tell me, how large a part of this drop are you that you meddle with God, to whom "all nations are as a drop from a bucket?"

(29) And why must we speak only of the heavens, the earth, the sea, and the nature of man? In our discourse, let us mount beyond the skies and come to the angels. Surely you know that a single angel equals in value this whole visible universe. Rather he is much more valuable. For if the whole world would not be worthy of a just man, as Paul says: " . . . of whom this world was not worthy,"[47] much less would it be worthy of one angel. For angels are far greater than just men.

(30) But still in heaven there are countless myriads of Angels, thousands upon thousands of Archangels, Thrones, Dominations, and Principalities. There are limitless hosts of

---

45 Cf. Is 40.15 (LXX). Chrysostom again uses the text of Isaiah to emphasize the great number of powerful nations and their insignificance when compared to the power of God.

46 Enumerations of the nations are a tradition in Christian literature, especially of those peoples converted to Christianity (M). Chrysostom's list covers not only Asia Minor and mainland Greece but Italy, Britain, and India. We find similar (but shorter) lists in Chrysostom's *Demonstratio quod Christus sit Deus* VI (PG 48.822), VII (ibid.), and XII (ibid. 830). Of course Chrysostom is still proving God's power by the ease with which these vast multitudes were created and the insignificance of their numbers as compared to God's creative might.

47 Cf. Heb 11.38. The just men are the patriarchs, prophets, and heroes of the OT, but the angels are far greater than they were. Again we have Chrysostom's favorite argument a fortiori.

spiritual powers and tribes beyond number.[48] God made all these powers with such ease that no words can explain it. The mere act of God's will was enough to make them all. An act of will does not make us tired. Neither did creating so many and such mighty powers weary God. The prophet revealed this when he said: "Everything which he willed he did in heaven and on earth."[49] Do you see that not only for creating the things on earth but also for the creation of the powers in heaven the mere act of his will was enough?

(31) Tell me. When you hear this, do you not weep for yourself, do you not bury yourself in the earth because you have lifted yourself to such a pitch of madness that you are playing the busybody and striving to meddle with God? You are treating him as something worthless when it is he alone whom you must glorify and adore.[50] Paul was a man filled with abundant wisdom. When he looked at the incomparable excellence of God and the worthlessness of human nature, he grew vexed with those who were meddling with the way God was governing the world and he was so deeply displeased that he said: "Man, who are you to answer God back?"[51] Who are you? Ponder first your nature. In no way can anyone find a name which can express your nothingness.

(32) But you will say: "I am a man. I have been honored with freedom." But this honor was not given to you so that you

---

48 As Daniélou explains, "powers" can be used in a generic sense of all the celestial powers, including the eight other choirs plus countless unknown choirs and tribes. More specifically, it is used to designate all the celestial powers which are outside the eight other choirs and whose categories are unknown to us on earth. See SC 28 bis Introduction, p. 42 and IV.11–12 below.

49 Cf. Ps 134 (135).6. The Psalm is a hymn of praise for God's many blessings including his creative activity. Cf. R. Murphy, JBC 35:151.

50 Here Chrysostom makes clear the proper attitude toward God ("whom you must glorify and adore") as opposed to that of the Anomoeans, who are meddlesome busybodies. See above, e.g., I.26 and n. 40; I.36.

51 Cf. Rom 9.20. According to J. Fitzmyer (JBC 53:100) Paul is not trying to silence his imaginary objector but rather to put the discussion (of God's freedom) on its proper level. God's control of the world is not to be judged by man's myopic view. Chrysostom will return to the rest of the verse presently.

might abuse and contradict your freedom; you have it so that you may use it to obey the one who gave you this honor. God did not give you this honor for you to insult him with it. He gave freedom to you so that you might give glory to him. But whenever a man is meddlesome and inquisitive about God's essence, he insults God. To refuse to be inquisitive about God's promises is to glorify him. But you are dishonoring him as long as you continue to be inquisitive and to search into his revelations and even into him who has revealed them.[52]

(33) I wish you to know that refusing to meddle with God's promises is to glorify him. To prove this to yourselves, listen to what Paul says about Abraham, his obedience, and the faith he showed in everything God said. "He did not consider his own body dead nor the dead womb of Sarah. Yet he did not question the promise of God but was strengthened in faith."[53] What Paul is saying is that nature and age were driving Abraham to despair, but faith was holding out to him hope of success. "And he was strengthened in faith and gave glory to God because he was fully persuaded that God could do whatever he promises."[54] Do you see that a man who is fully persuaded by whatever God shall reveal gives glory to God? Therefore, if the man who believes in God gives glory to him, the man who refuses to believe turns the dishonor done to God onto his own head. "Who are you to answer God back?"[55]

(34) Paul next wished to show how great a distance there is between God and man. True, he does not show how great this distance must necessarily be. But from the example he has given, we can understand that the difference is a still much greater one. What did Paul say? "Will something molded say to the molder, 'Why did you make me like this?' Does the potter

---

52 The Anomoeans' freethinking on the essence and revelation of God is an insult to God. Freedom is given to men that they may give glory to him.
53 Cf. Rom 4.19–20.
54 Cf. Rom 4.20–21. "Gave glory to God" is an OT expression (cf. 1 Sm [1 Kgs] 6.5; 1 Chr 16.28) which here formulates Abraham's reaction of grateful recognition of God's power to keep his promise. Cf. J. Fitzmyer, JBC 53:48.
55 Cf. Rom 9.20.

not have the right to make from the same lump of clay one vessel for a lofty purpose and another for a humble one?"[56]

(35) What do you mean, Paul? Am I to be subject to God in the same way the clay is to the potter? Yes, Paul says. For the distance between God and man is as great as the distance between the potter and the clay. Rather the distance is not merely as great but much greater. The potter and the clay are of one and the same substance. It is just as Job said: "I admit it as for those who dwell in houses of clay because we are ourselves formed from the same clay."[57]

(36) If a man seems more comely to look upon than clay, this difference was not produced by a change of nature but by the wisdom of the craftsman.[58] Why? Because you are no different from the clay. If you refuse to believe this, let the coffins and the cinerary urn convince you. And you will know that this is the truth if you have gone to visit the tombs of your forebearers. Therefore, there is no difference between the clay and the potter.

(37) But the distance between the essence of God and the essence of man is so great that no words can express it, nor is the mind capable of measuring it. Just as the clay follows the potter's hands in whatever way he draws or turns it, so must you be as mute and silent as the clay whenever God wishes to accomplish some purpose of his. Paul did not say what he said because he was depriving us of our freedom, heaven forbid, nor because he was destroying our power to choose. Rather, he spoke so that he might do more and more to curb the arrogance of our tongues.

---

56 Rom 9.20–21. The molded and the molder present a familiar OT motif. Cf. Is 29.16; 45.9; 64.7; Jer 18.6; Wis 15.7. In the OT the figure depicts God as the creator and governor of the universe possessing power, dominion, and freedom. Paul emphasizes the function of the thing molded, be it an unshapely pot or a beautiful vase. Chrysostom allows that the potter is far above the clay he molds but that both potter and clay, being both of the same substance, are infinitely inferior to God.

57 Cf. Jb 4.19 (LXX).

58 That man may be like the beautiful vase he owes to God, the creator, who possesses power, dominion, and freedom over the clay which he molds. But man is still clay.

(38) If you think it is a good idea, let us also look at this. Whatever was it which the Romans wished to learn, and why was Paul so vehement in curbing their tongues? Were they growing meddlesome with their inquiries into God's essence? By no means! No one of them ever had the boldness to do that. But what is far less sinful, they were seeking to learn God's ways of governance.[59] Why is one man punished? Why does another find mercy? Why does this man escape vengeance, while the other is overwhelmed with sufferings? Why did this man find pardon and another fail to find it? Such are the things they were seeking to learn. How do we know this? From the words Paul spoke just before the text I quoted. I mean when Paul said: "Therefore, he has mercy on whom he wills, and whom he wills he hardens. You will then say to me: 'Why, then, does he find fault? For who has opposed his will?' "[60] It was then Paul went on to say: "My friend, who are you to answer God back?"[61]

(39) Therefore, Paul is checking the tongues of those who seek to inquire out of curiosity into God's management of affairs. Surely God does not allow them to meddle in these matters. When Paul did not permit the Romans to meddle in these matters, what about you Anomoeans? Do you not think that you deserve to be seared with ten thousand thunderbolts? You are being meddlesome and pretending to know that blessed essence which manages all the universe. Is this not a mark of the ultimate madness? Listen to what the prophet says. Rather, listen to what God says through the prophet. "If I am a father, where is my honor? And if I am Lord, where is your fear of me?"[62] The one who has fear is not meddlesome, but falls down and worships. The one who has fear does not make inquiries out of curiosity. Instead, he gives praise and glory.[63]

---

59 The Romans are less arrogant in questioning God's governance in the matter of rewards and punishments than are the Anomoeans who pretend to know God as God knows himself, i.e., in his essence.
60 Rom 9.18–19. See NAB note ad loc.
61 Cf. Rom 9.20 and see n. 51 above.
62 Cf. Mal 1.6 (LXX).
63 See above Hom. II.32–33.

(40) Let the powers in heaven and also the blessed Paul instruct you in this. For the one who reproves others who fail God in these matters is not himself in the same sorry plight as they. Listen to what Paul says to the Philippians. He was showing them that his knowledge was imperfect, just as he had done in his letter to the Corinthians when he said: "We know in part,"[64] to prove that he did not yet have full knowledge. Now he takes up the same idea. "Brothers, I do not think of myself as having understood."[65] What could be clearer than these words? Paul's cry is louder than a trumpet blast as he instructs the entire world to be content and satisfied with the measure of knowledge which has been granted to it. No one should think that he has attained to full knowledge and understanding in this world.

(41) Tell me, Paul. What is it you mean? Do you have Christ speaking in you[66] and do you say: "I do not think of myself as having understood?"[67] Paul would answer: "The very reason I said that I have Christ speaking in me is that he taught me these things." So after Paul had said: "I do not think of myself as having understood,"[68] the Philippians would not have thought that they had complete understanding unless they were stripped utterly of the Spirit's help and unless they had rejected from their souls every influence which comes from him.[69]

(42) But someone may object and say: "And what is there to show that Paul is talking here about faith, knowledge, and

---

64 1 Cor 13.9 and see above Hom. I.10–11.
65 Phil 3.13. NAB translates: "I do not think of myself as having reached the finish line," where the "finish line" is the life on high in Christ Jesus (ibid. 15) to which Paul hopes to arrive at his resurrection from the dead (cf. ibid. 11). The verb used by Paul means basically to grasp or capture (e.g., a prize) but is often used in a secondary sense of to grasp with the mind. Obviously, in the context of 1 Cor 13.9, Chrysostom here takes the verb as meaning to understand.
66 2 Cor 13.3.
67 Phil 3.13.
68 ibid.
69 I.e., unless the Philippians were in the same sorry state as were the Anomoeans.

doctrines?[70] He may be talking about conduct and a way of life. Could he not mean: 'I consider myself imperfect in my conduct and in my way of life?' " Paul made it perfectly clear that this was not the case when he said: "I have fought the good fight, I have finished the race, I have kept the faith. From now on the crown of justification awaits me."[71] A man who had won the race and was going to receive the crown would never have said: "I do not think of myself as having understood,"[72] if he were talking about conduct. If this is what he was talking about, then there is no one who sees clearly and understands what things must be done and what things must be avoided. But these things are clearly known to all man, even to barbarians and Persians and the whole human race.

(43) To make my meaning still clearer, I am going to read what follows that passage.[73] After Paul had said: "Beware of the dogs, beware of workers of evil,"[74] and after he spoke at length about those who were introducing Jewish teachings which were illsuited to a non-Jewish situation, he went on to say: "The things that were gain to me I have considered loss because of Christ. But I will therefore consider all as loss so that I may be found not having justification from the law but the justification which comes from God through faith in Jesus Christ."[75] Then he tells us what sort of faith he means. He means the faith "of knowing him and the power of his resurrection and the sharing in his sufferings."[76]

---

70 Here Chrysostom's congregation is again faced squarely with the topic especially treated in this homily: the relationship between knowledge and faith (M).

71 Cf. 2 Tm 4.7–8. Death is near and Paul has persevered.

72 Phil 3.13.

73 Since the verses he will quote (not read) actually precede Phil 3.13, Chrysostom must mean by "follow" something such as putting 3.13 in its proper context.

74 Phil 3.2 and NAB note ad loc.

75 Cf. Phil 3.7–9.

76 Phil 3.10. On his resurrection, Jesus becomes Lord and "Son of God in power (Rom 1.4)." The risen Jesus posesses a power which is the vital principle of the new Christian life, the new creation (cf. 1 Cor 1.18; 6.14). This power is the glory bestowed by the Father (Rom 6.4) and it gradually brings about the transformation of the man of faith into an image of Christ himself (2 Cor 3.18; 4.6; Phil 2.21). This influence of Christ enables man to be identified with Jesus in his sufferings, death, and resurrection. See J. Fitzmyer, JBC 50:23.

(44) What is "the power of his resurrection?" Paul is telling us that we have been shown a new kind of resurrection. Many dead men on many occasions arose before Christ did.[77] But no one ever arose as Christ did. For all the others who arose returned into the earth again. Even though they were freed from the tyranny of death for a time, they were led back again under its sway. But when the body of the Lord arose, it did not return into the earth again but went up to heaven and destroyed all the tyranny of the enemy. And, along with himself, Christ made the whole world arise and now he is seated on the royal throne.

(45) As Paul pondered all these marvels, he showed us that no power of reasoning[78] will be able to describe such great and numerous wonders. Faith alone can teach them and make them clear. This is why he said that faith is: "to know the power of his resurrection."[79] If the process of reasoning cannot describe resurrection—for this is beyond human nature and the usual course of events—what power of thought will be able to explain his resurrection especially since it is so different from other resurrections? There is none. But faith alone is all we need if we are going to believe that a mortal body both rose up and went to immortal life, having neither limit nor end.

(46) In another place Paul expressed the same idea when he said: "Christ having risen dies no more; death no longer has power over him."[80] He said this to describe the double miracle: Christ's resurrection and the way he rose. That is why he said,

---

77 In 2 Kgs (4 Kgs) 4.25–37 we read how Elisha restored to life the son of the Shunammite woman, as also Elijah raised the widow's son from the dead in 1 Kgs (3 Kgs) 17.17–24. In the NT Jesus performs the same miracle by raising back to life the daughter of Jairus (Mk 5.21–43), the son of the widow of Naim (Lk 7.11–15), and Lazarus four days dead (Jn 11.1–46 and see Hom. IX below). Peter raised Tabitha to life after Christ's resurrection (Acts 9.39–41).

78 Again we see how inferior to faith are the processes of reasoning. See above Homilies I.23, 39; II.13, 24; below II.48, 49; III.6; V.30, 58.

79 Phil 3.10.

80 Cf. Rom 6.9. Unlike others who had been raised from the dead, Christ has totally conquered death by his resurrection. By this victory he has introduced men to a new mode of life and given them a new principle of life, the Holy Spirit. Cf. J. Fitzmyer, JBC 53:65.

"in faith to know the power of his resurrection."[81] And if reasoning processes cannot discover his resurrection, it is far less possible for them to discover his generation from above.

(47) When Paul was discussing the resurrection and also speaking of Christ's passion and cross, he entrusted these, too, to the power of faith. Then after he had brought up this whole question, he went on to say: "My brothers, I do not think of myself as having understood."[82] He did not say: "I do not think of myself as having known," but "as having understood." He testified neither to his total ignorance nor to complete knowledge. "I do not think of myself as having understood" are the words of a man who is making it clear that he has arrived at a certain point of his journey, that he is going on and will advance further, but he has not yet completely reached the end.[83]

(48) He gives this encouragement to others, too, when he says: "Let as many as are perfect have this attitude, and if in anything you are otherwise minded, God will reveal that also to you."[84] He did not say that the process of reasoning will instruct, but that God will reveal it. Do you not see that he is not talking about conduct and a way of life but about doctrines and faith? For conduct and a way of life do not require revelation, but doctrines and knowledge do. In another text he made the same point clear when he said: "If a man thinks he knows

---

81 Phil 3.10. Cf. above note 76. The power of the resurrection can be known only by faith in what God has revealed. The same is true for the Son's generation from above.

82 Phil 3.13.

83 Here Chrysostom shows the more basic meaning of the verb in Phil 3.13 which NAB translates "as having reached the finish line." See above note 65.

84 Cf. Phil 3.15. The mature man is well formed in the Christian life and is no longer a babe or neophyte (cf. 1 Cor 2.6; 14.20; Heb 5.13–14); however, he has not yet reached the summit of perfection (cf. J. Fitzmyer, JBC 30:23). God's help is necessary to reach this stage of knowledge and understanding.

something, he does not yet know anything."[85] He did not simply say: "He does not know," but: "He does not know it as he ought to know it."[86] For he does have knowledge, but it is not exact and complete knowledge.

(49) That you may learn that this is true, let us not talk about the things above but, if you wish, let us bring the discussion down to visible creation. Do you see the sky? We know that it keeps the shape of a vault and we learned this not by reasoning but from divine Scripture. That it covers the whole earth we also know and we know this because we heard it in the same way from Holy Scripture.[87] But we do not know what the essence of the sky is. If anyone should be confident that he knows its essence and be obstinate in maintaining that he has such knowledge, let him tell you what the essence of the sky is. Is it frozen crystals of ice? Is it a cloud which has become condensed? Is it air which has grown thicker? No one can give you a clear answer.[88]

(50) Do you still need proof of how mad those men are who say that they know God? You cannot tell what the nature of the sky is and you see it every day. Do you then profess to know perfectly the essence of God whom you cannot see? Who is so

85 Cf. 1 Cor 8.2. In context, this verse has to do with meats offered to idols and the conscience of men who eat or abstain from such food. Some Christians were rigorists in this matter and others more liberal. The knowledge underlying the judgment of conscience is neither exact nor complete; hence, no one should pass judgment on others whose conscience does not conform to his own. Chrysostom uses the text to distinguish between the knowledge we acquire by revelation and the knowledge we cannot gain by processes of reasoning. In Chrysostom's context we know that God exists but no creature, not even the Anomoeans, can know his essence. Cf. above Hom. I.20–22.

86 Cf. 1 Cor 8.2.

87 Cf. Gn 1.6–9. Of course the Bible is not the most scientific source of the knowledge man can have of physical phenomena.

88 Basil maintains the same thing in *Adversus Eunomium* III.6 (PG 29.668 A-B) as does Gregory of Nyssa in his *Contra Eunomium* II.71 (ed. W. Jaeger, vol. I, p. 247; PG 45.933 C).

imperceptive that he fails to recognize the ultimate madness of those who say that they know these things?[89]

(51) These are my reasons for encouraging all of you to speak to the Anomoeans mildly and with moderation. Try with all your might to treat them as you would treat people who have suffered a mental illness and lost their wits. Surely this doctrine of theirs is the offspring of their madness and of a mind swollen with great conceit. Their festering wounds cannot bear a touch of the hand nor endure too rough a contact. So it is that wise physicians cleanse such ulcers with a soft sponge.[90]

(52) Since these Anomoeans have a festering ulcer in their souls, let us take a soft sponge, wet it with pure and soothing water, and bathe the ulcer with all the words I have spoken to you. In this way let us try to restrain their swollen conceit and cleanse away all their pride. Even if they insult and outrage you, even if they kick at you and spit on you, however they treat you, my beloved, do not give up your corrective care. Many similar outrages must lie in wait for physicians who treat a man gone mad. In spite of everything, these physicians must not give up. Because of these very insults they must have pity and feel sorry for their patients since these insults are the symptoms of their sickness.

(53) I speak these words to the stronger ones among you, to those who can withstand harsh treatment, to those who can receive no hurt from associating with those men. If anyone should be somewhat weak, let him flee the company of the Anomoeans, let him run away from their gatherings so that the motive of friendship may not become a starting point for godlessness.[91] This is what Paul does. He personally mingles

---

89 Later Chrysostom will show that man cannot know even the essence of his own soul (cf. Hom. V.27–29) or that of an angel (cf. ibid. 26). How, then, could he know the essence of God? Anyone who maintains he does is utterly mad.

90 Medical metaphors are frequent in Chrysostom, especially where the ailments are spiritual rather than physical. Cf., e.g., P.W. Harkins, *St. John Chrysostom: Baptismal Instructions* (ACW 31 pp. 99–100; 105–8; 133–34; FOTC 68 pp. 35, 53, 94, 207, 214, and below Homilies II.52, 54; III.32; V.45, 53.

91 See above Hom. I.43.

with the sick and says: "I became like a Jew to the Jews, to those not subject to the law I became like one not subject to the law."[92] But he leads his disciples and those of lesser strength away from such associations when he exhorts and teaches them with these words: "Bad company corrupts good morals."[93] And again: "Come out from among them and separate yourselves from them, says the Lord."[94]

(54) If a physician visits a sick man, he often helps both the patient and himself. But if a man is one of the weaker sort, he does both harm to himself and to the invalid by exposing himself to contact with the sick. In no way will he be able to help the patient and he will bring great harm to himself from the sick man's illness.[95] This is what happens to those who look upon those suffering from ophthalmia because they themselves contract something from that sickness.[96] Those who mingle with these blasphemers also undergo this, if they be of the weaker sort, because they are drawing on themselves a great portion of the godlessness of the Anomoeans.

(55) Therefore, to prevent doing ourselves the greatest harm, let us avoid any association with them. Let us only pray for them and beseech the loving-kindness of God, who wishes all men to be saved and come to a knowledge of the truth,[97] to free them from this deceit and snare of the devil, and to lead

---

92 Cf. 1 Cor 9.20–21 and NAB note ad loc. The sick are the Jews and pagans. Being all things to all men, Paul observes the Mosaic law among the Jews but does not among the pagans. What Paul means is that he knows only the law of Christ, which is charity. So, in his own behavior, he respects the erroneous and scrupulous consciences of those who are sick. Cf. R. Kugelman, JBC 51:60.

93 1 Cor 15.33. Paul cites a popular proverb to warn the Corinthians to guard themselves against those who would corrupt their faith and morals. See R. Kugelman, JBC 52:24.

94 2 Cor 6.17. The verse is a free joining of Is 52.11 and Jer 51.45. In Isaiah the reference is to contact with whatever would cause ritual impurity; Paul raises the injunction to the moral plane. See J. O'Rourke, JBC 52:24.

95 See above Hom.I.43. The physician, like the strong Christian, is helped by helping. But the weaker Christian can be harmed by contact with the sick.

96 Ophthalmia or conjunctivitis is not so contagious, as popular belief held.

97 Cf. 1 Tm 2.4. Cf. below V.43. It is God's will that Christians pray for all men because it is his (salvific) will that all men be saved. Paul here describes salvation as "to come to the knowledge of the truth." We find similar phraseology in 2 Tm 2.25; 3.7; Ti 1.1. Cf. G. Denzer, JBC 57:18.

them back to the light of knowledge, that is, to God, the Father of our Lord Jesus Christ in union with the all holy Spirit, the giver of life, to whom be glory and power now and forever, world without end. Amen.

HOMILY III

HEN HARD-WORKING FARMERS SEE A FRUITLESS TREE growing wild and spoiling their labors, a tree which, with its rugged roots and thick shade, is destroying the plants they have cultivated, they lose no time in cutting it down. Often a wind which has arisen from some quarter of the sky joins with them to help in removing it by blowing the foliage off the tree. After shaking the tree violently, this wind snaps off limbs and strews them over the ground. In this way the wind does much to lighten the farmers' labor. We, too, are cutting down a wild and uncultivated tree, namely, the Anomoean heresy.[1] So let us call upon God to send us the grace of the Spirit to blow more violently than any wind and tear the heresy out by the roots and, in this way, relieve us of much of our toil.

(2) Surely it has often happened that land has been left uncultivated and has gotten no help from the farmer's hands. Then, from its own womb, it has put forth worthless weeds, an abundance of thorns, and wild trees. In the same way, the souls of the Anomoeans have been left untended and have gotten no benefit from the care which comes from the Scriptures. Of themselves and from themselves, they have put forth this heresy like a wild and uncultivated tree.[2] Paul did not plant it,

---

1 Chrysostom uses the proper noun or adjective "Anomoean" only five times in the course of Homilies I-V: in II.1; 2 and 16; and here in paragraphs 1 and 2. Mostly he refers to them as "heretics" (e.g., I.30; III. 11; IV.11). In my translation I have often added (or substituted) the proper noun or adjective "Anomoean" to make it perfectly clear to whom Chrysostom is referring. Here in his exordium, Chrysostom compares his task as a teacher to the toils of the farmer who must keep his arable land free from wild and uncultivated growth. As the wind helps the farmer, so the teacher needs the Spirit's help to root out heresy.

2 Ignatius of Antioch, in his *Epistle to the Trallians* 6.1 (ACW 1 [trans. J. Kleist, Westminster, Md. 1946]) p. 77, warns Christians that they must abstain from plants of alien growth, that is, heresy and partake exclusively of Christian food, that is, the Scriptures. Ignatius also calls heresy "the weed of the devil" in his *Epistle to the Ephesians* 10.3 (ibid. p. 64).

Apollos did not water it, nor did God make it grow.[3] Importunate curiosity planted it, the conceit of folly watered it, and a passionate desire for self-glory made it grow.[4] We also need the flame of the Spirit so that we may not only tear out this evil root but also burn it to ashes. Let us call on this God whom they curse and we bless. And let us also appeal to him to spur my tongue to run faster and to open your minds to a clearer understanding of what I say.[5]

(3) All our labor is on God's behalf and for his glory. Rather, our labor is for our own salvation. For no one can do God harm by dishonoring him nor can anyone increase God's glory by blessing him.[6] God always abides in his own glory; to bless him does not increase it, to curse him does not make it less. Men who glorify God as he deserves or, rather—since no one can give him such glory—those who glorify him to the best of their ability reap the profit of the praise they give him. But those who curse and disparage him compromise their own salvation.

(4) "He who has cast a stone into the air has cast it on his own head,"[7] as someone has said about those who blaspheme God. Surely, if someone takes a stone, as if it were a spear, and throws it at the sky, he cannot pierce the body of the sky, for he cannot throw it as high as that. Rather, he will receive the blow on the top of his own head just as the stone falls back on him who threw it. In the same way, the man who hurls blasphemies at that blessed essence of God would never do any harm to it. God's essence is much too great and far too high to receive any hurt. The blasphemer is sharpening his sword against his own soul because he has become so arrogant toward his benefactor.

---

3 Cf. 1 Cor 3.6.

4 Instead of God giving the increase, their mad and meddlesome curiosity has led the Anomoeans to glorify their own reason when they should have been giving glory to God.

5 Not only is the Spirit's aid necessary to root out and destroy heresy but it must also inspire the preacher and enlighten the minds of those who hear him.

6 God is impassible and, therefore, can suffer no harm or dishonor. His intrinsic glory cannot be increased because he is infinitely perfect. Hence honor or dishonor paid to him can only accrue to those who praise or curse him.

7 Cf. Sir (Ecclus) 27.25 (LXX). The verse exemplifies the inexorable law of retribution.

(5) Let us call upon him, then, as the ineffable God who is beyond our intelligence, invisible, incomprehensible, who transcends the power of mortal words. Let us call on him as the God who is inscrutable to the angels, unseen by the Seraphim, inconceivable to the Cherubim, invisible to the principalities, to the powers, and to the virtues, in fact, to all creatures without qualification, because he is known only by the Son and the Spirit.[8]

(6) I know that I will be charged with false and boastful talk because I maintained that God is incomprehensible to the powers above. But it is the very fact of this incomprehensibility which moves me to charge the Anomoeans with great madness and folly. It is not pretense or vain boasting to say that the creator is beyond the grasp of all creatures. But the Anomoeans are guilty of extravagant boasting when they say that they, by the weak processes of their own reason, can grasp and define the essence of God who cannot be comprehended by the powers above.[9] For the Anomoeans are no better than creatures who crawl on the ground[10] and they are so vastly inferior to the powers above.

(7) If I fail to prove what I promised, I would deserve to be charged with false and boastful talk. But I shall prove that God cannot be comprehended by the powers above. If, after that, you still confidently affirm and obstinately contend that you do know him, how many times would you deserve to be thrown over a precipice into perdition for pretending to have perfect

---

8 Chrysostom's list of negative divine epithets emphasizes the Anomoeans' boastful blasphemies in maintaining that they know God as God knows himself. Indeed, God's essence cannot be understood by men or angels because it transcends the grasp of all creation. Only the Son and Spirit who, together with the Father, constitute the Trinity can know, as distinct Persons, their own divine essence.

9 In Hom. II.19 Chrysostom joined the words madness and folly. As in that place, so, too, here the madness and folly are manifested in the abuses of the processes of reasoning which invariably lead to a destructive pride. This is the case with the Anomoeans whose mad folly and pride lead them to think they are superior to the angels.

10 This was the sentence meted to the serpent for tempting Eve in the garden of Eden. The Anomoeans, like the serpent, tempt others to think they will be like God and, as a consequence, will be punished. Cf. Gn 3.5 (and NAB note ad loc.) and 3.14. In Hom. IV.5 Chrysostom refers to the Anomoeans as "mere crawling creatures."

knowledge of that which is beyond the perception of all the spiritual powers?

(8) So come now, let us move on to prove these very points.[11] But once again, we must first turn our words to prayer. I say this because, oftentimes, when prayer accompanies a discourse, it will serve to provide us with a demonstration of the things we are seeking to prove.[12] Therefore, let us call upon "the King of kings and Lord of lords, who alone has immortality, who dwells in unapproachable light, whom no human being has ever seen nor can see. To him be honor and power forever Amen."[13] These are not my words. Paul spoke them. And notice, please, the piety and holy fear which are rooted in his soul. After he mentioned God, he did not dare to go on with a further explanation of doctrine until he had closed his discourse with a doxology and had paid the debt owed to God. If "the memory of a just man is praised,"[14] much more must God's name be mentioned with honor and worship.

(9) And Paul often does this at the beginning of his epistles. He first mentions God and then does not go on to his teaching until he pays to God the glory and praise due to him. Listen to how he speaks in his letter to the Galatians. "We wish you the favor and peace of God our Father and of the Lord Jesus Christ, who gave himself for our sins, to rescue us from the

---

11 The points Chrysostom will prove are three in number: (1) the equality of the Father and the Son; (2) that God is incomprehensible both to men and to the powers above; (3) that God can be seen by men or angels only by condescension and accommodation.

12 The points Chrysostom proposes to prove are all matters of doctrine. The prayers, all from Scripture, which he will introduce serve a double purpose: they will ask God's help in explaining the doctrine and they will provide the proof of the doctrine he is expounding (cf. paragraph 11 below).

13 Cf. 1 Tm 6.15–16. As G. Denzer points out (JBC 57:32), the phraseology and structure of these verses suggest that they were taken from an ancient Christian hymn (cf. 1 Tm 1.17; 3.16; 2 Tm 2.11–13). The titles "King of kings" and "Lord of lords" are found in the OT (e.g., Dt 10.17; 2 Mc 12.15; 13.4; Dn 2.37). Such titles were used by Oriental monarchs, and the primitive Church probably used the terms to show opposition to the divine honors paid to these rulers; but God "alone has immortality." ". . . Whom no human being has ever seen or can see:" cf. Jn 1.18; 6.46; 1 Jn 4.12. However, with the aid of grace, some kind of vision of God is available to man (Mt 5.8).

14 Cf. Pvb 10.7 (LXX). NAB reads: "The memory of the just will be blessed."

present evil age, as our God and Father willed—to him be glory
for endless ages. Amen."[15] And again in another place: "To the
King of ages, the immortal, the invisible, the only God of
wisdom, be honor and glory forever and ever! Amen."[16]

(10) Does Paul do this only in the case of the Father and not
in the case of the Son? Listen to how he has done this same
thing in the case of the only begotten. After he had said: "I
could even wish to be separated from Christ for the sake of my
brothers, my kinsmen according to the flesh," he went on to
say: "Theirs were the adoption, the covenants, the lawgiving,
the worship and the promises. From them came Christ, who is
God over all and blessed forever! Amen."[17] And it was only
after he paid glory and praise to the only begotten, as he had to
the Father, that Paul went on to explain his message. For he

---

15 Cf. Gal 1.3–5. The greeting formula combines the two notions of grace
(covenant favor) and peace which are rooted in the old priestly blessing of
Nm 6.24–26. But in Paul, "grace" has the connotation of the merciful
bounty of God manifested in Christ Jesus (cf. Rom 5.1–11). The two words,
grace and peace, invoke on the Galatians a share in the Messianic blessings
which are derived from both the Father and Christ (as equals). ". . . Who
gave himself for our sins" sounds the epistle's dominant note: salvation
through Christ according to the Father's plan. See J. Fitzmyer, JBC 47:8,
49:10.
16 Cf. 1 Tm 1.17. Another of the doxologies which are frequent in Paul's
epistles (cf. e.g. Gal 1.5; Rom 9.5; etc.). "King of ages" was an expression
current in post-exilic Judaism and is found in Jewish prayers. The entire
verse is probably a quotation from an early Christian hymn. See G. Denzer,
JBC 57:16.
17 Cf. Rom 9.3–5. Paul would heroically be willing to be cut off from Christ to
atone for the Jews who, despite the many privileges bestowed by God, had
failed to recognize their Messiah, "who is God over all and blessed forever."
Here obviously Chrysostom sees Paul as calling Christ "God", which clearly
makes him equal to the Father. This exegesis has been questioned because
slight changes in punctuation could change the meaning and make the
"one who is God over all" refer to the Father in a brief doxology which
comes after the enumeration of the privileges of Israel. Scholars are
divided on the question. Paul does not seem to call Christ "God" elsewhere,
except possibly in Ti 2.13, which may be deutero-Pauline. For two dis-
cussions of Rom 9.5 see J. Fitzmyer, JBC 53:97 and R. E. Brown, "Does the
New Testament Call Jesus God?" in Theological Studies 26 (1965) 545–73,
esp. 559–60. Both these eminent scholars present the evidence well.
Neither would reject Chrysostom's exegesis but each would claim a certain
probability for this passage as referring to Jesus as God.

heeded Christ's words: "So that all men may honor the Son just as they honor the Father."[18]

(11) And so that you may learn that the prayer itself will provide us with the proof, come now and let us bring the prayer before you. "The King of kings," Paul said, "The Lord of lords, who alone has immortality, who dwells in unapproachable light."[19] Stop the heretic and ask him what "Who dwells in unapproachable light" means. And pay heed to the accuracy with which Paul speaks. He did not say: "Who is an unapproachable light," but: "Who dwells in unapproachable light." Why? So that you may learn that if the dwelling is unapproachable, much more so is the God who dwells in it. But Paul did not say this to make you suspect that there is a house or place surrounding God. Rather, he wished you to have a deeper and superior knowledge that God is beyond our comprehension.

(12) However, he did not say: "Who dwells in incomprehensible light," but: "in unapproachable light," and this is much stronger than "incomprehensible." A thing is said to be incomprehensible when those who seek after it fail to comprehend it, even after they have searched and sought to understand it. A thing is unapproachable which, from the start, cannot be investigated nor can anyone come near to it. We call the sea incomprehensible because, even when divers lower themselves into its waters and go down to a great depth, they cannot find the bottom. We call that thing unapproachable which, from the start, cannot be searched out or investigated.[20]

(13) How will you heretics reply to that? If anyone will say that God may be incomprehensible to men, but not to angels nor to the powers above, tell me this. Are you an angel? Are

---

18 Cf. Jn 5.23.
19 1 Tm 6.15–16.
20 Notice that Chrysostom here gives a meticulous exegesis of a phrase by analyzing each term and its use in the phrase, by the exactness of the sacred writer in choosing his words, by what he had said and did not say, and why (M). Cf. Hom.IV.8.

you numbered among the throng of spiritual powers? Have you forgotten what your nature is? Let us grant that God is unapproachable only to men, although Paul did not add this qualification nor did he say: "Who dwells in a light unapproachable to men but which the angels can approach." Suppose, however, we make a concession and grant you this qualification. Are you not yourself a man? Suppose, then, that the angels can approach him. What difference does it make to you since you are the meddlesome busybody who is obstinately contending that God's essence is comprehensible to human nature?[21]

(14) But to let you know that God is unapproachable not only for men but also for the powers above, listen to what Isaiah says. And when I say Isaiah, I mean what the Spirit states, for every prophet speaks through the action of the Spirit.[22] What does Isaiah say? "And it came to pass in the year in which King Oziah died that I saw the Lord sitting on a high and lofty throne, and the Seraphim stood round about him. Each one had six wings; with two they covered their faces and with two they covered their feet."[23]

(15) Why, tell me, do they stretch forth their wings and cover their faces? For what other reason than that they cannot endure the sparkling flashes nor the lightning which shines from the throne? Yet they did not see the pure light itself nor the pure essence itself. What they saw was a condescension accommodated to their nature. What is this condescension? God condescends whenever he is not seen as he is, but in the way one incapable of beholding him is able to look upon him.

---

21 Despite the fact that man cannot even look upon an angel, the Anomoeans still maintain that they know the essence of God who is infinitely higher than any angel.

22 It is the action of the Spirit which gives the sacred writers their inspiration.

23 Cf Is 6.1–2 (LXX). Isaiah's vision occurs in the Temple of Jerusalem. The forms of the Seraphim are either semihuman or semibestial. They have six wings: two covering the face, two the feet, and two for flight (cf. J. McKenzie, DB 789). For Chrysostom the only important wings are the pair covering the face since the theophany is too much for them to look upon. Cf. Hom.IV.7.

In this way God reveals himself by accommodating what he reveals to the weakness of vision of those who behold him.[24]

(16) And it is clear from Isaiah's very words that, in his case, he saw God by such condescension. For he said: "I saw the Lord sitting on a high and lofty throne."[25] But God is not sitting. This is a posture for bodily beings. And Isaiah said: "On a throne." But God is not encompassed or enclosed by a throne; divinity cannot be circumscribed by limits. Nonetheless, the Seraphim could not endure God's condescension even though they were only standing near. For "the Seraphim stood round about him."[26] It was especially for this very reason that they could not look upon him, namely, because they were near. But Isaiah is not speaking of being near in place. He said: "And the Seraphim stood around him," because he wished the Holy Spirit to make it clear that even though the Seraphim are closer to God's essence than we men are, they still cannot look upon it just because they are closer. He is not hinting at place in a local sense; when he speaks of closeness in place, he is showing that the Seraphim are nearer to God than we men are.[27]

(17) And the fact is that we do not know God in the same way in which those powers above know him. Their nature is far more pure and wise and clear-sighted than man's nature. The blind man does not know that the sun's rays are unapproachable as does the man who can see. So we do not know the incomprehensibility of God in the same way as these powers do. The difference between a blind man and a man with sight is as great as the difference between us men and the powers above. So, even if you hear the prophet say: "I saw the Lord," do not suspect that he saw God's essence. What he saw was this

---

24 Here we have a definition of the term condescension by which, in a theophany, God accommodates himself to the weakness of vision of those who behold him. Notice that no creature, be he angel or man, sees God as he really is, i.e., in his essence. We have already seen the term in Hom I.35 (and note 60); we shall see it again in this and the following two homilies.

25 Cf. Is 6.1.

26 Cf. ibid. 2.

27 This theme is discussed often in the series of homilies *Vidi Dom.*, esp. in Hom.VI (PG 56.135–42).

very condescension of God.[28] And he saw that far less distinctly than did the powers above. He could not see it with the same clarity as the Cherubim.

(18) And why do I speak of that blessed essence of God? A man cannot even look upon the essence of an angel without fear and trembling.[29] To convince you that this is true, I shall present to you the blessed Daniel, God's friend,[30] a man who, because of his wisdom and justice,[31] approached God with confidence,[32] a man well approved for his many other virtuous actions. I shall show this blessed Daniel utterly weakened, broken up, and distraught because he was in the presence of an angel. And let no one think he experienced this because of his sins or a bad conscience. His soul's confidence in God had already been proved. Clearly, then, the blame for his condition belonged to the weakness of his nature.

(19) So this man, Daniel, fasted for three weeks, "and ate no desirable bread."[33] Neither wine nor meat entered his mouth; nor did he anoint himself with oil. It was then that he saw the vision since his soul had been made more fit to receive such an apparition because, by his fasting, it had become lighter and more spiritual. And what did Daniel say? "I have lifted up my eyes and looked, and behold a man clothed in linen (that is, a priestly garment) and his loins were girt with gold of Ophaz. His body was as Tharsis, his face was as the appearance of lightning, his eyes as lamps of fire, his arms and legs as the appearance of shining brass, the sound of his spoken words as

---

28 Here the term condescension does not mean God's condescension in itself but rather the form under which God chose to manifest himself as a consequence of his condescension (M).

29 Step by step, Chrysostom reinforces his argument by withdrawing successively from each order of creatures the power to contemplate those who are higher in the spiritual order (M). Man could not look upon the essence of an angel without a holy dread. How, then, could he look upon the essence of God? Chrysostom will use Daniel as his example.

30 God protected Daniel by sending his angel to close the lions' mouths so that they did him no harm after he had been cast into their den. Cf. Dn 6.23.

31 Cf. Dn 1.17, 20; 5.11.

32 Cf. Dn 6.11–12. He approached God in prayer.

33 Cf. Dn 10.3. Daniel's fasting is a preparation for mystical knowledge rather than a penance for sin. Cf. Chrysostom, De Poenit. V.1 (PG 49.307).

the voice of a multitude. I alone saw this vision, and the men who were with me saw it not; but a great amazement fell on them, and they fled in fear, and no strength was left in me, and my glory was turned into corruption."[34]

(20) What does he mean when he says: "My glory was turned into corruption?"[35] He was a handsome young man. But fear of the angel's presence affected him like a man on his deathbed. It spread a pallor all over his face, it destroyed the freshness of his youth, and drained all the color from the surface of his skin. This is why he said: "My glory was turned into corruption."[36] When a charioteer becomes frightened and lets go the reins, all his horses tumble down and the whole chariot is overturned. The same thing generally happens in the case of the soul when it is gripped by some terror or anguish. When the soul is frightened to distraction and lets the reins fall loose from its own faculties and powers of operation, which are rooted in each body's organs of sense perception, it deprives the limbs of their control. Then, because they have been deprived of the power which controls them, these limbs are buffeted on every side and become useless. This is what Daniel experienced at that moment.[37]

(21) What, then, did the angel do? He raised Daniel to his feet and said: "Daniel, man of desires, understand the words I

---

34 Cf. Dn 10.3, 5–8 (LXX). The description of the angelic visitor borrows heavily from Ez esp. chaps. 1, 9, 11. In turn it serves as a model for Rv 1–2. In verses 5–6 NAB reads "with a belt of fine gold round his waist. His body was like chrysolite;" JB reads "with a girdle of pure gold around his waist; his body was like beryl." Neither mentions Ophaz or Tharsis, cities famous for ornaments of gold or precious stones. The reactions of Daniel and his companions are reminiscent of the experience of Paul and his companions on the road to Damascus (cf. Acts 9 3–8).

35 Cf. Dn 10.8 (LXX). NAB reads: "I turned the color of death;" JB reads: "my appearance altered out of all recognition." From what Chrysostom goes on to say, we can imagine that Daniel's "glory" refers to his physical attractiveness which was destroyed by his fear of the angel as he saw him in condescension, so that he looked like one on his deathbed. Cf. Hom.IV.3.

36 Cf. Dn 10.8.

37 Fear of what he saw in the vision destroyed Daniel's power to operate as a natural unit. See Hom.IV.3–4, where Daniel's terror was driving his soul to escape his body. Chrysostom's purpose in using the vivid comparisons of Hom.III.20 and IV.4 is to prove to the Anomoeans the vast superiority of angels to men.

speak to you and stand upright because I am now sent to you."[38] And Daniel stood up all atremble. The angel began to speak to him and said: "From the day you gave your heart to be afflicted before God, your words were heard, and I have come because of your words."[39]

(22) Again Daniel fell to the ground,[40] just as happens to those who fall into a faint. Such people, once aroused, come back to their senses and see us clearly while we are holding them and sprinkling cold water on their faces. But often enough, as we hold them in our arms, they faint away again. And this is what happened to the prophet. His soul was frightened, he could not endure to look upon the presence of his fellow servant,[41] nor could he bear the brightness of that light. So he became troubled and confused, as if his soul was hurrying to burst from some chain binding it to the flesh. But the angel still held him fast.

(23) Let those Anomoeans listen who, out of curiosity, are investigating into the essence of the Lord of angels.[42] Daniel, to whom the eyes of the lions showed reverence,[43] Daniel, who had a more than human power in his human body,[44] could not endure the presence of his fellow servant but lay on the ground before the angel[45] and could not breathe.[46] For he said: "My bowels were turned within me at what I saw, and no breath was left in me."[47] But these Anomoeans, who are so far removed from the virtue of that just man, profess to know with all exactness the highest and first of essences, the very essence of God, who has created myriads of these angels. And yet Daniel did not have the strength to look upon a single one of them.

---

38 Cf. Dn 10.11 (LXX).

39 Cf. ibid. 12.

40 Cf. ibid. 9.

41 Fellow servant, here, and in the following paragraph, is the angel. Below (III.32) it is Chrysostom; in III.35, the priests (including Chrysostom) who instruct the congregation.

42 Cf. above note 29. This sentence also would seem to offer sound proof that Anomoeans were present in the church and listening to Chrysostom.

43 Cf. Dn 6.23 (LXX).

44 Cf. ibid. 4.

45 Cf. ibid 10.8–9.

46 Cf. ibid. 17.

47 Cf. ibid. 16–17.

(24) Let us bring our discourse back to our earlier prop-
osition and let us show that God, even by the accommodation
of condescension, cannot be seen by the Powers above. Tell me
this. Why do the Seraphim stretch forth their wings?[48] There is
no other reason than the statement made by the Apostle: "Who
dwells in unapproachable light."[49] And these heavenly virtues,
who are showing this by their very actions, are not the only
ones. There are powers higher than the Seraphim, namely, the
Cherubim. The Seraphim stood near: the Cherubim are the
throne of God.[50] They are not called this because God has need
of a throne, but so that you may learn how great is the dignity
of these very powers.

(25) Hear what another prophet has to say about the Cherubim. "And the word of the Lord came to Ezekiel, the son of
Buzi, by the river Chobar."[51] He stood by the river Chobar as
the prophet Daniel, in his day, stood beside the Tigris.[52] For
whenever God is going to reveal some sight beyond all expectation to his servants, he leads them out of the cities to a place
free from tumult. He does this so that their souls may not be
upset by any sight or sound; so that, while their whole being
enjoys full peace and tranquility, they may occupy themselves
with contemplating the things he shows them.

(26) What, then, did Ezekiel see? "Behold a cloud came
from the north, enveloped in brightness and flashing fire. And

---

48 Cf. Is 6.2. See also above Hom.III.14–15; below IV.7.
49 1 Tm 6.16.
50 The cherubim are not the throne of God. This statement seems to mean
   that these powers have great dignity because they serve as the "throne" of
   God and are superior to the seraphim who stand near it. The Arians seem
   to have discussed the hierarchy of the heavenly host only to have Cyril of
   Jerusalem point the finger of scorn at them for idle conjecture. Cf.
   L. McCauley, St. Cyril of Jerusalem, Catechesis 11.12 (FOTC 61 [Washington
   1969] 217): "Let these rash men tell me first how a throne differs from a
   domination, and then inquire into what concerns Christ. Tell me, what is a
   principality and what a power, what a virtue and what an angel; and then
   busy yourself with the Creator . . ." Chrysostom does not doubt the hierarchy of the heavenly host nor does he explain the superiority of the
   cherubim.
51 Cf. Ez 1.3.
52 Cf. Dn 10.4.

in the midst of it, something gleamed like electrum, and brightness was in it. Also in its midst was the likeness of four living creatures. They looked like this. Their form was human, but each had four faces and four wings.[53] They were tall and frightening. The backs of the four were filled with eyes set in a circle.[54] Over their heads something like a firmament could be seen, fearful as the appearance of crystal, spread out over their heads from on high.[55] Each had two wings covering its body. Above the firmament there appeared to be a sapphire stone with what looked like a throne upon it. And upon the throne was seated one who had the appearance of a man. Upwards from what resembled his waist, I saw what appeared to be electrum; downwards from what resembled his waist, I saw what looked like fire. The splendor which surrounded him was like the rainbow which is seen in the clouds on a rainy day."[56]

(27) And because Ezekiel wished to show that neither he, the prophet, nor those heavenly powers approached the divine essence in itself and in its pure state, he went on to say: "This was the appearance of the likeness of the glory of the Lord."[57] Did you see in both places, God's accommodation of condescension? There is no reason other than this that the heavenly powers hide themselves with their wings [even though they are wiser, more knowledgeable, and purer than we are].[58]

(28) How is this made clear to us? By their very names. The Angel is called by that name because he announces to men the things of God. The Archangel is called by that name because he rules the Angels. These heavenly virtues also have proper names which show us their wisdom and purity just as their wings reveal the loftiness of their nature. Gabriel is shown as flying not because angels have wings but so that you may know

---

53 Cf. Ez 1.4–6.
54 Cf. ibid. 19.
55 Cf. ibid. 22.
56 Cf. ibid. 25–28. For a summary of the vision see Hom.IV.9.
57 Ez 1.28.
58 The bracketed words are omitted from several MSS. They may represent a gloss (M).

that he comes down to human beings from places which are lofty and from a way of life which is spent on high. Certainly, in the case of the Angels and the Archangels, their wings show no more than the loftiness of their nature.

(29) The wings, then, reveal the lofty natures of the powers above; the throne shows that God rests upon them; the eyes show how clear-sighted they are; their closeness to the throne and their unceasing chanting of hymns signify that they are ever wakeful and never sleep. So, too, the name of one choir shows its wisdom; the name of another, its purity. For what is the meaning of Cherubim? Knowledge which has become full. And what is the meaning of Seraphim? Mouths of fire. Do you see how their names mean the wisdom of the one choir and the purity of the other?[59] Still, a heavenly power in which knowledge has become full cannot look upon God's accommodation of condescension without fear. If the Anomoeans' knowledge is limited, and Paul says: "We know in part . . . as in a mirror in a dark manner"—how great would their folly be if they think that they clearly see and understand what the heavenly powers cannot even look upon?[60]

(30) God is incomprehensible not only to the Cherubim and Seraphim but also to the Principalities and the Powers and to any other created power. This is what I wished to prove now, but my mind has grown weary. It is not so much the great number of arguments which tires me, but a holy dread at what I had to say. My soul shudders and has become frightened since it has dwelt too long on speculations about heavenly matters.

(31) Come, therefore, let me bring my soul down from the heavens and lead it away from its dread. Let me find refuge for it in my usual exhortation. And what is this exhortation? I urge you to pray for the Anomoeans, so that they may one day return to health. Just as we ask you to implore God in behalf of those who are sick, in the mines, in harsh slavery, or are

---

59 J. Daniélou (SC 28 bis Introduction 42–44) discusses the significance of the names of the choirs of angels, deriving his material chiefly from Homilies I–V.

60 A reductio ad absurdum again establishes the great folly of the Anomoeans. Cf. 1 Cor 13.9, 12; Hom.I.13, 18, 27, 31, 33.

possessed by demons,[61] much more do we bid you to implore
him on behalf of these Anomoeans, because their godlessness
is a greater evil than that of any demon. The madness of the
possessed has an excuse. The disease of the Anomoeans has
nothing to offer in its defense.[62]

(32) Now that I have made mention of the prayer for the
possessed, there is something I wish to talk about with your
loving assembly so as to eradicate a sinful sickness[63] from the
Church. It would be strange if we were trying with such care to
heal outsiders while we neglected a disease which ails our own
members. What, then, is this sickness? This immense throng is
applauding now and paying such sharp attention to what I am
saying.[64] But all too often, when the time comes which inspires

61 Chrysostom speaks at length on the prayer for the possessed in
  Hom.IV.31–41. We also find a precise allusion to the prayer which preceded the dismissal of the demoniacs below (III.42). In *Constitutiones
  apostolicae* 8.10, 14–15 (PG 1.1086–87; 1110–1114) we read of the prayer
  for the sick, those in the mines and prison, and those in harsh captivity
  (slaves) in the same order in which Chrysostom lists them. The possessed
  were dismissed after the prayer for them, as the catechumens and penitents
  had been dismissed before them, and the liturgy proper was ready to begin.
  See J. Daniélou, Introduction, (SC 28 bis) pp. 52–53.
62 Since the sickness of the Anomoeans springs from a self-willed pride in
  which their meddlesome speculations madly indulge, it has no excuse.
  Nonetheless Christians must pray for them (as well as for all the sick) so that
  they may abandon their idle curiosity and return to the health of humility.
63 The sickness—leaving the church after the homily and before the liturgy of
  the Eucharist—may have been due, at least in part, to his pluralistic
  congregation. In our Introduction (74 above) it was pointed out that, by
  imperial edicts, Christianity was the official religion of the empire and all
  Arian churches had been turned over to the orthodox. Furthermore, the
  people came to hear and applaud Chrysostom, who was already famous as
  an orator. So, when the homily was over, many had gotten all for which they
  had come. It certainly was an abuse, especially for orthodox Christians, and
  as early as the year 341 the Synod of Antioch passed a decree which
  excommunicated those who attended the Christian service to hear the
  Scriptures but did not join in the prayers and dishonored the eucharist. Cf.
  C. J. Hefele, *Histoire des conciles* 1.2 (Paris 1907) 715. For other details on the
  behavior of the Christians of Antioch in church see Chrysostom, *In act. apos.*
  XXIV.4 (PG 60.190); *De bap. Christi* (PG 49.370).
64 Chrysostom was frequently applauded by his congregation. In FOTC 68 he
  tells us in his first discourse *Against Judaizing Christians* (p. 3) that, after his
  first homily in this present series, there was great applause. But he also says
  in that same first discourse: "I am not now speaking for show or applause
  but to cure your souls (p. 15)." See also P. Albert, *S. Jean Chrysostome considéré
  comme orateur populaire* (Paris 1858) esp. Chap. 7; Baur 1.206–30, esp. 216.

the greatest religious awe,[65] I have searched for your throng and been unable to see it. I moaned in my deep grief that, while your fellow servant was preaching, the zeal of your throng was great, your eagerness reached a high pitch, people crowded against one another and stayed till the very end of the homily. But when Christ is about to appear in the holy mysteries, the church becomes empty and deserted.

(33) How can such conduct deserve pardon? By this carelessness of yours you destroy all my commendation for the zeal with which you listened. Who will not bring accusation against you, and against me, when he sees that the benefit derived from your listening runs off like water? If you were paying careful attention to what was being said, you would have proved your zeal by your deeds. But the fact that, after listening, you immediately run off is a sign that your minds neither grasped nor stored away any part of what I said. If my words were held in your souls, with all certainty they would have kept you here in the church and have sent you on to the awesome mysteries in a deep spirit of piety. But now, just as if you had been listening to some musician play the cithara,[66] as soon as the homily is over you walk out of church with no benefit to show for it.

(34) And what silly excuse do most of you give? I can pray at home, you say, but at home I cannot hear the homily and the instruction.[67] My friends, you are deceiving yourselves! Yes, you can pray at home, but not in the same way as you can in the church. In the church there is a large throng of spiritual fathers;[68] there, with one accord, a cry is sent up to God. When you call upon the Lord by yourself, he does not listen to you in the same way as when you invoke him along with your brothers. Here in church you have something more. Here you

---

65 The time of the eucharistic sacrifice.
66 The congregation has come to church as if to a concert for their entertainment.
67 Chrysostom offers the guilty ones' excuse as a straw man which he will presently demolish by showing the superiority of public prayer (especially the eucharistic prayer) to instruction and private prayer.
68 As in Hom.II.3, the "fathers" probably refer to visiting bishops. See note 4 on Hom. II.

have the oneness of mind, the unison of voices, the common bond of love, the prayers of the priests.[69] This is why the priests conduct the prayers. The prayers of a crowd are somewhat weak; but when they are caught up with the stronger prayers of the priests, they rise up to heaven together with them.

(35) Besides, what benefit would there be in a homily when prayer has not been joined to it? Prayer stands in the first place; then comes the word of instruction. And that is what the apostles said: "Let us devote ourselves to prayer and the ministry of the word."[70] Paul does this when he prays at the beginnings of his epistles so that, like the light of a lamp, the light of prayer may prepare the way for the word.[71] If you accustom yourselves to pray fervently, you will not need instruction from your fellow servants because God himself, with no intermediary, enlightens your mind.

(36) If the prayer of a single person is so powerful, much more so is the prayer which is offered along with many other people. The sinewy strength of such a prayer and the confidence that God will hear it is far greater than you can have for the prayer you offer privately at home. What makes this clear? Listen to Paul himself when he says: "He rescued us from the danger of death and continues to rescue us. We have hoped that he will never cease to deliver us if you all join in helping us by prayer in our behalf, so that God may be thanked for the gift granted us through the prayers of many people."[72] It was by this means, too, that Peter escaped from prison. "The Church prayed fervently to God on his behalf."[73]

(37) If the prayer of the Church helped Peter and led forth from the prison that pillar,[74] how is it, tell me, that you think

---

69 This mention of the role of the priest in the official prayer of the Church is also made more complete in *In 2 Cor.* 18.3 (PG 61.527B).

70 Acts 6.4.

71 See above Hom.III.9–12.

72 Cf. 2 Cor 1.10–11. As many had prayed for Paul's safety, so should many give thanks for it. Paul's teaching gives an important place to prayer, both of petition and thanksgiving. Cf. J. O'Rourke, JBC 52:9.

73 Cf. Acts 12.5.

74 Used figuratively as in Gal 2.9, where Paul refers to James, Cephas, and John as "pillars" (of the Jerusalem Church).

slightly of its power? What defense will you have for this action of yours? Listen to God himself when he says that he respects the throng of people which invokes him with affection. When he was defending his action in the case of the gourd plant against Jonah's complaint, he said: "You had pity on the gourd for which you suffered no distress nor did you rear it; shall I not spare Nineveh, the great city, in which dwell more than a hundred and twenty thousand persons?"[75] He does not mention the large number without purpose. He does so in order that you may learn that any prayer which is offered with a unison of many voices has great power.

(38) Now I wish to show this to you by an example from human history as well. As you know, ten years ago, some men were arrested for trying to seize supreme power. One of them—a man in a position of power—was found guilty of the charge. He was gagged and was being led to execution. Then the whole city ran to the hippodrome, even bringing the workmen from their shops. All the people came together from every side and rescued the condemned man from the imperial wrath, even though he deserved no pardon.[76]

(39) Because you wished to appease the anger of an earthly emperor, you all ran to him in a crowd, even bringing your wives and children. Now it is the king of heaven whom you are going to make favorable and well-disposed. Now you are going

---

75 Cf. Jon 4.10–11 (LXX) and NAB note ad loc. Chrysostom is not concerned with Jonah's anger at the loss of the plant which shaded him from the hot sun nor with his disappointment that his message to the Ninevites was heeded so that they repented. Chrysostom's point is that God hears the repentant prayers of the 120,000 inhabitants and spares the sinful city.

76 Montfaucon alludes to this incident (see above Introduction, *Notice* I.1–2) and names Theodore, secretary to Valens, as the imperial official and conspirator. (See G. Downey, *History* 401–02.) Chrysostom reports that Theodore was cruelly executed for his part in the plot. Cf. *Ad vid. iun.* 4 (PG 48.604) and Socrates, HE 6.35 (PG 67.504–05). Malingrey identifies the man Chrysostom speaks of here as Hierocles, son of Alypius. Cf. Ammianus Marcellinus, *Rerum gestarum libri* 29.1.44 (vol. 3 in Loeb Classical Library, trans. J. Rolfe [Cambridge, Mass. 1939]). According to Ammianus, Alypius, a former vice-governor of Britain, had all his goods confiscated and was exiled; Hierocles, on his way to death, "by a lucky chance" was reprieved. For Chrysostom, the "lucky chance" was the unanimity of the Antiochenes in suing for Valens' imperial pardon.

to rescue from his anger not one man, as you did then, or two, or three, or a hundred. Now you are going to set free from the snares of the devil all the sinners in the world and all those possessed by demons.[77] And what do you do now? You sit down at home instead of running together as a group so that God may respect the unison of your prayers and put aside his punishment of those sinners and demoniacs as well as forgiving you your own sins.

(40) Suppose, at that sacred moment, you should happen to be in the market place, or at home, or involved in pressing business transactions. Should you not grow more violent than any lion and burst every bond which holds you back? Will you not leave all this behind and hurry to join the others in their common prayer and supplication? My beloved, tell me this. What hope of salvation will you have at that sacred moment? It is not only men who are making their voices heard in that prayer, a prayer which is filled with the holiest fear and dread. Angels, too, fall down in adoration before their Lord. Archangels beg his favor. They have that sacred moment to fight for them as their ally; they have the sacrifice to lend them aid.[78]

(41) Men cut down olive branches and wave them in the paths of kings. They wave these branches to remind their rulers to be merciful and kind. But at that sacred moment, instead of olive branches, the angels are holding forth the Lord's body and they are calling upon the Lord in behalf of human nature, just as if they were praying in some such words as these: "We pray for these men whom you first deemed so worthy of your love that you laid down your own life. We pour forth our supplications for those for whom you yourself poured forth your blood. We call upon you in behalf of those for whom you offered this body of yours in sacrifice."

(42) This is why at this sacred moment the deacon has those who are possessed stand up and bids them to bow only their heads and to make their supplications by the posture of their bodies. For they are not permitted to join the prayers of the

---

77 Cf. above paragraph 31.
78 J. Daniélou, (SC 28 bis) Introduction, 58–60, attests to the presence at and participation in the eucharistic sacrifice of the angelic hosts. Cf. Rv 8.4.

assembly of their brothers. The deacon has them stand so that you may pity them both for their misfortune and because they cannot speak. He also does this so that you may use your own confidence in approaching God for their protection. Let us, then, keep all these things in mind and hurry to gather together at that moment so as to draw to ourselves God's mercy and to find grace and help in our time of need.

(43) You have shown praise for my discourse. You received my exhortation with loud applause. Now show your praise by your deeds. It takes no long time to prove your docility and your obedience. Right after the exhortation comes the prayer. That is the praise I seek, namely, the applause which you give by your very deeds.[79]

(44) Therefore, encourage one another to remain standing just as you have been standing. If anyone wavers from the ranks, take care to hold him back.[80] In this way you will receive a double reward, for your own zeal and for the concern you show for your brothers. And you will pour forth your own supplications with greater confidence in God because you have made God favorable to you. Then you can obtain blessings both in this world and the next through the grace and loving-kindness of our Lord Jesus Christ, to whom be glory forever and ever. Amen.

---

79 Chrysostom mentioned the applause of the congregation earlier in para-graph 32 (cf. note 64 above). Here he names the applause he really wants—praise proved by deeds. Cf. also Hom.V.59. He says much the same thing in *In epist. ad Rom.*4 (PG 48.369) where he specifies among the deeds "docility in your actions."

80 All Christians constitute one body in Christ. Hence the faithful have an obligation to fulfill a kind of apostolate by watching over each other's conduct during the services (M). See *In act. apos.* Hom.24.4 (PG 60.190). This will earn for the vigilant Christian a double reward.

HOMILY IV

RECENTLY[1] PROVED TO YOU that God is incomprehensible to men[2] and even to the Cherubim and Seraphim.[3] I should be satisfied now to put the question aside without bringing forward further arguments on this subject. But the chief purpose of my efforts and desire was not only to stitch shut the mouths of my Anomoean opponents but also to provide more and more instruction to your loving assembly.[4] So it is that again I take up the same question and advance my argument still further.

(2) The time I spend on these arguments will both increase your knowledge about the Anomoeans and will make my prize of victory over those heretics a brighter one, if my discussion clears away any remnant of their error which may still remain. In a pasture we must do more than cut down useless and harmful weeds at the level of the ground, for they grow again if their roots still lie below the earth. We must pull them up from the very womb and belly of the soil and set them naked in the heat of the sun so that they may readily wither away.[5]

(3) Come then, and let my discourse again lead you up to heaven.[6] I do not do this to play the busybody by making idle

---

1 The meaning of *prōēn*, which I have translated as "recently" is not always precise. It can mean "lately," "just now," or (usually in combination with *khthes*, "yesterday") it can be more definite and mean "the day before yesterday." In any event, the interval between Homilies III and IV could not have been too long, although the lengthy recapitulation of Hom.III with which Hom.IV opens could indicate that the third discourse *Against Judaizing Christians* interrupted the present series at this point. See Introduction 54 and note 69.
2 In Homilies I and II.
3 In Hom.III, esp. 6–7; 9–17; 29–30.
4 Chrysostom here states clearly the apologetic purpose of these homilies (to refute the Anomoeans) and his objective of instructing his congregation on this heresy.
5 Cf. above Hom.III.2–3.
6 Cf. above Hom.III.30–31.

investigations. I do it because I am anxious to root out the untimely contentiousness of those who have no understanding of themselves and who refuse to admit the limits of their human nature. This was the reason for my lengthy proof that not only the appearance of God but even of his angels was too much for that just man, Daniel, to endure. I did that when I recounted for you his whole story and showed you a Daniel who blanched, trembled, and was in a condition no better than men on their deathbeds. Why? Because his soul was striving to burst the bonds of his flesh.[7]

(4) When a dove spends its time in a cage, it grows tame and manageable. When it sees something to frighten it, it grows terrified, flies to the top of the cage, and looks for a way out through the windows in its desire to escape from its distress. In the same way, the soul of the blessed Daniel at that moment strove to fly out of his body. It rushed from one side to the other trying to escape. Had his soul succeeded, it would have deserted his body and flown away. But the angel quickly laid hold of it, freed it from its distress, and led it back again to its own lodging.[8]

(5) I told that story to the Anomoeans at that time so that they might learn the vast difference between a man and an angel. I was hoping that, when they realized how inferior they were to angels, they might return to their senses and rid themselves of the meddlesome curiosity which they display against their Master. The just man, Daniel, could not endure to look upon an angel for all the confidence he had in God. But these Anomoeans, who are so far below Daniel's virtue, have the curiosity to investigate not an angel but the very Master of the angels.[9]

(6) Daniel overcame the fury of lions;[10] we cannot even prevail over foxes.[11] He made a dragon burst asunder and conquered the nature of the wild beast because of his con-

---

7 Cf. above Hom.III.18–22, esp. 20.
8 Cf. Dn 10.10.
9 Cf. above Homilies I.34–36; III.6–8; 23.
10 Cf. Dn 6.17–24.
11 The Anomoeans are compared to foxes because of their craft and guile.

fidence in God;[12] we are afraid of mere crawling creatures.[13] He stopped a king who was raging like a lion; he showed himself and took a stand midway between the king and the barbarian army against which Nebuchadnezzar was rushing; he checked the king's anger, which was burning more vehemently than any fire, and brought into the light all that had been darkened.[14] But when Daniel, who brought these things to light, saw that an angel had come to him, he was gripped by a dizziness which plunged him into deep darkness.[15] What defense will those Anomoeans have for trying to take the blessed nature of God and to subject it to close investigation?

(7) On that other day when I spoke to you, I did not stop my discourse at this point; I even brought my statement of the case up to the point where it included those wise virtues above. We showed them turning aside their eyes, covering their faces with their wings, standing up straight on their legs, raising an unceasing cry of praise.[16] We did this because those spiritual powers reveal to us in every way their own astonishment and holy dread. Because they are wise and are closer to that ineffable and blessed essence, they know better than we do that it is incomprehensible and cannot be understood. And their increased wisdom increases their reverence and piety.[17]

(8) We also told you what the unapproachable is and that it is much greater than the incomprehensible. As the reason for this we showed that the incomprehensible is seen as incomprehensible after people have searched into it and tried to understand it. The unapproachable, from the very beginning, does not admit of investigation nor can anyone come near it.

---

12 Cf. Dn 14.23–27: Vulgate; Bel and the Dragon: LXX.

13 In Hom.III.6 the Anomoeans are said to be no better than creatures who crawl on the ground. Hence, they are vastly inferior to the powers above (who, like men, do not know God in his essence).

14 No mention of this event is found in the book of Daniel as it has come down to us (M). In fact, the historical Nebuchadnezzar is not mentioned in Dn. When his name occurs in Dn 1-4, he is only a fictitious character representing the Seleucid monarchy, particularly Antiochus IV Epiphanes. Cf. J. McKenzie, DB 610.

15 Cf. Dn 10.8–9.

16 Cf. Homilies I.35; III.14–17.

17 Cf. Hom.III.29.

To show this we needed a simile and we used the image of the sea.[18] We also told you that Paul did not say: "Who is an unapproachable light," but, "Who dwells in unapproachable light."[19] But if the dwelling is unapproachable, much more so is the God who dwells in it. Paul did not say this to limit God to a place but to prove all the more cogently that God can neither be comprehended nor approached.

(9) Furthermore, we brought forward other heavenly powers, the Cherubim. We showed how above them is a firmament, a crystal stone, the likeness of a throne, the appearance of a man, electrum, fire, and a rainbow. And after all these things, the prophet said: "This was the appearance of the likeness of the glory of the Lord."[20] By all these means we showed you the condescension and accommodation of God and that his very essence is too much for the virtues above to endure.[21]

(10) I did not recapitulate these matters for no reason. Since the promise I made constitutes a debt which I owe to you, I wish to know exactly what I have paid and what is the balance still owed.[22] This is what men who owe a balance on a debt do. They produce a tablet on which the entire account has been written down; after they have shown this to those who lent them money, they pay on the balance still due. I, too, have opened the recollections of your minds as I would open a tablet. I have pointed with my finger, as it were, at what has been paid on the account. Now I shall go on to pay the balance of what I owe.

(11) What, then, was there left for me to prove? That there are neither Principalities, nor Powers, nor Dominations, nor any other created virtues which have a perfect comprehension of God.[23] I say other virtues because such virtues do exist, but we do not even know their names. Think of how mad and

---

18 Cf. Homilies I.24, 29; III.11–15.
19 1 Tm 6.16 and Hom.III.11.
20 Ez 2.1.
21 Cf. Hom.III.24–29.
22 Cf. Hom.III.30.
23 Cf. below Hom.IV.17.

foolish the Anomoean heretics are! We do not even know the names of the master's servants, but they, like busybodies, are investigating into the very essence of the master himself. There are angels, archangels, thrones, dominations, principalities, and powers. However, they are not the only virtues who dwell in the heavens. There are tribes and nations without limit or number, and no words can set them before your minds.[24]

(12) Where is the evidence that there are more heavenly virtues whose names we do not even know? It was Paul who said this. He did so when he was speaking about Christ and said: "He seated him above every principality, power and virtue, and every name that can be given not only in this age but also in the age to come."[25] Do you see that there are names in heaven which are going to be known but which are unknown now? That is why Paul said: "Not only in this age but also in the age to come."

(13) And why is it a matter for wonder if these heavenly powers do not have a perfect comprehension of God's essence? It is no great task to prove this. Many of his plans for the world's redemption are not known to these very virtues above, nor to the principalities, the powers, and the dominations. Again we shall prove from Paul's own words that they learned some of God's plans at the same time we men did and that they did not know them before us. In fact, they not only learned them at the same time as we did but they even learned them through us.[26]

(14) Paul said: "It was unknown to other generations as it has now been revealed to his holy apostles and prophets that

---

24 This sentence is reminiscent of Rv 7.9 (M) where the reference is not to the choirs of angels but rather to the hosts of the elect.

25 Cf. Eph 1.21. See below Hom.V.35.

26 See NAB note on 1 Cor 2.10–16 which says: "Just as the individual is the only one cognizant of his own thoughts, which he alone can reveal, so it is with God and his plans for the salvation of humanity." See also Chrysostom *In Johannem* Hom.1.2 (FOTC 33) p. 6, where he says: ". . . from those awesome mysteries which even the angels did not know before they took place. They also have learned by the voice of John, along with us, and through us have acquired knowledge of what we have learned."

the gentiles are now coheirs, members of the same body, and sharers of his promise"—but the promises had been given to the Jews—"through the gospel of which I, Paul, became a minister."[27] And what makes it clear that the powers above learned this at the same time? What Paul said was said concerning men. Listen, therefore, to what follows. "To me, the least of all the saints, was given the grace to preach to the gentiles the unfathomable riches of Christ."[28] What does he mean by "unfathomable?" He means that which cannot be investigated or examined, not only what cannot be discovered but what we cannot even search out or of which we cannot find a trace.[29]

(15) Again let the Anomoeans hear how thick and continuous are the showers of darts which Paul shoots at them. If the riches are unfathomable, how could he who gave the gift of the riches fail himself to be unfathomable? ". . . To enlighten all men on the mysterious plan which was hidden in God so that now, through the Church, God's manifold wisdom is made known to the principalities and powers."[30] Did you hear how those powers above learned these things at that time and not before? For the king's attendant does not know what the king wills to do, ". . . so that now, through the Church, God's manifold wisdom is made known to the principalities and powers of heaven." See how great an honor was conferred on human nature that both with us and through us the powers above learned the secrets of the King.[31]

(16) But what clear evidence do we have that Paul is speaking about those powers which are above? Surely he knows the demons as principalities and powers and calls them by those names when he says: "Our battle is not against blood and flesh

27 Cf. Eph 3.5–7.
28 Cf. Ibid. 8.
29 Chrysostom's definition of "unfathomable" is practically identical with his definition of "unapproachable" (see Homilies III.12 and IV.8). He must look on the two words as almost synonymous.
30 Cf. Eph 3.9–10.
31 After he has humbled the Anomoeans and their pretentious reliance on human intelligence left to its own powers, Chrysostom shows here the honor God has done to human nature by sharing with it, through the Church, his plan of redemption (M).

but against the Principalities and Powers and the rulers of this world of darkness of the present age."[32] He does not say here that the demons learned, does he? By no means! He was speaking about those powers from above for, after he said in the earlier text, "the principalities and the powers," he went on to add, "in heaven."[33] In the earlier text the principalities and powers are in heaven; in the text just cited these principalities and powers dwell below heaven. This is why Paul calls them rulers of this world.[34] He is showing that heaven is inaccessible to them and that they manifest their whole dominion in this world only.

(17) Did you see how the powers on high learned these mysteries with us and through us? Let me now bring my discourse around to the payment of my debt.[35] Let me show you that neither the principalities nor the powers know God's essence. Who is it, then, who says this? It is no longer Paul, nor Isaiah, nor Ezekiel. But it is another holy vessel and instrument. It is John, the Son of Thunder himself,[36] the beloved of Christ, who leaned on the Lord's breast[37] and drank from there the divine waters.[38] What, then, did he say? "No one has ever seen God."[39] Truly he is the Son of Thunder. More clearly than

---

32 Cf. Eph 6.12. The words "of the present age" are not found in the NT text. Chrysostom omits the rest of the verse which reads: "the evil spirits in regions above." This addition would destroy his argument or call for subtle exegesis of his distinction between Principalities and Powers in heaven and the fallen Principalities and Powers whom he calls demons and rulers of this world of darkness. In 2 Cor 12.2 we find evidence for more than one area called heaven. J. O'Rourke, JBC 52:42, identifies the first as our earth's atmosphere, the second as the region of the stars, and the third as the Paradise to which Paul was snatched and where God dwells. Then the "evil spirits in regions above" might dwell below heaven and be called "rulers of this world of darkness," whose evil stands in contrast to the light of heaven. Then Chrysostom's distinction is valid.

33 Cf. Eph 3.10.

34 "Rulers of this world" aptly describes the function which people of Paul's time considered the fallen angels to have through their control over human events. See J. Grassi, JBC 56:40.

35 Cf. Homilies III.30; IV 10; VII.7

36 Cf. Mk 3.17.

37 Cf. Jn 13.25; 21.10.

38 Cf. Jn 7.37–38.

39 Jn 1.18.

a trumpet call he sent forth a word whose sound suffices to confound the contentious.

(18) Let us see what objection might be urged against what he said. Tell me, John, what do you mean when you say: "No one has ever seen God?" What shall we think about the prophets who say that they saw God? Isaiah said: "I saw the Lord sitting on a high and exalted throne."[40] And, again, Daniel said: "I saw until the thrones were set, and the Ancient of days sat."[41] And Micah said: "I saw the God of Israel sitting on his throne."[42] And, again, another prophet said: "I saw the Lord standing on the altar, and he said to me: 'Strike the mercy seat.' "[43] And I can gather together many similar passages to show you as witnesses of what I say.

(19) How is it, then, that John says: "No one has ever seen God?" He says this so that you may know that he speaking of a clear knowledge and a perfect comprehension of God. All the cases cited were instances of God's condescension and accommodation.[44] That no one of those prophets saw God's essence in its pure state is clear from the fact that each one saw him in a different way. God is a simple being; he is not composed of parts; he is without form or figure. But all these prophets saw different forms and figures. God proved this very thing through the mouth of another prophet. And he persuaded those other prophets that they did not see his essence in its exact nature when he said: "I have multiplied visions, and by the ministries of the prophets I was represented."[45] What God was saying was: "I did not show my very essence but I came

---

40 Is 6.1. See Homilies III.14, 16; XI.26 for Isaiah's vision.
41 Cf. Dn 7.9. For Daniel's vision of God see Hom.XI.25; and of the angel, Hom.III.18–23.
42 Cf. 1 Kgs (3 Kgs) 22.19 and NAB note ad loc. See also below Hom.XI.26.
43 Am 9.1 (LXX). In the vision the Lord tells the prophet Amos that there will be no escape from his wrath.
44 Recall Chrysostom's definition of condescension given above in Hom.III.15.
45 Hos 12.11 (LXX). The text probably means that God constantly instructs his people and remains near to them through the many visions and messages sent to them through the prophets. The wording of the text is quite different in NAB but the meaning is perhaps not far removed from LXX. Chrysostom's interpretation fits his purpose well.

down in condescension and accommodated myself to the weakness of their eyes."

(20) However, John does not say only of man that: "No one has ever seen God."[46] This was proved by what I have said—I mean by the prophetic utterance which states: "I have multiplied visions, and by the ministries of the prophets I was represented."[47] It is also clear from what God said to Moses. When he wished to see God face to face, God said to him: "No one shall see my face and live."[48] So that point is clear and we can agree upon it. John was not talking only about our human nature but also about the powers above when he said: "No one has ever seen God." For this reason he brought forward the only begotten to teach this doctrine. So that no one may say: "How is this proved?" he went on to add: "The only begotten Son, who is in the bosom of the Father, himself has revealed this."[49] In this way John provides a trustworthy witness and teacher for this doctrine.

(21) If John wished to show here only the same truth which Moses had shown, there would have been no need to add that the only begotten had revealed this. For, without this addition in John's text, it would not be the case that only the only begotten had revealed it. For long before John spoke these words (as if they were words he had heard from the only begotten), Moses, the prophet—just as if he had heard it from God—made this truth clear to us. But John brings in the only begotten as his witness because he was about to go beyond what

---

46 Cf. Jn 1.18. The rest of the verse reads: "It is God the only begotten, who is in the bosom of the Father, who has himself revealed him." See also Mt 11.27 and NAB note ad loc.

47 Hos 12.11 (LXX).

48 Cf. Ex 33.20 (LXX). Moses' request to see God's glory (Ex 33.18) is impossible since the sight of God is too much for mortal man to bear (cf. Gn 32.30; Dt 4.33; Jgs 6.22–23 etc.). The obscure and enigmatic description of Ex 33.21–23 probably indicates that although his request was refused, Moses was granted a knowledge of God superior to that accorded to ordinary men or even to other prophets. The language and thought of these verses are reminiscent of Elijah's divine confrontation in 1 Kgs (3 Kgs) 19.9–13. Cf. J. Huesman, JBC 3:94.

49 Cf. Jn 1.18. Chrysostom reads "Son" for "God" of the NT. See n. 46 above and n. 55 below.

had been said to Moses and to reveal that not even the powers above see God. Therefore, he brought forward the only begotten to teach us this truth.

(22) You must understand here that the "sight" of the powers above is their knowledge. The powers above are spirits[50] and do not have pupils or eyes or eyelids. What is sight for us is knowledge for them. So when you hear that, "No one has ever seen God," you must understand that the words you hear mean that no one knows God in his essence with complete exactness.[51] As for the Seraphim, when you hear that they turned away their eyes and covered up their faces, and that, again, the Cherubim did the same thing,[52] you must not understand that they have eyes or pupils. Such a form and appearance belongs to bodies. What you must believe is that, by these terms, the prophet was hinting at the knowledge of these powers above.

(23) And so, when the prophet says that they could not endure to look upon God, even though God was condescending and accommodating himself to their weakness, he means just this: they cannot endure to comprehend him with a pure and perfect knowledge; they dare not look fixedly at his essence pure and entire; they dare not look at him even after he has accommodated himself to them. And to look fixedly means to know.

(24) The evangelist, John, knew that knowledge of such matters is beyond human nature and that God is incomprehensible to the powers above. This is why he brought in to teach us this doctrine the one who is seated at the right hand of God and who has a perfect knowledge of these things.[53] And John did not simply say "the Son," even though, had he said only that, it would have been enough to curb the tongues of the shameless Anomoeans. Many are called by the name of Christ, but there is one Christ; many are called lords, but there

---

50 As pure spirits, the powers above are totally immaterial and have no dependence either on bodily parts or functions. See below Hom.V.4.
51 Cf. above Hom.IV.11 and below Hom.IV.23.
52 Cf. above Hom.III.14–15; 29–30.
53 Cf. above Homilies IV.12; 29; V.25. See also Ps 109(110) 1.1.

is one Lord; many are called gods, but there is one God.[54] So, too, many are called sons, but the Son is one. The addition of the article is enough to show the special excellence of the only begotten.

(25) Still, John was not satisfied with this, but after he said: "No one has ever seen God," he went on to add: "The only begotten Son, who is in the bosom of the Father, himself has revealed this."[55] First he said "only begotten," and then, "Son." Since the name of son is so common, and since many people therefore detract from his glory and consider that he is one of many—for the name of son is common to all men—John has put in the first place that which is his special excellence, that which belongs only to him and to nobody else, namely, the title "only begotten". From this title you may believe that the common title of son is not common but is peculiar to him and belongs to no other as it does to him.

(26) To make my meaning clearer, I shall say the same thing again, but in fuller detail. The name *son* belongs to men and it belongs to the Christ. But it belongs to us by analogy; it belongs to Christ in its proper sense. The title *only begotten* is his alone and belongs to no one else, even by analogy. Therefore, from the title which belongs to no one else but to him alone you must

---

54 Cf. 1 Cor 8.5–6. Although the pagans speak about many gods and many lords, the Christian knows that there is really only one God, the Father and Creator of the universe who has made us for himself, and only one Lord, Jesus Christ, through whom all things were made and through whom we are brought to the Father. Cf. R. Kugelman, JBC 51:55. Chrysostom here points out the analogous use of the names Christ (anointed), lord, and god, but the primary analogates are Jesus Christ, our Lord, and our God. So, too, in the argument which follows, "son" can be and is used analogously, but the primary analogate is the only begotten Son.

55 Cf. Jn 1.18. Again Chrysostom reads "Son" for "God" of the NT. See K. Aland, et al., *Novum Testamentum Graece* (Stuttgart 1979). R. Brown, "Does the New Testament Call Jesus God?" *Theological Studies* 26 (1965) 553–54 accepts the reading which calls Jesus "God" which is supported by the best Greek MSS and by the recently discovered Bodmer papyri dating from circa A.D. 200. Chrysostom's reading, Brown reports, is supported by some early versions, by a good number of later Greek MSS., and by some Greek and many Latin Fathers. "Only begotten" occurs four times in the Johannine writings and in three of them it is combined with "Son" (Jn 3.16, 18; 1 Jn 4.9). Brown remarks that the combination in Jn 1.18 may reflect a scribal tendency to conform.

understand that the title of *Son*, which belongs to many, is his in its proper sense and meaning. This is why John first said, "only begotten," and then, "Son."

(27) If these two titles do not satisfy you, John says, let me mention another, a third designation, which is crass and on a human level but which can still lead such creatures as crawl on the ground[56] up to an understanding of the glory of the only begotten. What is this title? "Who is in the bosom of the Father."[57] The expression is a crass one, but it can prove genuine sonship if we understand it in a sense which befits God.

(28) When you hear the words "throne" and "the seat at the right hand,"[58] you do not understand a throne nor a place nor a circumscribed space; from the expressions "throne" and "the sharing of a place to sit," you must think of an honor which is precisely the same and equal. In the same way, when you hear the word "bosom," you must not think that there is a bosom or a place; from the expression "bosom," you must understand the Son's closeness to and confidence in the Father who has begotten him. To say that the Son dwells in the bosom of the Father shows us and brings before our minds much more clearly his closeness to the Father than do the words "seated at the right hand." For the Father would not let himself have the Son in his bosom unless the Son were of the same essence, nor could the Son endure to dwell in the Father's bosom if the Son were of a nature inferior to the Father's.[59]

(29) Therefore, since he is the Son, since he is the only begotten, and since he dwells in the Father's bosom, he knows perfectly all that the Father knows. This is why the evangelist

---

56 Again, the Anomoeans. See above Homilies III.6 and IV.5.

57 Jn 1.18. The expression denotes complete intimacy, a community of life. Cf. B. Vawter, JBC 63:46.

58 Cf. above Hom.IV.7; Is 6.1; Dn 7.9; 1 Kgs (3 Kgs) 22.19; Heb 12.1 for "throne".

59 Here we see Chrysostom's proof that the Father and the Son are one in essence and that the Son is equal to the Father in power and majesty, divinity of nature, and oneness in knowledge—all of which Arius and the Anomoeans would deny. In IV.27 Chrysostom mentions for the first time "the glory of the only begotten," by which he means the equality of the Father and the Son. He will continue this theme in Hom.V and develop it at length in Homilies VII–XII.

used these expressions to bring before your minds the perfect knowledge which the Son has of the Father. For John was talking about knowledge. If, then, John is not talking about the Son's knowledge of the Father, why did he speak of the bosom? If God is not a body—and he certainly is not—and if John is not making known the genuine sonship and the closeness of the Son to the Father, the word bosom has been used in vain and without reason. Why? Because it fulfills no purpose for us. But it was not uttered in vain. God forbid! The Spirit says nothing in vain. Here he is revealing the closeness of the Son to the Father.

(30) After the evangelist made the great revelation that not even the creatures on high see God, that is, that they do not have an exact knowledge of God, he wished to bring forward a trustworthy teacher of this truth. Therefore, John set down these words so that you might never thereafter doubt him but believe him in all things, just as you would believe the Son, the only begotten, who dwells in the bosom of the Father. Unless someone should be obstinate and wish to be so shameless as to contradict me, I maintain that this is proof of the Son's eternity. From the words spoken to Moses: "I am who am,"[60] we understand that God is eternal. So, too, from the expression: "Who is in the bosom of the Father," we can understand that the Son is in the bosom of the Father from all eternity.[61]

(31) I have proved to you by all these arguments that the essence of God is incomprehensible to every creature. There now remains for me to show that the Son and the Holy Spirit alone know God with full and perfect knowledge.[62] But let me put that off for another discourse so as not to bury your minds under a mound of arguments. Let me now turn my words to my customary exhortation.

(32) What is this usual exhortation of mine? I urge you to hold fast to earnest prayer with a sober mind and watchful

---

60 Ex 3.14.
61 Arius held that only the Father was without beginning; the Son was generated and, hence, there was a time when the Son was not, for whatever has origin must begin to be. Therefore, according to Arius, the Son could not have been eternal. See Introduction 27.
62 Cf. Homilies V.6–7; VII.7.

soul.[63] Not long ago I spoke to you on this and saw that you all readily complied with what I said.[64] It would be absurd for me to find fault with you when you are careless and not to praise you when you do what is right. So today I wish to praise you and to express to you my gratitude for heeding that exhortation of mine.

(33) I will express my gratitude by instructing you on the reason why that prayer precedes the other prayers[65] and why, at that moment, the deacon orders the demoniacs and those possessed by the distress of madness to be brought in and then bids them to bow their heads.[66] Why, then, does he do this? Because the power and activity of the demons is a painful shackle; it is difficult to deal with it; it is a chain which is stronger than any iron.

(34) When a judge appears in court and is about to take his seat at the high tribunal, the jailers lead from their cells all the prisoners and make them sit in front of the barred door and the screen which covers the entrance to the court. The prisoners are unwashed and slovenly; their hair is long and unkempt; their clothes are ragged and tattered. So, too, when Christ is going to take his seat, as it were, at the high tribunal and to reveal himself in the mysteries themselves, our spiritual fathers have ordained that the demoniacs be led in just as the jailers bring in the prisoners.[67]

(35) The purpose of this is not that the possessed give an accounting of their faults, as those prisoners must do, nor that they undergo punishment or torture. Rather, the reason is so

---

63 Cf. 1 Pt 5.8; 1 Thess 5.6; Hom V.47; ACW 31 pp. 78, 106, 116, 272.
64 Cf. Hom.III.31, 35–44.
65 The prayer for the demoniacs preceded the prayers for the candidates for baptism and for those doing penance.
66 Cf. Hom.III.42. See also J. Daniélou, Introduction (SC 28 bis) 52.
67 The scene Chrysostom paints is a dramatic one, In court the judge will ascend the tribunal to sit in judgment over the prisoners who have neglected themselves and have no others to care for them. In the church the tribunal is the altar where Christ will soon reveal himself in the eucharistic mysteries. Before him now stand not those guilty of crimes but those possessed by demons. The pitiable state of the demoniacs should rouse not only the pity of the Christian congregation but also their united prayers to implore Christ to have mercy on their brothers who are possessed. See also Chrysostom, In 2 Cor. hom 18.3 (PG 61.527).

that all the people of the city here present in the church may raise their united prayers of supplication in the demoniacs' behalf. In this way all of you, with a loud cry and with one accord, are begging and imploring our common Master to have mercy on those possessed.[68]

(36) So it was that we brought accusations against those who, at that time, left such a prayer behind them and, at that sacred moment, left the church to busy themselves elsewhere.[69] But now I wish to find fault with you who stay inside. It is not because you remain in church but because, while you do stay here, you show a disposition no better than those who left to busy themselves outside. How is this so? It is because you keep talking to one another at that sacred moment which is filled with holy fear and trembling.[70]

(37) What are you doing, my friends? Do you see standing close to you such a large crowd of prisoners who are your brothers and do you keep talking about things which have nothing to do with them? Is not the sight of them alone enough to frighten you and bring you to feel sympathy for them? Is your brother in chains, and do you feel no concern?[71] Tell me this. What excuse will you have for being so unsympathetic, so inhuman, and so cruel? While you chatter away, while you show your brother no concern and make such small account of him, are you not afraid that some demon may not leap out of his soul and, with no trace of fear, enter into yours? Why

---

68 J. Daniélou conjectures from this passage that the "loud cry with one accord" was "Lord, have mercy." See Introduction (SC 28 bis) 53. Cf. also above Hom.III.41–44.

69 See above Hom.III.36. There Chrysostom chides those who leave the church immediately after the homily and do not remain for the moment when Christ will appear in the mysteries.

70 The sacred moment is the prayers and petitions of the faithful—including the prayer for the demoniacs. See *Constitutiones apostolicae* 8.7 (PG 1.1078–81). See also F. E. Brightman, ed., *Liturgies Eastern and Western* vol. 1 (Oxford 1967) 5–6. During these prayers it would seem that many of the faithful who had remained in the church chattered among themselves and did not heed the prayers or make the responses. Chrysostom finds fault with such an unbecoming attitude on the part of the faithful in his Homily *De bap. Christi* 4 (PG 49.370).

71 If the congregation cannot be moved by sentiments of reverence and brotherly love, at least a feeling of fear for themselves should make their attitude toward the demoniacs one of prayerful pity.

should he be afraid? In you he has found a soul unoccupied and swept clean; he has found a house with an open door.[72]

(38) Would it not be fitting that, at that moment, you all join together and send forth streams of tears, that all your eyes be wet with weeping, and that groans and lamentations rise up from the whole assembly? After they shared in the mysteries, after they received the benefits of baptism, after they were enrolled in the army of Christ,[73] that wolf was able to snatch them like lambs from the fold and to keep them in his power. Can you look at this disaster and hold back your tears? How can such action as yours deserve a defense? Are you unwilling to share in your brother's pain? At least wake up and fear for yourself.

(39) Tell me this. If you were to see your neighbor's house engulfed in flames, even if he were your bitterest enemy, would you not run to quench the fire because you were afraid that the flames might make their way along the street and set fire to your own front doorway? Think of this in the case of the demoniacs, too. The power and activity of the demons is a kind of fire and conflagration which is hard to control. Be careful, then, for fear that the demon may make his way along the street and seize hold of your soul. Whenever you see that he is nearby, flee with all speed to the Master.[74]

---

72 A demon ousted from a soul it has possessed seeks a new restingplace as we read in Lk 11.24–26, a text which must have been on Chrysostom's mind. The unfeeling Christian may manifest an external cleanliness, but this is not enough to keep him from being at risk of possession by a demon. It may house a pride far worse than the condition of the demoniacs. Cf. C. Stuhlmueller, JBC 44:106.

73 The mysteries here mentioned are the mysteries of initiation. Cf. ACW 31.49, 134, 148, 150. Even after a Christian has received the benefits of baptism (ibid. 227–28, 246) and been enrolled in the army of Christ (ibid. 43, 182, 205, 334 n. 53) he is still vulnerable to possession by a demon.

74 If love for our neighbor will not move us to help quench the demon's flames which are destroying his house, self-interest should lead us to lend a hand before the fire spreads to our own home. If we flee to Christ with the help of our prayers, the demon will see the futility of attacking us. Such self-interest is not the most lofty motive but it is efficacious.

(40) Then, after the demon sees that your soul is fervent and wide awake, he will judge that your mind will never be vulnerable to his assaults. But if he sees you yawning and careless, he will quickly enter into you as he would go into a deserted inn. If he sees that you are awake, attentive, and grasping onto the heavens themselves, he will never be so bold as to look you in the face. So, even if you hold your brothers in scorn, at least take thought for yourself and shut the door to your soul in the face of the evil demon.

(41) Nothing is so likely to block his assaults against us as is constant prayer and supplication.[75] That very exhortation of the deacon when he says, "Let us stand up straight,"[76] was not instituted as part of the liturgy by chance or without reason. It was done so that we might straighten up our thoughts which were dragging along the ground. It was also done so that we might first cast aside the weakness which comes to us from the affairs of daily life and then be able to make our souls stand straight before God.

(42) It is true that when the deacon bids us to stand straight this command is given not to the body but to the soul. Let us listen to Paul who has used this expression in the same way. When he was writing to men who had fallen down and given up in the face of the troubles which were attacking them, he said: "Straighten up your drooping hands and your weak

---

75 Cf. Eph 6.18.

76 Cf. Homilies III.14; IV.7; J. Daniélou, Introduction (SC 28 bis) 54; *Constitutiones apostolicae* 8.12 (PG 1.1091; Brightman p. 13). Malingrey, in commenting on Hom.IV.7, says that "standing up straight on their legs" doubtless corresponds in Chrysostom's thought with a liturgical attitude which betokens attention and respect. The Jewish liturgy recommends for the prayer of the eighteen benedictions that both feet be kept side by side and the legs well stretched out. This attitude, by itself, is sufficiently significant, she says, to be found in the heavenly liturgy which Chrysostom thinks of after the fashion of the earthly liturgy. The deacon's exhortation: "Let us stand up straight" does explain both the attitude attributed to the angels around God's throne and the expression "standing up straight on their legs" of Hom.IV.7.

knees."[77] What should our response be, then? Should we say that he is talking about the hands and knees of the body? By no means! He is not speaking to runners and boxers and wrestlers. By these words he was exhorting people to rouse up the strength of the reasoning powers within them because these had been weakened by temptations.[78]

(43) Think by whose side you are standing, think of those with whom you will call on God. It is with the Cherubim. Think of those with whom you are joining to form this choir, and this will be enough to sober you. Although you wear a body around you, although you are entangled with flesh, reflect on the fact that you have been deemed worthy to join with the spiritual powers above to praise in song the common Master of all.[79] But if anyone has allowed himself to lose his zeal and goodwill, let him not share in those sacred and mystic hymns. Let no one keep his thoughts on the affairs of daily life at that sacred time. Let him rid his mind of all earthly things, let him transfer himself entirely to heaven and let him stand next to the very

---

77 Heb 12.12. This verse is addressed to those who are enduring trials. Perhaps the author of Hebrews had in mind those who had undergone persecution as described in Heb 10.32–34. Chrysostom, joining the text to the deacon's exhortation "Let us stand up straight before the Lord with fear and trembling" (Brightman p. 13) is clearly thinking of the verse in a liturgical context. J. Daniélou, Introduction (SC 28 bis) 54 notes that the explanation given by Chrysostom for the standing position is found elsewhere in connection with the formula *anō tas kardias* (Lift up your hearts), e.g. in Cyril of Jerusalem, *Catechesis mystagogica* 5.4 (PG 33.1111–14) and in Theodore of Mopsuestia, *Les homélies catéchètiques de Théodore de Mopsueste* (ed. R. Tonneau and R. Devreesse in *Studi e testi* 145, Vatican City 1949) 539.

78 Temptations do have a debilitating effect on our intellects and wills which can distort our moral judgments and blunt our desire to show our love for God and neighbor during the mysteries.

79 In this paragraph we may have an allusion to the Cherubic hymn whose introduction into the eastern liturgy is usually placed in the late sixth century. In was sung by the choir at the Great Entrance. Perhaps in the light of the present passage the Cherubic hymn's introduction should be put at an earlier date (M). The eastern liturgies stress a much more active role for the angelic choirs than do the western.

throne of glory and raise his all holy hymn to the God of glory and majesty.[80]

(44) This is why we are bidden at that sacred moment to stand straight up. For to stand straight up is merely to stand in a manner which befits one who is a mere human being to stand before God, that is, "with fear and trembling,"[81] with a soul that is sober and vigilant.[82] These words do apply also to the soul, as Paul again makes clear when he says: "Stand fast thus in the Lord, beloved."[83] For if the bowman is going to shoot his arrows so that they hit the mark, he first concerns himself with his own stance. After he has positioned himself exactly facing his target, he then gets busy and shoots his arrows. If you are going to shoot your arrows at the devil's wicked head, concern yourself first with the posture of your thoughts. Then take a straight, upright, and unencumbered stance so that the arrows you shoot at him will find their mark.[84]

(45) This is what I have to say about prayer. But in addition to your negligence in the matter of the prayers, the devil has devised another thing which makes me most discouraged. We must build a barricade against this assault of his. What, then, is this wickedness which the evil demon works upon us? When he

---

80 Again in this paragraph we most probably have another reference to the liturgy where, again, the choir of men is likened to the choir of angels. The allusion is clearly to the *Trisagion* of the eucharistic prayer. This hymn, borrowed from Is 6.3, again affirms that the Church on earth is invited to share in the heavenly canticle of the Seraphim (M). For the Cherubic hymn see the Glossary of Technical Terms in Brightman, 573; for the *Trisagion* cf. ibid. 590. Judging by the content, the two hymns may have been identical by the time of the liturgy attributed to Chrysostom (cf. ibid. 377). See also J. Daniélou, Introduction (SC 28 bis) 55, who cites Chrysostom's *Vidi Dom.* I.1 (PG 56.97–98) and *De Poenit.* Hom.9 (PG 49.345), which connect the *Trisagion* with the eucharistic prayer.
81 Cf. Phil 2.12. NAB reads: "with anxious concern," but the Greek text has: "with fear and trembling."
82 Cf. above note 63.
83 Phil 4.1.
84 Again we have a comparison which recaptures life and which, by its precision of detail, makes an action visible to us as it unrolls before our eyes. Cf. Homilies II.51 and 52; III.1 and 2; 41 and 42; IV.2, 4; V.48 (M).

saw how you were, united as if into one body, and how strictly your attention was fastened on my words, he did not send any of his servants who, by their counsel and advice, would try to turn you away from listening to me. He knew that no one of you would put up with anyone advising you to do that.

(46) But he did send some robbers and pickpockets to mingle among you and had them ready on more than one occasion to snatch from the many people gathered here the money which they had tied up in their purses. And this has happened in this church many times to many people. But I do not wish this to continue to happen. Nor do I wish your eagerness to hear me to be quenched because, as has happened to many of you, you have lost your money. Therefore, I counsel and advise all of you that nobody come into the church carrying money.[85] In that way, your eagerness to hear the homily will not become for those thieves an opportunity for evildoing. Then the pleasure which comes to you from spending your time here will not be effaced by the theft of your money.

(47) The devil contrived this not to make you poorer but to let the loss of your money make you feel deeply disgusted and lead you away from your eagerness to hear the homily. He once stripped Job of all his possessions not to make him poorer but to strip him of his piety.[86] The purpose of the devil's zeal was not to take away Job's possessions—he knows that money is nothing—but so that, through the loss of his material pos-

---

85 The devil, through his agents, will go to any length to undermine piety and attention during the homily and the liturgy. The preventive measure which Chrysostom suggests might meet with something less than universal approval from the financial committees of today's parish councils.

86 The devil, or Satan, in the book of Job, is the Adversary or prosecutor who spies on men's wrongdoings and reports them to the Master (cf. Jb 1.6–12; Zec 3.1); in Jb he is not yet the "devil" of later Judaist and Christian theology. To understand him as such would distort our understanding of the book of Job. Cf. R. A. F. MacKenzie, JBC 31:12.

sessions, he might cast Job into a sin of the soul.[87] And if the devil cannot do that, he will never think that he has accomplished anything.

(48) Now that you know the devil's purpose, beloved, whenever he snatches away your money either through thieves or by some other means, give glory to your Master. In this way, you will have gained greater profit and you will deal your enemy a double blow—you did not take your loss in bad grace, and you gave thanks to God. But if the devil sees that the loss of your money leaves you downcast, if he prevails upon you to take it in bad grace and to blame it on the Lord, he will never stop doing this. However, if he sees that you do not blaspheme the God who made you and that you even give him thanks for each of the terrible things which happen to you, the devil will stop leading you into temptations. Why? He knows that the test of troubles becomes for you a reason for giving thanks. He is only making your crowns brighter and increasing the prizes you will gain.

(49) This is what happened with Job. After the devil took away Job's possessions and wounded his body, he saw Job giving thanks. So he no longer dared to attack Job but he went away. Why? He had suffered a disgraceful and irreparable defeat; he had made God's athlete shine with greater splendor. Since, then, we, too, know this, let us fear one thing only—sin. Let us endure the other things with courage: loss of money,

---

87 The "sin of the soul" would be blasphemy—"to curse God and die (Jb 2.9)," as Job's wife suggested to him. See FOTC 68, page 31. This purpose of the devil would be much more in keeping with the later Christian concept of Satan. Job's wife's advice, according to MacKenzie (JBC 31:15), shows that she reacts as the Adversary had expected Job would. She feels that God has now shown himself to be Job's enemy and that Job should express that fact before he dies. Indeed, blaspheming God will bring the punishment of death but will free him from his disaster. Cf. FOTC 68, page 226, where Chrysostom says that Job's wife's words had quite the opposite effect—they gave him great strength so that he even reproached her. He chose to feel pain, to endure hardship, and to suffer ten thousand terrible things rather than curse God and so find release from his terrible troubles.

bodily sickness, business reverses, abuse, slander, and whatever other trouble may come upon us. It is not the nature of these things to harm us; in fact they can give us the greatest help. As long as we put up with them and are grateful, they will bring us even richer rewards. You surely see that, after Job received all the victory crowns for his patience and courage, he had regained twofold all the things he had lost.[88]

(50) You will regain all your losses, not twofold or threefold but a hundred fold, if you endure them with courage.[89] And you will be heirs to eternal life. May it come to pass that you all gain this by the grace and loving-kindness of our Lord Jesus Christ, to whom be glory now and forever, world without end. Amen.

---

88 Cf. Jb 42.10.
89 Courage in hearing and holding to the gospel message is the measure of our reward, as is seen in the parable of the seed in Mt 13.8–23 and Lk 8.4–15.

HOMILY V

HEN A SPEAKER IS GOING TO TAKE UP a rather lengthy topic, it will require several discourses. It cannot be completed in one or two or three days but needs several more. In such a case, I think a teacher must not impose his entire instruction on the minds of his hearers suddenly and all at once. I think he should divide his whole topic into several parts and, by means of this division, make the burden of his argument light and easy to grasp. For surely, speech, hearing, and each of our senses has measures and rules and established bounds. If a man tries to go beyond these limits, he finds that he has lost his power to perceive.[1] Tell me this. What is sweeter than light? What is more pleasant than sunshine? Still when we spend too long a time with these sweet and pleasant things, they become burdensome and oppressive.

(2) This is why God established the law that night follow day, so that night could take our tired eyes, close our lids, and lull our pupils to sleep. In this way the night rests our weary power of vision and makes it ready to see more serviceably on the following day. Wakefulness and sleep are opposites to each other, it is true. But when we use them with reasonable moderation, they are also very pleasant for each other. This is why,

---

1 Chrysostom's advice is sound and explains why he gives only a partial treatment of the same general topic over the course of several homilies. Strangely, the advice comes in what proves to be the longest of the homilies in the series on the incomprehensibility of God. Chrysostom gives the same caution in *De Laz.* III.1 (PG 48.991) using the example of a mother who feeds her child his first solid food a little at a time so the child will not reject it, and in *Vidi Dom.* III.1 (PG 56.112), where he points out that oil should be added to a lamp drop by drop so as not to quench the flame.

even though we call the light sweet, in like manner we also call sleep sweet, even if sleep takes us away from the light.[2]

(3) So it is that the lack of proper proportion is always oppressive and burdensome; reasonable moderation is always sweet and useful and gentle. Therefore, although a fourth and even a fifth day have already passed since I started to speak to you on God's incomprehensibility, I am not even today ready to complete this discussion.[3] But after I shall have spoken to your loving assembly at a length which has due regard for proper proportion, I have decided that I will then let your minds again have some rest.[4]

(4) At what point did I stop in my recent discourse? I must take it up from there because, in spiritual teaching, there is a kind of succession and progression. In the last homily we were telling you that the Son of Thunder said: "No one has ever seen God. The only begotten Son, who is in the bosom of the Father, himself declared him."[5] Today we must learn where

---

2 Night and sleep, which keep men from going beyond the measure of their strength, are also praised by Chrysostom in his treatise on divine providence. See A.–M. Malingrey, *Sur la providence de Dieu* VII. 26–29, SC 79 (Paris 1961) 123–25. (M).

3 "A fourth and even a fifth day" presents a problem. Montfaucon, in a footnote (PG 48.736), would rightly exclude Hom.I from this time frame but then states that the four or five days must start from Hom.II. This cannot be the case. Discourses I and II of the series *Against Judaizing Christians* certainly interrupted the series *On the Incomprehensible Nature of God*. Cf. FOTC 68.1 note 1. But the opening paragraph of the third discourse *Against Judaizing Christians* (FOTC 68 p.37) says: "Once again a pressing need has interrupted the sequence of my recent discourses." The plural "discourses" shows that there must have been at least two. What follows (ibid.) shows that the interrupted series was again the series *On the Incomprehensible Nature of God* since he says: "I must put aside my struggles with the heretics for today . . ." Since he opens Hom. IV with a lengthy recapitulation of Hom.III, it would seem more likely that the second interruption came after Hom.III of the present series. Then the interval of four or five days would embrace Homilies IV and V (and possibly III). See Hom.IV.1 note 1 and Introduction 54 and note 69.

4 This decision might indicate Chrysostom's intention to end his discussion of God's incomprehensibility (Homilies I-V), or, after a brief interval, to move on to a second stage of his battle against the Anomoeans, in which he will treat of the "glory of the only begotten" or the equality and con-substantiality of the Father and the Son in Homilies VII-X. See Hom.VII.7.

5 Cf. Jn 1.18. Cf. Hom.IV. 17–30. The Son of Thunder is the evangelist John, as we learn from Mk 3.17.

the only begotten Son of God declared this. John is the one who tells us: "He replied to the Jews and said: 'Not that anyone has seen the Father except him who is from God, he has seen the Father.' "[6] Again, he here means "know" when he says "see."[7]

(5) However, John did not simply say: "Nobody knows the Father" and then stop.[8] Why? He did not wish anyone to think that this statement applied only to human beings. He wished also to show that neither the Angels nor the Archangels nor the powers above know the Father, as he made clear by what follows. For after he said: "Not that anyone has ever seen the Father," he went on to add: "Except him who is from God, he has seen the Father."[9] If he had simply said, "Nobody," many of those who heard him might perhaps have considered that this was said only about our human nature. But, as it is, because he said, "Nobody," and then added, "Except the Son," by this further mention of the only begotten, he excluded all created beings.

(6) Why then, someone objects, does he also exclude the Holy Spirit?[10] By no means does he exclude the Holy Spirit, for the Spirit is not a part of creation. The word, "Nobody" always is used to express the exclusion of creatures alone. If the question is about the Father, it does not exclude the Son. If it is about the Son, it does not reject the Spirit. To make this very point henceforth clear, namely, that the word "Nobody" was not used to reject the Spirit but to express the exclusion of creatures in this very matter of knowledge, which John says belongs to the Son alone, let us listen to what Paul says when he is speaking to the Corinthians.

(7) What, then, does Paul say? "Who knows a man's innermost self but the man's own spirit within him? Similarly, no

---

6 Cf. Jn 6.46. The NT text omits "He replied to the Jews and said," although the printed editions and MSS include it as part of Chrysostom's citation.

7 Cf. Homilies IV.23,29; V.25, where Chrysostom again identifies "know" and "see."

8 Cf. Hom.IV.24–30.

9 Cf. Jn 6.46.

10 Chrysostom was aware of the objection as we saw in Hom IV.31 but there he postponed his answer. He gives it now in the present and following paragraph.

one knows what lies in the depths of God but the Spirit of God."[11] Here the words "no one" do not reject the Son. And when they are applied to Christ, they do not exclude the Holy Spirit. This makes it clear that what I said is true. If John intended to exclude the Spirit when he said: "No one has seen the Father except the one who is with God,"[12] it would be strange for Paul to say that, just as a man knows the things which are his, so the Holy Spirit knows perfectly the things of God.

(8) The word "one" is used in the same way as "no one," and has the same force and power.[13] Consider this. Paul says: "One God, the Father from whom are all things, and one Lord, Jesus Christ, through whom are all things."[14] If the Father is said to be one God, it excludes the Son from being God; if the Son is said to be one Lord, it excludes the Father from being Lord. But surely the Father is not excluded from being Lord because of Paul's words: "One Lord, Jesus Christ." Therefore, neither is the Son excluded from being God because of the words: "one God, the Father."[15]

(9) If the Anomoeans should say in reply that the Father is called one God because the Son is God, but not on the same level as the Father, what follows from the premises they set down? They then must say—for we would not say it—that the Son is called one Lord because the Father is Lord, but not on the same level as the Son. But if to say this is impious, neither

---

11 Cf. 1 Cor 2.11.

12 Cf. Jn 6.46. Chrysostom would allow for no contradiction in the Scriptures, especially on such an important point of dogma.

13 In paragraph 6, "nobody" is used to express the exclusion of creatures alone, as is "no one" in 1 Cor 2.11 in paragraph 7. Never do these words exclude the divine Persons of the Trinity, who are not creatures. The same is true of "one", which excludes creatures but never the divine Persons when it is a question of one God and one Lord.

14 Cf. 1 Cor 8.6.

15 Chrysostom's explanation is directly opposed to the teaching of Eunomius, the Anomoean heresiarch. Eunomius, starting with the terms *agennētos* (unbegotten) and *gennēma* (begotten, offspring), affirms a radical difference in nature between the Father and the Son. He says in his *Apologia* 7 (PG 30.841): "For neither of them can be equal to the other, since, in truth, the maker must exist before what comes into being, and what comes into being must be second to the maker (M)."

would the first statement have any basis in truth. Just as the expression "one Lord" does not exclude the Father from being perfect Lord nor does this title bestow Lordship on the Son alone, so the expression "one God" does not exclude the Son from being true and genuine God, nor does this title show that Godhead belongs only to the Father.

(10) That the Son is God and, while still remaining the Son, is God on the same level as the Father becomes clear from the very addition of the word "Father." If this name of God belonged only to the Father and if it could not designate for us another personal reality[16] but only that first and unbegotten personal reality,[17] inasmuch as the name "God" can belong to and denote only that personal reality, the addition of the name "Father" would serve no purpose.

(11) If the additional designation of "Father" were not meaningful, it would be enough to speak of "one God", and we would know who was meant. But since the name of "God" is common to the Father and the Son, Paul would not be making it clear of whom he was speaking if he were only to say "one God." So the addition of "Father" was needed to show that he was speaking of the first and unbegotten personal reality. The name of God would not suffice to show this, since this name is common to him and to the Son.

(12) Some names are common to several; others are proper to one. There are common names to show that the essence is exactly the same; there are proper names to characterize what

---

16 The word translated as "personal reality" is *hypostasis*. This word, prior to Arianism, could have been used as a synonym for *ousia* (essence) but, starting with the Trinitarian quarrels, it took on an extremely precise technical meaning which opposed it to essence. Malingrey points out that we know that this technical sense was the meaning given to the term by the orthodox at Antioch in Chrysostom's day thanks to a text of Epiphanius in his *Panarion* (PG 42.468). There Epiphanius is proving that Meletius (cf. Introduction 41–42) and his followers do not deserve to be considered as heretics because they agree that the Father, Son, and Holy Spirit are of the same substance and are three personal realities, one essence and one Godhead.

17 Chrysostom no doubt uses the term *agennētos* (unbegotten) on purpose because it is the basis for the whole theology of Eunomius. But by linking it with "first," he implies that there exist second and third personal realities, equal in dignity to the first (M).

is proper to the personal realities.[18] The names "Father" and "Son" characterize what is proper to the personal realities; the names "God" and "Lord" show what is common. Therefore, after Paul set down the common name of "one God," he had to use the proper name so that you might know of whom he was speaking. He did this to prevent us from falling into the madness of Sabellius.[19]

(13) It is clear from Paul's text that the name "God" is not greater than the name "Lord," nor is the name "Lord" inferior to the name "God."[20] Throughout the whole Old Testament, the Father is constantly called Lord. We read, "The Lord, your God," "the Lord is one,"[21] and again, "You shall adore the Lord, your God, and him only shall you worship,"[22] and still again, "Great is our Lord, and great is his power: and of his wisdom there is no number,"[23] and still again, "Let them know that *Lord* is your name; you alone are the most high over all the earth."[24]

(14) Therefore, if this name of Lord were inferior to the name of God and unworthy of that divine essence, there would be no need for saying: "Let them know that *Lord* is your name." Again, if the name of God were greater and more holy than the name of the Lord, there would be no need that the Son, who, according to the Anomoeans, is inferior to the Father, be given a title from a name which belongs to the Father and is proper to

---

18 As in paragraphs 5–8 above, Chrysostom again applies a grammatical technique to his exegesis. Basil does the same in his *Contra Eunomium* I.8 (PG 29.528–29).
19 For Sabellius and Sabellianism see Introduction 16. Cf. also FOTC 33.78,389; 41.292,301; SC 28 bis 281 note 5.
20 As Malingrey points out, when, in the Jewish tradition, one did not wish out of respect to use Yahweh, the proper name for God, the word Adonai (Lord) was substituted for it. LXX does the same when it translates both Yahweh and Adonai by the word *Kyrios* (Lord). This is why Chrysostom makes no distinction between the passages which show either of these names when he cites OT texts.
21 Cf. Ex 20.2 and Dt 6.4. Actually the LXX text reads: "The Lord is our God, the Lord is one."
22 Cf. Dt 6.13. Again the LXX differs slightly. The whole verse reads: "You shall fear the Lord your God, and him only shall you adore; you shall cleave to him, and by his name you shall swear."
23 Ps 146 (147).5.
24 Ps 82 (83).19.

the Father alone. But this is not true, not at all true. Neither is the Son inferior to the Father, nor is the name of Lord less worthy than the name of God. Hence the Scripture has used these titles with no difference of meaning for both the Father and the Son.

(15) You have heard, therefore, that the Father is called Lord. Come now, and let me show you that the Son is called God.[25] "Behold, the virgin shall be with child, and shall give birth to a son, and they shall call his name Immanuel; which means, 'God is with us.' "[26] Did you see how both the name "Lord" is given to the Father, and the name "God" is given to the Son? In the Psalm, the sacred writer said: "Let them know that *Lord* is your name."[27] Here Isaiah says: "They shall call his name Immanuel."[28] And again, he says: "A child is born to us, and a son is given to us: and his name shall be called Angel of Great Counsel, God the Strong, the Mighty One."[29] Look, please, at the understanding and the spiritual wisdom of the prophets.[30] To prevent anyone from thinking that they were

---

25 Basil develops this point at greater length in his *Contra Eunomium* 4 (PG 29.672–73).

26 Cf. Is 7.14. However, Chrysostom quotes the text as found in Mt 1.23. See note on Is 7.14 in NAB.

27 Cf. Ps 82 (83).19.

28 Cf. Is 7.14.

29 Cf. Is 9.6 (LXX). Chrysostom quotes this same text in his *Demonstratio contra Judaeos et gentiles quod Christus sit Deus* 2 (PG 48.815–16) but at greater length; both the *Demonstratio* and the present homily omit "whose government is on his shoulder" after "a son is given to us." What follows "Messenger of Great Counsel" is not found in all MSS of the LXX; Rahlfs omits it from his LXX text but includes it in his critical apparatus. The words omitted from Rahlfs' text ("God the strong, the mighty one"), however, are essential to Chrysostom's argument. Various English translations generally support Chrysostom's citation (e.g., NAB: "God-Hero;" JB: "Mighty-God;" King James: "the mighty God;" Challoner: "God the Mighty"). Although the titles given in the text may have been intended to describe an ideal king of Israel, Christian tradition has, with one voice, seen the fulfillment of the promise in Christ. Cf. F. Moriarty, JBC 16:21. JB, in a note ad loc points out that the Christmas liturgy applies these titles to Christ, presenting him as the true Immanuel.

30 As in Hom.I.23 and in Hom.III.14, it is clear that Chrysostom uses the term "prophets" to include all who speak through the action of the Spirit whether in the OT or NT. So it is that he takes his arguments from Isaiah, Baruch, Paul, and John.

referring to the Father when they spoke simply of God, they first made mention of the divine plan of salvation.[31] For surely, the Father was not born of a virgin nor did he become a little child.[32]

(16) Another prophet spoke of the Son in somewhat the same way: "This is our God, nor will another be reckoned as comparing to him."[33] And of whom does he say this? He does not say it of the Father, does he? Of course not! Listen to how he mentioned the divine plan of salvation, as well. After he said: "This is our God, nor will another be reckoned as comparing to him," he went on to add: "He found out all the way of knowledge and gave it to Jacob his servant and to Israel his

---

31 The plan of salvation is God's plan for the world of which the most striking manifestation is the Incarnation (M). J. Daniélou, in his Introduction (SC 28 bis) 49–50, quotes a passage from Gregory of Nyssa which fleshes out what Chrysostom hints at when he speaks of the plan of salvation. In his *In Canticum 8* (ed. W. Jaeger, vol. VI, pp. 254–57; PG 44.948B–949B) Gregory says (in part): It is not only human nature which has been instructed in the divine mysteries by this grace (of the coming of Christ), but the Principalities and the Powers in heaven also perceived the varied wisdom of God when it was made manifest by the Incarnation of Christ . . . . Up to then, in fact, the heavenly powers perceived only the simple wisdom of God. Now, through the Church, they have perceived clearly God's varied wisdom because they see how the Word becomes flesh, how life is intermingled with death . . . . This is why . . . the friends of the Spouse (the angels) were moved when they perceived in this mystery another mark of the divine wisdom . . . . I would dare to say that after they saw through the Spouse (the Church) the Spouse's own beauty, they marvelled at what is invisible and incomprehensible to all beings. For God made the Church his body. If, then, the Church is the body of Christ and Christ is the head of the body, giving form to the body in his own likeness, perhaps, while contemplating the one alongside the other, they saw the invisible in it (the Church). And just as those who cannot look at the disk of the sun see it through its reflection in the water, so the angels immerse their eyes in a pure mirror—the figure of the Church—and contemplate the Sun of justice as if through its manifestation. Cf. Hom.IV.13–15.

32 Cf. Is 7.14 and Mt 1.23.

33 Bar 3.36. Baruch was Jeremiah's secretary.

beloved. Afterwards he was seen upon earth and he conversed with men."[34]

(17) And Paul said: ". . . from whom is the Christ according to the flesh, who is over all things, God blessed forever, Amen."[35] And again: "No fornicator or covetous one has an inheritance in the kingdom of Christ and God."[36] And still again: ". . . through the appearance of our great God and Savior Jesus Christ."[37] And John calls him by the same name of God when he says: "In the beginning was the Word, and the Word was with God; and the Word was God."[38]

(18) Yes, the Anomoeans say, but show us this. Where does the Scripture put the Son together with the Father and call the Father Lord? I shall not only show you this. I will also prove that the Scripture calls the Father "Lord" and the Son "Lord" and that it calls the Father "God" and the Son "God." And it gives the same titles to each in the same texts. Where can we

---

34 Cf. ibid. 37–38. Chrysostom quotes Bar 3.36–38 (attributing the verses to Jeremiah) to prove that Christ was both God and man in his *Demonstratio* 2 (PG 48.815). Both here and in the *Demonstratio* a difficulty arises from the way in which Chrysostom uses the text, understanding "he" (i.e., God) as the subject of the verbs "was seen" and "conversed." Both NAB and JB give "she" (i.e., "understanding") as subject of these verbs. Even though both Greek and Latin Fathers have applied this to the Incarnation, the context of Bar 3 requires that Wisdom (or understanding) be the subject of the two verbs. The personification of Wisdom and the idea of her dwelling among men occur also in Sir (Ecclus) 24 (see NAB note ad loc.). But Bar 3.38 may refer in a fuller sense, as does Chrysostom, to the Messiah, through whom revelation has been brought to perfection. See P. Saydon, *A Catholic Commentary on Holy Scripture* (London 1953) 598.

35 Rom 9.5 and NAB note ad loc.

36 Cf. Eph 5.5

37 Cf. 2 Tm 1.10. Aland's text does not have "of our great God" nor are these words found in the English translations. This hurts Chrysostom's argument, although a note ad loc. in JB says the appearing of Christ refers to the Incarnation and redemption. This implies that Christ is not only Savior but also God. It seems more likely that Chrysostom is quoting not 2 Tm 1.10 but part of Ti 2.13 which reads: ("as we await our blessed hope) the appearing (of the glory) of our great God and Savior Jesus Christ." Or we may have a conflation of the two similar texts. Chrysostom quotes the full text of Ti 2.13 in Hom VIII.22.

38 Jn 1.1.

find this? Once, when Christ was speaking to the Jews, he said: " 'What do you think of the Christ? Whose son is he?' And they said to him: 'David's.' He said to them: 'How then does David in the Spirit call him *Lord*, saying, "The Lord said to my Lord: Sit at my right hand?" ' "[39] Do you see how both Father and Son are called Lord?

(19) Do you wish to find out where the Scripture puts together the Father and the Son and calls the Father "God" as well as calling the Son "God?" Listen to the prophet, David, and the apostle, Paul, as they make this very point very clear to us. "Your throne, O God, stands forever and ever: the scepter of your kingdom is a scepter of righteousness. You have loved justice and hated wickedness: therefore God, your God, has anointed you with the oil of gladness beyond your fellows."[40] And again, Paul added his witness to this when he said: "Of his angels he says, 'He makes his angels winds.' Of his Son, 'Your throne, O God, stands forever and ever.' "[41]

(20) For what reason, the Anomoeans will say, here in this other passage did Paul call the Father "God" and the Son "Lord?"[42] In the text to which they refer, Paul did not do this by chance or without purpose, but because he was talking to Greeks who were infected with polytheism. He did it so that they might not say: "While you are accusing us of speaking of many gods and many lords, you are yourself caught in these charges because you spoke of gods and not of God." So Paul accommodated himself to their weakness and called the Son by another name, but by a name which has the same force and meaning as "God."[43]

(21) To show that this is true, let us read this other passage to which the Anomoeans refer. Then you will understand

---

39 Cf. Mt 22.42–44 and Ps 109 (110).1. Matthew's text shows certainty of the Davidic authorship of the Psalm whose purpose is to show the transcendent superiority of "my Lord (the Messiah)" to the author, David. The command to sit suggests the enthronement in a place of honor, at the right hand of God. See NAB notes on Ps 110 and FOTC 68, p. 194 and nn. 65 and 66.

40 Cf. Ps 44 (45).7–8 and NAB note on 45.7.

41 Cf. Heb 1.7–8. See also Ps 103 (104).4 (LXX) and NAB ad loc., as well as M. Bourke, JBC 61:70.

42 Cf. 1 Cor 8.6 and paragraph 8 above in this homily.

43 Cf. paragraphs 8 and 9 above in this homily.

clearly that what I said is not just guesswork on my part. "Now about things offered to idols we know that we all have knowledge . . . 'Knowledge' inflates but love upbuilds . . . Now as for food sacrificed to idols we know that there is no such thing as an idol in the world, and that there is no other God but the one God."[44] Do you not see that Paul is addressing these words to men who believe that there are many gods?

(22) "Even if there are many so-called gods and many so-called lords either in heaven or on earth,"—again Paul is doing battle with those polytheists—"there are, to be sure, many such 'gods' and 'lords,'—that is, 'so-called'—"but for us there is one God the Father, from whom all things come; and one Lord Jesus Christ, through whom everything was made."[45] Paul added the word "one" so that those men might not think that he was reintroducing polytheism. He called the Father "one God" without excluding the Son from being God just as he called the Son "one Lord" without excluding the Father from being Lord.[46] He did this because he was correcting their weakness and because he did not wish to give them an occasion for falling into error.

(23) This is why the prophets revealed the Son of God to the Jews in a somewhat dim and scanty fashion rather than with clear and obvious statements. After the Jews had just been set free from the error of polytheism, they would have fallen back into the same disease if they were again to have heard of one person who is God and another person who is God. This is why, throughout the Old Testament, the prophets are constantly saying: "There is one God, and there is no God except for him."[47] The prophets were not denying the Son—God forbid!—but they wished to cure the Jews of their weakness and, meanwhile, to persuade them to give up their belief in the many gods which did not exist.

(24) Therefore, when you hear the words "one" and "no one" and similar expressions, do not diminish the glory of the

---

44 Cf. 1 Cor 8.1,4.
45 Cf. ibid. 5–6.
46 Cf. paragraphs 8 and 9 above in this homily.
47 Cf. Dt. 4.35; Is 45.5,21.

Trinity but, by these terms, learn the distance which separates the Trinity from created beings.[48] As Scripture also says in another place: "For who has known the mind of the Lord?"[49] That this is the case here and that the sacred writer does not exclude either the Son or the Spirit from this knowledge was proved by what I said before. When? When I brought in as my witness the text which reads: "For who knows a man's innermost self but the man's own spirit within him? Similarly, no one knows what lies in the depths of God but the Spirit of God."[50]

(25) And again, it is the Son who says: "No one knows the Son except the Father and no one knows the Father except the Son."[51] And indeed in another text he also says this same thing: "Not that anyone has seen the Father except the one who is from God; he has seen the Father."[52] At the same time he stated the fact that he knows the Father perfectly and he set forth the reason why he knows him. And what is the reason? It is because the Son is "the one who is from God."[53] And, again, the proof that the Son knows the Father perfectly rests on the fact that he is "the one who is from God." For it is on this account that the Son has clear knowledge of the Father, namely, that he is from God; and the fact that he is from God is a sign and indication that he knows him clearly.[54] For an inferior essence would not be able to have clear knowledge of a superior essence, even if the difference between them were slight.[55]

---

48 Cf. paragraphs 6–9 above in this homily.

49 Cf. Is 40.13; Rom 11.34.

50 Cf. 1 Cor. 2.11 and cf. paragraph 7 above in this homily.

51 Cf. Lk 10.22.

52 Cf. In 6.46.

53 Socrates, *Historia ecclesiastica* 2.10 (PG 67.201), informs us that those who used this formula attributed it to Lucian of Antioch. On the question of the origin of the Son, the Anomoeans followed the Arians, some of whom claimed that the Son comes from nothing (is created) and others held that the Son is of a substance other than that of the Father (M).

54 This refutes two points of Eunomian doctrine: 1. Man knows of God all that God knows of himself; and 2. The knowledge which the Son has of the Father is no different from the knowledge other creatures have of the Father (M).

55 Gregory of Nyssa, in his *In Ecclesiasten hom. 8* (ed. W. Jaeger, vol. V. p. 414; PG 44.732A) says the same thing.

(26) Listen to what the prophet said about the angels and about human nature. This will show that the difference between the two is slight. After the prophet had said: "What is man that you are mindful of him, or the son of man that you let your mind dwell on him," he went on to say: "You made him a little less than the angels."[56] However, even if the difference is small, since some difference does exist, we do not know perfectly the essence of the angels. Even though we seek to know their essence ten thousand times, we cannot discover it.[57]

(27) But why do I speak of the essence of the angels when we do not even know well the essence of our own souls? Rather, we do not have any knowledge whatsoever of that essence.[58] If the Anomoeans obstinately contend that they do know it, ask them of what the essence of the soul consists. Is it air, a breath, a wind, or fire? They will say it is none of these. Why? Because all these are bodies, but the essence of the soul is not bodily. Although they do not know the angels or their own souls, nonetheless they stubbornly maintain that they have exact knowledge of the master and creator of all things. What folly could be worse than this?

(28) And why should I speak of what kind of essence the soul has? It is not even possible to say how it exists in our body. What answer could anyone give to this question? That it is extended throughout the bulk of the body? But that is absurd. To exist that way is proper only to bodies. That this is not the way that the soul exists in the body is clear from this example. If a man's hands and feet are amputated, the soul remains whole and entire and is in no way mutilated by the maiming of the body.

---

56 Cf. Ps 8.5 and 6.

57 Cyril of Jerusalem, *Cathechesis* 6.6 (FOTC 61, p. 151; PG 33.545B) offers a similar argument for the angels' knowledge of God according to the capacities of the various choirs.

58 As he did with the nature of the sky in Hom.II.42–50, Chrysostom now shows that we do not have knowledge of our own souls, their essence, nor how they exist in our bodies. This lack of precise knowledge is aimed at Eunomius and the Anomoeans who are refuted on this point also by Basil in *Adversus Eunomium* III.6(PG 29.668A) and by Gregory of Nyssa in his *In Ecclesiasten hom. 8* (ed. W. Jaeger, vol. 5, p. 416; PG 44.732D). It was a commonplace of Greek philosophy of the Christian era to insist on the limits of human knowledge.

(29) Then it does not exist in the whole body but has it been gathered together in some part of the body? If that is true, the rest of the parts must be dead, because whatever lacks a soul is altogether dead. But we cannot say that. What we must say is that we know that the soul is in our bodies but that we do not know how it is there. God has shut us off from this knowledge of the soul for a reason. What is that reason? So that, out of his great superiority, he might curb our tongues, hold us in check, and persuade us to remain on earth and not to meddle out of curiosity with matters which are beyond us.[59]

(30) So as not to build up our conclusions on such questions from reason alone, come, let us again turn our argument to the Scriptures. John says: "Not that anyone has seen the Father except the one who is from God; he has seen the Father."[60] What does this mean, the Anomoeans will object. This text did not testify that the Son has perfect knowledge. What John did make clear is that creatures do not know the Father when he said: "Not that anyone has seen the Father." And again he did make it clear that the Son knows the Father when he added: "Except the one who is from God; he has seen the Father."[61] However, he has not yet shown that the Son knows the Father perfectly and in the same way as the Father knows himself.

(31) The Anomoeans will say that it is a possibility that neither a creature nor the Son knows the Father clearly, but that the Son knows him more clearly than a creature. However, they will say, it is possible that the Son does not have a perfect comprehension of the Father. For John says that the Son sees and knows what the Father is. He has not yet proved that the Son knows him perfectly and in the same way as the Father knows himself. Do you wish me to refute this from the Scriptures and from the very words of Christ? Then let us listen to what he says to the Jews: "Just as the Father knows me and I

---

59 Cf. Hom I.36.
60 Cf. Jn 6.46.
61 Cf. ibid.

know the Father."⁶² What more perfect knowledge do you wish than this?

(32) Put this question to the man who would contradict you. Does the Father know the Son perfectly, does he have perfect and total knowledge of him, does nothing which concerns the Son escape him, and is his knowledge complete? Yes, he answers. Then, when you hear that the Son knows the Father as the Father knows the Son, search no further, because their mutual knowledge is perfectly equal. And surely in another place the Son made this point clear when he said: "No one knows the Son except the Father, and no one knows the Father except the Son and anyone to whom the Son wishes to reveal him."⁶³

(33) However, the Son does not reveal as much as he knows but as much as we have the capacity for knowing.⁶⁴ If Paul does this same thing, Christ does it with all the more reason. And Paul said to his own disciples: "I could not talk to you as spiritual men but only as men of flesh, as infants in Christ. I fed you with milk and did not give you solid food because you were not yet ready for it."⁶⁵ The Anomoeans will say that Paul spoke these words only to the Corinthians. Suppose I show that there were other things which Paul knew, things which no man knew before him. Suppose I show that even though he was the only man to know these things, he took this knowledge with him

---

62 Jn 10.15. The text loses some of its argumentative power when it is not taken in isolation but in its proper context, in which the mutual knowledge of the Good Shepherd and his sheep is compared to the mutual knowledge of the Father and the Son, of which it is an extention. Cf. B. Vawter, JBC 63:117. However, Chrysostom's grasp of Johannine Christology and of such texts as Jn 3.16–18; 5.19–23; 7.16; 8.28–29; and esp. 10.38 may justify his use of Jn 10.15 as proof that the Son has perfect knowledge of the Father.

63 Cf. Mt 11.27 and NAB note ad loc.

64 Cf. Hom III.15 and note 24. Also cf. Cyril of Jerusalem, *Catechesis* 6.6 (FOTC 61, p.151), who expresses the idea of condescension and accommodation by saying that the only begotten reveals to each according to his individual capacity.

65 Cf. 1 Cor 3.1–2.

when he departed this life. Where can we discover this? In the Epistle to the Corinthians. For it was there that Paul said: "I heard words which cannot be uttered, words which no man may speak."[66]

(34) Nonetheless, even this very man, who at that time heard words which cannot be uttered, words which no man can speak, has only a partial knowledge, a knowledge which falls far short of the knowledge to come. For the same man who said this also spoke those other words, namely: "We know in part and we prophesy in part,"[67] and, "When I was a child, I spoke as a child, I understood as a child, I thought as a child,"[68] and, "Now I see as in a mirror in an indistinct image, but then face to face."[69]

(35) So it is that all the fraud of the Anomoeans is refuted from these texts. When we do not know the essence itself, not that it is but what it is, it would be the height of folly to give it a name. Besides, even if it were clear and known, it would not be safe for us, of ourselves and by ourselves, to give a name or title to the essence of the master. Paul did not dare to give names to the powers above. He did say: "He seated Christ high above every principality, every power, every virtue, and every name that can be given not only in this age but also in the age to come."[70] He did teach us that there are names for the powers above and that we will know them in the age to come. But he did not have the boldness himself to give them names other than "the powers above." Nor would he have dared, out of idle curiosity, to concern himself about any other names.

(36) Therefore, what excuse or defense could those men deserve who do dare to have such curious concern about the

---

66 Cf. 2 Cor 12.4. Paul finds here that his vocabulary fails him and, in this sense, he cannot speak. "Words that cannot be uttered" was a technical expression in the language of the Greek mystery religions for teachings which were not to be revealed to the uninitiated. Cf. J. O'Rourke, JBC 52:42.

67 Cf. 1 Cor 13.9. Cf. Homilies I.11,13,17,31,33; II.40; III.29.

68 Cf. 1 Cor 13.11. Cf. Hom. I.15.

69 Cf. 1 Cor 13.12. Cf. Homilies I.18; III.29. Here Chrysostom means "know" by "see" as he does, e.g., in Hom.IV.23 and 29.

70 Cf. Eph 1.20–21. Cf. Hom.IV.12.

essence of the Master? Since his very essence is beyond our powers of comprehension, we must flee from these Anomoeans as we would from those who have lost their wits. It is clear that God is unbegotten. But no prophet has said, no apostle has hinted, nor any evangelist suggested that this is the name of his essence. And this is very reasonable. If men were ignorant of the essence itself, how could they entertain the idea of calling it by a name?

(37) But why do I speak of the divine Scriptures when the absurdity of the Anomoeans is so obvious and their iniquity is so excessive that not even the pagans, who had wandered so far from the truth, ever tried to say anything like this? For no pagan ever dared to set down a definition of the divine essence or to encompass it with a name. And why do I speak of the divine essence? In their speculations on the nature of incorporeal beings, the Greeks did not set down a complete definition of this nature but gave an obscure statement and description rather than a definition.[71]

(38) What is the wise objection and argument of these Anomoeans? They say: "Do you not know what you are adoring?" First and foremost, we should not have to reply to this objection because the Scriptures afford such strong proof that it is impossible to know what God's essence is. But since our purpose in speaking is not to arouse their enmity but to correct them, come, let us show that being ignorant of God's essence but contending obstinately that one does know his essence, this is really not to know him.

(39) Tell me this. Suppose that two men are obstinately arguing with each other about whether they can know how large the sky is. Suppose that one of them says that it is impossible for the human eye to encompass it, and the other would contend that it was possible for a man to measure the

---

71 All Christian apologetics of the first centuries tends to show that the pagans had a confused knowledge of God such as Chrysostom shows when he says: "a vague and obscure statement or description rather than a definition (M)."

entire sky by using the span of his hand.[72] Which of these two would we say would know the size of the sky? Would it be the one who argues how many spans wide the sky is? Or would it be the one who admits that he does not know? Surely, the man who admits he does not know the size of the sky when he sees its magnitude will have a better understanding of how large the sky is. When it is a question of God, will we not use the same discretion? Would it not be the ultimate madness if we failed to do so?

(40) All that we are required to know is that God exists; we are not asked to be busybodies and be inquisitive about his essence. Paul shows us this. So listen to what he says. "Anyone who comes to God must believe that he exists."[73] Again, when the prophet was censuring a man for his impiety, he did not accuse him because he did not know what God is but because he did not know that God exists. For he said: "The fool says in his heart: 'There is no God.' "[74] So it was not his failure to know what God's essence is that made the man impious; it was his failure to know that God exists. All that piety requires for religion is for us to know that God exists.

(41) Still the Anomoeans have another well-practiced argument. What is that? Scripture says: "God is spirit."[75] Tell me, then. Does this bring his essence to light? Will anyone accept that argument if he has even drawn a little way near to the

---

72 As a measure of length a span is a half cubit. A cubit is the length of the arm from the elbow to the tip of the middle finger. A span of the hand is the distance from the tip of the thumb to the tip of the little finger when the hand is stretched out (M).

73 Cf. Heb 11.6. The rest of the verse reads: "and that he rewards those who seek him." M. Bourke, JBC 61:63, notes that the two objects of belief should probably be understood as synonymous. What must be believed is not the mere fact of God's existence, but his existence as the one who has entered into gracious relations with man.

74 Cf. Ps 13 (14).1. and Ps 52 (53).2 where both verses read exactly the same and give a counterstatement to Heb 11.1. "The fool" is a practical atheist and, therefore, an impious man. See R. Murphy, JBC 35:31.

75 Jn 4.24. The text is taken from the incident of Jesus' encounter with the Samaritan woman at the well. In 4.10 Jesus had told the woman that, had she asked him, he would have given her living water. B. Vawter (JBC 63:77) points out that, in the biblical sense, spirit does not define God's nature so much as it describes his life-giving activity.

doors of the divine Scriptures? According to that argument, God will also be fire, just as it has been written that God is spirit, so has it been written: "Our God is a consuming fire,"[76] and again: "A fountain of living water."[77] Not only will God be a spirit and a fountain and a fire; he will also be a soul, a wind, a human mind, and other things far more absurd than these.[78] Surely there is no need to detail all these things in my discourse; nor is it necessary to imitate the Anomoeans' madness.

(42) Surely, this word "spirit" has many meanings. For example, it can refer to our own souls. Paul tells us this when he says: "Hand such a man over to Satan that his spirit may be saved."[79] Spirit may also mean a wind, just as when the prophet says: "You will break them with a strong wind."[80] And spirit is also called a gift of the Spirit in this passage: "The Spirit himself gives testimony to our spirit,"[81] Paul says. And again: "I will pray with the spirit but I will also pray with the understanding."[82] Spirit is called anger in the passage where Isaiah says: "Did you not meditate with a harsh spirit to slay them?"[83] The help sent by God is also called spirit: "The spirit which is before our face, our anointed Lord."[84] According to the Anomoeans, then, God will be all these things for us and will be compounded of as many elements as these many things are.

---

76 Heb 12.29. Cf. Dt 4.24; Is 33.14.

77 Cf. Jer 2.13.

78 Convinced as Chrysostom is of the incomprehensibility of the divine essence, he finds it absurd to reduce it to created things whether they be material or immaterial.

79 Cf. 1 Cor 5.5.

80 Cf. Ps 47 (48).8 (LXX).

81 Cf. Rom 8.16. The rest of the verse reads: "that we are children of God." J. Fitzmyer, commenting on this text in JBC 53:85, says that the vital dynamism that constitutes sonship comes from the Spirit as well as the power whereby man recognizes his status. This is the gift of the Spirit to which Chrysostom refers.

82 Cf. 1 Cor 14.15. The verse occurs in a passage discussing the charismatic gifts of tongues and interpretation, both gifts of the Spirit. "To pray with the spirit" seems to refer to the gift of tongues, which must be complemented by the prayer of the understanding or the gift of interpretation.

83 Is 27.8 (LXX).

84 Cf. Lam 4.20 (LXX). Cf. NAB note ad loc. and G. Wood, JBC 36:33, who remarks that Yahweh was the source of all life and blessing.

(43) But let us not act foolishly by bringing forward matters which need no refutation. Come, let us put an end here to our discussion with the Anomoeans and let us turn our whole attention to the question of prayer.[85] The more impious they are, all the more let us intercede for them and beg God that they may some day give up their madness. For this will be acceptable in the presence of God, our Savior, ". . . who wishes all men to be saved and to come to a knowledge of the truth."[86]

(44) Therefore, let us never stop making intercession on their behalf. For prayer is a mighty weapon, an unfailing treasure, a wealth which is never expended, a harbor that is always calm, a foundation for tranquility. Prayer is the root and source and mother of ten thousand blessings. It is more powerful than the empire itself.

(45) Oftentimes, for all that he wears the crown, the emperor falls sick, he lies in his bed, and is burning up with fever. Physicians, armed guards, servants, and generals stand around him. But the physicians' skill, the presence of his friends, the attendance of his servants, the variety of medications cannot ease him. Neither the magnificence of his retinue, nor the abundance of wealth, nor any other human resources can soothe that sickness. But if a man who has confidence in God enters the room, touches the emperor's body,[87] and merely offers a sincere prayer in his behalf, the sickness is banished. What wealth, the throng of servants, medical knowledge even the emperor's own dignity and station did not effect, the prayer of one poor man often enough, a poor beggar, has accomplished.

---

85 Chrysostom turns his argument from refutation of the Anomoeans to a plea for prayers for their conversion and cure and an encomium of prayer (paragraphs 43–50), a discussion on true humility (paragraphs 51–55), the need for confessing one's faults (paragraphs 56–59), and of surrender to Christ (paragraphs 60–63).

86 1 Tm 2.4 and Hom. II.55. G. Denzer points out (JBC 57:18) that here Paul clearly affirms the universal salvific will of God but does not enter into the problem of its relationship to free will in man's salvation. Salvation is here described as "to come to a knowledge of the truth," as it is in 2 Tm 2.25 and Ti 1.1.

87 Probably the imposition of hands is meant. It was with this gesture that Christ cured the sick (cf., e.g., Lk 5.13; Mk 5.23 and 41). The apostles did the same (cf. Acts 5.12; 28.8).

(46) I am not talking of a prayer lightly and carelessly offered but of one made in earnest, which comes from an afflicted soul and from a contrite heart. This is the kind of prayer which mounts up to heaven. This kind of prayer is like water. As long as water flows over level ground and enjoys plenty of room, it does not leap up to the sky. But when irrigators put barriers on the ground to pen the water into ditches, because it is now crowded and cramped, it darts upward to the sky more speedily than any arrow. So it is, too, with the human mind. As long as it enjoys full freedom from fear, it is relaxed and spreads itself far and wide. But when the pressure of affairs on earth has cramped its course so that it is indeed afflicted and bruised, it sends upward to heaven prayers which are pure and strong.

(47) So that you may know that the prayers which are uttered in time of affliction would have the best chance of being heard, hear what the prophet says: "In my affliction I cried to the Lord, and he listened to me."[88] Therefore, let us stir up our conscience to fervor, let us afflict our soul with the memory of our sins, not so that it is crushed by anxiety, but so that we may make it ready to be heard, so that we make it live in sobriety and watchfulness[89] and ready to attain heaven itself. Nothing puts carelessness and negligence to flight the way grief and affliction do. They bring together our thoughts from every side and make our mind turn back to ponder itself. The man who prays in this way, in his affliction, after many a prayer, can bring joy into his own soul.

(48) A large gathering of clouds at first makes the air murky. But after the clouds send down continuous showers and empty themselves of all their rain, they make the air calm and bright. In the same way, as long as distress and anguish stay cramped and compressed in our hearts, they darken our thinking. When they are emptied and evaporate through the words of our supplication and the tears which flow from our eyes as we pray, they bring a great brightness to the soul. Why?

---

88 Ps 119 (120).1 (LXX).
89 Cf. 1 Thess 5.6 and 1 Pt 5.8. See also Homilies IV.32; VI.30; VII.3,6,59.

Because, like the rays of the sun, God's help has entered into the soul of the man who is praying.

(49) But what are the coldhearted words offered by many men as an excuse for not praying? "I lack the confidence to speak freely to God," they say, "I am filled with shame and cannot open my mouth." Your pious caution was spawned by Satan. Your words are a cloak for your own careless indifference. It is the devil who wishes to lock the doors which give you access to God. Do you lack the confidence to approach and to speak freely to him? If you really believe that you lack this confidence, then your confidence is really great and this in itself is a great help. But to think that you have this freedom to speak on your own merits is, on the other hand, a cause for shame and deserves the ultimate condemnation.

(50) Suppose you perform many acts of virtue. Suppose you have no awareness of evil in yourself. But then suppose that you believe that, on your own merits, you possess the freedom to approach and speak to God. Then you are depriving yourself of all benefit from your prayer. Yet even if you carry the burden of ten thousand sins on your conscience, you will still find great freedom to approach and speak to God, as long as you are convinced that you are the least of all men.[90]

(51) However, it is no humility to think that you are a sinner when you really are a sinner. But whenever a man is conscious of having done many great deeds but does not imagine that he is something great in himself, that is true humility. When a man is like Paul and can say: "I have nothing on my conscience," and then can add: "But I am not justified by this,"[91] and can say again: "Christ Jesus came to save sinners of whom I am the chief,"[92] that is true humility. That man is truly humble who does exalted deeds but, in his own mind, sees himself as

---

90 This passage completes Chrysostom's discussion of *parrhēsia*, the confidence and freedom to approach God and speak to him. This can be either a virtue (confidence in God) or a vice (culpable boldness). It is the virtue which Daniel possessed (cf. Hom.IV.5) and which is characterized by humility. Cf. Homilies II.21; III.18,36,42,44; IV.5,6; V.45,49,50,62.
91 Cf. 1 Cor 4.4.
92 Cf. 1 Tm 1.15.

lowly.[93] However, in his ineffable loving-kindness, God welcomes and receives not only the humble-minded but also those who have the prudence to confess their sins. Because they are so disposed toward him, he is gracious and kind to them.

(52) To learn how good it is not to imagine that you are something great picture to yourself two chariots. For one, yoke together a team consisting of justice and arrogance; for the other, a team of sin and humility. You will see that the chariot pulled by the team which includes sin outstrips the team which includes justice. Sin does not win the race because of its own power, but because of the strength of its yokemate, humility. The losing team is not beaten because justice is weak, but because of the weight and mass of arrogance. So, humility, by its surpassing loftiness, overcomes the heaviness of sin and is the first to rise up to God. In the same manner, because of its great weight and mass, pride can overcome the lightness of justice and easily drag it down to earth.[94]

(53) To help you to see that the one team is swifter than the other, recall to your mind the Pharisee and the publican. The Pharisee yoked a team consisting of justice and pride when he said: "I thank you, O God, that I am not like the rest of men, robbers, greedy, nor like this publican."[95] What madness! His self-claimed superiority to all human nature did not satisfy his arrogance, but he even trampled the publican, who was standing nearby, under the foot of his great haughtiness. And what did the publican do? He did not try to evade the insults, he was not troubled by the accusation, but he patiently accepted what was said. But the dart shot at him by his enemy became for him

---

93 This definition is completed by another which Chrysostom gives in *In Philip.* Hom.VI.2 (PG 62.236) where he says: "What, then, is humility? It is to think humble thoughts. But he is not a humble man who thinks humble thoughts because he is forced to do so; rather, he is humble who humbles himself."

94 Chrysostom's example of the two chariots is reminiscent of Plato's *Phaedrus* 246a–48c and its myth of the chariots of gods and men. Chrysostom now makes an easy transition from his mythical example to the parable of the Pharisee and the publican, which explains perfectly the meaning of his myth.

95 Cf. Lk 18.11.

a curing medication, the insult became a word of praise, the accusation became a crown of victory.

(54) Humility is such a blessing and so profitable that we do not feel the sting when others abuse us, nor do we act like wild beasts when our neighbors insult us. Such things can produce for us a great and genuine good, as happened in the case of the publican. He took the insults and put aside the burden of his sins. He said: "Be merciful to me, a sinner,"[96] and he left justified rather than his detractor. Words were better than deeds, and what was said surpassed what was done. The Pharisee put forward his justice, his fasting, and the tithes he gave. The publican spoke mere words but laid aside the burden of his sins. God not only heard his words but he saw the intention with which he uttered them. He also saw the publican's soul humble and contrite, he had mercy on him and treated him with loving-kindness.

(55) I tell you this not so that we may fall into sin but so that we may be humble. If a publican, the lowest form of iniquity, not by humble-mindedness but by simply admitting what he was, won for himself such great favor from God, how great will be the divine assistance which will come upon those who have done great and good deeds but who do not believe that they, of themselves, are something great?

(56) Therefore, I exhort, I entreat, and I beg you never to stop confessing your faults to God. I am not leading you onto a stage before your fellow servants nor do I force you to reveal your sin to men. Open your conscience before God, show him your wounds, and beg him for medication to heal them. Do not point them out to someone who will reproach you but to one who will cure you. Even if you remain silent, God knows all things. Tell your sins to him so that you may be the one who profits. Tell them to him so that, once you have left the burden of all your sins with him, you may go forth cleansed of your

---

96 ibid. 13.

faults and free from the intolerable need to make them public.[97]

(57) The three young men endured the furnace and gave their lives to confess their faith in the Lord.[98] Nonetheless, after so many deeds of such great virtue, they said: "We cannot open our mouths; we have become a shame and a reproach to your servants and to those who revere you."[99] Why, then, do you open your mouths? They reply: "So that we may say this very thing, namely, that we cannot open our mouths and so that in that very way we may win the Master over to our side."[100] The power of prayer quenched the force of fire, it curbed the wrath of lions, it brought an end to wars, it stopped battles, it quelled storms, it drove out demons, it opened the gates of

---

97 This paragraph (as do numerous other places in Chrysostom's works) seems to show that auricular confession to a priest was neither required nor practiced at Antioch in the fourth century. In his *De Sac.*, 3.5,6 (PG 48.643–44), Chrysostom tells us that the priest can absolve sins twice: once through baptism and then, if one has sinned afterwards, through the last anointing. But he often speaks of a third kind which takes place between God and the sinner alone, if the sinner repents and shows a firm purpose of amendment. As well as the present paragraph, there are many other passages in the same vein. See, e.g., Hom.VI (*On the Blessed Philogonius*) below, paragraphs 30–37; ACW 31, p.38; FOTC 68, pp. 61,63 n.; *De Laz.* Hom IV.4 (PG 48.1012). The question of whether Chrysostom can be taken as a witness for auricular confession has been disputed. P. Galtier, "St. Jean Chrysostome et la Confession," *Recherches de sciences religieuses* 1 (1910) 209–240; 313–50, thinks he can. But Baur 1.361–62 finds his arguments unconvincing, and actually summarizes the present paragraph (p. 362) as part of his own proof. Also on the negative side is H. Keane, "The Sacrament of Penance in St. John Chrysostom," *Irish Theological Quarterly* 14 (1919) 305–317. G. Bardy, "St. Jean Chrysostome," DTC 8.1. 683 also states that Galtier's arguments are inconclusive.

98 Cf. Dn 3.19–23. The three boys (Shadrach, Meshach, and Abednego) are bound and thrown into the fiery furnace, but it is their executioners who are devoured by the flames. The young men miraculously go unscathed. They do give witness to their God and, hence, are martyrs; they do not, however, lay down their lives for him. Cf. FOTC 68, pp. 87,98,118.

99 Cf. Dn 3.33 (LXX).

100 The three youths have done great deeds but they cannot open their mouths to boast of them because they cannot believe that, of themselves, they are something great. Rather, they are a shame and a reproach. That is all they can say, but, by confining themselves to this confession, they hope to win God's favor and forgiveness.

heaven, it cut asunder the chains of death, it put sickness to flight, it beat off insults and abuse, it made shaken cities stand. Prayer removed blows inflicted from above, it took away the plots and treachery of men, and, in a word, every dread event.

(58) Again, I am not talking of prayer which comes merely from the lips; I am talking of prayer which rises up from the bottom of the heart.[101] When trees send their roots deep into the earth, they are not broken or torn up even by ten thousand assaults of the winds. Why? Their roots are strongly and tightly bound deep in the earth. So it is with prayers. Those which are sent up from deep within the heart, because they are securely rooted, lift themselves up to heaven, and no sophistries of the mind can turn them aside by their assaults. This is why the prophet said: "Out of the depths I have cried to you, O Lord."[102]

(59) I say this not only that you may show your approbation of them by your deeds.[103] If you tell men your personal misfortunes, if you describe to them in tragic tones the evils which have befallen you, you may find some consolation in your distress, that is, if you think that talking about your troubles will make them evaporate. But if you share with your Master the sufferings you feel in your soul, it is much surer that you will receive comfort and consolation in abundance. People often grow weary of a man who comes to them with his wailing and bitter laments. At times they even push him from their path to get rid of him. But God does not act in this way. He lets the wailing man come to him and even draws him to himself. Even if it takes you all day to share your misfortunes with God, he will love you all the more and will grant your petitions.

(60) Surely Christ proved this very thing when he said: "Come to me all you who labor and are burdened, and I will give you rest."[104] Now he calls us, let us not fail to heed him.

---

101 As did the prayer of the three young men.
102 Cf. Ps 129 (130). 1.
103 See above Homilies I.47; III.43. Also cf. FOTC 68, p.3; *De stat.* 5.7. (PG 49.79).
104 Mt. 11.29.

When he draws us to himself, let us not leap away from him. Even if we have ten thousand sins on our soul, then all the more let us run to him. Men have been burdened with as many faults before. And they were the ones he invited to come to him when he said: "I did not come to call the just but sinners to repentance."[105] And in this text he means those who are oppressed with burdens, those who are in distress, those who are laboring under the weight of their sins. God is called a God of consolation, a God of mercy.[106] Because he is constantly working to encourage and console those who are distressed and afflicted even if they have sinned ten thousand times.

(61) Just let us abandon ourselves to him. Just let us run to him. Let us not stand aloof from him. Then, by the experience of this very test, we shall learn the truth of his words. No existing thing will be able to cause us grief or distress if our prayer is made in perfect earnest. For, whatever evil will come upon us, we shall easily drive it off through prayer.

(62) And what is strange if the power of prayer can do away with the troubles which come from our human condition? Does not prayer easily quench the evil nature of our sins and make them disappear? Do we wish to complete the course of this life with ease? Do we wish to put aside all the sins we have inflicted on ourselves? Do we wish to stand with confidence before the tribunal of Christ? Then let us never cease to prepare for ourselves a proper medication for this, a medication compounded from our tears, our zeal, our persevering care, and from our patient endurance.

(63) In this way we shall enjoy continuous health and gain blessings for the life to come. May it come to pass that we all win these through the grace and loving-kindness of our Lord Jesus Christ, with whom be glory to the Father together with the Holy Spirit, now and forever, world without end. Amen.

---

105 Cf. Mt 9.13.
106 Cf. 2 Cor 1.3.

HOMILY VI

ODAY I WAS PREPARING TO STRIP for the struggles against the heretic Anomoeans and to pay off the balance of my debt to you.[1] But the feast of Blessed Philogonius,[2] which we are celebrating today, has summoned my voice to recount his virtuous deeds. And I must show full obedience to this summons. For if a man who speaks ill of his mother or father dies the death,[3] it is clear that a man who speaks well of them will have full enjoyment of the rewards of life. If our parents in the flesh should enjoy such good will from us, so

---

1 Although Hom. VI constitutes another break in the sequence of Chrysostom's attack against the heretic Anomoeans, it comes at a time when Chrysostom was passing to the second stage of that attack. He has proved that God's nature is incomprehensible to every creature and has introduced the second part of his argument, the "glory of the only begotten," the consubstantiality of the Son with the Father, in Homilies I–V. But he has yet to complete his discussion of the Son's consubstantiality and will do so in the remaining homilies. Also the break comes at a fortunate time, since the feast of Christmas was only five days off. As Montfaucon says in *Notice* II.1 above, Hom.VI follows Homilies I–V in the older MSS and in the edition of Fronto Ducaeus. Therefore, Montfaucon keeps the same order, especially since Hom.VI is followed by Homilies VII and VIII in the same sources. Also, the opening sentence shows that Hom.VI constitutes an interruption, and that more discourses against the Anomoeans will follow so that Chrysostom can pay off the balance of his debt (cf., e.g., Hom.IV.10). Hence, we have not disturbed the established order.

2 Since the present homily offers practically the sole source of our information on St. Philogonius, perhaps there is no need to present any biographical note on him. However there are brief accounts in the Bollandists' *Acta sanctorum*, vol. 4 (Venice 1748) 30–31; H. Delehaye et al., *Propylaeum ad Acta Sanctorum Decembris* (Brussels 1940) 594–95; A. Butler, *The Lives of the Saints*, Vol. 12, (ed. by H. Thurston and D. Attwater) (London 1938) 209–210; Edmund Venables, "Philogonius, bishop of Antioch," in *A Dictionary of Christian Biography*, vol. 4, eds. William Smith, Henry Wace (London 1887) 389–90.

3 Cf. Lv 20.9 and Ex 21.17. Chrysostom sees the converse of what these texts prohibit in the fourth commandment. He then extends the commandment from parents in the flesh to those in the spirit, i.e., "Fathers" or bishops, even though they be deceased.

much the more would this hold true for our parents in the spirit.

(2) And this is especially so since our praise and approval do not make the souls of the departed shine with greater brightness, but the blessed ones do make better men of those who are gathered here–both of us who speak and of you who listen to their praises. But after Philogonius mounted up to heaven, he would have no need for praise from men on earth. Why? Because he has entered into a better and more blessed fortune. But while we are still pilgrims here on earth, we need many an exhortation and from every source. We are the ones who must have words of praise and encouragement from Philogonius so that we may rise up and imitate him.

(3) A wise man once exhorted us to do this when he said: "The memory of the just man will be praised."[4] But he did not say this because he meant that the departed souls are helped by our praise. He said it because those who praise the departed derive the greatest benefits from remembering them. Since, therefore, we have so much to gain from keeping their memory sacred, let us not reject the wise man's words but, rather, let us heed them. And today is a time well suited to recount the virtuous deeds of Philogonius. For today marks the anniversary of his entrance into a life of peace and calm in heaven. There, in heaven, he has moored his ship in a harbor in which there can be no suspicion of future shipwreck,[5] fear, or pain. And what is so strange about it if the harbor of heaven is free from every fear? For Paul was speaking to men still living in this life when he said: "Rejoice always, pray without ceasing."[6]

(4) But in this life there are diseases, insults, untimely deaths, false accusations, envious acts, and many reasons to grow despondent. Here we find anger, evil lusts, countless

---

4 Pvb 10.7. The wise man is Solomon.
5 To suffer shipwreck in harbor was proverbial for undergoing unforeseen disaster. Cf. Chrysostom, *In Matt* 15 (PG 57.235) and 26 (PG 57.342), as well as *Baptismal Instructions* (ACW 31, p.38).
6 1 Thess 5.16–17. J. Forestell, JBC 48:28, points out that even on earth Paul depicts Christianity as not merely a series of obligations but as a way of life oriented to God in joy, prayer, and thanksgiving. A fortiori this is true of life in heaven.

treacheries, daily anxieties. On earth we encounter a constant succession of evils which bring sufferings on us from every side. Yet Paul said to men still living here on earth that we could rejoice always if we would lift our heads a little above the surging waves of everyday affairs and keep our lives under good control. But after we depart this life, it is a far easier thing to obtain this blessing. Then, all these troubles have been taken away and there are no diseases, no sufferings, no grounds for sinning. Then, those coldhearted words "what's mine" and "what's yours" no longer exist to bring every dread evil into our lives and to cause countless conflicts.

(5) That is why I say that the saintly Philogonius is a happy soul. His life was changed and he did put aside this city here with us. But he mounted up to another city, the city of God. He left this Church here but he is a citizen in the Church of the firstborn who are enrolled in heaven.[7] He left these festivals here on earth but he entered into the festal gathering of the angels. For up in heaven there is a city, there is a Church, there is a festival. Hear what Paul says: "You have come to the city of the living God, the heavenly Jerusalem, and to the Church of the firstborn who are enrolled in the heavenly Jerusalem, and to the Church of the firstborn who are enrolled in heaven, and to countless angels in festal gathering."[8] He calls everything in heaven a festal gathering not only because of the throng of the powers above but also because of the abundance of blessings and the continuous joy and pleasure there.

(6) What makes a festal gathering on earth? The assembled throng, the abundance of goods for sale. Wheat, barley, all kinds of products, flocks of sheep, herds of cattle, clothing, and many other such things are brought in for some to sell and others to buy. Someone will ask: "What one of those things is to be found in heaven?" In heaven there are no such things. But in heaven there are things which are far more solemn and august.

---

7 Cf. Heb 12.23.
8 Cf. ibid. 22–23. The Church Triumphant is a continuation and culmination of the Pilgrim Church on earth.

(7) In heaven, we find no wheat, no barley, no different kinds of products. But we do find everywhere in heaven love, the first fruit of the Spirit.[9] We find joy and pleasure and peace and goodness and mildness in great abundance. There are no flocks of sheep nor herds of cattle. But, to be sure, the spirits of just men who have been made perfect, the goodness of souls, and the virtuous deeds of men whose characters are sound can be seen everywhere in heaven.[10] We see no garments or cloaks but we see crowns more valuable than any gold, than any contest prizes or rewards, and ten thousand blessings stored up for those who live upright and virtuous lives on earth.[11]

(8) In heaven the throngs which come together are much larger, holier, and more august. Nor are the crowds made up of city dwellers or country folk. Instead, in one place in heaven, we find myriads of angels, in another place, thousands of archangels, elsewhere, companies of prophets, in another place, choirs of martyrs, battalions of just men, and many various groups of people in whom the Lord has been well pleased.

(9) Truly, this is a marvellous festal gathering. What makes it greater than all others is the fact that, in the midst of the assembly, moves the king of all who are gathered there. After Paul had said: "To countless angels in festal gatherings," he went on to say: "And to God the judge of all."[12] And who ever saw a king coming to a festival? Here on earth no one has ever seen it. But those who are there in heaven constantly behold their king. They can see him in their midst and they can also see how he sheds on all who are gathered there the brightness of his own glory.[13]

---

9 In Gal 5.22–23 Paul lists love as the first fruit of the Spirit, and also adds joy, peace, goodness, and mildness along with patient endurance, kindness, generosity, faith, and chastity. It may be, however, that here Chrysostom is referring to Rom 8.23, where Paul is speaking of the Christian's destiny of glory. See NAB note on Rom 8.18–27 and J. Fitzmyer, JBC 53:22.

10 Perhaps a reference to Rom 8.16–17. See NAB note ad loc.

11 Cf. 1 Cor 25–26; 2 Tm 2.5,4.8; 1 Thess 2.19; Jas 1.12; 1 Pt 5.4.

12 Cf. Heb 12.22–23.

13 Cf. Heb 1.3 and NAB note on verses 1–4. Marvellous as will be the vision of the blessed, it will still be limited by their capacity to perceive.

(10) Festivals here on earth often end at noon. Not so the festal assembly in heaven. Nor does that festival wait for the months to return in their cycle, nor for the revolving years, nor for the counting of days. The festival in heaven continues with no interruption. Its blessings have no limit, the feast itself knows no end, it can neither grow old nor waste away, it does not die nor does it decay.[14] In heaven there is no tumult or disturbance such as on earth. There everything is in proper order and well arranged. There, voices rise in rhythmic harmony, as if blending with the lyre in the sweetest music, to praise the master who created heaven and earth. There, as if it were in a hallowed sanctuary during the divine mysteries, the soul completes its ritual of initiation.[15]

(11) Today[16] marks the anniversary of the day when the blessed Philogonius withdrew from this world and entered into that holy and ageless inheritance which was appointed for him. What discourse could there be which could do justice to a man who was deemed worthy of such a happy fortune? No words could do so. Tell me, then. Shall we remain silent on that account? And yet, why did we come together? Shall we admit that our words cannot reach the heights of his deeds? Yet this is the very reason why we must speak. When our words cannot match the deeds we praise, we fulfill the greatest purpose of a panegyric. For when a man's virtuous acts go beyond ordinary human nature, it is obvious that it lies beyond the powers of the human tongue to praise them.[17]

(12) Philogonius will not reject my words on that account. Rather, he will imitate his master. When the widow put into the collection box only two small coins,[18] the master did not give

---

14 Unlike the earthly riches of Mt 6.19 which moths and rust corrode, where thieves break in and steal.

15 Possibly a reference to baptism which makes one a child of God and heir to heaven.

16 "Today" was December 20, five days before the Feast of the Nativity of Christ, in the year A.D. 386, some forty-two years after the death of Philogonius in 324.

17 Despite his protests, Chrysostom has spoken most eloquently about the overflowing peace and joy of heaven, but his words are well within the capacity of his congregation to understand.

18 The incident of the widow's mite is recounted in Lk 21. 1–4 and Mk 12.41–44. Chrysostom alludes to it again in Hom.VIII.12.

her a recompense worth only two coins. Why was that? Because he paid no attention to the amount of the money; what he did heed was the wealth of her soul. If you calculate by the value of her money, her poverty is great. If you bring her intention into the light, you will see that her store of generosity defies description. Therefore, I, too, give what I have, even if my slender talents have little value.

(13) Certainly, my ability falls far short of the generosity and magnanimity of the noble and just Philogonius. But it would be the strongest proof of his generosity if he does not reject my small talent but does the same thing which rich men do. For rich men first accept from the poor small amounts of which they have no need. But then they open their own purses and hand over money as a gift to those who gave what they could. In this same way, Philogonius has accepted praise from the words I speak, praise of which he has no need. Then, in return, he will repay me by his deeds, the blessings of which I am in constant need.[19]

(14) Where, then, shall I begin my words of praise? From what other point than from the office which the grace of the Spirit entrusted to him?[20] It is true, that, in the civil sphere, the offices men hold by no means can give proof of the virtue of those to whom they have been entrusted. On the contrary, they often serve to accuse the officeholder of evil acts. Why? Because the protection given to and by friends, the cheating, the flattery, and other far more disgraceful things usually have their effect on such offices and on those who hold them.[21] But when God selects a man by his vote, when God's hand touches a holy head, the divine vote is not bought with a bribe, God's judgment cannot be held suspect. The dignity of God, who elects him, would put beyond all dispute God's approval of him whom he has elected.[22]

---

19 This offers clear evidence of why we should pray to the saints in heaven. They will intercede for us and win for us the graces we need.
20 Philogonius became bishop of Antioch in the year 318.
21 Political chicanery and official misconduct are limited to no one era.
22 Until the sixth century bishops were frequently elected by the votes of clergy and laity (CE 2.583). Chrysostom sees the hand of God as directing the election.

(15) The character of Philogonius makes it clear that God did choose and elect him. He was taken from the marketplace and led to the episcopal throne. He had shown himself to be a man of outstanding piety and distinction during his earlier life when he had a wife and daughter[23] and was involved in the practice of law. In fact, the splendid virtue of his former life, which so far outshone the sun, immediately established that he was worthy of the episcopal office. So he was brought from the tribunal of the courts to the bishop's tribunal. In his earlier life, he defended men against plotters and made the innocent win out over the guilty. When he came to the bishop's throne, he defended men against the insolent assaults of demons.

(16) That he was deemed deserving of this office by a great grace of God is a strong proof of his virtue. How strong? Listen to the words Christ spoke to Peter after the resurrection. Christ asked him: "Peter, do you love me?" And Peter replied: "Lord, you know that I love you."[24] What did Christ then say? He did not say: "Throw away your money. Fast from food. Live the hard life. Raise the dead. Drive out demons." Christ

---

23 The history of the question of priestly and episcopal celibacy is a complicated one. What is standard in the Roman Church today cannot be said to be of apostolic origin or universal in patristic times or even today in the Eastern Churches. A recent book by C. Cochini, *Origines apostoliques du célibat sacerdotal* (Paris 1981) is a learned attempt to show that clerical celibacy dates back to the earliest days of the Church as a matter of rule, but his work is criticized on grounds of historical method by R. Balducelli in his article, "The Apostolic Origins of Clerical Continence: A Critical Appraisal of a New Book," *Theological Studies* 43 (1982) 693–705. He concludes that the legitimation of clerical celibacy is still an unfinished task. As for apostolic origin (even allowing for some uncertainty as to the precise meaning of "bishop"), it seems settled by Paul in 1 Tm 3.2, where he says: "A bishop must be irreproachable, married only once . . . " and in Ti 1.6, where he says the same thing for presbyters, adding that they must be the father of children who are believers. Paul also says that a deacon should be the husband of one wife (1 Tm 3.12). In patristic times, canon 23 of the Spanish Council of Elvira in 295–303 imposed celibacy on the three higher orders of the clergy, but the restriction was far from universal, especially in the East and for those who were married before ordination. See H. Thurston, "Celibacy of the Clergy," CE 3.481–88. Of course, Philogonius may have been a widower before his accession to the see of Antioch.
24 Cf. Jn 21.16. Chrysostom uses the words by which Christ commissioned Peter as prince of the apostles to show that Philogonius was not only a man of virtue but also deserving of his episcopal office.

did not bring forward or command any of these things or any other miracle or act of virtue. He passed all these by and said: "If you love me, feed my sheep."[25] Why did Christ say this? Because he wished to show us not only what is the strongest sign of love for him but also to point out the love which he himself shows for his sheep. So now he makes this the strongest proof which Peter can give of his love for him. For Christ's words practically mean: "He who loves my sheep loves me."

(17) And look how many things Christ endured for his flock. He became a man,[26] he took upon himself the form of a servant,[27] he was spat upon,[28] he was slapped in the face,[29] and, finally, he did not refuse to die the most shameful death.[30] For he poured forth his blood on the cross.[31] Therefore, if a man wishes to win esteem in the eyes of Christ, let him show his concern for these sheep, let him seek what is helpful for all, let him be anxious to care for his brothers. God holds no virtuous act in greater esteem. That is why Christ said in another place: "Simon, Simon, Satan has desired to have you that he may sift you as wheat. But I have prayed for you, that your faith may not fail."[32]

---

25 Cf. Jn 21.17. Christ is here passing on his own office as Good Shepherd to Peter, who must love the sheep as did Christ, even to laying down his life for them. This will be the measure of Peter's love for Christ. Fraternal charity is loving one's brothers as Christ loves us; he who loves Christ's flock loves Christ.

26 Cf. Jn 1.14.

27 Cf. Phil 2.7.

28 Cf. Lk 18.32.

29 Cf. Mt 26.67.

30 Cf. Phil 2.8. Dt 21.23 says that everyone who is hanged on a gibbet is accursed. Paul quotes this text in Gal 3.13, applies it to Christ, but tells us that Christ redeemed us from the curse of the Law by himself becoming a curse for us. Cf. also 1 Pt 2.8.

31 Chrysostom has a beautiful section on the glory of the cross in his *Demonstration Against the Pagans on the Divinity of Christ* (PG 48.826–27).

32 Cf. Lk 22.31–32. C. Stuhlmueller (JBC 44:159) points out in this prediction of Peter's triple denial of Christ that Satan got his wish and that God permitted Peter to be severely tempted, just as he placed Job in the hands of Satan (cf. Jb 1.12; 2.6). Stuhlmueller (ibid.) also points out that "faith" is here to be taken in the biblical sense of loyal attachment to Jesus through trust, love, and confidence. In that kind of faith in Jesus Peter never collapsed.

(18) "What return, then, will you make to me for this concern and care of mine?" Christ asks. What is the return for which he is looking? He seeks a return in kind. For he said: "When you turn back to me, you must strengthen your brothers."[33] And so it was that Paul, too, said: "Be imitators of me as I am of Christ."[34] And how, Paul, did you become an imitator of Christ? "By pleasing all men in every way, by not seeking my own benefit but the benefit of all men, so that they might be saved."[35] Again, in another place, Paul said: "Christ did not please himself but pleased many."[36] Therefore, nothing could be so great a mark or sign of the man of faith who loves Christ as would be his care for his brothers and his concern for their salvation.

(19) Let these words ring loud in the ears of all the monks who dwell on the mountain tops and who in every way have crucified themselves to the world.[37] Let them, in proportion to the power which is theirs, help those who rule and direct the churches, let them encourage these leaders with the anointing of their prayers, their unity of mind, their love.[38] Unless they

---

33 Cf. Lk 22.32. Just as Jesus has prayed for Peter and this strengthened him in his faith, so Peter is to strengthen all the apostles and the faithful. This is Chrysostom's reason for mentioning the prediction of Peter's temptation at this point. C. Stuhlmueller (JBC ibid.) notes that Peter, who was in a sense the greatest among the brethren, through the experience of his temptation, has become the least; but by being one with them, he will know how to lead them.

34 In 1 Cor 4.16 Paul begs the Corinthian Christians to imitate him. R. Kugelman (JBC 51:26) says that Paul is their father because he has begotten them in Christ. Hence, they must follow his example. In doing so, they will be following Christ and measuring up to the ideal of the new life they have received. In 1 Cor 11.1 Paul says: "Imitate me as I imitate Christ." Kugelman (ibid. 51:67) notes that in imitating Paul's selfless example in seeking salvation for all, the Corinthians will be imitating Christ, the perfect exemplar of renunciation for the salvation of men.

35 Cf. 1 Cor 10.33 and see ibid. 9.22.

36 Cf. Rom 15.3.

37 In the eighth of his *Baptismal Instructions* (ACW 31.119–21; 280–83) Chrysostom greets monks from the countryside (who were present at his postbaptismal Instruction) with words of praise for their way of life and virtuous deeds.

38 The Church is one Body in Christ; the monks whose lives are devoted to work and prayer must, as members of that body, show a special concern for the bishops, who are Christ's vicegerents on earth.

help in every way the bishops who have been appointed to their office by God's grace and who have taken upon themselves the anxieties of so many concerns, these monks must know that, even if they are living far away, they have lost the sum total of their way of life and have cut off the source of all their wisdom.[39]

(20) Where do we have the strongest proof of a bishop's love for Christ? This will make it clear. Let us see how our bishop[40] handled his episcopal duties. This will require no further words from me because your own zeal and earnestness are in themselves proofs of this point. If someone goes into a vineyard and sees the vines putting forth their leaves and heavy with grapes because they have been protected and guarded by fences on every side, he will need no word or further proof to learn how excellent a farmer the vintner is. So, too, if someone comes in here to our assembly and sees you, the spiritual vines, and the fruits you put forth, he will need no discourse or instruction to learn what sort of bishop has been put in charge of you. As Paul said: "You are my epistle which has been written and read."[41] For the river reveals its source and the fruit its root.

(21) Therefore, I ought to have spoken of the time when Philogonius undertook this office, and this would by no means have been the smallest part to my panegyric. And it would also have served quite adequately to prove how virtuous a man he was. When he assumed the episcopal office, there were great

---

39 In the Christian context, wisdom is the true doctrine, the Christian way of life, and it is often associated with piety. As applied to monasticism, it means the moral and ascetical life. Cf. H. Graef, trans., *St. Gregory of Nyssa: The Lord's Prayer and the Beatitudes*, ACW 18 (Westminister, Md. 1954) 190 n.93 on *philosophia*. See also ACW 31.119–20.

40 The bishop referred to here is Flavian, who succeeded Meletius as bishop of Antioch in 381.

41 Cf. 2 Cor 3.2. This is an allusion rather than an exact citation. The text reads: "You are my epistle, known and read by all men, written on your hearts." J. O'Rourke, JBC 52:13, notes that "written on your hearts" indicates men who are tractable and docile. God's grace cannot affect those who will be obdurate.

difficulties and many grounds for discontent.[42] A persecution
had just ended,[43] and traces of those trying times still remained. The situation still required considerable correction.
And we must add to these troubles the fact that an heretical
sect, which had its beginning in his day, was throwing obstacles
in his path even though, in his wisdom, he foresaw all that they
would do.[44]

(22) I would like to speak at greater length on this matter
but I must hasten to turn my discourse to another topic, and
that a necessary one. Therefore, I leave it to our own bishop to
complete the panegyric because he is our common father and a
zealous follower of the blessed Philogonius.[45] Furthermore, he
has a more exact knowledge of all events of those earlier days.[46]

(23) So now I shall proceed to another path of preaching. A
feast day is about to arrive and it is the most holy, august, and
awesome of all feasts; it would be no mistake to call it the chief
and mother of all holy days. What feast is that? The day of

---

42 Downey, *History*, 331–37 recounts several incidents from these days including a famine, revival of pagan cults and the cult of the emperor, a
   petition that Christians be banished from Antioch and its territory, a
   rupture between the emperors Maximinus and Constantine (which led to
   civil war).
43 The persecution started in 303 under Diocletian. After his abdication
   (305) it was continued under Maximinus. Licinius, who succeeded Maximinus, at first in accord with Constantine, emperor of the West, tolerated
   freedom of belief. But later Licinius altered his official position on
   religion and dismissed Christians from all court positions and from civil
   service because Christians were thought to favor Constantine. Another
   imperial rupture was inevitable. A civil war followed; on his defeat in 324,
   Licinius was executed, and Constantine became sole emperor. See
   Downey, *History*, 331–37.
44 This is a clear reference to Arius and the Christological and Trinitarian
   heterodoxy which would harrass orthodox Christianity for years to come.
45 It was not uncommon for several preachers (especially bishops, either
   resident or visiting,) to address the congregation on the same day.
46 Philogonius died in 324, some twenty-three years before Chrysostom was
   born. Hence Flavian, who must have been considerably older than Chrysostom, might well have a more exact knowledge of "those earlier days."

Christ's birth in the flesh.[47]

(24) It is from this day that the feasts of the Theophany,[48] the sacred Pasch,[49] the Ascension, [50] and Pentecost[51] had their source and foundation. Had Christ not been born in the flesh, he would not have been baptized, which is the Theophany or Manifestation; nor would he have been crucified, which is the Pasch; nor would he have sent down the Spirit, which is Pentecost. So it is that, just as different rivers arise from a source, these other feasts have their beginnings from the birth of Christ.

(25) Not only for this reason is it right that the day of Christ's birth should enjoy the principal place but also because what occurred on this day provides a much stronger reason for us to experience a holy fear and trembling[52] than all the others do. For the fact that Christ, who became man, also died was a

---

47 Chrysostom will now change his theme to the feast of the Nativity and the proper attitude for a true Christian celebration of it. One should approach the altar and receive the eucharist, but only after he has truly repented and been reconciled. Since the feast of St. Philogonius was celebrated on December 20, Christmas was only five days off. Cf. below paragraph 30.

48 Although all three of the great Cappadocian Fathers (Basil, Gregory of Nazianzus, and Gregory of Nyssa) use Theophany for the feast of the Nativity, Chrysostom makes it clear that he means by it the Epiphany. Nor does he mean by this name the coming of the magi but rather the feast celebrated in commemoration of the baptism of Jesus in the Jordan, when the Spirit of God descended like a dove and the voice was heard from the heavens, saying: "This is my beloved Son. My favor rests on him." Cf. Mt 3.13–17.

49 In Christian usage, the sacred Pasch included the period from the Last Supper, through the passion, death, and resurrection of Christ.

50 Perhaps the Ascension was outside the scope of the Gospel narratives. Its account is found in Mk 16.19 (a later addition—see NAB note on Mk 16.9–20) and in Lk 24.51. Since the account of the Ascension is also found in Acts 1.9, C. Stuhlmueller (JBC 44:180) notes that some would think that the account does not belong to Luke's Gospel.

51 The descent of the Holy Spirit is recounted in Acts 2.1–4. See NAB nn. ad loc.

52 The Incarnation and birth of Christ are moments which should arouse in us even greater fear and trembling than other events in God's plan of redemption, which are consequents of the fact that the Word became flesh and dwelt among us. Cf. J. Daniélou, Introduction, (SC 28 bis) 30–39.

consequence of his birth. Even though he was free from any sin, he did take upon himself a mortal body, and that should make us marvel. That he who is God was willing to become man, that he endured to accommodate himself to our weakness and to come down to our level is too great for our minds to grasp. It makes us shudder with the deepest holy fear; it fills us with terror and trembling.

(26) This is what amazed Paul when he said: "Wonderful, indeed, is the mystery of our religion."[53] How wonderful? "God was manifested in the flesh."[54] And again in another place: "God is not taking to himself the angels but he is concerned with taking to himself the children of Abraham; therefore, it was right for him to become like his brothers in every way."[55] This is why I especially greet and love this day. This is why I set before your eyes his love so that I may make you share in it. And this is why I ask and beg all of you to be here in church for that feast with all zeal and alacrity. Let each of us leave his house empty so that we may see our master wrapped in swaddling clothes and lying in a manger. This is a sight which is filled with holy fear and trembling. It is incredible and beyond our every expectation.

(27) What defense or excuse will we have when, for our sake, he comes down from heaven, but we do not even leave our homes to come to him?[56] The magi were strangers and foreigners from Persia. Yet they came to see him lying in the

---

53 Cf. 1 Tm 3.16 and the rest of the verse (which Chrysostom does not quote in its entirety). As G. Denzer (JBC 57:22) notes, the "mystery" is Christ himself. The remainder of the verse seems to have been borrowed from an ancient Christian hymn.

54 Cf. 1 Tm ibid. The words quoted are the first line of the portion of the hymn Paul seems to be quoting. See G. Denzer, ibid.

55 Cf. Heb 2.16,17. M. Bourke (JBC 61:18) remarks that this entire section of Heb deals with the Incarnation but that verse 16 has a wider reference because the present tense of the verb suggests a continuing help rather than the single event of the Incarnation.

56 For a Christian to make no effort to be present at the eucharistic mysteries on the feast of Christ's birth is a mark of the ultimate in sloth and tepidity; such a response to the first step in God's plan of salvation is utterly indefensible. Even the pagan magi made a long and arduous journey to pay homage to Jesus shortly after his birth.

manger. Can you, a Christian, not bear to give a brief measure of time to enjoy this blessed sight? If we shall present ourselves in a spirit of faith, there is no doubt but that we shall truly see him as he lies in the manger. For the table of this altar takes the place of the manger.

(28) And surely the master's body will be lying on this altar, not wrapped in swaddling clothes, as it was after his birth, but clothed all about by the Holy Spirit.[57] Those who have been initiated understand what I am saying.[58] The magi adored him, but that was all. If your conscience is without stain when you come forward, we shall allow you even to receive that body and then to go off to your home. Do you, therefore, come forward and bring your gifts, not such gifts as the magi brought,[59] but gifts which are far holier and more august. The magi brought gold; you bring a temperate and virtuous spirit. They brought incense; you must offer pure prayers, which are the incense of the soul.[60] They brought myrrh; you must bring a humble and contrite heart[61] along with alms.[62]

---

57 Just as it was by the power of the Holy Spirit that Mary conceived and bore the child Jesus, so, too, it is by that same power of the same Spirit that Jesus is present, flesh and blood, soul and divinity, on the altar, through the ministry of the priest, at the liturgy of the eucharist.

58 Only the baptized who have experienced the *traditio symboli* and rebirth in Christ through the waters of regeneration could know the marvels wrought at the mysteries. Catechumens (who would be present for the homily) had to leave the church before the liturgy proper began. Like the magi, they could adore but could not receive the eucharist.

59 Gold, frankincense and myrrh, as we read in Mt 2.11, and as Chrysostom enumerates them in the following sentence.

60 We should recall here Chrysostom's encomium of prayer given in Hom.V.44–59. In the same homily (60–63) he stressed the power of prayer to reconcile us to God despite the countless sins which may stain the soul.

61 Hom.V.51–55 also points out that our prayer must come from a humble and contrite heart if we are to win forgiveness for our sins.

62 Almsgiving was regarded as a highly efficacious social virtue in the Golden Age of patristic literature in both East and West. The motives for this high regard were deeply theological: identification of Christ and the poor, and atonement for sin. See B. Ramsey, "Almsgiving in the Latin Church: The Late Fourth and Early Fifth Centuries," *Theological Studies* 43 (1982) 226–59.

(29) If you come forward with these gifts, you will enjoy and share in this sacred table with great trust and confidence. Why do I speak these words at this time? I know for sure that on that day many will come forward and lay hostile hands on that spiritual sacrifice.[63] We must not do this to the harm and condemnation of our souls.[64] We must approach the altar to win salvation for ourselves. That is why, now, before that day, I beg and beseech you, only after you have cleansed yourselves in every way are you to approach these mysteries.

(30) Let no one say to me: "I am so ashamed. I have a conscience filled with sins. I am carrying the heaviest of burdens." The period of five days is time enough to cut away the multitude of your sins if you are sober and watchful[65] and if you pray. Do not look to the shortness of the time but consider the loving-kindness of the master. The people of Nineveh drove off God's great wrath in three days.[66] The narrow span of time did not deter them, but after their eager souls won for them the master's loving-kindness, they were able to accomplish the whole task.

(31) After the harlot had come to Christ, in a brief moment of time, she washed away her every reproach and disgraceful deed.[67] Even though the Jews were accusing Christ because he

---

63 Chrysostom is referring to those who will partake of the eucharist unworthily because they are unrepentant.

64 Cf. 1 Cor 11.27–29.

65 Cf. 1 Pt 5.8. This is one of Chrysostom's favorite admonitions. See Homilies IV.32,44; V.47; VI.30; VII.3,6,59.

66 The story of Nineveh's conversion is told in Jon 3.1–10. The LXX reports that Jonah proclaimed the Lord's threat that the city would be destroyed in three days. Its inhabitants repented immediately, and the Lord turned aside his wrath. NAB says that the city would be destroyed in forty days. Chrysostom, of course is basing his time frame on the LXX reading.

67 Cf. Lk 7.37–50. When compared with Mt 26.6–13, Mk 14.3–9, and Jn 12.1–8, Luke's account gives rise to many difficulties, as C. Stuhlmueller notes in JBC 44:76. Evidently, during the period of oral transmission, details of one account passed over into another so that the identity of the woman, the host of the supper, the place of the action, the time in Jesus' life the action occurred, and various other details have become ensnarled. Since Chrysostom's present theme is sincere repentance and immediate remission of sins, Luke's account fits in best with his argument. The harlot has been identified with Mary Magdalen, but there is no basis for the identification except that Mary also anointed Christ's feet (Jn 12.3). However, that occurred at Bethany just before Jesus' triumphal entry into Jerusalem. See J. McKenzie, DB 552–53. Luke's account places the event in a different place and early in Christ's public life.

let her come to him and gave her such freedom and confidence, Christ curbed their tongues, freed her from her sins,
accepted her earnestness and zeal, and then sent her away.
Why did he do this? Because she had come to him with a warm
heart, a soul on fire, and a fervent faith. She first loosened her
hair, sent forth streams of tears from her eyes, took hold of
those sacred feet, and emptied her jar of ointment upon them.

(32) She used the things with which she cast her spell on
men as medication to effect her repentance and conversion.
She poured forth her tears through the eyes which she had
used to arouse the eyes of licentious men. She dried the feet of
Christ with the curling hair with which she tripped up many a
man and turned him to sin. She anointed his feet with the
perfume with which she enticed her many lovers. You, too,
must make God favorable to you and appease him again with
the same things you used to anger and provoke him.[68] Did you
provoke him by stealing money? Then you must appease him
with money by giving back what you have stolen to those whom
you wronged, and by giving back an amount over and above
what you stole.[69] You must say, as Zacchaeus did: "I give back
four times of all that I stole."[70]

(33) Did your tongue anger God by insulting and abusing
many men? Then win back God's favor by your tongue as you
send pure prayers up to him, as you speak well of those who
insult you, as you praise those who speak ill of you, as you give
thanks to those who wrong you.[71] This does not require many
days or years but only the right intention and purpose. Then
all is set straight in a single day. Stand aloof from wickedness,
take a firm hold on virtue, stop doing evil, promise never to

---

68 Satisfaction for sin is best made by that which led the sinner to do wrong:
e.g., a tongue which lied must be used to tell the truth.

69 One suspects that Chrysostom intends that the amount "over and above"
restitution should be given as alms.

70 Cf. Lk 19.8. Since Zacchaeus was a tax collector, his theft would probably
have been by defrauding the taxpayer or the state. The "four times" seems
to refer to OT statutes of restitution such as we find in Ex 21.37 and Nm
5.5–7.

71 Again, the way to give satisfaction for sin is best made by that with which
the sinner did wrong; here it is the sinful tongue atoning by prayer, by
returning insults with praise and thanking those who did harm. In this
way the penitent proves his right intention and finds his sinful tongue
providing him with the opportunity to practice virtue.

commit these sins again, and this will be enough to excuse you.[72] I solemnly affirm and I give you my pledge that if each of us who is in sin turns away from his past evil deeds and truly promises God that he will never go back to them again, God will ask for nothing else by way of a greater excuse. He is a God of loving-kindness and of mercy. Just as the woman in labor is eager to give birth to her child, so God desires to pour forth his mercy, but our sins stop him short.[73]

(34) Therefore, let us tear down this wall and, from this time on, let us bid everything farewell for these five days and begin to observe the feast. Away with the business of the law courts! Away with the business of the City Council! Away with daily affairs together with their contracts and business deals! I wish to save my soul. "What does it profit a man if he gain the whole world but suffer the loss of his soul?"[74] The magi went forth from Persia. You go forth from the affairs of daily life. Make your journey to Jesus; it is not far to travel if we are willing to make the trip. We need not cross the sea nor climb the mountain crests. If you prove your piety and full compunction, you can see him without leaving home,[75] you can tear down the whole wall, remove every obstacle, and shorten the length of the journey. As the prophet said: "I am a God who is near at hand and not a God afar off,"[76] and: "The Lord is close to all who call upon him in truth."[77]

(35) But, as it is, many of those who do believe have come to a high pitch of folly and contempt. Even though their souls are weighted down with countless sins and they feel no concern for themselves, they still approach this table on feast days with no thought or preparation. They do this because they fail to

---

72 If the sinner would have his sins forgiven, he must avoid future temptation and have a firm purpose of amendment.
73 If we refuse to repent, we frustrate God's mercy; he made us free and he will not take away his gift to us even if we abuse it.
74 Mt 16.26.
75 This does not mean that Chrysostom approves the sloth and tepidity which keep a Christian at home rather than attending the eucharistic liturgy (cf. above paragraph 27 and note 56); rather it means we can see Christ without leaving town and making a long journey.
76 Cf. Jer 23.23. NAB poses this as a question.
77 Ps 144 (145). 18.

realize that it is not the feast day nor the assembly but a pure conscience and a life freed from sin which make the time right for communion.[78] The man whose conscience is free from fault should approach this table every day.[79] But for the man who is in the grip of his sins and is unrepentant, it is perilous to approach this table even on the feast. For surely coming once a year does not free us from the reproach of our sins if we draw near to the table with an unworthy heart. In fact, our condemnation is the greater because, even though we come but once a year, on that one occasion we approach the table with an uncleansed soul.

(36) Therefore, I exhort all of you not to take in your hands these divine mysteries[80] because you feel that the feast forces you to do so. If ever you should be going to share in this holy sacrificial offering, I urge you to cleanse your hearts many days before. How? By repenting, praying, giving alms, and devoting your efforts to things of the spirit.[81] Do not, like a dog, turn yourself back again to your own vomit.[82]

---

78 Even though they are unworthy, many thoughtless Christians approach the altar because it is the feast of Christ's Nativity. But the feast does not make the time right; first, they must repent their sins and cleanse their souls.

79 Montfaucon notes (PG 48.867) that at Alexandria the eucharistic liturgy was celebrated three times a week. At Antioch there would seem to have been no restriction. But see Baur 1.190–91, 197. St. Augustine tells us that his mother, Monica, had attended Mass daily (*Confessions* 9.13.36, trans. V. Bourke in FOTC 21.261). See also *Against Judaizing Christians* (FOTC 68.xxiv,60). The present passage seems to confirm the practice to which Augustine and Chrysostom allude.

80 This is a clear reference to the practice of receiving communion in the hand. Cf. Chrysostom's *Baptismal Instructions* (ACW 31.177;329–31, where sources are quoted, e.g., Theodore of Mopsuestia, *Catechesis* 16.27–28 [trans. R. Tonneau and R. Devreesse in *Studi e testi* 145 (Vatican City 1949) 577–79] and Cyril of Jerusalem in *Catechesis* 22.21–22 [PG 33.1124B–25B]). For the custom of the communicants' signing their senses with the eucharist see F.J. Dölger, "Das Segnen der Sinne mit der Eucharistie," *Antike und Christentum* 3 (1932) 231–44.

81 Notice that, again, there is no mention of auricular confession to a priest. See Hom. V.56 and note 97. For almsgiving as an atonement for sin see B. Ramsey, art. cit. in *Theological Studies* 43 (1982) esp. pp. 241–47, where several Latin Fathers are cited or quoted on this point.

82 Cf. Prv 26.11 which in the LXX reads: "As when a dog goes to his own vomit and becomes abominable, so is a fool who returns in his wickedness to his own sin." Chrysostom is urging a firm purpose of amendment which will keep the sinner from returning to or repeating his sin.

(37) Is it not foolish to show such great concern for material things? Yet, many days beforehand, because the feast is coming, you select the best clothes from your wardrobe and get them ready. You buy new shoes. You prepare a more sumptuous table. You think of many means to provide for yourself in every way. You overlook nothing which will brighten your appearance and make you look stylish and smart.[83] But you take no account of your soul. It is neglected, clothed in shoddy garments, unwashed, wasted with hunger, and you let it stay uncleansed. Will you bring here to church your stylish body but overlook your soul, which is half clad and filled with disgrace? Your fellow servants see only your body, and it does them no harm no matter how you have neglected it. But the Master sees your soul and he inflicts the greatest punishment on it since you have been careless and negligent about it.

(38) Do you not know that this table is filled with a spiritual fire? Fountains gush forth with water, but this table has a kind of mysterious flame. Therefore, do not carry corn stalks or wood or hay as you approach it. You might cause a more destructive conflagration and burn your soul to ashes as it shares in the mysteries.[84] Instead of flammable things bring precious stones, gold, and silver so that you may render them purer and then depart with your profit in your heart.[85] If you have any wickedness there, drive it out and banish it from your soul. Does one of you have an enemy who has treated him with the greatest injustice? Let that man do away with his hostility; let him keep in check his soul, which is burning and swollen with hate, so that there may be no tumult or commotion in his heart.[86]

---

83 External preparations for the feast are no substitutes for true repentance since they do not cleanse the soul of its guilt.

84 The sinner should recall Paul's warning in 1 Cor 11.27–29. To approach the altar with unrepented sins on our souls is to feed fuel to a fire which will destroy us.

85 We must approach the eucharist not with the destructive fuel of unrepented sins on our souls but with gifts that cannot be destroyed by the spiritual fire of the altar, gifts which its flames will purify rather than destroy.

86 This sentence recalls the words of Jesus' new law against anger, abusive language, and contempt as recorded in Mt 5.22–25. Reconciliation will replace hatred and anger in the sinner's soul with peace.

(39) You are going to receive your king in communion. And when your king comes into your soul, it must be very tranquil and still. Your thoughts must be marked with the deepest peace. But you were treated most unjustly and you cannot bear to put aside your anger. Why, then, do you do even greater wrong and more serious harm to yourself? Whatever your enemy may do to you, he will not treat you as badly as you treat yourself if you refuse to be reconciled to him and if you keep trampling underfoot the laws of God.[87]

(40) Did your foe outrage you? Tell me, is that why you outrage God? To refuse to be reconciled to the enemy who has caused you pain is not the act of a man who is taking revenge on his foe. It is the act of a man who is outraging God, who gave us these laws. Therefore, do not look back on the foe who is your fellow servant; do not look back on how deeply he has harmed you. Rather, put God before your mind and the fear of him which you should feel. Force yourself to be reconciled to the enemy whose countless evil acts have caused you pain. Then, consider that the greater the violence you will endure in your own soul, the greater will be the honor you will enjoy from God, who gave these commandments.

(41) Just as you receive him here with great honor, so will he receive you in heaven with great glory. He will give you an infinitely richer reward because you obeyed his laws.[88] May all of you come to this reward by the grace and loving-kindness of our Lord Jesus Christ, with whom be to the Father glory, honor, power, and worship, together with the Holy Spirit for ever and ever, world without end. Amen.

---

87 Again we should recall the words of our Lord on loving our enemies, which we read in Mt 5.43–48.
88 The man who has repented and cleansed his soul will be like the blessed of the beatitudes (Mt 5.3–12) and will enjoy the same rewards.

HOMILY VII

 GAIN THE CHARIOT-RACES ARE ON,[1] and again our congregation has shrunk.[2] However, as long as you are present, our assembly could not shrink. If a farmer should see his crop in full bloom and ready for harvest, he makes little account of the fact that the leaves are falling. Since you are here as my harvest, neither do I now feel such great distress because I see that the fallen leaves are being swept away. I do grieve for the laxity of those who are not here, but still the earnestness of the loving assembly of you who are present consoles me in the pain I feel for those who are absent. Sometimes those absentees do attend our services. But, even then, they are not really present. Their bodies are here, but their minds are wandering far and wide. In your case, however, even when you are taken away from our assembly, even then you are among us. Your bodies may be elsewhere, but your minds are here in the church.

(2) I did wish to deliver a long discourse against our absentees but I have no desire to reproach those who are neither present nor listening to my words. To reprove them would

---

1 The preceding homily was delivered on December 20, 386. Hom.VII was given early in January 387, because Chrysostom mentions in Hom.VII.7 that recently he had proved the incomprehensibility of the divine essence to all created beings (cf., e.g., Hom.IV.11, 17); indeed it is clearly understood only by the three divine Persons (cf. Homilies IV.31 and V.6). The mention made of the chariot races in the opening sentence of Hom.VII led Montfaucon to conjecture that the exact date when the present homily was delivered was Sunday, January 5, 387, the day when the games in the circus were held in 387 (cf. above *Notice* II.5).

2 The opening of this exordium is quite similar to those found, e.g., in Chrysostom's sixth *Baptismal Instruction* (ACW 31.93–94); *De Laz.* 7 (PG 48.1043–46); *In s. Lucianum* (PG 50.519–21); *De Anna* 4 (PG 54.660–62); *In Rom.* 12.20 (PG 51.171). On the spectacles of the circus and the theater see Baur 1.86–90.

make it look as if I were fighting against shadows.[3] So, I shall keep my words for a time when they are here. Now, however, I shall try to guide your loving assembly, by God's grace, to your customary meadow and to the sea of the Holy Scriptures.[4] But you must pay heed and stay alert. In the case of people who are making a voyage, even if everyone else is asleep, as long as the helmsman alone is awake and alert, there is no danger. His watchfulness and navigational skill before all else, suffice to keep the ship safe.

(3) But here in church it is not the same. Even if the preacher is watchful and sober,[5] but his hearers fail to show the same vigilance, his discourse will sink in the sea and perish. Why? Because he has found no one's mind ready to hear his words. Therefore, we must be sober and watchful.[6] The merchandise and cargo in which I deal concern more important things. We are not voyaging after gold and silver and perishable things. Our journey looks to the future life and the treasures of heaven. And the paths which lead to these we will find here in church.[7] Furthermore, we will find that they are more numerous than the pathways over the land and sea.

(4) But if we lack the skill and knowledge to follow these paths, we will suffer the worst of shipwrecks. Therefore, none of you who is sailing with me must show the fearfulness of passengers who sleep aboard a ship. Rather, you must show the same watchfulness and concern as the helmsman does. While all the others are asleep, the helmsman sits at his tiller, carefully marks the pathways in the waters, and looks at the sky so far above him. And all the while the course of the stars, like a kind of finger, points out the path for him so that he may safely steer his ship.

---

3 Perhaps an echo of Plato, *Apology* 18d.

4 Chrysostom speaks of frolicking about in explicating the Scriptures, "as if I were sporting in some meadow" in his *Against Judaizing Christians* (FOTC 68) 72.

5 Cf. 1 Pt 5.8. Watchfulness and sobriety are very important virtues to Chrysostom. See Homilies IV.32, 44; V.47; VI.30; VII.6, 59.

6 Cf. ibid.

7 Rather than at the circus, chariot races, and in other worldly pursuits and pleasures.

(5) A person who has no knowledge of the sea could not sail in full daylight with such confidence and ease as the helmsman sails in the middle of the night, when the sea shows itself in a more formidable mood. Why is this? The helmsman is wide awake and quite calm as he puts to practice his skill in sailing. He keeps careful watch not only on the pathways of the sea and the courses of the stars but also on the assaults of the winds. The helmsman's wisdom and knowledge are great. So it is that many a time when the blast of a more violent gale has struck his ship and is about to swamp it, he has the wisdom to make many a quick change in the angle of his sails. He runs before the wind and puts an end to all danger from the gale. By pitting his skill against the violence of the winds' blasts, he snatches his vessel from the storm.

(6) Those sailors voyage over waters we can see and hear and feel. Although they are searching for this world's goods, they continuously keep their minds watchful and alert. All the more must we keep ourselves prepared in the same way they do. Surely, the careless man faces a greater danger, while the sober man is more secure.[8] This ship of ours is not constructed of timbers but is joined fast together by the divine Scriptures. The stars in the sky do not guide us on our way but the Sun of Justice[9] steers our ship on its course. As we sit at the tiller, we are not waiting for the blasts of wind; we are waiting for the gentle breath of the Spirit.

(7) Therefore, we must be alert and keep careful watch for the paths which we must follow. The rest of my discourse will

---

8 Again we have an echo of 1 Pt 5.8.

9 Cf. Mal 3.20 (NAB); 4.2 (LXX). C. Stuhlmueller, JBC 23:68 notes that the Sun of Justice was a common symbol in the ancient Near East. The sun, always one of the principal gods, was thought to provide warmth and life, light and law. Cf. J. Finegan, *Light from the Ancient Past* (2nd ed., Princeton 1959) 96–97. The Bible uses the same symbolism but identifies the deity as the one God, Yahweh. Cf. Ps 18(19).4–11. Chrysostom uses the Sun of Justice to mean Yahweh in *Against Judaizing Christians* (FOTC 68.5), and Christ in his *Baptismal Instructions* (ACW 31.56, 166) and in *De Laz.* 7 (PG 48.1046). In the present passage Chrysostom seems to mean the Holy Spirit. In any event, all three divine Persons are one God.

again concern itself with the glory of the only begotten.[10] Recently, I proved that the comprehension of God's essence lies far beyond the wisdom of men, angels, archangels, and, in a word, all creation.[11] I also demonstrated that the divine essence is well-known and clearly understood by the only begotten and the Holy Spirit alone.[12] Now my discourse moves on to a second stage of my wrestling with the heretics.[13] Now we ask whether the Son and the Father have the same power and might, whether they are of the same essence. Rather, this is not a question we are asking, because, by the grace of Christ, we have already found this to be true and we hold firmly to it. But now we are preparing to prove this very thing to those who shamelessly oppose these truths.[14]

(8) To be sure, I feel a blush of shame as I make ready to assail them with my arguments. Who will not laugh at me for trying to prove and demonstrate truths which are so obvious? Still, what sort of condemnation should not await the man who asks whether or not the Son is of the same nature and essence as the Father? Such a question not only contradicts the Scriptures but also is against the opinion common to all men and contrary to the very nature of things. That the one begotten is of the same substance as the one who begets is true not only of

---

10 Here we come on a phrase which, for Chrysostom, seems to be synonymous with consubstantial with the Father. He speaks of the only begotten in Homilies III.10; IV.20, 21, 25, 26, 27, 29, 30; V.4, 5, and in all these places he is demonstrating the equality of the Son with the Father in power, knowledge, and understanding. He will use the phrase "the glory of the only begotten" frequently in the following homilies, where his point will be the consubstantiality of the Father and the Son.

11 Cf. Hom.IV.11–23.

12 Cf. Homilies IV.31; V.6–8.

13 There are two possibilities for the relation between Homilies I–V and VII–X. Either we have two series of which the first deals principally with the incomprehensibility of God's nature (I–V) and the second with the consubstantiality of the Son with the Father; or we have one series consisting of two stages, as Chrysostom says. The second seems the more probable. Chrysostom now demonstrates that the Father and the Son are one in power and essence.

14 It would seem that a goodly number of Anomoeans had not succumbed to the lure of the chariot races but were present to hear Chrysostom's arguments.

men but also of animals. You could see the truth of this even in the case of trees.[15]

(9) Would it not be absurd for this law to remain fixed for plants and animals and beasts, while only in the case of God does it alter itself and change? However, so that I may not seem to be making these assertions on evidence drawn from things in our own world, let me take my proof from the Scriptures themselves and let me start my discourse on this question from this source. Then, we who believe will not make ourselves a laughing stock, but those who reject this belief and doctrine will be ridiculed and scorned because they are opposing what is so evident even when they are looking the truth straight in the face.

(10) "What is so evident," they say. "If he is of the same substance (*homoousios*) with the Father because he is called the Son, then we, too, can be of one substance with the Father. For, surely, we, too, are called his sons. The Psalmist says: 'I have said: You are gods, and all of you are the sons of the most High.' "[16] Oh, how shameless they are! How extreme is their folly! How clearly they show their madness in every way! When we were starting our discourses on the incomprehensibility of God, they were obstinately striving to claim for themselves what belongs to the only begotten alone, namely, that they know God as perfectly as God knows himself.[17] Now, when our discourse is concerned with the glory of the only begotten, they are obstinately striving to bring him down to the cheapness of their own level when they say: "We, too, are called sons."[18]

---

15 Some philosophers might find fault with this argument because it fails to draw a distinction between specific essence and individual essence. But it is the sameness of the specific divine essence (possessed by all three Persons of the Trinity) which is at issue.

16 Ps 81(82).6. Christ's own comment on this verse is found in Jn 10.35 ("He called them gods to whom the word of God was addressed.") Since it is a question of the Son's consubstantiality, however, the key clause in the verse is "all of you are sons of the most High."

17 Chrysostom no doubt is referring to such passages as Hom.I.20–23, 30–33, where the Anomoeans pretend to possess the fulness of knowledge, including knowledge of God's incomprehensible essence. See also Hom.V.5–8.

18 Again Chrysostom argues from analogy. We are all sons, but the only begotten Son is the primary analogate.

(11) But this does not in any way make us of the same substance (*homoousios*) with God. You are called a son, but he is the Son. In your case it is only a word; in his, it is a reality. You are called a son but you are not called the only begotten, as he is. You do not live "in the bosom of the Father;"[19] you are not the "brightness of his glory;"[20] you are not "the exact representation of his being;"[21] you are not "in the form of God."[22] If, then, what I said in my earlier discourses did not persuade you, let yourself be won over by these texts, and many more than these. They testify to the nobility and excellence which belong to him.

(12) When he wishes to show that his essence is in no way different from the Father's, he says: "He who has seen me has seen the Father."[23] When he wishes to show that his power differs from the power of others, he says: "I and the Father are one."[24] When he wishes to show that his power is equal to the Father's, he says: "For as the Father raises the dead and grants life, so the Son also grants life to those whom he wishes."[25] When he wishes to show that he is to receive identical worship with the Father, he says: "So that all men may honor the Son

---

19 Cf. Jn 1.18 and See Hom.IV.17–22, 25, 27, 30; V.4, 7.

20 Cf. Heb 1.3.

21 Cf. ibid.

22 Cf. Phil 2.6.

23 Cf. Jn 14.9. During the discourse at the Last Supper, Philip asked Jesus to "show us the Father" (ibid. 8). As B. Vawter comments (JBC 63:144), this would have been an extraordinary manifestation, and the response of Jesus (ibid. 9) shows that Philip must learn that the only vision of God vouchsafed in this world is through Jesus Christ. Jesus' reply, for Chrysostom, is clear evidence that Father and Son are one in essence.

24 Jn 10.30. Again the comment of B. Vawter (JBC 63:119) is much to the point. Father and Son are one in mind, will, and action. Jesus does not say merely that he and the Father are "at one" but are "one thing." This was how the Jews understood him, for they accused him of blasphemy and picked up rocks with which to stone him.

25 Jn 5.21. One exercise of the Son's divine power will be the raising of the dead to life. As B. Vawter remarks (JBC 63:84) this also means not only the final resurrection, of which Christ's resurrection is the principle (cf. 1 Cor 15.20–23), but the gift of new life in the here and now, the life of grace which is the beginning of the life of glory (cf. Jn 11.25–26).

just as they honor the Father."[26] And when he wishes to show he has the same authority to amend the law, he says: "My Father works, and I work."[27]

(13) But these heretics ignore all these texts. They do not understand the name "Son" in its proper meaning because they, too, have been honored by being greeted as sons. So they bring the Son down to the same cheap level as themselves when they quote the Psalmist's words: "I have said: You are gods, and all of you are sons of the most High."[28] Because of the fact that you are greeted as sons, you are saying that the Son is no greater than you and, for this reason, is in no way a true Son. Then, because you have been greeted as gods (since God gave you a share in this name), perhaps you will be obstinate and contend that the Father is no greater than you. For just as the Psalmist called you sons, so also did he call you gods. However, even though you are called gods, you do not dare to say that, in this case, the name has no difference in meaning but you agree that the Father is true God.[29] In the same way, in the case of the Son, you must never be so bold as to thrust yourself forward and say: "I, too, have been called a son. Since I am not of the same essence as the Father, neither should the Son be of that same essence."[30]

(14) Yet, all the texts I have enumerated show that he is a true Son and of the same essence as the Father. When the Son says that he is of the same form and an exact representation,[31] what is he proving to us other than that his being is no different from the Father's? For in God there is neither form nor face. But the heretic will say: "You cited these texts; now quote the

---

26 Jn 5.23.
27 Cf. Jn 5.17 and NAB note ad loc. Cf. Hom.XII.42, 48, 50, 52.
28 Cf. Ps 81(82).6 and NAB note on Ps 82.6.
29 The Anomoeans here admit that the name "gods" is applied to them by analogy, i.e., the name is applied to God and men in meaning partly the same and partly different. Therefore, men are not divine as God is.
30 Here the Anomoeans apply the name son to the only begotten Son and to themselves in the univocal sense. As applied to Christ and themselves, it has exactly the same meaning. Therefore neither they nor Christ can be of the same essence as the Father.
31 Cf. Phil 2.6 and Heb 1.3 and see paragraph 11 above.

ones which show the opposite." What texts show the opposite? "Texts such as that which shows that he prays to the Father. If he has the same might and is of the same substance and does all things with power, why does he pray?"

(15) I shall not only cite those texts but I shall also carefully set forth all the others in which he is spoken of as lowly and abased. But first I must tell you that I can give many reasons which justify the texts where he is spoken of in lowly fashion. You, however, can give no explanation for the passages which show him as exalted and glorious other than that he wished to show us his nobility and excellence. If this were not the case, there would be a conflict and contradiction in the Scriptures. He did say: "For as the Father raises the dead and grants them life, so the Son also grants life to those to whom he wishes,"[32] and the other things I quoted. And, again, he did pray whenever he had to pray. And there you see a contradiction. But if I set forth the reasons, all cause for doubting is removed.

(16) What are the reasons why both he and his apostles said many lowly and abasing things about him? The first reason is also the most important, namely, that he was clothed with flesh and he wished all men, both of those days and of later ages, to believe that what they saw was not simply a shadow or an apparent form but a true nature.[33] And the apostles did say many lowly and human things about him, as he did about himself. Even at that, the devil was able to persuade some pitiful and miserable men to deny the plan of redemption and to dare to say that he did not take on flesh. By doing this, they took away the entire basis of his humanity. If Christ had not said these lowly and human things about himself, how few there would have been who would not have fallen into this ruinous doctrine?

---

32 Cf. Jn 5.21 and see note 25 above.
33 The plan of salvation rests on the Incarnation whereby Christ, while remaining God, took upon himself a true human nature and became like us in all things except sin. Those who held that his human nature was a mere phantom and that Christ was not truly man were the Docetists. See the Index s.v. Docetism. Cf. paragraph 34 and 47 below.

(17) Do you not still hear, even today, that Marcion,[34] Manichaeus,[35] Valentinus,[36] and many others denied the plan of redemption in the flesh? This is why Christ says many things which are human and lowly, things which fall far short of that ineffable essence of his. He does so to prove and guarantee the plan of redemption. The devil has striven with all his strength to take this faith away from men because he knew that if he destroys man's belief in the plan of redemption, it would be all over with most of the things we hold as true.

(18) Over and above this reason, there is also another, namely, the weakness of the men who heard him.[37] Those who

---

34 Marcion, born in Pontus ca. 110, a Gnostic heretic whose Christology is that of Docetism. The archheretic denounced in Polycarp's *Epistle to the Philippians* (7.1) is Marcion. Quasten 1.78 quotes the pertinent passage. "For everyone who shall not confess that Jesus Christ is come in the flesh is antichrist: and whoso shall not confess the testimony of the Cross is of the devil: and whoso shall distort the words of the Lord to his own desires, and say that there is neither resurrection nor judgment, this is the firstborn of Satan." For fuller accounts of Marcion and the Marcionites see J. P. Arendzen, "Marcionites," CE 9.645–49; A. A. Stephenson, "Marcion," NCE 9.193–194; F. L. Cross, *The Early Christian Fathers* (London 1960) 64–65; H. Jonas, *The Gnostic Religion* (2nd ed. Boston 1963) 137–46.

35 Manichaeus or Mani (which is a title or term of respect rather than a proper name) was born in Babylonia ca. 215. He professed a religion of pure reason as opposed to "Christian credulity." He was a true Gnostic who held that salvation is to be gained by knowledge. His Christology was pure Docetism since his Christ only appeared to be a man who seemed to live, suffer, and die to symbolize the light (as opposed to the darkness) suffering in this world. For fuller accounts of Manichaeus and Manichaeism see J. P. Arendzen, "Manichaeism," CE 9.591–97; J. Ries, "Manichaeism," NCE 9.153–60; G. Bardy, "Manichéisme," DTC 9.2. 1841–95.

36 Valentinus, one of the most influential of the Gnostic heretics, was Egyptian-born but died in Crete ca. 160. He held that man, the highest being in the lower world, shares in both a spiritual and material nature. The work of redemption consists in freeing the higher, the spiritual, from its servitude to the lower, and this work was the mission of Christ and the Holy Spirit. The Christology of Valentinus is extremely confusing. But he is clearly a Docetist since he held that Christ did not have a real body and, therefore, did not suffer. For fuller accounts see J. Quispel, "The Original Doctrine of Valentine," *Vigiliae christianae* 1 (1947) 43–73; P. J. Healy, "Valentinus and Valentinians," CE 15.256; G. W. MacRae, "Valentinus," NCE 14. 518–19; H. Jonas, *The Gnostic Religion* (2nd ed. Boston 1963) 174–205; G. Bardy, "Valentin," DTC 15.2. 2497–2519.

37 This is part of the process of condescension and accommodation, which Chrysostom defined in Hom.III.15. Here, however, it is a case of Christ speaking in his human nature and suiting his words to the limited capacities of his listeners.

were then seeing him and hearing him for the first time could not accept the more sublime words of his teaching. What I am saying is not guesswork and I shall try to prove this to you from the Scriptures themselves. I shall also try to show that if he were ever to say anything great, sublime, and worthy of his glory—but why do I say great, sublime, and worthy of his glory?—if ever he were to have said anything beyond the grasp of human nature, the men who heard him would be upset and scandalized. But if he ever were to say something in a lowly and human fashion, they would run to him and accept what he said.

(19) The heretic will ask: "Where can I see this?" You can see it especially in the Gospel of John. When John said: "Abraham your father rejoiced that he might see my day. He saw it and was glad. They said: You are not yet fifty years old and have you seen Abraham?"[38] Do you see how they reacted to him as if he were a mere man?[39] What, then, did he say to them? He said: " 'Before Abraham came to be, I am.'[40] And they took up stones to cast at him."[41] And when he was speaking at length about the mysteries, he said: "The bread which I shall give for the life of the world is my flesh."[42] And some of his disciples then said: "This is a hard saying. Who can listen to it?"[43] And what was the result? "From this time on many of his disciples turned back and no longer went about with him."[44]

(20) Tell me, what was he to do? Was he to waste his time constantly by speaking more sublime words, frighten off the souls he hunted, and drive everyone away from his teaching?

---

38 Cf. Jn 8.56–57 and NAB note ad loc.

39 And, therefore, not divine. In his *Demonstration*, Chrysostom constantly affirms the divinity of Christ by stating that he was "no mere man."

40 Cf. Jn 8.58–59. B. Vawter, JBC 63:48, states that this is one of Jesus' most emphatic affirmations concerning his divine nature. Certainly the Jews took it as such and considered Jesus' statement as blasphemous.

41 Cf. ibid. 59. Vawter (ibid.) comments that many have objected to this verse because the temple courtyard was not a likely place for stones to be found. However, the fact that Herod's temple was still under construction would explain the presence of stones and other debris.

42 Jn 6.51 and NAB note ad loc.

43 Jn 6.60.

44 Jn 6.66.

This would not be in keeping with God's loving-kindness. Surely, when he said again: "He who hears my word will not taste death forever,"[45] the Jews asked him: "Do we not say well that you have a devil? Abraham died and the prophets died, and you say that he who hears my word will not taste death?"[46] And is it any wonder that the crowds felt this way when even their leaders shared this feeling?[47]

(21) Nicodemus was himself one of their leaders and, in a spirit of good will, he came to Jesus and said: "We know that you are a teacher come from God."[48] But he could not accept Christ's words on baptism because they were far too strong for his weakness. For Christ had said: "Unless a man be born of water and the Spirit, he cannot see the kingdom of God."[49] Then Nicodemus fell prey to human suspicions and asked: "How can a man be born when he is old? He cannot enter a second time into his mother's womb and be born again, can he?"[50] How did Christ reply? "If I told you about earthly things and you did not believe, how will you believe if I tell you about the things of heaven?"[51] All Christ was doing was offering a defense and explaining why he did not continually speak of his birth from above.

---

45 Cf. Jn 8.51. To accept Jesus' teaching will lead to eternal life.

46 Cf. ibid.

47 Pharisees were among the crowd (cf. Jn 8.12) and probably were the ones offering objections to Jesus' discourse.

48 Jn 3.2. Nicodemus was a Pharisee who secretly came to Jesus at night. This event preceded the discourses to which Chrysostom alludes in paragraphs 19 and 20.

49 Cf. Jn 3.5 and NAB note ad loc. Since Nicodemus replies with verse 4, it would have been more apposite if Chrysostom had quoted instead verse 3, which reads: "Unless a man be born from above, he cannot see the kingdom of God (cf. NAB note ad loc.)." Of course, Chrysostom's citation could either be a conflation of verses 3 and 5 or a copyist's confusion of the two verses. Nicodemus' reply (verse 4) does add the word anōthen, "from above" (from verse 3?) Furthermore, anōthen can have a temporal meaning, "again", and verse 3 and 4 could mean "be born again" or "reborn."

50 Cf. Jn 3.4.

51 Jn 3.12. B. Vawter, JBC 63:69, says that up to this point Jesus has been speaking of what should be comparatively easy to understand, at least by analogies. In this sense, rebirth and the presence of the Spirit are "earthly things." If Nicodemus cannot understand these, if they cannot bring him to faith in Jesus' true character, then he is obviously in no position to receive the revelation of "heavenly things," that is, mysteries of which faith alone can provide the basis for understanding.

(22) Again, at the very time of the crucifixion, after his countless miracles, after many a demonstration of his power, when he said: "You will see the Son of Man coming upon the clouds,"[52] the high priest could not endure what Jesus said and tore his garments.[53] How, then, would he have had to speak to those men who would put up with nothing sublime? It is no wonder that he said nothing at all great or lofty about himself to men who were so weak and were crawling along the ground.[54]

(23) What I have already said would be enough to prove that this was the reason and excuse for the lowly and abject words he spoke while here on earth. And I shall try to make this clear from the opposite side. You just saw that if Christ ever said anything great or lofty, the people were scandalized, they were upset, they turned away, they reviled him, and they avoided him. Now I shall try to show you that, if he said anything lowly or mean, they ran to him and accepted his teaching.

(24) At another time, he said: "Of myself I can do nothing; I preach only what my Father has taught me."[55] Then, those who before had turned away from him immediately ran to him. Since the evangelist wished to show us that they believed because what Jesus said was lowly and humble, he gave us an indication of this when he said: "When he was speaking these things, many believed in him."[56] And in many other places you can find that this same thing happened. This is why Christ often said that this same thing happened. This is why Christ often said many things in a quite human fashion and, again, why he often said much which was not spoken in a human fashion but in a way suited to God and worthy of his nobility and excellence. He spoke as man when he was accommodating himself and condescending to the weakness of those who heard him. He spoke as befitted his divinity when he was

---

52 Cf. Mt 26.64.
53 Cf. ibid. 65.
54 Chrysostom describes the Anomoeans as "crawling along the ground" in Homilies III.6 and IV.27. Here, of course, he means the Jews of Christ's own day.
55 Cf. Jn 8.28.
56 Jn. 8.30.

taking care to give a sound and correct statement of his doctrines.

(25) If his accommodation and condescension penetrated all he said, it would have done harm to men of later ages in their conception of his dignity.[57] So he did not neglect this portion [of his future Church]. Even though he foresaw that men of his own day would not listen but would revile him and turn away, nonetheless he did speak as he did so as to establish the very point I mentioned and to show the reason why he intermingled lowly statements with the sublime. And this reason was that they were not yet able to accept the lofty and sublime things he was saying.[58]

(26) If he were not willing and ready to accommodate himself, it would be useless to teach sublime doctrines to those who would not listen or turn their attention to them. As it is, even if it were of no benefit to them, yet it did instruct us, it did prepare us to have a suitable conception of him, and it did persuade us that he changed to a more lowly mode of discourse because these people could not yet accept the lofty and sublime things he was saying. Therefore, when you see that he is saying lowly and humble things, do not think that this is a mark of any meanness in his essence. See it as an accommodation and condescension on his part because the understanding of his hearers was weak.

(27) Do you wish me to give you a third reason? He did and said things which were lowly and humble not only because he was clothed in flesh and because of the weakness of those who heard him but also because he wished those who were listening to be humble in their minds and hearts. And this is the third reason. If someone is teaching humility of heart, he does this not only by what he says but by what he does. He is moderate in both word and deed. Christ said: "Learn of me because I am meek and humble of heart."[59] And again in another place: "The Son of Man did not come to be served but to serve."[60]

---

57 I.e., Christians of later ages might have found it difficult to accept that Christ was divine as well as human.
58 See paragraph 18 above.
59 Cf. Mt 11.29.
60 Cf. Mt 20.28.

When he taught us to be humble and never to run for the first places[61] but in every case to accept being regarded as inferior, he persuaded us to this both by what he said and what he did. And this gave him many an opportunity to speak in humble and lowly fashion.

(28) I can also give you a fourth reason which is no less important than the ones I have already mentioned. What is this reason? It is to prevent us from ever falling into a belief that there is only one person in God because the three realities of the three persons are so ineffably close. Even though Christ rarely said anything on such a topic, some men have already slipped into this impious doctrine. When Sabellius, the Libyan, heard Christ saying: "The Father and I are one," and "Whoever has seen me has seen the Father,"[62] he took the closeness shown to the Father as expressed in these words and turned it into a basis for impiety and a belief that the Father and the Son were one person and not two distinct personal realities.

(29) These are not the only reasons. Christ was also trying to prevent anyone from believing that he was the first and unbegotten substance and from supposing that he was greater than the Father who had begotten him. Certainly it is clear that Paul feared this very thing, namely, that someone might at some time surmise that this was the case and hold to this wicked and unholy belief. So after Paul had said: "For he must reign until he shall put his enemies under his feet,"[63] and then had added: "He has put all things under his feet,"[64] he then went on to say further: "Except the one who subjected all things to him."[65] And Paul would not have gone on to note that exception unless

---

61 Cf. Lk 14.7–11.

62 Jn 10.30; 14.9. Sabellius (3rd century), as Chrysostom says, held that Father and Son were but a single Person. He became the leader of the Monarchians and was excommunicated by Pope Callistus ca. 220, but his Modalist followers were still strong until the fifth century. See above Introduction 16 and notes 24 and 25 for literature.

63 1 Cor 15.25. NAB's translation replaces the Greek pronoun *autos* with "Christ" in English and reads, "Christ must reign," while the Greek says, "He must reign." Cf. Ps 109(110).1.

64 Cf. 1 Cor 15.27.

65 Cf. ibid. The meaning is that the Father, who subjected all things to Christ, is excluded from among the things subjected.

he felt a fear that somehow some such diabolical belief might arise.

(30) Oftentimes, too, when Christ was trying to soften the ill will of the Jews, he retreated from the sublimity of what he was saying and often made his reply in the light of the suspicious minds of those who were talking with him. This was the case when he said: "If I bear witness concerning myself, my witness is not true."[66] He spoke in this way because he was striving to refute the suspicion of the Jews. Surely, he did not wish to show that his witness was untrue. What he was saying was this: "You Jews suspect my witness and do not consider it as true because you do not wish to accept me when I am speaking about myself."

(31) And we can find many other reasons, too. We could give many explanations for the lowliness and humility of his words. But I want you heretics to give just one reason for his sublime teachings other than the one I have already mentioned, namely, his wish to show us his own nobility and excellence.[67] But you could not give any other explanation.

(32) A person who is great might speak of himself as something small, and this would involve no accusation or charge. Rather, this is a mark of his modesty and goodness. But if a lowly person should ever say something great about himself, he will not escape accusation. His words are a mark of imposture and pretense. This is why we all praise a man who is lofty and sublime when he speaks about himself in lowly fashion. But no one will praise the lowly man if he should ever boast that he is greater than he is.

(33) The result of this is that even if the Son were far inferior to the Father, as you heretics say he is, then he ought never to have said anything to prove that he is equal to the

---

66 Jn 5.31. As B. Vawter (JBC 63:86) says, Jesus here accepts the general principle in human jurisprudence that a man is not to be taken simply at his own word. He needs the testimony of others. In verse 36 he brings forward a supportive witness: the works the Father has given him to do testify that the Father has sent him. But the Jews do not believe the Father because they do not hear the Father nor do they have the Father's words abiding in their hearts.

67 Cf. above paragraph 15.

Father. This would be imposture and pretense. However, the fact that he who is equal to the Father says something which is lowly and demeaning about himself gives us no cause to accuse him. Rather, this is a high commendation and deserves our greatest admiration.

(34) I would like to make what I said still clearer and I would like you all to know that I am not launching an attack against the divine Scriptures. So come, now, and let us take up the first of the reasons we mentioned. Let us show where, because he is clothed in flesh, he speaks words which are beneath the dignity of his divine essence. And if you wish, let us put before our minds the very prayer which he made to the Father.[68]

(35) But pay careful attention to me for I wish to recount the entire matter to you from a somewhat lofty point of view. There was a supper on that holy night on which he was going to be betrayed. I call it a holy night because the countless blessings, which would come throughout the world in accordance with the plan of redemption, had their beginning on that night.[69] It was on that night when the traitor was sitting with the eleven disciples and, while they were at supper, that Christ said: "One of you will betray me."[70] Please keep these words in mind so that, when we come to the prayer, we may see why he prayed as he did.

(36) Please consider, too, the solicitude of the Master. He did not say: "Judas will betray me." He did not make the traitor's act more shameless by accusing him in the presence of the others. But when Judas' conscience pricked him and he said: "Is it I, Lord?," Christ said to him: "You have said it."[71] Not even at that time did he permit himself to make a specific accusation against Judas but he did let Judas disclose his own guilt. But not even this made Judas a better man. For he received the morsel and then went out.[72]

---

68 The prayer to the Father is that uttered during Christ's agony in the garden, recounted in Mt 26.39.
69 The Last Supper marked the institution of the Holy Eucharist and led up to the passion, death, resurrection and ascension of Our Lord.
70 Mt 26.21.
71 Mt 26.25.
72 Cf. Jn 13.30. This morsel was not the Eucharist. See CCHS 1005.

(37) After Judas left, Jesus turned his attention to his disciples and said: "You will all be scandalized because of me."[73] When Peter denied this and said: "Even though all shall be scandalized, I will never be scandalized,"[74] again Jesus said: "Amen I say to you, before a cock crows, you will deny me thrice."[75] When Peter again denied he would do so, Jesus let him alone. What Jesus was telling Peter was: "You do not believe what I say and you keep denying my words. But your very own deeds will persuade you that you must not contradict your Lord." And again, I ask you, please remember these words and keep them in mind. Recalling them will be useful for us when we are examining Christ's prayer.

(38) Christ spoke of the betrayer, he foretold that all would run away, he predicted his own death. "I shall smite the shepherd and the sheep will be scattered."[76] He foretold who was going to deny him, when he would do so, and how many times it would happen. He predicted everything accurately. After he had foretold all these things as a sufficient proof that he possessed knowledge of what was going to happen, he went to a certain villa to pray. The heretics say that the prayer is the prayer of the divinity;[77] we say it is the prayer of the plan of redemption.

(39) You be the judges and, by the very glory of the only begotten, cast your vote so as to show favor to no man. Even if I am pleading my case before friends,[78] I pray and beseech you

---

73 Cf. Mt 26.31. As J. McKenzie says (JBC 43:185), "scandalized" means that the apostles' messianic hopes for Jesus will be disappointed. NAB translates it: "Your faith in me will be shaken."

74 Cf. Mt 26.33. J. McKenzie (JBC ibid.) points out that Peter's excessive self-confidence will be followed by a fall more grievous than the fall of the others; the rest will be offended and their faith shaken, but Peter will deny Christ three times before dawn.

75 Cf. Mt 26.34. Jesus predicts Peter's triple denial.

76 Cf. Mt 26.31. J. McKenzie (JBC ibid.) notes that, as given here, the text is an inexact quotation of Zec 13.7 which reads: "Smite the shepherds and draw out the sheep, and I will bring my hand against the little ones." But the point is clear; the group will be helpless when they lose the leadership of Jesus, until the Spirit descends upon them.

77 But the divinity would be a divinity inferior to the Father's.

78 This proves that Chrysostom's purpose is not only to refute the heretics but also to instruct and confirm the orthodox in his congregation.

that your judgment be impartial and not made to win my favor
or to win the enmity of the heretics. That the prayer is not a
prayer of the divinity is especially clear from this: God does not
pray; it is a mark of his divinity to be worshipped. God receives
a prayer; he does not offer one. Still, because the heretics are so
shameless, I shall try to make it clear to you from the very
words of the prayer that it belongs to the plan of redemption
and to Christ's weakness in the flesh.[79] For whenever Christ
says something of a lowly nature, what he says is so mean and
lowly that the surpassing humility of his words can persuade
even those who are extremely obstinate and contentious that
the words he speaks fall far short of that sacred and ineffable
essence.[80]

(40) Let us, then, turn to the words of the prayer. "Father, if
it is possible, let this cup pass away from me; yet not as I will but
as you will."[81] Let us question those heretics at this point. Does
Christ not know whether it is possible or impossible? A short
while before, at the supper, he said: "One of you will betray
me."[82] And: "It is written, 'I will smite the shepherd, and the
sheep will be scattered.' " And: "You will be scandalized because of me."[83] And when he spoke to Peter, he said: "You will
deny me," even: "You will deny me three times."[84] But now,
when he is praying, does he not know whether it is possible or
impossible? Tell me. Who could say that, no matter what his
frame of mind?

(41) If the time ever comes when no prophet, no angel, no
archangel will know what Christ did not know, it could be that
the obstinate heretics will have some basis for their argument.
But what they say that Christ did not know is so clear and
obvious to all that even we humans have an accurate knowledge of it. How then, will the heretics find excuse or pardon

---

79 The Incarnation is the cornerstone of the plan of redemption. It was
    God's will that the Son became man to set men free.
80 I.e., Christ's divine nature as the only begotten Son.
81 Cf. Mt 26.39.
82 ibid. 21.
83 Cf. Mt 26.31.
84 Cf. ibid. 34.

for maintaining that Christ said "if it is possible" because he really did not know whether it was possible or not?

(42) It is clear that his servants, the prophets, had exact knowledge of what I am discussing. They also knew that he had to undergo death and that he had to suffer this death on the cross. Many years before, David made both these things clear when he spoke in the person of Christ and said: "They have pierced my hands and feet."[85] And David proclaimed what was going to happen as if it had already occurred. Why? Because he was showing that it is impossible for this not to have happened, just as it is impossible for what has already happened not to happen. Again, Isaiah foretold this same death when he said: "He was led as a sheep to the slaughter and was dumb as a lamb before his shearer."[86] When John saw this lamb again, he said: "Behold the Lamb of God, who takes away the sin of the world."[87] And he spoke these words as a prediction.

(43) Notice that the Lamb was not mentioned merely as a lamb, for John added the words "of God." Since there was another lamb, namely, the Jewish lamb, John spoke in this way to show that the Lamb of which he was speaking is the Lamb of God. The Jewish lamb was offered only for the Jewish nation; the Lamb of God was offered for the whole world. The blood of the Jewish lamb only kept wounds from the body; the blood of the Lamb of God cleansed all the world. The blood of the Jewish lamb could not do what it did by its own nature; it had that power because it was a type of the Lamb of God.

(44) So where are those who were saying that Christ is a Son and we are sons?[88] Where are those who are trying to drag him

---

85 Cf. Ps 21(22).18 and NAB note ad loc.

86 Cf. Is 53.7.

87 Cf. Jn 1.29. The exact meaning of "Lamb of God" is not sure in the minds of many modern biblical scholars. Some (as does Chrysostom) see a reference to the Passover lamb; others (and probably Jn) see it as referring to the servant of the Lord of Is 53.7–12, where the servant is compared to a lamb and is said to bear the iniquities of many. The words "who takes away the sins of the world" seem to favor the servant figure, since the Passover lamb, although it protected the people of Israel from destruction, had no connection with sin. For further interpretations see B. Vawter, JBC 63:52. Notice that Chrysostom sees the Baptist as speaking these words as a prediction of the passion.

88 See above paragraphs 10–11.

down to our cheap and mean condition because we share in the same title? Look! [You heard] *lamb* and *Lamb*, one name indeed but an infinite difference between each nature. When you hear a common designation here, let no thought of equality enter your mind. So, when you hear *son* and *Son* in this context, do not drag the only begotten down to your mean condition. But why must I speak of what has already been proved? If the prayer is a prayer made by his divinity, Christ will be revealed as attacking, contradicting, and fighting against himself.[89] For he who said in this prayer: "Father, if it be possible, let this cup pass from me,"[90] because he shrank back from and shunned the passion, was the same Christ who said, in another place, that the Son of Man must be betrayed and scourged.[91]

(45) Then, after he had heard Peter say: "Far be it from you, O Lord; this will never happen to you,"[92] Christ objected to this so strongly that he said: "Get away from me, Satan (*satana*)! You are an obstacle (*skandalon*) in my path. These thoughts of yours are men's thoughts, not God's."[93] Even though a short while before he had praised Peter and had called him blessed, he now called him Satan. Christ did not do this to insult Peter. What he wished to show by this affront was that Peter had not spoken from his heart. Indeed, what Peter said was so unlike his usual self that Christ did not hesitate to call him Satan even though he was Peter.

(46) Again, in another place, Christ said: "I have greatly

---

89 Because God does not pray; it is a mark of his divinity to be worshiped. Cf. above paragraph 39.

90 Cf. Mt 26.39.

91 Cf. Lk 18.31–33; Mt 16.21; Mk 8.31.

92 Cf. Mt 16.22.

93 Cf. ibid. 23. Peter's remonstrance to Christ's prediction of his passion, death, and resurrection occurs immediately after Peter's confession that Jesus is the Messiah, the Son of the living God (ibid. 16; cf. NAB notes ad loc.). Jesus' response to this confession was to name Peter the rock on which he would build his Church and to entrust to him the keys of the kingdom (ibid. 18–19 and NAB notes ad loc.). This makes Jesus' rebuke all the more telling. As J. McKenzie remakrs (JBC 43:116), the revelation of Jesus as Messiah was more easily received than the revelation that the Messiah must suffer, die, and rise. Peter's opposition to this makes him an obstacle (*scandalon*) and an adversary (*satana*) to the fulfillment of the plan of redemption. See below Hom.VIII.28.

desired to eat this Pasch with you."[94] Why, then, did he say "this Pasch" even though at other times he had observed this feast with them? Why, then? Because the cross would follow this Pasch. And, again, he said: "Father, glorify your Son so that your Son may glorify you."[95] To be sure, in many places we find him foretelling the passion,[96] desiring that it come to pass,[97] and saying that this was the reason he had come into the world.[98] How is it, then, that in his prayer he says: "If it be possible?" He is showing the weakness which belongs to a human nature. And human nature would prefer not to be torn from the present life; it would draw back and shrink from death.[99] Why? Because God has implanted in human nature a love for the life of this world.

(47) Even after he had said so many things of this sort, some men still made so bold as to maintain that Christ had not assumed flesh.[100] What would they have dared to say if Christ had said nothing of this kind? Here we have the reason why, in those places in which he foretells his passion and desires that it come to pass, he speaks as God; but, as man, he shuns it and prays to avert it. Nonetheless, he shows us that he went wil-

---

94 Cf. Lk 22.15.

95 Cf. Jn 17.1. Glory is a complex theological concept which evolves throughout the OT and exhibits several aspects. Its basic meaning is weight and, as applied to men, it connotes importance. The glory of God appears as a brilliant light visible to men only when it is veiled by a cloud. Later OT books show it as a visible manifestation of God's divinity and a recognition of that divinity. In the synoptic gospels glory reflects the OT uses of the word, as does Acts, but adds the brilliance of the glory of Jesus which is manifested by anticipation in his Transfiguration. Once we do read (Lk 24.26) that Jesus will arrive at his glory through his passion and death. Paul adds the hope that Christians will rise to glory. They will be glorified with Christ by sharing in his passion. In John the mutual glory of Jesus and the Father is prominent. In the present text, the glorification of Jesus is his passion, death, and resurrection. This is the supreme manifestation of the holiness of the Father and his greatest saving act. See J. McKenzie, DB 313–15. Also B. Vawter, JBC 63:45 and 70:30–32.

96 E.g., Mt 16.21; 17.22–23; 20.18–19; Mk 8.31; 9.31; 10.33–34; Lk 9.22, 44; 17.25; 18.31; Jn 10.12, 17.

97 E.g., Mt 23.37; Lk 13.34; 22.15.

98 E.g., Jn 3.16, 17; 6.51; 8.12; 12.47; 13.1; 18.37.

99 Christ has a true human nature and human nature shrinks from death. See below paragraphs 52–53.

100 I.e., the Docetists. See above paragraphs 16–17 and notes 33–36.

lingly to his passion when he said: "I have the power to lay down my life and I have the power to take it up. No one takes it from me, but I lay it down of myself."[101]

(48) How is it, then, that he says: "Not as I will, but as you will?"[102] And why do you wonder that, before the crucifixion, he was so eager to give a guarantee that his flesh was true flesh? Even after the resurrection, when he saw the disciple who doubted, he did not refuse to show him both his wounds and the marks of the nails and to submit his scars to the touch of the hand. In fact, he said: "Feel and see; for a spirit does not have flesh and bones."[103] This is why he did not, from the very beginning, assume a mature manhood. He allowed himself to be conceived, born, nourished with milk. He spent so long a time in this world so that he might prove that he was true flesh both by the length of his days on earth and by every other means. Angels often appeared on earth in the form of man, as did God himself. But their appearances were not in true flesh but by an accommodation and a condescension.

(49) To prevent you from thinking that his coming to earth was an accommodation, as those others were, and to give you solid grounds for truly believing that his was real flesh, he was conceived, born, and nurtured. That his birth might be made manifest and become common knowledge, he was laid in a manger,[104] not in some small room but in a lodging place before a throng of people.[105] This was the reason for the swaddling clothes and also for the prophecies spoken long before. The prophecies showed not only that he was going to be a man but also that he would be conceived, born, and nurtured as any child would be. Isaiah proclaimed this when he said: "Behold, the virgin will conceive and bear a son, and they will call his

---

101 Cf. Jn 10.18. Chrysostom inverts the first and second parts of the verse.
102 Cf. Mt 26.39.
103 Cf. Lk 24.39.
104 Cf. Lk 2.6–7.
105 The "throng of people" either was or included the shepherds (Lk 2.8–18) and, later, the magi (Mt 2.9–11).

name Immanuel. He eats butter and honey."[106] And again, the same prophet said: "A child is born to us, a son is given to us."[107] Do you see how these prophecies foretold his infancy?

(50) So ask the heretics these questions. Is God afraid? Does he hesitate and shrink back? Does he feel pain? If they answer that he does, stay away from them and make them stand at the devil's side, or even deeper in hell than the devil. For even Satan will not dare to say this. But if they say that none of these feelings is worthy of God, then tell them that neither does Christ pray as God.

(51) Furthermore, if the words of Christ's prayer are the words of God, there is another absurdity involved. For the words not only reveal a struggle but they point to two wills opposed to each other: one, the Son's, and the other, the Father's. Christ's words: "Not as I will but as you will"[108] are the words of one who is making this clear. But those heretics never conceded this. When we constantly quote the text: "The Father and I are one"[109] in connection with his power, they keep saying that this was said in connection with the will because they maintain that the will of the Father and of the Son is one.[110]

(52) However, if the will of the Father and the Son is one, how is it that Christ says in this text: "Yet not as I will but as you

---

106 Cf. Is 7.14 and NAB note ad loc. See Hom.V.15.
107 Cf. Is 9.5 and NAB note ad loc. See also Hom.V.15.
108 Cf. Mt 26.39.
109 Jn 10.30.
110 The doctrine that there is one divine will because there is only one divine Person grows out of Modalistic Monarchianism and Docetic Christology such as that held by Marcion, Manichaeus, and Valentinus (see above paragraph 17 and notes 34–36). The Anomoeans would deny that both a divine nature and a human nature are united in the one Person of the Logos "without confusion and without change, without severance and without separation." If rightly understood, this statement of the Council of Chalcedon (A.D. 451) implies one subject of predication and a twofold principle of operation—one Christ to whom, by reason of the hypostatic union, both human and divine actions are attributed, and two natures from each of which its own proper activity proceeds without interference from the other. See B. J. Otten, *A Manual of the History of Dogmas*, vol. 1 (3rd ed. St. Louis 1922) 422. As Chrysostom understands it (in simpler terms), Christ is one divine Person possessing two natures and two wills, of which the one nature and will are divine, while the other nature and will belong to him as true man. Each nature and will has its own proper activities.

will?"[111] For if this statement had been made with a view to his divinity, there is a contradiction, and many absurdities arise from it. But if it was said in his flesh, the statement is reasonable, and there could be no grounds for blame or reproach. If the flesh does not wish to die, it should not be condemned. To shun death is according to its nature.[112] And Christ gives abundant proof of every aspect of his human nature—except sin.[113] And he did this so as to block up the mouths of the heretics.

(53) Therefore, when he says: "If it is possible, let this cup pass from me" and "Not as I will but as you will,"[114] he is showing nothing other than that he is clothed in flesh, and that the flesh fears death. For it is a mark of the flesh that it fears death, shrinks back from it, and struggles against it. At that time, he left his flesh deserted and stripped of any divine power of operation to show its weakness and to confirm its nature. At other times, he conceals it so that you may know that he is not merely a man.

(54) If he never showed forth anything except what was proper to man, people would have believed that he was only a man. If he never accomplished anything except what was proper to his divinity, no one would ever have believed in the plan of redemption. This is why he varies and mingles both his words and his deeds. He does not wish to provide an excuse or pretext for the mad sickness of Paul of Samosata,[115] of Marcion, and of Manichaeus.[116] This is why, as God, he foretells what will come to pass and, as man, he shrinks back from it.

(55) I would like to have gone through all the other reasons, too. I would like to have shown from his very deeds that, just as

---

111 Cf. Mt 26.39.
112 Cf. above paragraph 46.
113 Cf. Heb 4.15.
114 Cf. Mt 26.39.
115 Paul of Samosata, a bishop of Antioch about the year 260 held to a modalist form of Adoptionism which denied the divinity of Christ and held that Jesus was a mere man to whom God had revealed himself more than to any other prophet. Cf. G. Bardy, *Paul de Samosate* (Louvain-Paris 1923). Chrysostom calls his teachings "mad" and "insane" in his *Commentary on John* (FOTC 33, pp. 45, 81, 164, 393) and links his name with Marcion (ibid. 41.4). See Cayré vol. 1, 175–76.
116 For Marcion and Manichaeus see above notes 34 and 35.

in this case his prayer showed the weakness of the flesh, so again, in other places, he prayed so as to set aright and correct the weakness of his hearers.[117] We must not think that everything which he said in a humble and lowly vein was said only because he was clothed in human flesh. He also spoke in this way because of the other reasons I mentioned.[118] But so that the abundance of topics still to be discussed may not overwhelm and destroy the many things I have already said, I will put a stop to my discourse against the heretics and postpone to another day what I have still to say against them. Now I shall again turn to exhort you to pray.

(56) It is true that I have often spoken to you on this subject. But there is still a need to speak on it even at this time. Clothes which have been dipped in dye just once have a color which easily fades. Those which the dyers frequently dip in and draw out of the vat keep the brightness of this color unchanged. This also happens where our souls are concerned. When we hear the same words time and time again, we accept the teaching; like a cloth dipped in dye, we do not easily reject it.

(57) Therefore, let us not listen as if my words were trifling or incidental. There is nothing which has as much power or more power than prayer. A king clad in a purple robe is not so splendid as the man who, because he is praying, is adorned by his conversation with God. Suppose the whole army is present, along with many generals, state officials, and consuls. At that moment, suppose someone comes forward and holds a private conversation with the king. He turns every eye to himself and makes everyone regard him as worthy of greater respect. Surely, it would be the same with those who pray.[119]

(58) Consider, then, how great a thing it will be when the angels are present, when the archangels are standing there together with the seraphim, cherubim, and all the heavenly powers. Suppose, then, that this mere human can come forward and, with great confidence, can converse with the king of

---

117 Cf. above paragraphs 18–26.
118 Cf. above paragraphs 27–30.
119 For a similar passage and argument see Chrysostom's *Baptismal Instructions* (ACW 31) 115.

these heavenly powers. How great an honor would it take to match this? Not only honor but the greatest benefit could come to us from prayer, even before we obtain our request. As soon as a man has raised his hands to heaven, as soon as he has called upon God, he has immediately put away human affairs. In his mind, he has gone over to the future life and, thereafter, thinks of the things of heaven. He has nothing in common with the life of this world, as long as he is praying and as long as his prayer is offered with diligence and care.

(59) Then, even if anger boils up, it is easily cooled. If passion flares forth, the flames are readily quenched. If envy consumes us, it is not difficult to drive it away. The same thing happens which the prophet says happens when the sun rises. What did he say? "You made the darkness and it was night. In it all the wild beasts of the forest will go forth, even young lions roaring for prey and to seek meat for themselves from God. The sun arose and they were gathered together and shall lie down in their dens."[120] At sunrise, then, every wild beast is driven off and slinks away to its lair. So, too, when a prayer, like a ray of the sun, arises from our tongue and comes forth from our mouth, our mind is enlightened, all the savage passions which destroy our reason slink away and flee to their own lairs, if only our prayer is diligent, if only it comes from a watchful soul and sober mind.[121] Should the devil be on hand when we pray, he is driven off; should a demon be there, he slinks away.

(60) When a master is talking with his servant, no other servant—even one who has the confidence and freedom to address the master—would dare to come forward and disturb the conversation. Much less would any of those who have given offense and are deprived of this freedom to speak be able to disturb us while we are conversing with God and showing him the esteem which befits him.

(61) Surely, prayer is a harbor for those caught in a storm; it is an anchor for those tossed by the waves; it is a staff for those who stumble. Prayer is a treasure for the poor, security for the rich, a cure for the sick, a safeguard for those in good health. It

120 Ps 103(104).20–22.
121 Cf. 1 Pt 5.8.

keeps our blessings inviolable and quickly changes our ills to good. If temptation comes, it is easily repelled. If loss of possessions or any of the other things which cause grief to our souls befall us, prayer is quick to drive them all away. Prayer is a refuge from every sorrow, a basis for cheerfulness, a means for continual pleasure, a mother for our philosophy and way of life.[122]

(62) Even if the man who can pray with diligence is destitute of all things, he is richer than any other man. Yet, one who has been robbed and deprived of prayer may sit on the very throne of a king, but he is poorer than the poorest man. Was Ahab not a king and did he not have treasures beyond telling of silver and gold?[123] But since he did not have prayer, he went around searching for Elijah, a man who had neither a cloak to clothe him nor a place to lodge.[124] All he had was a sheepskin.[125] Tell me, Ahab, what does this mean? You have so many storehouses and are you looking for a man who has nothing? "Yes," he says. "For of what use are my storehouses to me since this man has locked up the heavens and made all my possessions worthless?"[126] Do you see how Elijah was more wealthy than Ahab? Until Elijah spoke, the king and his whole army were in dire need.

(63) What a marvellous thing! He did not have a cloak but he locked off the heavens. He locked off the heavens for this very reason, namely, because he did not have a cloak. Because he possessed nothing here on earth, for this very reason he gave proof of his great power. For he merely opened his lips and caused countless treasures of blessings to be brought down from the heavens. O, the mouth which had within it the

---

122 "Philosophy", in the Christian context, is the true doctrine, the Christian way of life, and it is often associated with piety. Cf. H. Graef, *St. Gregory of Nyssa* (ACW 18) 190 note 93 on *philosophia*.

123 Cf. 1 Kgs (3 Kgs) 20.3–17.

124 Cf. ibid. 19.9. Elijah had to take shelter in a cave.

125 Cf. ibid. 19.13. Elijah had a rough wooly skin (*mēlōtē*), not an outer garment made of cloth (*himation*).

126 These words of Ahab do not appear in 1 Kgs, but in 1 Kgs (3 Kgs) 17.1 Elijah swears to Ahab that no rain will fall on Israel except "by the word of my mouth." The drought lasted for three years. See J. McKenzie, DB 231–32.

fountains of rain! O, the tongue which made the showers pour down! O, the voice which teemed with countless blessings![127]

(64) Let us turn our eyes constantly on this man who was poor yet rich, who was rich because he was poor. Then let us scorn the things of this life and long for the things of the life to come. For in this way we shall win all the good things both here and hereafter. May all of you gain these blessings by the grace and loving-kindness of our Lord Jesus Christ, with whom be glory to the Father, together with the Holy Spirit now and forever, world without end. Amen.

---

127 The end of the drought is recounted in 1 Kgs (3 Kgs) 18.41–45 but the story is told with much less drama than Chrysostom's words imply.

HOMILY VIII

ESTERDAY[1] WE RETURNED FROM WAR, from a war and battle with the heretics. Our weapons were stained with blood, the sword of my discourse was red with gore. We did not strike down their bodies but we did destroy their arguments and "Every proud pretension which raises itself against the knowledge of God."[2] For such is the kind of battle this is and, therefore, such is the nature of the weapons. Paul instructed us on both these points when he said: "For the weapons of our warfare are not carnal, but powerful before God for demolishing strongholds and destroying arguments and every proud pretension that raises itself against the knowledge of God."[3]

(2) It would be fitting to mention again the fortunes and misfortunes of war which occurred yesterday. At least it would benefit those who were not here then if we should again give an account of the battle lines, the conflict, the victory, the trophies of the enemy's rout. But I do not wish to make you more careless.[4] So I shall pass over this account in the hope that those

---

1 Evidently the present homily was delivered on the day following the delivery of Hom.VII; it also follows Hom.VII in the older MSS and in the edition of Fronton du Duc, as Montfaucon tells us in *Notice* II.1 above. Chrysostom's description of his battle with the heretics as a bloody one is, of course, rhetorical exaggeration, as he immediately explains.

2 Cf. 2 Cor 10.5.

3 Cf. ibid. 4–5. Paul sees the preaching of the gospel as a warfare. Anything opposed to God and his ways can be called an enemy stronghold. The arguments are the fallacious arguments raised up against Paul's teaching. The knowledge of God is belief in and service of God according to the principles of the gospel, and their application to concrete cases. See J. O'Rourke, JBC 52:33.

4 To recapitulate yesterday's arguments might make more careless those who had preferred the chariot races to Chrysostom's homily and the mysteries. Therefore, the absentees must learn the contents of Hom.VII from those who were present.

of you who did not come yesterday may feel stung by this loss and become more earnest to hear again, one after another, the topics I shall touch upon today. If anyone of yesterday's absentees is earnest and alert, he will find out what I said then from those who were here. Certainly, those who heard me showed such enthusiasm that they went home only after they had listened to my every word and had let nothing I said escape them.

(3) Therefore, you will find out what I had to say from them. But what I have to say today I myself will tell you. I will put before you an objection which the sons of the heretics[5] have advanced against me. What is this objection? Yesterday[6] I was discussing the power of the only begotten and I showed that his power is equal to the power of the Father who begot him. And I spent many a word on this subject. Although they[7] were stunned and confounded by the arguments I gave, they have now advanced against me a gospel text spoken in a different place, a text which they suspected had also been spoken with a contradictory meaning. They raised their objection by saying: "Indeed, it is written: 'But as for sitting at my right hand and at my left, that is not mine to give. That is for those for whom it has been prepared by my Father.'"[8]

(4) I again give your loving assembly the same exhortation which I always give. Today I warn and advise you not to go

---

5 "Sons of the heretics" may mean disciples of the heretics or members of some Anomoean guild or association. This conjecture is based on the expression "sons of the prophets" found in the "prediction–fulfillment" stories of e.g., 1 Kgs (3 Kgs) 20–42. As P. Ellis says (JBC 10:41), the men in these stories are not prophets but disciples or, as the Hebrew expression puts it, "sons of the prophets," i.e., men of strong Yahwistic faith who lived a common life in loose associations or guilds. See *Against Judaizing Christians* (FOTC 68.74–77 and notes). The "sons of the heretics" may have formed a similar heretical group among the Anomoeans.

6 The word used for "yesterday" here is *prōēn* and may refer only to Hom.VII. Or it may mean "recently" (see Hom.IV.1 note 1) and then it could include Homilies IV and V, which also discuss the equality of power of the Son and the Father.

7 "They" would be the "sons of the heretics" who were present to hear all three homilies (IV, V, VII) or certainly Hom.VII. Evidently the chariot races did not blunt their zeal for argumentation and debate.

8 Mt 20.23.

merely to what is written but to search out the meaning of what is said. If a person should busy himself simply with the words, if he should search for nothing more than what has been written, he will fall into many errors.[9] The written words say that God has wings when the prophet says: "You will protect me in the shadow of your wings."[10] But we will not on that account say that God's spiritual and indestructible essence is winged. If we cannot say this about men, much less can we say it about the undefiled, invisible, and incomprehensible nature of God.[11] What, then, are we to understand by the wings? The help, security, shelter, defense, and unconquerable aid which God gives us.[12]

(5) Again, the Scriptures speak of God as asleep when the psalmist says: "Arise! Why do you sleep, O Lord?"[13] He does not say this to make us suspect that God sleeps. This would be the utmost madness. By the word "sleep" the psalm shows God's patience and forbearance toward us. Another prophet has said: "You will not be like a man who sleeps, will you?"[14] Do you not see that we need much help from our understanding and reason when we are searching into the treasure house of the divine Scriptures? If we listen to the words only, if we do

---

9 Chrysostom does not here mean that one must search for allegorical meanings in the Scripture as did the school of Alexandria. He means that the literal meaning must not be simply read and accepted. The reader must search into what he reads to discover the deeper meaning of the text before him. The examples which follow make this clear.

10 Ps 16(17).8.

11 The literal meaning is indefensible a fortiori.

12 As R. Murphy says in JBC 35:34, this psalm is the lament of an individual unjustly accused. The "wings" are an allusion to the wings of the cherubim over the Ark on which Yahweh is enthroned. Yahweh and his angels will help and defend the accused, who is seeking the shelter and security which come from God.

13 Cf. Ps 43(44).24. R. Murphy (JBC 35:60) characterizes the psalm as a lament of the community during some catastrophe that we can no longer specify. Israel's suffering is a martyrdom, a bearing witness, a motive to move God to intervene. Because of God's patience and forbearance with the sins of Israel, he is thought of as sleeping, as hiding his face. Now the Israelites pray for God to arise to help and redeem them.

14 Jer 14.9 (LXX). NAB reads: "Why are you like a man dumbfounded?" Again we have a collective lament of the Israelites who are suffering from a drought. Their hope is in the forbearance of God.

not think but take the words as they come, not only will those absurdities follow but many a conflict will be seen in what has been said.

(6) One man says that God sleeps, and another says that he does not sleep. Yet both statements are true if you understand the words in the proper way. The man who says that God is sleeping is pointing out God's forbearance and patience; the one who says he is not sleeping makes clear that God's nature is pure and undefiled. Since we need so much help from our understanding and reason, let us not take simply in one sense the statement: "It is not mine to give, but it belongs to those for whom it has been prepared by my Father."[15] This statement does not take away Christ's power nor does it cut off his authority. Rather, it shows his great care and wisdom and foresight in behalf of our human race.

(7) To prove that he is Lord and can mete out punishment or honor, listen to what he himself said when he spoke these words: "When the Son of Man will come in the glory of his Father, he will set the sheep at his right hand and the goats on the left. And he will say to those on his right hand, 'Come, blessed of my Father, take possession of the kingdom prepared for you from the foundation of the world. For I was hungry, and you gave me food; I was thirsty, and you gave me drink.' Then he will say to those on his left hand, 'Depart from me, you cursed, into the fire which was prepared for the devil and his angels. For I was hungry, and you gave me no food; I was thirsty, and you gave me no drink; I was a stranger, and you did not take me in.' "[16] Did you see his perfect judgment and how he gives both honor and punishment? He can award crowns and he can visit with vengeance. Some he leads into the kingdom and others he sends down into Gehenna.[17]

(8) But notice the great care he shows for us here. When he was speaking to those who would receive crowns, he said:

---

15 Mt 20.23.
16 Cf. Mt 25.31–43 which Chrysostom summarizes with some omissions and changes.
17 Gehenna is the place of fiery punishment for the wicked. See J. McKenzie, DB 299–300.

"Come, blessed of my Father, take possession of the kingdom prepared for you before the foundation of the world."[18] But he did not say to those who would be punished: "Depart from me, you cursed, into the fire prepared for you," but, "Into the fire prepared for the devil."[19] What he is saying is this: "I have made ready the kingdom for men. But it was not for men that I prepared Gehenna but for the devil and his angels. If you showed by the life you lived that you deserve punishment and vengeance, you would be correct in setting that down to your own account." And see how strong is his inclination to show his love for mankind. Even though they had not yet entered the contest, crowns were prepared for them beforehand, and prizes had been made ready for the victors. For he said: "Take possession of the kingdom prepared for you before the foundation of the world."[20]

(9) And you could see something somewhat like this in the parable of the ten virgins.[21] When the bridegroom was about to arrive, the foolish virgins said to the wise ones: "Give us some of your oil."[22] But the wise ones said: "No, for fear that there may not be enough for you and for us."[23] But the Scripture is not speaking here about oil or a lamp flame; rather, it is speaking about virginity and love of one's fellow man. It puts virginity in the place of the lamp flame and almsgiving in the place of the oil. It does this to show that virginity has great need of love for one's fellow man and cannot reach salvation without it.[24]

(10) But who are those who sell the oil? None other than the poor, for they give rather than take. Surely, you must not think of giving alms to the poor as an expense but as a source of income. It is not an outlay of money but it is a profitable

---

18 Cf. Mt 25.34.
19 Cf. ibid. 41.
20 Cf. ibid. 34.
21 We find this parable in Mt 25.1–13.
22 Cf. Mt 25.8.
23 Cf. ibid. 9.
24 The point seems to be that as the lamp flame needs oil, so virginity must give alms. Those virgins who had no oil (and therefore gave no alms) were shut out of the wedding feast. See below paragraphs 14–15.

business.[25] For you get back more than you give. You give
bread and get back eternal life. You give a coat and get back a
garment of immortality. You give your house to be shared and
you get back a heavenly kingdom. You offer perishable things
and you receive things which last forever.[26]

(11) But someone will say: "How could I give alms? I am a
poor man." When you are poor, then most of all can you give
alms.[27] Because the rich man is drunk with abundance of his
wealth, because he is sick with a very severe fever, because he is
gripped by insatiable desire, he always wants to increase his
possessions.[28] The poor man is free from this illness and
cleansed of this disease. Therefore, he will give more readily of
what resources he has.

(12) An amount of wealth does not by its nature produce
almsgiving, but the amount of good intention does.[29] There
was a time when that widow put two small coins in the collection box and she surpassed those who were proud of their
wealth.[30] And the other widow entertained that lofty soul with a
handful of meal and a little oil.[31] Their poverty proved to be no

---

25 The poor give their oil, i.e., the opportunity for almsgiving. And almsgiving makes possible an exchange of temporal for eternal goods. Hence, it is
a profitable business. See B. Ramsey, art. cit., *Theological Studies* 43 (1982)
247.

26 We have here an echo of Mt 25.35–36.

27 See B. Ramsey, art. cit. 240–41, who cites Augustine, Ambrose, and
Jerome in support of his position.

28 The man of wealth who fails to give alms is like the greedy rich fool in the
parable recounted in Lk 12.16–21, who grew rich for himself instead of
growing rich in the sight of God. Cf. Ramsey, art. cit. 240.

29 Ramsey (ibid. 240–41) quotes St. Jerome, *Treatise on the Psalms* 112(111)
where Jerome says (CCSL 78.233): "is a person in such a position, who has
nothing to give to anyone else, to be numbered among the unjust? But the
failure to give alms is a sin on the part of one who has something to give,
while one who has nothing to give is blameless so long as he has the desire
to give."

30 Cf. Mk 12.41–44; Lk 21.1–4; Hom.VI.12 for the incident of the widow's
mite.

31 Cf. 1 Kgs (3 Kgs) 17.8–17. Again we have an example of a widow in
extreme poverty, but because her intention is good and she believes the
promise of the Lord, she gives to Elijah ("that lofty soul") from her small
store. This widow lived in Zarepheth (modern Sarafend) nine miles south
of Sidon near the coast. Cf. P. Ellis, JBC 10:40 and P. Fannon, *A New
Catholic Commentary on Holy Scripture*, ed. R. Fuller et al. (London 1969)
336.

hindrance to either of these women. Do not, then, make idle and senseless excuses. God does not demand a large contribution but he does require a wealth of good intention. The spirit of almsgiving is not shown by the measure of what has been given but by the willingness of those who give.[32]

(13) Are you poor and more poverty-stricken than any man? Surely, you are not more destitute than that widow who surpassed the rich and far outdid them in generosity. Are you in want of the very necessity of food to eat? Surely, you are not in greater need than the widow of Sidon. She had fallen to the extreme depths of hunger and was expecting soon to die.[33] The throng of her children[34] stood around her, but not even in these circumstances did she hestitate to give what little she had. Yet, with her extreme poverty she bought boundless wealth. She turned her handful of meal into a threshing floor and her little jug into an oil press.[35] From a little, she made an abundance gush forth.

(14) But let us stop our constant digressions and return to the point we were making. When the bridegroom was about to come, the virgins were talking to each other. The sensible ones sent the foolish ones to the oil dealers, but it was already too late for them to buy oil. And this is quite reasonable. Dealers are found only in the present life. After one departs from this world, and the theater audience has dispersed, one cannot find a remedy for the things which have already happened. There is neither pardon nor defense but, for all future time, one must pay the penalty.[36]

---

32 We have a proof of this in the narrative of the rich man and Lazarus in Lk 16.19–31. The rich man was not condemned for his wealth but for his unwillingness to share it with those in need.

33 Cf. 1 Kgs (3 Kgs) 17.12.

34 Only one son is mentioned in the Scriptural account. When he later fell sick and stopped breathing, Elijah brought him back to life and restored him to his mother. Cf. 1 Kgs (3 Kgs) 17.17–24.

35 Cf. ibid. 16.

36 The parable of the virgins is really teaching the Christian community to be ever ready to meet the Lord at his second coming. Chrysostom sees in the parable not only the coming of the bridegroom but the day when he will separate the sheep from the goats and judge the living and the dead.

(15) And this is what occurred at the time of the wedding. When the bridegroom came, the sensible virgins went in because their lamps were lighted. But the foolish ones came too late to get in. When they knocked on the doors of the bridal chamber, they heard those dreadful words: "Go away. I do not know you."[37] Do you not see that here again he rewards with honor and metes out punishment, that he gives crowns and takes vengeance, that he both welcomes and sends away since he is the master of two kinds of judgments? You could see this also in the parables of the vineyard[38] and of the five, two, and one talents.[39] The servants who received the five and the two talents were welcomed by their master, and he put them in charge of more important affairs. But he ordered the servant who had received one talent to be bound and thrown into the darkness outside.

(16) But what is this shrewd argument of these heretics? Rather, what is this argument which is so filled with madness? The heretics admit that Christ says that he has the power to grant crowns and to chastise, to take vengeance and give rewards. But they then add that Christ also said that it was not his to grant the highest place of dignity or the loftiest honor.[40] Still, if you heretics know that nothing has been taken from his power to judge, why will you never put aside this untimely obstinacy of yours?

(17) Listen to Christ again when he says: "The Father does not judge any man but he has given all judgment to the Son."[41]

---

37 Cf. Mt 25.12.
38 Cf. Mk 12.1–9. E. Mally (JBC 42:70) calls this unique among Jesus' parables because it is an allegory of how Israel's rejection of the prophets was climaxed by the slaying of Jesus, and how God consequently dispossessed Israel of its birthright. An early Christian would have been more likely to answer the question asked in verse 9 by speaking of the son's return, referring to Christ's parousia.
39 Cf. Mt 23.14–30 and see Lk 19.12–27. This parable appears to have no reference to the parousia either hidden or overt. It does, however, show a master capable of two kinds of judgments—rewards or punishments. This, of course, is precisely what Chrysostom is out to prove.
40 As in the case of the sons of Zebedee. Cf. Mt 20.23.
41 Cf. Jn 5.22. Just as the Son has the power to raise the dead to life, he also has the work of judgment, a divine prerogative the Father has "given" to him (cf. ibid. 3.35).

If, therefore, he has all judgment, nothing has been taken from his power of judgment. He who has all judgment has the power to grant crowns to all and to exact punishment from all. Your loving assembly must not understand the words "he has given" in any human sense. The Father has not given what the Son did not already have, the Father did not beget a Son who was imperfect, the Son did not have something added to him after he was begotten. The words "he has given" mean this: the Father begot the Son just as he himself is, that is, perfect and complete.

(18) The evangelist has used this expression so that you may not think that two Gods have been begotten but so that you may see both the root and the fruit and so that you may not think that the power of judgment was added to the Son after he was begotten. When the Son was asked in another place: "Are you, then, a king,"[42] he did not say: "I received the kingdom," he did not say that the kingdom was given to him after he was begotten, but he said: "This is why I was born."[43]

(19) If he was born a perfect and complete king, it is also clear that he is a judge and arbiter. For it is especially the mark of a king that he makes decisions and judgments both to grant honors and to punish. And another source might help you to see that he has the power to grant heavenly honors. So we shall bring forward the man who is better than all men, we shall show that Christ granted this man a crown. Then what excuse will you heretics have to deny in the future that Christ has this power to reward?

(20) Who is the one who is better than all men? Who other than that tentmaker,[44] that teacher of the entire world,[45] the one who coursed over land and sea as if equipped with wings, the chosen instrument,[46] the attendant of Christ the bride-

---

42 Cf. Jn 18.33.
43 Ibid. 37. As B. Vawter says (JBC 63:162), Jesus is not a worldly king, but a king who has "come into the world," and the essence of his kingship is to "testify to the truth."
44 Cf. Acts 18.3.
45 Cf. 1 Tm 2.7.
46 Cf. Acts 9.15.

groom, the one who planted the Church,[47] the wise builder,[48] the preacher,[49] the one who ran the course and who fought the good fight,[50] the soldier,[51] the trainer of athletes, the one who left memorials of his own virtue everywhere in the world. He was snatched up to the third heaven before his own resurrection,[52] he was caught up into paradise, he shared in the ineffable mysteries of God, he heard and spoke such things as human nature cannot speak, he enjoyed a richer grace and manifested it in many more labors.[53]

(21) To learn that he toiled more than all others, listen to him as he says: "I have labored more than any of them."[54] But if he endured more labors than all, he will receive a richer crown. "For each will receive his own reward in proportion to his labor."[55] If he will receive a crown greater than the other apostles (and no one of the apostles was his equal, but he was greater than they), it is clear that he will enjoy the loftiest honor and privilege. And who is the one who will crown him? Listen to him as he says: "I have fought the good fight, I have finished the course, I have kept the faith. For the rest, there is laid up for me a crown of justice, which the Lord, the just Judge, will give to me on that day."[56] And, "the Father does not judge any man but he has assigned all judgment to the Son."[57]

(22) And it is clear that the Son will crown him not only from this text but from the text which I now quote: "Yet not to me only but also to those who love his coming."[58] And whose coming is this? Listen to him as he says: "The saving grace of God has appeared to all men, instructing us, in order that, rejecting ungodliness and worldly lusts, we may live tempera-

---

47 Cf. 1 Cor 3.6.
48 Cf. ibid. 10.
49 Cf. 1 Tm 2.7.
50 Cf. 2 Tm 4.7.
51 Cf. ibid. 2.3.
52 Cf. 2 Cor 12.2.
53 Cf. ibid. 11.23.
54 1 Cor 15.10.
55 Cf. ibid. 3.8.
56 Cf. 2 Tm 4.7–8.
57 Cf. Jn 5.22.
58 2 Tm 4.8.

tely and justly and piously in this world, looking for the blessed hope and glorious coming of our great God and Savior, Jesus Christ."[59]

(23) Our battle against the heretics has come to an end, we have raised up our trophy for their rout, and we have brought home the victory. We have proved from all we said that Christ has the power to honor and to punish because he has all judgment, because he crowns the man who is better than all others, and because he has proclaimed him a victor. He also gave honors and meted out punishments in those parables to which I referred.

(24) Now we must drive all upset and doubt from the minds of our brothers and instruct them why it was that Christ said: "It is not mine to grant this."[60] For I think many of you are finding difficulty with these words. Therefore, to remove your difficulties and to quiet the disturbance in your souls, make your minds ready and pay attention to what I say. And I, too, must work harder. For waging war and teaching are not the same, nor is it as easy to correct one's own brother as it is to wound a foe. In the tasks of teaching and correcting I must take greater pains so as not to overlook the limb which is lame or to pass over the heart which is troubled. I am telling you not to be upset or disturbed at what I am saying. For I am going to maintain that to give a place in the kingdom is neither a prerogative of the Son nor is it a prerogative of the Father.

(25) And I proclaim in a voice louder and clearer than a trumpet's call that this is not the Son's to give nor is it the Father's. For if it was the Son's, it would also be the Father's. This is why Christ did not simply say: "That is not mine to give." What did he say? "That is not mine to give but it belongs to those for whom it has been prepared."[61] He is showing that it belongs neither to him nor to the Father but to certain others. What do the words mean? I think your anxiety has increased

---

59 Cf. Ti 2.11–13.

60 Cf. Mt 20.23. Chrysostom has ended his battle with the heretics by proving that the power of judgment belongs to Christ and that it is his prerogative to reward or punish. Now he will turn to the instruction of the orthodox in his congregation to explain why a place of honor in the kingdom is earned by those for whom it is prepared.

61 Cf. Mt 20.23.

and your souls are still more troubled and disturbed. But do not be afraid. For I shall not stop until I give you a solution. So bear with me while I go back a little further in my discussion. If I do not do this, I cannot fix everything clearly in your minds. What, then, do the words mean?

(26) The mother of the sons of Zebedee, James and John, came up to Jesus along with her sons as he was approaching Jerusalem. And she said to him: "Command that my two sons may sit, one at your right hand and one at your left hand."[62] Another evangelist says that the sons themselves made this request of Christ.[63] However, there is no discrepancy in the two accounts, although we must not pass over even these little things. The two brothers had sent their mother before them. After she had opened the door and had already spoken for them, they then presented their own petition and spoke these words even though they did not understand what their petition meant.

(27) They were apostles but they were still far from perfect. They were like fledgling birds in a nest, whose feathers were not yet firmly fixed. And you must understand that, before the crucifixion, there was much that they did not know. This is why Christ reproved them and said: "Are you still without understanding? Do you not know nor understand that it was not about bread that I said to you to beware of the leaven of the Pharisees?"[64] And at another time he said: "Many things I have to say to you, but you cannot bear them now."[65] Not only did

---

62 Mt 20.20–23. The petition asks for the first two places in the kingdom, which Zebedee's wife seems (as did her sons and the other disciples) to have thought of as an earthly one. The request may reflect some recollection of Jesus' promise that his followers would take their places on twelve thrones to judge (i.e., to rule) the twelve tribes of Israel. Cf. Mt 19.28. See H. Wansbrough, "St. Matthew," *A New Catholic Commentary on Holy Scripture*, ed. R. Fuller et al. (London 1969) 939.

63 Cf. Mk 10.35–40 where we find no mention of the mother of James and John. Chrysostom's explanation of the apparent discrepancy seems simplistic but could be valid. See H. Wansbrough, "St. Mark," op. cit. 971.

64 We seem to have here a conflation of Mt 15.16 and 16.11. Lk 12.1 makes it clear that the leaven of the Pharisees is hypocrisy. The main point here is the disciples' lack of understanding.

65 Jn 16.12. As B. Vawter says (JBC 63:151), even at the very end of his public life, there is much that Jesus cannot say and that must await the enlightening activity of the Holy Spirit after the resurrection.

they fail to understand the loftier things but oftentimes, because of their fear and cowardice, they forgot what they heard. He reproached them for this when he said: "No one of you asks me, 'where are you going?' But because I have said these things to you, sorrow has filled your heart."[66] And, again, when he was speaking of the Helper,[67] he said: "He will bring all things to your mind and will teach you."[68] And he would not have said, "He will bring to your mind," unless they had put out of their minds many of the things which he had said.

(28) I did not say these things without purpose. I said them because at one time Peter clearly made a perfect profession of faith but at another time it is just as clear that he had forgotten everything. Once he had said: "You are the Christ, the Son of the living God,"[69] and was called blessed for these words. Shortly afterwards, he committed such a sin that he was called Satan. For Christ said: "Get behind me, Satan. You are a stumbling block to me, because you do not savor the things of God but those of men."[70] What could be less perfect than the one who does not judge by God's standards but by those of men? Christ was speaking to Peter about the cross and resurrection.[71] But Peter failed to understand the profundity of Christ's words, the mystery of his teachings, and the salvation which would come to the world. So he took Christ aside and privately said to him: "May you be spared, Lord! God forbid that this happen to you!"[72]

(29) Do you see that they clearly understood nothing about the resurrection? The evangelist pointed out this very thing when he said: "As yet they did not know that he had to rise from the dead."[73] Even if they failed to understand this, they

---

66 Cf. Jn 16.5–6.
67 The Helper is the Holy Spirit, the Paraclete.
68 Cf. Jn 14.26. As B. Vawter says (JBC 63:146), it will be the function of the Spirit, following the glorification of Jesus, to complete the revelation of Christ by enlightening the Church concerning the true and full meaning of what Jesus has done and said.
69 Mt 16.16.
70 Cf. ibid. 23 and see Hom.VII.45.
71 Cf. ibid. 21 and Hom.VII.46, note 96.
72 Cf. Mt 16.22.
73 Cf. Jn 20.9 and NAB note ad loc.

were in much deeper ignorance of other things, such as the kingdom of heaven, that we are chosen as the first-fruits, and his ascension into heaven.[74] They were still confined to the ground and not yet able to fly aloft.

(30) Such was the understanding they had. They expected that the kingdom would come to him immediately in Jerusalem because they had no better grasp of what the kingdom of heaven really was. Another evangelist hinted at this when he said that they thought of it as a human kingdom. They were expecting him to enter into it, but not to go to the cross and death. Even though they had heard it ten thousand times, they could not clearly understand.[75]

(31) Since they had not yet gotten a clear and exact knowledge of his teachings, they thought that he was going to this visible kingdom and would rule in Jerusalem. So the sons of Zebedee caught up with him on the road. Because they thought they had found the opportune moment, they put their request to him. They had broken away from the throng of the disciples and, just as if the whole situation had turned out exactly as they wanted, they asked about the privilege of the first seats and about being first among the others. They asked for this because they thought everything was finished and the whole business was over and done with. They made their request because they thought that now was the time for crowns and rewards.

(32) But their request showed how utterly ignorant they were. This is not mere conjecture on my part nor does its truth depend on how plausibly I say it. To show that this is true let me bring forward a proof from Jesus himself, who understands what is secret and hidden. Listen to what he said to them after they had made their request. "You do not know what you are asking for."[76] What could be clearer than this proof? Do you see that they did not understand what they were asking for when they were talking to him about crowns and rewards and

---

74 Cf. 2 Thess 2.13.
75 Cf. Lk 24.5–12; Mt 8.31–33.
76 Mk 10.38.

the privilege of the first seats and honors even before the contest had begun?

(33) Christ was hinting at two things when he said: "You do not know what you are asking for."[77] One was that they were talking about the kingdom and that he had said nothing about this. There had been no announcement or promise about this visible kingdom on earth. The other thing was that, when they sought at this time the privilege of the first seats and the honors of heaven, when they wished to be seen as more illustrious and splendid than the others, they were not asking for these things at the right time but at a time which was all wrong. For this was not the right time for crowns or prizes; it was the time for struggles, contests, toils, sweat, wrestling rings, and battles.

(34) This, then, is the meaning of the words "You do not know what you are asking for."[78] You were talking about these rewards even though you had not yet endured toils, nor stripped for the contests. While the world still needed to be set straight, while godlessness still prevailed in power, while all men were being destroyed, you have not yet made your dash from the starting gate. You have not yet stripped yourselves for the wrestling ring.

(35) "Can you drink this cup which I shall drink and can you be baptized with the baptism with which I am baptized?"[79] Here Christ was calling his crucifixion and death a cup and a baptism. He called his cross a cup because he was coming to it[80] with pleasure; he called his death a baptism because by it he cleansed the world. Not only on this account did he call his death a baptism but also because of the ease with which he would rise again. For just as one who is baptized in water easily rises up because the nature of the water poses no hindrance,[81] so, too, Christ rose with greater ease because he had gone down into death. And this is why he calls his death a baptism..What Christ means by his question is this: "Can you be slain and die? For

---

77 Ibid.
78 Ibid.
79 Cf. ibid. (second half of verse).
80 Savile's text reads "he was drinking it" for "he was coming to it."
81 Chrysostom is naturally thinking of baptism by immersion which was the common practice in his day.

now is the right time for these things, namely, for death and danger and toils."

(36) What was their answer? They said, "We can,"[82] even though they did not know the meaning of his question. Yet they promised that they could do it because they hoped they would be repaid. Christ says to them: "You will drink the cup and you will be baptized with the baptism with which I am baptized?"[83] And by these words he meant death. And so it came to pass because James was beheaded with a sword and John died many times over.[84] However, "To sit at my right hand and at my left hand is not mine to give, but it belongs to those for whom it has been prepared."[85]

(37) What he is saying is this. "You will die and you will be slain and you will win the honor of martyrdom. However, for you to be in the first places is not mine to give; that belongs to those who are contending for the prize more eagerly and with greater earnestness." To make my meaning clearer, let us suppose that a man is a judge at the contests. Let us then suppose that a mother has two sons entered in the games. Let us suppose that she takes her two sons and comes up to the judge and says: "Command that my two sons receive the crown."

(38) What does the judge answer? The very same thing, namely, it is not mine to give. "I am a judge," he says, "and I do not make my decisions as a favor nor because people come forward to request or beg me. I distribute the prizes according to the outcome of the contests." And this above all is the mark of a good judge: he does not merely award prizes at random; he awards them to pay honor to courage. And this is what Christ is doing. He does not speak in this way to detract from his own essence. Rather, he speaks as one who is making it clear

---

82 Cf. Mk 10.39.
83 Cf. ibid., the remainder of the verse.
84 James was beheaded under Herod Agrippa in the year A.D. 42 (cf. Acts 12.2). See also, D.H. Farmer, *The Oxford Dictionary of Saints* (Oxford 1978) 207–08. As far as is known, John died a natural death but must have undergone many trials before he died. For biographical details on John (often legendary) see *Butler's Lives of the Saints* vol. 4, ed. and revised by H. Thurston and D. Attwater (New York 1965) 620–23.
85 Cf. Mt 20.23.

that it is not his alone to give but it is the contestants' to take. If it were his alone, all men would have been saved and would have come to a knowledge of the truth.[86] If it were his alone, there would not be differences in honor. For he made all of us and feels concern equally for all.

(39) But there are differences in honor. Listen to what Paul says and how he makes this clear. "One is the glory of the sun, and another the glory of the moon, and another of the stars; for star differs from star in glory."[87] And again: "If anyone builds on this foundation with gold, silver, precious stones . . ."[88] Paul spoke in this way to make clear the variety of virtue. And he said this also to show that it is impossible for those who are snoring and slumbering to enter the kingdom of heaven. That prize must be won by many tribulations.

(40) Because they enjoyed abundant love and confidence before God, [James and John] thought that they would receive other honors as well. Because Christ wished to prevent men from growing more careless and lax since they were expecting further honors, he led them away from this erroneous surmise when he said: "It is not mine to give,"[89] but yours to take, if you should show the willingness to do so. He said this so that you might show greater earnestness, more pains, and abundant zeal. He was saying: "I grant crowns to deeds, I give honors to pains, I award the prize to him who sweats. In my eyes, the strongest proof is the proof which comes from deeds."

(41) Do you see that he was not speaking idly when he said that it did not belong to him nor to the Father but to those competing in the contests, to those who were toiling and suffering hardship? This is why he said to Jerusalem: "How often did I wish to gather your children together as a hen

---

86 Cf. 1 Tm 2.4 where, as G. Denzer says (JBC 57:18), Paul clearly affirms the universal salvific will of God but does not enter into the problem of its relationship to free will in man's salvation. Again, on 1 Tm 4.10, Denzer says (JBC 57:24), that the salvific will of God and the redemptive work of Christ extend to all men but in a special way to Christians. Cf. Homilies II.55 and V.43.
87 1 Cor 15.41.
88 Cf. ibid. 3.11–12.
89 Cf. Mt 20.23.

gathers together her chicks, but you would not? Behold, your house is abandoned."[90] Do you see that it is impossible for any of the careless and lax, for any of the indolent, for any of those lying on their backs asleep ever to be saved?

(42) From this we also learn another and a mysterious truth. Bearing witness[91] is not enough to give the highest honor or the loftiest place of privilege. You see how Christ foretold to [James and John] that they would bear witness to him but that by no means would they get the first places.[92] For surely there are some who can show that they have done greater things. Christ made this clear when he said: "You shall drink of the cup that I drink, and you will be baptized with the baptism with which I am to be baptized; but as for sitting at my right hand or my left, that is not mine to give."[93]

(43) Of course, Christ does not have men sit at his side. What he is speaking of is the enjoyment of greater honor, getting the first places, being higher than all others. He talks of sitting at his right hand or his left because he is condescending and accommodating himself to what they suppose is the case. For they were seeking the first places and to be seen as greater than all others. Now this is the very thing which Christ is saying. Bearing witness alone cannot make you appear as greater than the rest and in a higher place than all the others. You will die. But for you to enjoy the highest honor is not mine to give. That belongs to those for whom it has been prepared."[94]

---

90 Cf. Lk 13.34–35. The "house" in verse 35 is the Temple.

91 This translates the Greek word *martyrion*. G. Lampe, *A Patristic Greek Lexicon* (Oxford 1961) 829 s.v., gives: "testimony, evidence, proof," as some of the meanings of the word. "Bearing witness" seems to fit the present context best. H. Delehaye's study "Martyr et Confesseur," *Analecta bollandiana* 39 (1921) 20–49, in discussing the early evidence for the meaning "witness," cites Acts 1.21–22, where the emphasis is on the selection of an eyewitness (*martyr*) for the public ministry of Christ. A similar nuance for the meaning "witness" for *martyr* and its cognate *martyrion* (bearing witness) is found in Origen (184/85–253/54) in his *Commentary on the Gospel According to John* 2.210. For evidence of Chrysostom's usage of the term *martyr* to designate a witness who sealed his testimony with his blood, see *In s. Lucianum* (PG 50.522).

92 See above paragraphs 34–36.

93 Cf. Mk 10.39–40.

94 Cf. ibid.

(44) Tell me this. For whom has it been prepared? Let us see who these blessed and thrice blessed ones are. Let us see who enjoy those shining crowns. Who, then, are they and for what deeds do they appear in such bright glory? Listen to what Christ says. The ten were indignant because James and John had broken away from the group and wanted to crown themselves with the highest honor. Now see how Christ corrected the indignation of the ten and the ambition of the two. He called them and said: "The rulers of the Gentiles lord it over them, and their great men exercise authority over them. But among you this is not so. Let him who wishes to be first among you be the last of all."[95] Do you see that this is what [James and John] wanted, namely, to become first, greater, higher, and, as I might say, rulers over them? This is why Christ took a stand against them and brought to light their secret ambition when he said: "Let him who wishes to be first among you be the servant of all."[96]

(45) What he is saying is that, if you wish the privilege of the first place and the highest honor, seek the place which is last, seek to be less worthy, more humble, less important than all, and to rank yourselves below the others. This is the virtue which gives this honor. And we have a most profitable example in the verse which follows, where he says: "For the Son of Man did not come to be served but to serve, and to give his life as a ransom for many."[97] What he is saying is this. "You can see that to humble themselves is what makes men glorious and remarkable if you look at what happened to me, even though I have no need for honor and glory.[98] Still it was by my humility that I accomplished countless good deeds." For before he humbled himself and became man, everything had perished and was destroyed. But after he humbled himself, he exalted all things.[99]

---

95 Cf. Mk 10.42–43.
96 Ibid. 44.
97 Ibid. 45.
98 Christ is the Son of the Father who has crowned the only begotten with honor and glory and has put all things under his feet. Cf. Heb 2.7–8.
99 The Incarnation and plan of redemption renewed the face of the earth.

(46) He erased the curse,[100] he triumphed over death,[101] he opened paradise.[102] He struck down sin, he opened wide the vaults of the sky, he lifted our first fruits[103] to heaven, he filled the whole world with godliness. He drove out error, he led back the truth, he made our firstfruits mount to the royal throne. He accomplished so many good deeds that neither I nor all men together could set them before your minds in words. Before he humbled himself,[104] only the angels knew him. After he humbled himself, all human nature knew him. You see how his humbling of himself did not make him have less but produced countless profits, countless deeds of virtue, and made his glory shine forth with greater brightness. God wants for nothing and has need of nothing. Yet, when he humbled himself, he produced such great good, increased his household, and extended his kingdom.[105]

(47) Why, then, are you afraid that you will become less if you humble yourself? If you do humble yourself, you will become more exalted, you will be great, you will be illustrious, you will be renowned on every side. But this will happen only when you are satisfied to become less, to face dangers, and to be put to death. First you must seek to serve, to attend to and care for all men. If you will become exalted by humbling yourself, you must be ready to do and suffer all things.

---

100 The curse is probably the Old Law (cf. Gal 3.10–13).

101 The "fires of death" may be the "trial by fire" of 1 Pt 4.12 (persecution). More likely, the reference would be a text like 2 Tm 1.10, where Christ's appearance on earth as Savior of mankind "has robbed death of its power and has brought life and immortality into clear light through the gospel."

102 Cf., e.g., Lk 23.43; 2 Cor 12.4.

103 In 1 Cor 15.20 Paul says: "Christ is now raised from the dead, the first fruits of those who have fallen asleep." Just as the offering of the firstfruits was the symbol of the dedication to God of the entire harvest, so the resurrection of Christ involves the resurrection of all who are in him. The Christian who is incorporated in Christ by baptism shares in his risen life. This final fruit of redemption in Christ will be realized for the Christian at the Lord's parousia when the dead rise in glory. See R. Kugelman, JBC 51:84.

104 I.e., before his Incarnation.

105 In his *Demonstration*, Chrysostom proves that Christ is no mere man but that his power is divine by the growth of the Church and the miraculous spread of the gospel message all over the known world. Cf. PG 48.813–14; 830–33.

(48) Ponder this, my beloved, and then let us be fully prepared to pursue humility.[106] When we shall be insulted and spat upon, when we shall be subjected to every humiliation, when we shall be dishonored and scorned, let us endure all this and be glad. Nothing is so likely to exalt us and win us glory and honor, nothing is so likely to show us as great as is the virtue of humility. May it come to pass that, while we succeed in gaining this virtue in its perfection, we may obtain all the blessings which have been promised through the grace and loving-kindness of our Lord Jesus Christ, with whom be glory and honor and worship to the Father and the Holy Spirit now and forever, world without end. Amen.

---

106 Chrysostom's exhortation to humility is not only a telling weapon against the pride and boastfulness of the Anomoeans; it also urges the orthodox in his congregation to practice the humility of Christ. In this way they may hope to attain a high place in heaven. Cf. also Hom.V.51–55 and passim in all the homilies.

HOMILY IX

ODAY,[1] LAZARUS, WHO WAS RAISED FROM THE DEAD, gives us the solution to many different problems. However, the passage which was read[2] has also, in some ways, given an opportunity for argument to the heretics and a pretext to the Jews[3] to oppose our position. However, their argument and opposition are not founded in the truth—heaven forbid!—but arise from their malicious souls. For many of the heretics are saying that the Son is not like the Father.[4] Why? Because, they say, Christ had need of prayer to raise Lazarus back to life; if he had not prayed, he would not have brought him back from the dead.[5]

(2) And how, they say, will the one who prayed be like to the one who received the prayer? For the Son offers the prayer, but the Father received the prayer of his suppliant Son.[6] But

---

1 The authenticity of this homily has been questioned by an English scholar named Hales, who aided H. Savile in preparing his Eton edition of Chrysostom in 1612. As discussed above in the Introduction (paragraphs 68–71) this judgment is certainly in error because Chrysostom refers back to the present homily on three occasions in Hom. X. Montfaucon points this out in Notice III.5. Hales objected to the method of treatment and manner of invention, which he considered inferior to Chrysostom's rhetorical skill. Montfaucon (ibid. 7) offers for consideration the possibility that this homily is an improptu work, done offhand, and delivered ex tempore to meet the arguments of the heretics based on the gospel read in that day's liturgy. This homily may not be the best in the series against the neo-Arian heretics, but it is certainly not spurious.

2 "The passage which was read" seems to be a sure indication that the story of the raising of Lazarus (e.g., Jn 11.1–46) was the gospel reading assigned for that day's eucharistic liturgy.

3 The Jews would, of course, join the Anomoeans in denying the divinity of Christ. Judaizing Christians may have shared with them in this denial.

4 This is precisely the origin of the name Anomoean and also describes one of the chief tenets of their doctrine. Cf. Introduction, paragraph 35.

5 Cf. above Hom. VII.39.

6 But see below paragraphs 17 and 18.

their argument is really a blasphemy because they do not understand that Christ prayed by way of a condescension and accommodation to the weakness of those who were present.[7] Tell me this. Who is the greater? Is it the one who washes a man's feet or the one whose feet he washes? Surely, you will never say that he who washes is greater than the one whose feet he washed.

(3) But our Savior did wash the feet of the traitor Judas, for Judas was with the other disciples.[8] Who, then, was the greater? Was the traitor Judas greater because Christ his master washed his feet? Heaven forbid! But which is the greater act of humility? Is it to wash feet or to offer a prayer? There is no question but that washing feet is the more lowly act. If Christ did not decline to do the more humble task, how would he decline to do what was more lofty? Everything Christ did in raising Lazarus was done because of the weakness of the Jews who were present, and I shall prove this as my discourse moves forward.

(4) And surely the Jews,[9] too, took a pretext from this incident to oppose our position. For they asked: "How do the Christians hold that this man is God when he did not even know the place where the dead Lazarus was lying?" And it is true that the Savior did ask the sisters of Lazarus, Martha and Mary: "Where have you laid him?"[10] Therefore, the Jews say: "Do you see that he did not know? Do you see his weakness? Is this man God? He did not even know the place!" I shall discuss it with them, even though I do not hold with what they say. I

---

7 For the incident of condescension and accommodation see above Hom.III.15.

8 For the incident of the washing of the feet at the Last Supper cf. Jn 13.1–11.

9 These Jews are the Jews of Antioch, contemporaries of Chrysostom. More likely they were Judaizing Christians (because they show familiarity with the NT) who seem to have joined with the Anomoeans in denying the divinity of Christ.

10 Jn 11.34. Chrysostom has three homilies (62–64) in his *Commentary on John* (FOTC 41.165–205) which treat of the raising of Lazarus at much greater length and throw considerable light on the present homily.

shall tell them because I wish to reject and bring dishonor on their objection.[11]

(5) You Jews are saying that Christ did not know because he said: "Where have you laid him?"[12] Then the Father also failed to know, in paradise, where Adam was hiding. For the Father went about as if he were looking for Adam in the garden. And then he said: "Adam, where are you,"[13] just as if he were asking "Where did you hide yourself?" Why did God not first mention the place where Adam used to approach him with confidence and talk with him? "Adam, where are you?"[14] And what did Adam say? "I heard your voice as you walked in the garden; I was afraid because I am naked and I hid myself."[15] If you, Jew, are calling this ignorance, then call Christ's question ignorance also. Christ indeed did ask the women who were with Martha and Mary: "Where have you laid him?"[16] But do you call this ignorance?

(6) What, then, will you say when you hear God asking Cain: "Where is your brother Abel?"[17] What will you say? If you call this a fault of ignorance on the part of the Father, then call Christ's question a fault of ignorance. Listen to another proof from the sacred Scriptures. God said to Abraham: "The outcry against Sodom and Gomorrah has to come to me. Therefore I shall go down and see whether or not their actions match the outcry against them which has come to me, so that I may know."[18]

(7) The one who knows all things before they come to pass, the God who searches hearts and minds,[19] he who knows the

---

11 Again, Chrysostom seems to mean Judaizing Christians. Orthodox Jews were not likely to be present at services in a Christian church and, hence, Chrysostom could not have carried on a discussion with them as he does here.
12 Cf. Jn 11.34.
13 Cf. Gn 3.9.
14 Ibid.
15 Ibid. 10.
16 Jn 11.34.
17 Cf. Gn 4.9.
18 Cf. Gn 18.20, 21. E. Maly (JBC 1:65) points out that the theology of these texts is primitive.
19 Cf. Ps 7.10.

thoughts of men[20] is the one and only one who has said: "Therefore, I shall go down and see whether or not their actions match the outcry against them which comes to me, so that I may know."[21] If that means that God does not know, then Christ's question means that Christ did not know. But neither was the Father in ignorance in the Old Testament nor, in the New Testament, did the Son fail to know. What, then, did the Father mean when he said: "I shall go down and see whether or not their actions match the outcry against them which comes to me, so that I may know?"[22]

(8) What the Father is saying is this: "A report came to me. But I wish again to test this rumor more exactly in the light of the facts. I do not do this because I do not know. I do it because I wish to teach men not to heed words alone nor to believe them recklessly if someone speaks them against another." Men must believe what they hear only after they have first made an exact search and considered well the proof in the light of the facts. And this is why God said in another Scriptural passage: "Believe not every word."[23] For nothing is so destructive of men's lives as for a person to give quick credence to whatever people say. The prophet David was proclaiming a divine revelation when he said: "Whoever slanders his neighbor in secret, him have I banished and pursued."[24]

(9) You saw how there was no fault of ignorance in the Savior when he said: "Where have you laid him?"[25] Nor was there any want of knowledge in the Father when he said to Adam: "Where are you,"[26] or when he said to Cain: "Where is your brother Abel,"[27] or when he said: "I shall go down and see whether or not their actions match the outcry against them which comes to me, so that I may know."[28] Is it not time now to

---

20 Cf. Ps 93 (94).11.
21 Cf. Gn 18.21.
22 Ibid.
23 Cf. Sir (Ecclus) 19.15 LXX (19.14 in NAB).
24 Cf. Ps 100 (101).5.
25 Cf. Jn 11.34.
26 Cf. Gn 3.9.
27 Cf. Gn 4.9.
28 Cf. Gn 18.21.

form ranks against those who say that it was through weakness that Christ first prayed and then raised Lazarus to life?

(10) I urge you, beloved, to pay careful attention. Lazarus died, and Jesus was not there but in Galilee. And he said to his disciples: "Our friend Lazarus is asleep."[29] Because they thought he was talking about Lazarus literally being asleep, they said to him: "Lord, if he is asleep, [his life] will be saved."[30] Therefore, Jesus told them plainly: "Lazarus is dead."[31] And then the Savior came to Jerusalem to the place where Lazarus was lying. The sister of Lazarus came to meet him and said: "Lord, if you had been here, my brother would not have died."[32] If you had been here! Woman, you are weak. At that moment Martha did not know that even if Christ were not bodily on the spot, he was present through the power of his divinity.[33] But she was measuring the teacher's power by his bodily presence.

(11) That is why Martha said to him: "Lord, if you had been here, my brother would not have died."[34] That is why she then went on to say: "Even now, I am sure that God will give you whatever you ask of him."[35] So it was in response to her request that the Savior prayed. For God has no need of prayer to raise a dead man to life. He had raised others from the dead, had he not? When he was at the town gate and met a dead man being carried to burial, he merely touched the litter and raised the corpse to life.[36] At that time he had no need to pray to restore the dead man to life, did he? And again, in another place, he only spoke a word to a dead child. He said, "Talitha koumi," that is, "little girl, get up."[37] And he gave her back to her

---

29 Jn 11.11.
30 Cf. Jn 11.12.
31 Jn 11.14.
32 Cf. Jn 11.21.
33 I.e., by his divine omnipresence.
34 Jn 11.21.
35 Ibid. 22.
36 Cf. Lk 7.11–15 and NAB note ad loc.
37 Cf. Mk 5.40–42 and see Hom.X.20 below. Chrysostom quotes Mk where the original Hebrew or Aramaic is preserved and translated.

parents in good health. He had no need to pray at that time, did he?

(12) But why do I speak of the master? Even his disciples by a word alone restored the dead to life. Did not Peter raise Tabitha from death by his word?[38] Did not Paul work many miracles by the touch of his cloak?[39] Hear now what is more incredible than these signs and wonders. The shadow of the apostles restored the dead. For the Scripture says: "The people carried the sick on mattresses so that at least Peter's shadow might fall on one or another of them, and immediately they were raised up."[40] What, then? Did the shadow of the disciples raise the dead and did the master need prayers to restore the dead to life?

(13) But the Savior prayed because of the weakness of the woman. For Martha had said to him: "Lord, if you had been here, my brother would not have died. Even now, I am sure that God will give you whatever you ask of him."[41] Then it was as if Christ had said: "Martha, you asked for prayers, and I give you prayers. The fountain is before you. Whatever size vessel a man brings, he fills it to the brim. If it is a large vessel, he gets much water. If it is a small one, he gets a little water."

(14) So Martha asked for prayers, and the Savior gave her prayers. Someone else had said: "I am not worthy for you to come under my roof. But only speak the word, 'Be it done to you,' and my boy will be cured."[42] And the Savior said to him:

---

38 The story of Peter's raising Tabitha from the dead is recounted in Acts 9.36–41.

39 That God worked many miracles through Paul is well attested in the NT (cf., e.g., Acts 15.12; Rom 15.18–19; 2 Cor 12.12) but one finds there no mention of the touch of his cloak. Perhaps Chrysostom derived this detail from one of the apocryphal Acts. See Quasten 1.130–33.

40 Cf. Acts 5.15–16. The text in Acts omits "and immediately they were raised up." It seems hardly likely that, as Chrysostom suggests, corpses were carried on the mattresses in search of the revivifying shadow of Peter. Chrysostom may mean "as good as dead" or merely be guilty of a rhetorical exaggertion. Certainly, the text of Acts specifies that the victims are sick; but in Acts 5.16 we read that the sick and those troubled by unclean spirits were all cured.

41 Jn 11.21–22.

42 Cf. Mt 8.8.

43 Ibid. 13.

"Be it done to you according to your faith."⁴³ Another man said: "Come and cure my daughter."⁴⁴ And Christ said to him: "I shall follow you."⁴⁵ Therefore, the physician applies the cure as men wish and desire it, just as at another time a woman secretly touched the hem of his robe and secretly she was cured.⁴⁶ And Martha said: "I am sure that God will give you whatever you ask him."⁴⁷ Because she asked for prayer, the Savior gives her a prayer. But it was not because he had need to pray; it was because he was accommodating himself to her weakness.⁴⁸ He was showing her that he was not opposed to God but that whatever he does, the Father also does.⁴⁹

(15) In the beginning, God shaped man, and man was an image of both the Father and the Son. For God said: "Let us make man to our image and likeness."⁵⁰ Again, when he wished to bring the thief into paradise, he immediately spoke the word and did bring him in.⁵¹ Christ had no need to pray to do this even though he had kept all men after Adam from entering there. For God put there the flaming sword to guard paradise.⁵² But by his own authority Christ opened paradise and brought in the thief.

---

44 Cf. ibid. 9.18.
45 Cf. ibid. 19.
46 Cf. Mt 9.20–22 and Lk 8.43–48.
47 Cf. Jn 11.22.
48 Since Chrysostom's prime concern is rebutting the arguments of his opponents against the divinity of Christ, his prime answer is that Jesus is praying through condescension and to accommodate himself to men's weakness. Elsewhere (e.g., Hom.VII. 16,26–30 etc.) he stresses the importance of the Incarnation in the plan of redemption.
49 See Homilies VII.12 and XII.41–42. Cf. also Jn 5.17 and NAB note ad loc.
50 Cf. Gn 1.26. As E. Maly says (JBC 2:20) "image" ordinarily means an exact copy or reproduction. The implication that man would be as God is softened by the addition of "likeness" which means there will be a resemblance or similarity between God and man but not an identity. But what Chrysostom is stressing here is the equality in power between Father and Son. "Let us" connotes a quasi-consultation between the divine Persons on creating a creature who will have the power to know and to choose. See Hom.XI.13, 17, 20, 24.
51 Cf. Lk 23.43. Cf. Chrysostom, *De cruce et latrone* 2 (PG 49. 409–11) where, on the cross, Christ promises paradise to the good thief.
52 Cf. Gn 3.24. As E. Maly says (JBC 2:29), the flaming sword is probably seen here as a flash of lightning zigzagging back and forth as a symbol of the divine anger.

(16) Master, did you bring a thief into paradise? Did your Father send Adam out of paradise for a single sin, and did you bring in the thief who was guilty of countless crimes and ten thousand acts? Did you bring him in with such ease and with a single word? And Christ says: "Yes, I did. But my Father did not oust Adam by himself and without me, nor did I bring the thief into paradise by myself and without the Father. My bringing in the thief is also the Father's act, and my Father's ousting of Adam is also my act because 'I am in the Father and the Father is in me.' "[53]

(17) So that you may see that raising the dead Lazarus was not the effect of Christ's prayer, listen to him as he prayed. What did he say? "I give you thanks because you have heard me."[54] What, then, is this? Is it a form of prayer? Is it a type of supplication? "I give you thanks because you have heard me. Yet I knew that you always hear me."[55] If you know, O Lord, that the Father always hears you, why, then, do you bother the Father with what you already know?

(18) "I know," Christ says, "that the Father always hears me, but: 'I spoke because of the people standing nearby, that all may know that you sent me.' "[56] He made no prayer for the dead man, did he? He did not beseech the Father that Lazarus might rise from the dead, did he? He did not say: "Father, command death to obey," did he? He did not say: "Father, command hell not to shut its gates but to be ready to give the dead man back," did he? What he did say was: "I spoke because of the people standing nearby, that all may know that you sent me."[57] What happened, then, was not a sign or wonder but a lesson and instruction for those who were standing nearby.

(19) You saw that he did not make the prayer for the dead man's sake but for the sake of the unbelievers standing nearby. He said: "That they may know that you sent me."[58] But the

---

53 Cf. Jn 10.38 and 14.10.

54 Cf. Jn 11.41. No specific request is mentioned, nor is it necessary since the divine will of the Father and of the Son are always at one.

55 Ibid. 41–42.

56 Cf. ibid. 42. Chrysostom is stressing the point that he is accommodating himself to the weakness of those standing nearby.

57 Cf. Jn 11.42.

58 Cf. ibid.

heretics ask: "How can we know that he sent you?" I urge you to pay very exact attention. Christ is saying: "Look, by my authority I summon the dead man. By my own power I command death. I call the Father 'Father,' I call Lazarus forth from the tomb. If it is not true that I call the Father 'Father,' then let it be untrue that I call Lazarus from the tomb. But if the Father is truly my Father, let the dead man obey my command so that his return to life may instruct those nearby."

(20) What was Christ's command? "Lazarus, come forth!"[59] When Christ prayed, the dead man did not arise. He arose when Christ said: "Lazarus, come forth!" O the tyranny of death! O the tyranny of the power which took possession of that soul! My prayer was uttered, O Hell, and do you still refuse to let his soul go? "I do refuse," Hell says. But why? "Because I was not commanded to do so. I am a prison guard here and I have in my possession one who is subject to me. If I am not commanded to do so, I will not set him free. The prayer was not made on my account but for the unbelievers who are nearby. If I am not commanded to do so, I will not set free one who is in my keeping. I am waiting for the word of command to free his soul."[60]

(21) "Lazarus, come out here!" The dead man heard the command of his master and immediately he broke the laws of death. Let the heretics be ashamed and perish from the face of the earth! Surely, Christ's word has proved that the prayer was not uttered to raise the dead man but because of the weakness of the unbelievers who were, at the moment, nearby.[61] "Lazarus, come forth!" Why did he call the dead man by name? Why? If he were to have given a general command to all the dead, he would have raised all those in the tomb back to life.

---

59 Cf. ibid. 43.

60 Hales argues that this paragraph with its apostrophies and personification of hell sounds like the work of a more youthful talent but not like Chrysostom's solid arguments (cf. *Notice* III.8). Montfaucon suggests (ibid. 11) that many such apostrophes and personifications are found in Chrysostom's works. Undoubtedly, the paragraph does give us a rhetorical tour de force such as we might expect in an extemporaneous homily.

61 Cf. Jn 11.43. Christ's command is not part of his prayer, but Chrysostom maintains that Christ's reason for it is to accommodate the weakness of those who are present. See above paragraph 2.

But he did not wish to raise them all. That is why he said: "Lazarus, come forth! I am calling you alone to come back for a time. And I am calling you before the throng here present, so that, by raising one dead man to life, I may prove my power over those who are going to die.[62] For I, who have raised one man, will raise up the whole world. For I am the resurrection and the life."[63]

(22) "Lazarus, come forth!" And the dead man came forth bound with bandages.[64] What marvellous and unexpected things Christ did! He loosed the soul from the bonds of death. He burst open the portals of hell.[65] He shattered to bits the gates of bronze and the bolts of iron. He set free the soul of Lazarus from the bonds of death. Could he not also undo the bandages which swathed the dead man? Yes, he could. But he commanded the Jews to undo the bandages with which they had bound Lazarus when the placed him in the tomb. He did this so that they might recognize the marks of the very bonds which they had put on him. He did this so that, by their own experience, they might learn from the very things which they themselves had done that this is the same Lazarus whom they had placed in the tomb. He also wished them to learn that he is

---

62 Hales finds Chrysostom's reasoning spurious here. Montfaucon, however, argues that if a decision (on authenticity) has to be made from the spuriousness of reasoning of this sort, a great number of other homilies which are clearly authentic would have to be removed from the series of genuine works (*Notice* III.9).

63 Jn 11.25. B. Vawter notes (JBC 63:125) that Jesus affirms Martha's belief in a resurrection to come, with the significant addition that its power is to be found in himself. Physical death is the common lot of mankind, but faith in Christ will bring the believer to life again in the resurrection (cf. Jn 6.40).

64 Cf. Jn 11.44. After the body of a deceased person was washed and anointed with ointments and spices, it was wrapped in linen bandages before burial. Cf. J. McKenzie, DB 110.

65 This common translation means the power of death as J. McKenzie notes (JBC 43:114) in commenting on Mt 16.18. Hell or Sheol is the biblical abode of the dead (cf. J. McKenzie, DB 800–801). In the OT "gates" is used for a fortified city itself (cf. Gn 22.17, 24.60, and Is 14.31). Hence, by shattering the gates, Christ is opening the stronghold of death to set free the soul of Lazarus.

the Christ who, according to the gracious purpose of the Father, came into the world and who has power over life and death.[66]

(23) To you, O Christ, be glory and power together with your eternal Father and your all-holy and life-giving Spirit, now and forever, world without end. Amen.

---

66 Cf. Jn 6.38–40. The omission of Chrysostom's usual exhortation may well be another indication that this homily was delivered ex tempore.

HOMILY X

URING THE PAST SEVERAL DAYS,[1] I have delivered many panegyrics. In them I took as my theme the struggles of the Apostle [Paul] and I took delight in recounting his spiritual acts of virtue. Now, indeed, it is time for me to finish repaying my debt to you,[2] and there is nothing to keep me from doing so. Because so many days have intervened, I know that you have forgotten how much I still owe you. However, I shall not on that account hide my debts but I will be very eager to pay them off. I do not do this only because I am in your debt but because it is also profitable for me.

(2) In the case of contracts in the material order, it is profitable for a borrower to forget about the man who lent him money. But when the contract is in the spiritual order, there is profit for the one who is going to pay off a debt, however large, if those who are going to be paid constantly remind him of his obligations. For in this material world, the repayment of the money releases the borrower from obligation. The money passes over to the one who is repaid, the resources of the one who pays his debt are diminished, while the wealth of the one who is paid increases. But this is not so with spiritual debts. There, it is possible to pay off the money and still hold on to it. And the strangest part is that we keep the money we owe most of all at the time when we are making the payment to others.

---

1 The "past several days" does not give a clear indication of the interval between Homilies IX and X. The reference to "many panegyrics" on the Apostle is certainly a reference to the seven homilies *De laudibus s. Pauli* given very early in 387 according to Montfaucon, although not necessarily on successive days.

2 Chrysostom uses the same example of repayment of a debt above in Hom.IV.10 and 17. Here, however, he speaks of finishing the repayment, which hints that his series is drawing to an end. And indeed this is the final homily delivered against the Anomoeans at Antioch.

(3) However, my profit is diminished and my resources are lessened if I keep my wealth buried in my mind under constant guard or if I never share it with anyone. But if I take what is in my mind and communicate it to everyone, if I let a large number of people partake and share in everything I know, my spiritual wealth will increase.[3] Surely, it is true that he who shares with others increases the wealth he has on hand, while the one who conceals his wealth diminishes his whole profit. I have as witnesses to this the men to whom the talents were given, five thousand to one, two thousand to a second, and one thousand to a third. Two of them doubled the money entrusted to them and for this they were honored. The third man kept the money to himself and shared with no one. Therefore, he could not double his money and for this he was punished.[4]

(4) As we listen to this parable and fear the punishment it recounts, let us produce for our brothers what good we have; let us not hide it away, but let us publically share it with all men. When we share with others, then we grow all the more wealthy. When we make many share as partners in our business enterprise, then will we increase our own abundance. You think that your glory is diminished when you share with many the knowledge of things which you alone know. Indeed, that is the very time when your glory and your profits will increase. I mean the moment when you trample malice underfoot, when you quench the fire of envy, when you show the great love you have for your brother. If you walk around as the only one who possesses knowledge of something, men will turn away from you and hate you as a jealous person and misanthrope. God will exact from you as a wicked person the ultimate penalty.[5]

(5) In addition to all this, grace itself will quickly abandon and desert you. Even when grain is kept lying in storehouses, it

---

3 Here we see the paradox of paying a spiritual debt, where unselfish sharing with others benefits both him who gives and him who receives.
4 Cf. the parable of the talents in Mt 25.14–30. Chrysostom alludes to the same parable in Hom.VIII.15.
5 J. McKenzie (JBC 43:176) sees the same lesson in the parable as Chrysostom does. Talents, especially those given to disciples of Christ, grow with use and wither with disuse.

is consumed because the worm eats it up.[6] But if it is brought out to the fields and planted, it finds new life and is multiplied. So, too, if a spiritual discourse is kept constantly locked in the heart, it is quickly quenched because the soul is eaten up and destroyed by an envy which makes it shrink and waste away. But if the discourse is planted in the souls of our brothers like seeds in a fertile field, the treasure is multiplied both for him who possessed it and for those who receive it.

(6) A fountain from which water is constantly drawn becomes purer and gushes forth in greater abundance; if it is covered over, it becomes choked. In the same way, if we constantly draw from our spiritual gift and words of instruction, if we continuously give them to all those who are willing to draw from them, they will then gush forth all the more. But if they are buried under an envy which is reluctant to share with others, they are choked off and finally quenched.[7] Since, then, it is so profitable for me, come and let me, to the best of my ability, make public payment of what I owe and discharge my whole debt to you.[8] But first let me recall to your minds the order·and sequence of the arguments which constitute the debt which I am under obligation to pay.

(7) You know and recall that, in my recent discourses on the glory of the only begotten, I enumerated several reasons why he condescended and accommodated himself in the manner in which he spoke.[9] I also said that on many occasions Christ spoke in humble and lowly language not only because he was clothed in flesh and his hearers were weak but also, in many

---

6 Cf. Mt 6.19. Chrysostom sees Matthew's destructible treasure as grain which can be planted in the fields of people's minds and in this way find new life and be multiplied. Again, this benefits both those who give and whose who receive. Cf. also the parable of the sower and the seed recounted in Lk 13.4–9 and Christ's explanation of its meaning (ibid. 18–23).

7 The metaphor changes but the lesson is the same as in the parable of the talents: use results in growth, disuse quenches and withers what we have to share.

8 The "whole debt" is another indication that this homily is the last of the Antioch series.

9 This is a clear reference to Hom.VII.16–30.

instances, he was teaching us to be humble in our thoughts.[10] At that time we discussed those reasons at sufficient length as well as when we recalled to your mind the prayer he made at the raising of Lazarus[11] and the prayer he offered on the cross itself.[12] I clearly proved that he uttered one of these prayers as a guarantee of the plan of redemption[13] and the other to correct the weakness of those who heard him, even though he had no need of help himself.[14]

(8) And listen to this as a proof that he did many things while he was teaching men to be humble in their thoughts. He poured water into a basin and, as if this were not enough, he tied a towel around his waist and brought himself to the utmost lowliness when he began to wash his disciples' feet.[15] And, along with the other disciples, he even washed the feet of the traitor.[16] Who would not be struck with wonder at this? He washed the feet of the one who was going to betray him.

(9) When Peter put him off and said: "You will never wash my feet,[17] Christ did not pass him by but said to him: "If I do

---

10 Cf. Hom. VII.16–18, 24, 26–27, 53–55; VIII.44–48; IX.3,11,19–21.

11 Cf. Hom.IX.17–19. This is the first of the references back to Hom.IX which guarantees the authenticity of Hom.IX. See Introduction 68–71 and Hom.IX note 1.

12 The only words spoken by Jesus on the cross discussed in the earlier homilies are those he spoke to the thief when he promised to bring him into paradise (see Hom.IX.15–16). Chrysostom must mean by the cross the whole passion event. With regard to a prayer uttered at that time Chrysostom must here be referring to Christ's prayer during the agony in the garden: "If it be possible, let this cup pass away from me; yet not as I will but as you will." Chrysostom discusses this prayer in Hom.VII.40,41,44,48,51–53.

13 This is true for the prayer uttered in Gethsemane where Christ's humanity, assumed according to the plan of redemption, experiences a natural fear of death.

14 The prayer at the raising of Lazarus was in condescension and accommodation to those around him (Jn 11.42) as we see in Hom.IX.17–19 and, in the present homily, below paragraph 18.

15 This is a repetition of, if not an allusion to the same incident recounted in Hom.IX.2–3. Cf. Jn 13.1–11.

16 Although Jn does not specify that Jesus washed Judas' feet, he must have been present because the washing occurred very shortly before Jesus predicted he would be betrayed by one of the apostles (Jn 13.21). Chrysostom states clearly in Hom.IX.3 and in the present paragraph that the traitor was present and that Jesus washed his feet. Cf. Jn 13.4–5.

17 Cf. Jn 13.8.

not wash your feet, you have no share with me."[18] Then Peter said: "Lord, not only my feet, but my hands and head as well."[19] Do you see the reverence of this disciple both when he refused and when he agreed? Even though his statements were contradictory, both were spoken from a fervent mind. Do you see, in every respect, how impetuous and worldly-minded he was?

(10) But, as I was going to say to prevent you from suspecting that Christ had a lowly nature because of the lowliness of what he did, listen to what he said to them after he washed their feet. "You call me Lord and teacher, and you say well, for so I am. If, then, I, the Lord and teacher, wash your feet, you also should do this for one another. For I have given you an example, that as I have done to you, so also you should do for each other."[20]

(11) Do you see that he did many things so as to give an example? A teacher who is full of wisdom stammers along with his stammering young students. But the teacher's stammering does not come from a lack of learning; it is a sign of the concern he feels toward the children. In the same way, Christ did not do these things because of the lowliness of his essence. He did them because he was condescending and accommodating himself to us.[21]

(12) And we must not simply pass over this. If we examine his very action by itself, see what absurdity will follow. If the one who washes is seen as more lowly than the one who is washed—and Christ is the one who washes while the disciples are those who are washed—then Christ will be more lowly than

---

18 Ibid.

19 Ibid. 9.

20 Ibid. 12–15. B. Vawter points out (JBC 63:140) that in these verses we have an explanation of Jesus' action in the washing of the feet. Not only do the disciples and all Christians share in the fruits of Jesus' lifework but they must also imitate its spirit. It is their duty to practice the humility signified by this act.

21 As a sign of his love and concern, the wise teacher comes down to the level of his stammering students. So Christ, who is Lord and teacher, comes down to the lowly state of his disciples so that he may instruct them by his example. But Christ's condescension and accommodation must not be construed as any diminution of his divine essence.

the disciples. But not even a madman would say that. Do you see, then, how wrong it is not to know the reasons why Christ did everything he did? Rather, do you see how good it is to examine all his actions with great care?[22] We must not simply say that Christ said or did something which was humble and lowly. We must also add the reason why. That is what Christ did here in the incident of the washing of the feet.

(13) Christ also hinted at the same thing in another place. First he said: "In fact, who is the greater, he who reclines at table or he who serves the meal?"[23] Then he added: "Isn't it he who reclines? Yet I am in your midst as the one who serves you."[24] He said this, and did this, because he was showing that, in many cases, he took on himself the meaner things so that he might teach the disciples and, at the same time, win them over to practice moderation.

(14) And it is clear that he endured these humiliations to teach the disciples and not because his nature was inferior. For, in another place, he said: "You know that the rulers of the gentiles lord it over them. It is not so among you. Let whoever wishes to be first among you be the servant of all. The Son of Man has not come to be served but to serve."[25] If, then, he came to serve and to teach humility, do not be upset. Do not let your heart sink if you should see him at any time or in any place acting or speaking as a servant.

(15) In this way, too, he offered many of his prayers with the same purpose. Surely, they came to him and said: "Lord, teach us to pray, as John taught his disciples." [26] Tell me, what was he to do? Was he to refuse to teach them to pray? But this is why he came, that he might lead them into the perfect way of life. Did he have to teach them? Therefore, he had to pray.

---

22 This is salutary advice for Scripture-reading and meditation.

23 Cf. Lk 22.27.

24 Ibid. Another example of Jesus' humility is here shown by his choosing the lower place.

25 Cf. Mt 20.25–28 (with omissions).

26 Cf. Lk 11.1. Christ replied to his request with the "Our Father." See R. Brown, "The Pater Noster as an Eschatological Prayer," *Theological Studies* 22 (1961) 175–208. See also Mt 6.9–13. The version in Mt gives seven petitions in the "Our Father" while that in Lk shows only five.

(16) But, the heretics will say, he had to do this only by his words. However, teaching by words does not usually persuade those who are being instructed as does teaching by deed and example. Surely, this is why he did not teach the disciples to pray merely by his own words. Rather, he constantly taught by example and he spent whole nights long in the desert praying.[27] He did this to teach us and to admonish us that, whenever we are going to converse with God, we must flee from the noise, the confusion, and the crowds. Instead, we should go off to a place which is deserted and go at a time when our solitude will not be interrupted. A mountain does not offer the only solitude; a room where there is no clamor or uproar is just as much a place of solitude.

(17) You must know that he prayed so as to condescend and accommodate himself to us. I have already proved this—especially by what I said about the events which occurred in the raising of Lazarus.[28] But other things also make this clear. For example, why is it that he did not pray in the case of his greater miracles but did pray when the wonders he wrought were less striking? If he prayed because he needed the Father's help and because his own power was inferior, he should have prayed and called on his Father to help him in all his miracles. If not in all, he should at least have done so in his greater miracles.[29]

(18) But we find that he does the opposite. He did not pray when he worked the greater miracles because he was showing us that, when he did pray, he did so in order to teach others and not because of any lack of power. Surely, when he blessed the loaves of bread, he did look up to heaven and pray.[30] He did

---

27 As he did, e.g., before selecting the twelve. Cf. Lk 6.12.

28 Here we have the second of the clear references back to Hom.IX on which Montfaucon bases his argument for the authenticity of Hom.IX. See Introduction 68–71; Montfaucon's *Notice* III.4,6; Homilies IX.1 note 1; X.11 above and paragraph 18 below.

29 Chrysostom here makes effective use of an argument a fortiori.

30 Cf. Mt 14.19; Mk 6.41; Lk 9.16; Jn 6.11. All four evangelists report the multiplication of the loaves and fishes to feed the five thousand. NAB note on Mt 14.19 points out that the ritual of blessing and distribution anticipates the Last Supper. Chrysostom sees the rite of blessing as applying to all food.

this because he was teaching not to taste the food on the table until we first gave thanks to God, who had made the food for us to eat. When he raised many from the dead, he did not pray; he prayed only when he restored Lazarus to life. As we said in our earlier discourse, the reason for this was that he was correcting the weakness of those who were then present.[31] And he, himself, gave this as the reason when he clearly stated: "I spoke because of the people standing nearby."[32] In that discourse, I gave sufficient proof that it was not the prayer but his words which raised the dead man to life.[33] Watch carefully now, so that you may have a still clearer knowledge of this.

(19) Whenever there was need to punish or to honor, to forgive sins or to make laws, whenever Christ had to do any of the much greater things, you will not find him calling on his Father to help. Nor will you find him praying. All these things, as you will discover, he did on his own authority. And I shall enumerate each of them. You must consider with great care how, in none of these instances, does he stand in need of prayer.

(20) He said: "Come, blessed of my Father, and take possession of the kingdom prepared for you."[34] And again: "Depart from me, accursed ones, into the fire made ready for the devil and his angels."[35] See how he punishes and rewards with all authority and has no need of prayer? Still again, when he had to cure the body of the paralytic, he said: "Stand up, pick up your mattress, and walk."[36] When he had to free the child from death, he said: "Little girl, get up."[37] When he had to free the paralytic from his sins, he said: "Have courage, son, your sins are forgiven."[38]

---

31 Here we have the third reference back to Hom.IX. This and the other references (cf. notes 11 and 28 above) make it certain that Hom.IX is not spurious.
32 Cf. Jn 11.42 and Hom.IX.17–19.
33 See Hom.IX ibid.
34 Mt 25.34. Cf. Hom.VIII.8.
35 Mt 25.41. Cf. Hom.VIII.8.
36 Cf. Mk 2.9–11.
37 Cf. Mk 5.41. Cf. also Hom.IX.11.
38 Mt 9.2. This refers to the cure of the paralytic at Capernaum. In Hom.XII.11–28 Chrysostom discusses the cure of the paralytic at the pool of Bethesda.

(21) And again, when he had to rebuke the demons, he said: "I say to you, wicked spirit, come out of him."[39] When he had to hold the sea in check, he said: "Quiet, be still!"[40] When he had to cleanse a man in the grip of leprosy, he said: "I do will it. Be made clean."[41] When he had to make a law, he said: "You have heard that it was said to your forefathers, 'You shall not commit murder.' What I say to you is: Whoever shall say to his brother, 'You fool,' will be liable to the fires of Gehenna."[42] Did you see that he did everything with the authority of a Master? He hurled some into gehenna, he led others into the kingdom, he cured the paralytic, he drove off the demons to their death, he forgave sins, he rebuked demons, he held the sea in check.

(22) And yet, tell me, which is the greater miracle? Is it to lead into the kingdom and to hurl into Gehenna, is it to forgive sins and make laws with authority, or is it to multiply loaves? Is it not clear and does not everybody agree that the last is not so great as the others? But, nonetheless, he did not pray when he performed the greater miracles because he was showing that, even when he did pray in the lesser miracles, he did not pray because his power lacked strength but because he was teaching those who were nearby at the time.[43]

(23) So that you may know how great a miracle it is to forgive sins, I bring forward a prophet as my witness. This prophet

---

39 Cf. Mk 5.8. This incident occurred in the Gerasene territory when Jesus drove out of a demoniac an evil spirit named Legion and sent a host of demons into a herd of swine. The herd leaped off a cliff and was drowned in the lake. Cf. Mk 5.13.

40 Cf. Mk 4.39 for the calming of the storm.

41 Mt 8.3 and see below paragraph 44 where Chrysostom explains why Jesus said: "I do will it. Be cured." See J. McKenzie (JBC 43:56) who states that "leprosy is loosely used throughout the Bible for unspecified skin diseases which were as common in the Near East of NT times as they are today. The type of disease is not pertinent to the miraculous character of the cure."

42 Cf. Mt 5.21,22 (in part). As J. McKenzie says (JBC 43:35), Jesus forbids both murder and anger, the passion which leads to murder. So, too, expressions of anger in speech (even if violent action does not follow) are totally forbidden. By getting to the roots of anger, the prohibition against murder is made all the stronger. "Gehenna" here is a place of death and destruction where sinners are punished by a fire which is eternal (cf. Mt 18.8. See J. McKenzie, DB 300).

43 Cf. Jn 11.42 and see Hom.IX.18–19 and paragraph 18 above.

shows that to forgive sins is the work of no one else but of God alone when he says: "Who is a God like you cancelling iniquities and passing over sins?"[44] And bringing souls into the kingdom is much greater than destroying death. Yet he did lead souls into the kingdom and he did this by his own power.[45] To pass laws is not the task of those who are subjects but of those who rule. The very nature of what is done proclaims this, for it belongs only to kings to make laws. The Apostle shows this when he says: "Regarding virgins I have not received any commandment from the Lord, but I give my opinion as one who is trustworthy, having obtained mercy from the Lord."[46] Since Paul was a servant, he did not dare to add to what had been ordained by law from the beginning.

(24) Christ did not act as Paul did.[47] With great authority he cites the old laws and then introduces laws of his own. To make laws without any qualification belongs only to royal power. But we find Christ both making laws himself and amending the old laws.[48] If this is the case, what argument is left for those who are so shameless as to oppose him? This surely makes it clear that Christ is of the same essence as the Father who begot him.

(25) So that what I am saying may become still more clear, let us go to the very place in the Scriptures where Christ speaks of the Law. After Christ had gone up on the mountainside, he sat down. When everyone was standing nearby, he began to speak: "Blessed are the poor in spirit, the lowly, those who show mercy, the clean of heart."[49] Then, after those beatitudes, he said: "Do not think I have come to abolish the Law and the prophets. I have come not to abolish them but to fulfill them."[50]

---

44 Cf. Mi 7.18.
45 As he did in the case of the good thief on the cross. See Lk 23.44. Cf. Homilies VIII.46; IX.15–16.
46 1 Cor 7.25.
47 Paul was the servant, but Christ, as the Son and equal in power with the Father, was the author of the Law.
48 Christ did this in the cases of murder (cf. Mt 5.21–26), adultery (ibid. 27–30), divorce (ibid. 31–32), swearing oaths (ibid. 33–37), retaliation (ibid. 38–42), hatred of enemies (ibid. 43–48).
49 Cf. Mt 5.3,5,7,8.

(26) Who even suspected that? Or what had he ever said in contradiction of the Old Testament to make him speak in this way? He said: "Blessed are the poor in spirit,"[51] that is, the humble and lowly. But the Old Testament also said that. "My sacrifice to God is a contrite spirit; a heart contrite and humbled God will not spurn."[52] Again Christ said: "Blessed are the lowly."[53] Yet, when Isaiah was speaking in the person of God, he also said this. "To whom shall I look with respect but to the lowly and meek and to the man who trembles at my words?"[54]

(27) Christ said: "Blessed are those who show mercy."[55] Again, this concept is scattered throughout the Old Testament. For example, Sirach says: "Rob not the poor man of his livelihood. Reject not the supplication of the afflicted."[56] And there is many a mention of mercy and loving-kindness in the books of the Old Covenant. Christ said: "Blessed are the clean of heart."[57] David also said this. "A clean heart create in me, O God, and a steadfast spirit renew within me."[58] And if anyone goes through the remaining beatitudes, he will find that they are in strong agreement with the Old Testament.

(28) Since Christ had said nothing to contradict the Old Testament, why did he go on to say: "Do not think I have come to abolish the Law and the prophets?"[59] It was not because of what he had said that he made this correction but because of what he was going to say. He was going to start to extend the

---

50 Mt 5.17. As J. McKenzie says (JBC 43:34), Jesus' mission was not to annul the Law and the prophets (i.e., the whole collection of OT books) but rather to fulfill them, i.e., to bring the Law to perfection, to give it that finality the Pharisees believed it already possessed. Jesus affirms indirectly that the Law is imperfect, unfinished; he will perfect and finish it. Chrysostom will go on to show that the beatitudes and the New Covenant do not contradict the OT Law but are in strong agreement with it.

51 Cf. Mt 5.3.
52 Cf. Ps 50 (51).19.
53 Cf. Mt 5.5.
54 Cf. Is 66.2.
55 Cf. Mt 5.7.
56 Cf. Sir (Ecclus) 4.1,4.
57 Cf. Mt 5.8.
58 Ps 50 (51).12.
59 Mt 5.17.

commandments and he did not wish his disciples to think that any increase he made in them involved a contradiction of them nor that the new additions were in conflict with the old laws. That is why he said: "Do not think I have come to abolish the Law and the prophets,"[60] that is, "I am going to say things more perfect than what was said before." For example: "You have heard, 'You shall not commit murder.' But I say, 'You shall not become angry.' You have heard, 'You shall not commit adultery.' But I say, 'Anyone who looks lustfully at a woman has already committed adultery.' "[61] And there are so many similar statements.

(29) However, do not think that making the Law perfect abolishes it; it is not an abolition but a fulfillment. What Christ did with bodies he also did with the Law. What did he do with bodies? When he came and found many limbs maimed and all of them weak and deficient, he made them perfect and restored them to their proper and healthy condition. In these acts and in all he did, he made it clear that he was the one who had established the old laws and that he was the one who had created our human nature.[62]

(30) How eager he was to prove this is made especially clear when Christ cured the blind man. He was passing by and saw a blind man. So Christ made mud, smeared it on the sightless eyes, and said to the blind man: "Go wash in the pool of Siloam."[63] When he had raised the dead man to life by his command alone,[64] when he had performed so many other miracles by a mere word,[65] why, in this case, did he add an act, make mud, and plaster it on the blind man's eyes? Is it not clear

---

60 Ibid.

61 Cf. Mt 5.21,22; 27,28.

62 The analogy between fulfilling the Law and restoring maimed limbs to health is a powerful one. Chrysostom here uses it as an example and proof that Christ, as the Son who acts with the Father and with equal power, both gave the old Law and created human nature. As human nature can be maimed but brought to perfection by Christ, so, too, can he who gave the old Law bring it to fulfillment in the New Covenant.

63 Cf Jn 9.6–7.

64 As in the case of Lazarus. See Jn 11.43 and Hom.IX.20–22. For other instances see Lk 7.11–15, Mk 5.41, and Homilies IX.11; X.20.

that he did this so that, when you hear that God took dust from the earth and formed man, you may learn from what happens here that Christ is the one who formed man in the beginning?[66] If he did not wish to prove this, what he did when he made the mud would be idle and unnecessary.

(31) Furthermore, he wanted you to learn that the mud he used did not help him in restoring the blind man's sight. Plastering his eyes with a mere command instead of with that mud would have been more than enough. That is why he added a command and said: "Go, wash in the pool of Siloam."[67] For after he showed by the manner of his workmanship who it was who had made man in the beginning, he then said to the blind man: "Go, wash in the pool of Siloam."

(32) A first class sculptor might wish to demonstrate his own skill by using one of his own works. And so, when he is molding a statue, he leaves out a part so that, by the omission, he may prove his skill and ability to make the statue whole. In the same way, when Christ wishes to prove that it is he who has made the whole man, he left this man imperfect. He did this so that, after he came along and gave him his sight by restoring the part which had been omitted, he might implant in us faith and belief that it was he who made the man whôle.[68]

(33) And notice what part he uses to show this. He does not restore a hand or foot but restores sight to the eyes, which are

---

65 Cf., e.g., Mt 8.3 (and paragraphs 21 above and 44 below); Mk 1.41; Lk 6.24; Jn 2.7–8.

66 Chrysostom sees the act of smearing the blind man's eyes as a symbol of the Son acting in concert with his Father, in creating man from clay (cf. Gn 1.26; 2.7, and Hom.IX.15). B. Vawter, in commenting on Jn 9.6–7 (JBC 63:115), notes that, in the primitive Church, Christians saw in this episode a sacramental symbol of baptism. Spittle was commonly believed to have medicinal properties. The verb "smeared" means, literally, "anointed," and anointing from earliest Christian times was part of the ritual of baptism. The name of the pool, Siloam, which means "one who has been sent," has significance in Jn because Jesus is the one sent by the Father to give light. And it was in the waters of this pool that the blind man gained his sight, just as, in the pool of baptism, the newborn Christian gains new sight and new life. Strangely Chrysostom never refers to this episode in his *Baptismal Instructions* (ACW 31).

67 Cf. Jn 9.7.

68 And in doing this Christ proves that he is equal to the Father in power.

the fairest of our parts and the most necessary. Surely, no part of us is more valuable than our eyes. Since he could mold the fairest and most necessary part—I mean the eyes—it is quite clear that he can shape a hand, a foot, and all the other limbs.[69]

(34) O those blessed eyes! They became a spectacle for all who were nearby, they drew all men to themselves, and by their beauty they spoke and taught all who were standing close by how great is the power which Christ has. Surely, what happened was unexpected and a paradox. A blind man was teaching those with sight how to see. Christ made this clear when he said: "For judgment have I come into this world, so that the sightless may see, and the seeing become blind."[70]

(35) O blessed blindness! The sight which he did not receive from nature he received from grace. Nor did the delay he suffered cause a loss to be compared to the profit he gained from the manner in which the cure was accomplished. What could be more wonderful than those eyes which Christ's blameless and holy hands deigned to plaster over with mud? What happened in the case of the sterile woman also happened here.[71] She was in no way harmed by the delay. But she became much more illustrious because she conceived and bore a child not by nature's laws but by the laws of grace. In the same way,

---

69 Again an argument a fortiori.

70 Cf. Jn 9.39. As was the case with other words and works of Jesus, the sequel to the miraculous cure was a strong reaction on the part of the Pharisees. First they summon the man's parents and then the man himself for questioning. Later Jesus seeks out the man he had cured and elicits from him an act of faith and belief. But Jesus' reply to this confession is paradoxical: "For judgment have I come into this world." B. Vawter explains this part of Jesus' reply in commenting on Jn 3.17–18 when he says (JBC 63:71) that Christ had been sent into this world to bring eternal life, but willful unbelief makes Jesus the occasion of condemnation. Thus unbelief is its own condemnation, and the unbeliever passes judgment on himself (cf. Jn 12.31). But if the unbeliever puts aside his unbelief and makes an act of faith in Jesus and his mission, that man will see. But the effect of the judgment brought about by Jesus' call to faith is that many, like the Pharisees in this episode, who falsely believe that they already possess the light, will reject the revelation of God and, hence, be blind (JBC 63:116).

71 This reference would be to Elizabeth, wife of Zechariah, and mother of John the Baptist. Cf. Hom.II.9–16.

the blind man was not harmed by his past blindness but even gained the greatest profit from it. For he was deemed worthy, first, to behold the Sun of Justice and, then, to see the sun in the sky now made visible to his own eyes.[72]

(36) I say this so that we may not feel upset or take it with bad grace when we see ourselves or any others suffering from misfortunes. If we endure everything which happens to us with a sense of gratitude and patience, every misfortune will come to an end which is profitable for us and filled with many blessings. But this is what I wished to say. Christ took bodies which were imperfect because they lacked something and he made them perfect and complete. In the same way, he took the Law, which was imperfect, he corrected it, formed and molded it, and brought it to a more perfect state.[73]

(37) When you hear me say that the Law was imperfect, do not think that I am accusing him who made the Law. The Law was not imperfect because of its own nature; it became imperfect with the passage of time. At the time it was made, the Law was quite perfect and exactly suited to the natures of those who received it. But when, through Christ's instruction, nature thereafter advanced to a more perfect state, the old Law became less perfect, not because of its own nature but because of the progress in virtue which came from the instructions Christ gave.

(38) Suppose a bow and arrows were made for a prince to practice with rather than for fighting wars and for use in battles. Surely, these weapons become useless when the prince has grown and has learned to excel in warfare. The same thing has happened with our nature. When we were in a less perfect condition and we were learning to train ourselves by practice, Christ gave us suitable weapons which we could carry with ease. When later we were grown up and matured by our advances in virtue, those weapons became less suitable because we had advanced in perfection. This is why Christ came and put in our hands other and better weapons.

---

72 For the Sun of Justice see Hom.VII.6, esp. note 9.
73 See above paragraphs 24–30.

(39) Consider the great prudence and wisdom Christ shows when he cites the old Laws and then proposes the new. For he said: "You have heard that it was said to your forefathers, 'You shall not commit murder.' "[74] Tell us, O Christ, who said this? Did you say it, or did your Father? But he does not tell us who said it.

(40) Why did he remain silent on this point? Why did he fail to make it clear who had said it? Why did he bring forward the Law without naming the person who made it? The reason was this. If he were to have said: "You shall not commit murder, but I say to you that you shall not become angry,"[75] his words would have seemed offensive because of the foolishness of those who were listening. They were not yet able to understand that, in making these new Laws, he was not overturning the older Laws but was adding to them. Those who were listening would have said to him: "What do you mean? Did your Father say, 'You shall not commit murder,' and do you say, 'You shall not become angry?' " Christ wished to keep anyone from thinking that he was opposing the Father or saying something more than the Father had said, as if he were wiser than the Father. That is why he did not say: "You have heard from the Father."

(41) Again, if he were to have said: "You have heard that I said to your forefathers," this, no less than the former notion, would have seemed too much for those listening to him to endure. See what happened when he said: "Before Abraham came to be, I am."[76] They tried to stone him. What would they have done if he were to have added that he also had given the Law to Moses? This is why he said nothing about himself nor about the Father. He let that pass and said: "You have heard that it was said to your forefathers, 'You shall not commit murder.' "[77]

(42) When Christ supplied what was missing in the defective bodies, he taught the people who it was who had made man in

---

74 Cf. Mt 5.21.
75 Cf. ibid. 22.
76 Cf. Jn 8.58.
77 Cf. Mt 5.21.

the beginning.[78] He does the same thing here. By correcting the Law and by adding what was missing, he teaches us who it was who had also given the Law in the beginning. This is why he made no mention either of himself or of the Father when he was speaking of man's creation. In this case, too, he named no person but left this indefinite when he said: "The creator, at the beginning, made them male and female."[79] In his words he said nothing as to who the creator was; but by his deeds he taught us who had created man when he supplied what was missing in defective bodies.

(43) So, too, here, when he said: "You have heard that it was said to your forefathers,"[80] he kept silent as to who had said it but, by his very deeds he revealed that he was the one. For he who supplied what was missing was the one who, in the beginning, had introduced the Law. Furthermore, he cites the old Laws themselves. He does this so that those who were listening may learn, by comparing the old and the new, that what he says is not said in opposition to the Father, and that he has the same power as the Father who begot him. The Jews understood this and they were struck with wonder. And struck with wonder they were indeed. Listen to the evangelist who made this clear when he said: "The crowds were in admiration at his teaching, for he was teaching them as one having power and not as their Scribes and Pharisees."[81]

(44) The heretic says: "What, then, if they misinterpreted this?" Christ did not find fault with them, did he? He did not rebuke them, did he? Instead, he confirmed their opinion. For immediately after, a leper came up to him and said: "Lord, if you will, you can make me clean." And what did Christ say? "I do will it. Be made clean."[82] Why did he not simply say: "Be

---

78 See above paragraphs 29–35.
79 Cf. Mt 19.4 and Gn 1.27.
80 Cf. Mt 5.21.
81 Cf. Mt 7.28–29. The Nestle-Aland *Novum testamentum graece*, 26th ed. (Stuttgart 1979) excludes "and Pharisees" from the text as an intrusion but accepts it as a variant reading in the critical apparatus to verse 29.
82 Cf. Mt 8.2,3. Christ confirms his equal power with the Father by the miracles he performs on his own authority.

made clean?" Indeed, the leper did testify that Christ had the power when he said: "If you will do so." But so that you may not believe that the words: "If you will to do so," belong only to the leper's opinion, Christ himself added his own words: "I do will it. Be made clean." In this way, he purposely showed that the power was his in every respect and that he does all he does on his own authority. If this were not so, then what he said would be idle and unnecessary.

(45) We have learned, therefore, that Christ has power in all things. Should we, then, see him, in some other place, doing or saying something humble and lowly, remember that he is doing so either for the reasons I recently enumerated[83] or because he wished to bring his hearers to humility of mind.[84] But let us not on that account bring on him the discredit of a mean and lowly essence.

(46) He endured to assume the very flesh of a man. But he did this out of a spirit of humility and not because he was inferior to the Father.[85] What is the evidence for this? And yet the enemies of the truth are spreading the word around that the reason he took on flesh was because of his inferiority to the Father. For they are saying: "If he were equal to the Father who begot him, why did the Father not take flesh upon himself?[86] Why was it the Son who put on the form of a servant?[87] Is it not clear that the Son assumed this form because he was inferior to the Father?"

(47) Indeed, if inferiority was the reason why the Son put on our human nature, then the Spirit, who is inferior to the Son, as they say (for we would not say that), should have been made flesh. For if the Father is greater than the Son because the Son was made flesh but the Father was not made flesh, the Spirit

---

83 Cf. Hom.VII.16–30; 53–55.

84 Cf. Hom.VIII.44–48; above paragraph 7.

85 This was all part of the plan of redemption.

86 This was not part of the plan of redemption but an objection tainted with the teachings of the Monarchians, Patripassians, and Sabellians. See Introduction 16 and notes. Also cf. Jn 1.14 (and NAB note ad loc.) which offers a sublime refutation of the Anomoean position.

87 Cf. Phil 2.7. The heretics make a correct reference to Scripture but draw an unwarranted conclusion, as Chrysostom will presently prove.

will be greater than the Son for this same reason. For the Spirit did not take on flesh.[88]

(48) But we do not wish to prove this by demonstrative arguments. Come, therefore, and let us prove it from the Scriptures themselves. Let us show that he took flesh upon himself because of his humility. Paul had exact knowledge of these things. Whenever he is going to exhort us to something profitable for us, he draws his examples of virtue from heaven itself. For example, he often counsels us on charity and love. So when he wished to urge his disciples to love each other, he brought Christ before them and he said: "Husbands, love your wives, just as Christ also loved the Church."[89]

(49) Again, when he was talking about almsgiving,[90] he did this same thing. This is why Paul said: "You know the graciousness of our Lord Jesus Christ—how being rich he becomes poor for your sakes, that by his poverty you might become rich."[91] What Paul means is something like this. Just as your Master became poor by taking on flesh, so you must

---

88 This argument is a perfect reductio ad absurdum for all the orthodox who hold to the creed of Nicaea. The Anomoeans would probably look on it as sound logic, and as proof that all three divine Persons cannot be perfectly equal in power and Godhead. Perhaps Chrysostom realized this because he will now seek the source of his argument from Scripture rather than from logic.

89 Eph 5.25. Cf. J. Grassi, (JBC 56:38), who points out that this verse offers a particular application of Eph 5.1 ("Be imitators of God as his dear children"), where the Christian is invited to make his life a sacrifice of love for others as Christ did. When husband and wife do this by subjection and love, or mutual self-giving, their married love will be a visible sign that they are imitating and sharing in Christ's action of loving his Church and giving himself up for her. For the idea of Christ giving himself up for others see Gal 2.20.

90 Paul's plea for alms was for the poor in Jerusalem.

91 2 Cor 8.9. J. O'Rourke, (JBC 52:28) explains that Jesus was rich because he is Son and equal to the Father, possessing the fulness of the Godhead. However, he took to himself a human nature, becoming thereby a part of this world of weakness and death, so that those who believe in him might be made rich. Paul appeals to this profound truth of faith even in a secondary matter, the collection of alms for the Church of Jerusalem. The collection, however, was not of secondary importance as a manifestation of Christian charity, because it was motivated by a desire to make concrete the union existing among Christians. This unity assures that the alms of those with greater means will always be shared with those in greater need, wherever they may be.

become poor in money. For just as poverty of honor did him no harm, so, too, poverty in money matters will not be able to hurt you but will produce great wealth for you.

(50) Again, when he was speaking to the Philippians about humility, he brought the example of Christ before them and said: "In humility let each one regard the others as his superiors."[92] And then he went on to say: "Have this mind in you which was also in Christ Jesus,[93] who, being in the form of God, did not think it robbery to be equal with God, but he emptied himself, taking the nature of a servant."[94]

---

92 Cf. Phil 2.3. Chrysostom probably also has in mind Jesus' instruction to the twelve found in Mk 10.42–45, which we find discussed in Hom.VIII.44–45. According to J. Fitzmyer, (JBC 50:16), Paul fears that petty jealousies are at work among the Philippians and is counselling humility, selflessness, and concern for others as a remedy. Chrysostom may have chosen to quote the verse form Philippians here because he now intends to cite the verses which almost immediately follow it.

93 Cf. Phil 2.5. This verse is subject to controversy as to its precise meaning. J. Fitzmyer (JBC 50:16) sees verse 5 as open to two interpretations. First, as translated above, the meaning would be that Paul is exhorting the Philippians to an imitation of Christ, whose humility and abasement would serve the Christian as his model for conduct. But, second, if rendered: "Have for one another that attitude which you also have in Christ Jesus," the stress is not on the moral imitation of Jesus but on the vital principle of new Christian communal life.

94 Cf. Phil 2.6–7. Here we have what appears to be a portion of an early liturgical hymn. According to J. Fitzmyer (JBC 50:19), if "form" is understood in this hymn to refer to Jesus' possession of that quality associated through condescension and accommodation with the external manifestation of Yahweh in the OT, then it can be said that he was of divine status. According to W. Arndt and F.W. Gingrich, *A Greek-English Lexicon of the New Testament and Other Early Christian Literature* 4th ed. (Chicago 1952) 108, s.v. *harpagmos*, the usual meaning of "robbery" is here next to impossible because the state of being equal to God cannot be equated with the act of robbery. However, *harpagmos* can be taken as equal to *harpagma*—a change from the abstract to the concrete which is grammatically justifiable—and then have the meaning of "prize" or perhaps "privilege." Fitzmyer (JBC ibid.) suggests that the word should be taken in a passive rather than an active sense and be translated as "a prize (or booty) held fast, snatched to oneself." He finds this meaning most in keeping with the context. Jesus did not treat the status of divine glory (i.e., being equal to God) as a privilege or possession to be clutched so tenaciously that it might be exploited in the future. Although Jesus possessed divine equality, he did not stand on this dignity. He did not empty himself of divinity but of the status of glory by his Incarnation to take upon himself the condition of a servant. Being equal to God, he did not cease to be equal when he became man and abased himself.

(51) Therefore, if Christ allowed himself to put on flesh because he was inferior to the Father in nature, what was done would not be an act of humility.[95] Then it would have been idle and unnecessary for Paul to bring this in when he was exhorting his disciples to be humble. For it is an act of humility when an equal obeys an equal. And Paul himself pointed this out when he said: "Who being in the form of God, did not think it robbery to be equal to God, but he emptied himself taking the nature of a servant.[96]

(52) What does he mean when he says: "He did not consider it robbery to be equal with God, but he emptied himself, taking the nature of a servant?" He means that, when someone has stolen something which does not belong to him and continues to keep it, he would not choose to give it up even though he is afraid and cannot feel confident that he will keep what he has stolen.[97] But the man who has a possession which cannot be taken away from him feels no fear even though his possession is hidden away.[98]

(53) For example—to make what I say clear by an illustration—suppose the same man has a servant and a son. If the slave shouts out demands for his freedom—a freedom which in no way is his to demand—and if he opposes his master, then he cannot be brought to undertake any menial work or to obey any command. Why? Because he is afraid that this very work may hurt the freedom he has demanded. He is afraid that obeying any command may put an obstacle in his path. For he has stolen an honor and holds it contrary to what he deserves.

(54) But the son will not beg off from doing any menial work

---

95 For an inferior to abase himself is not an act of humility. But Jesus is equal to the Father and, hence, he is not an inferior in his divine nature, even though he assumes a human nature. This is a true act of humility.
96 Cf. Phil 2.6–7.
97 Chrysostom obviously understands *harpagmos* as meaning "robbery." Hence, we have translated it that way.
98 The Son's divinity and equality with the Father cannot be taken away even though it may be hidden by the human nature Christ assumed at the Incarnation. He now possesses two natures, divine and human, in one reality as a Person.

because he knows that, even if he carries out all the services of his father's servants, his own freedom has in no way been hurt but remains unchanged. Doing the work of servants cannot take away the honor and nobility which are his by nature. Why? He does not have his nobility because he has stolen it as the servant did. He has it by reason of his very birth and from his first day on earth it was his by inheritance.

(55) This is what Paul was making clear about Christ. Since Christ was free by nature and a true son, he had not seized equality with the Father by theft. Therefore, since he had no need to hide this equality, with full confidence, he took on himself the nature and form of a servant. He knew full well that condescension and accommodation in no way could lessen his glory. For his glory was not alien to him or brought in from outside himself; it was not given to him by robbery; it was not another's glory which did not belong to him. Christ's glory was truly and genuinely his by nature.[99]

(56) This is why he took the form and nature of a servant. He knew well and firmly believed that this could in no way do him harm. Therefore, in no way did it harm him but, even in the form of a servant, he kept the same glory. Do you see that the very taking of flesh upon himself is a proof that the Son is equal to the Father who begot him, and that this equality is not alien to him nor brought in from outside himself? Do you see that this equality does not come and go but is strong and unalterable, the kind of equality a son is likely to have with his father?

(57) Therefore, let us propose all these arguments to the heretics. At least, as far as it depends on our efforts, let us lead them away from their evil heretical belief and let us bring them to the truth. As for ourselves, let us not think that faith alone is enough for our salvation. We must also feel concern for our own conduct and give an example of the most perfect life. In

---

99 Father and Son are equal in power and glory since these are qualities which belong to the one Godhead, which is equally possessed by all three divine Persons. The glory of the Godhead may be concealed by the Son's human nature but will reappear at the hour of his exaltation (cf. Jn 17.5).

this way, we shall have made ready for ourselves a profitable benefit from two sources, from faith and from good works.[100]

(58) I recently[101] urged you to excel in virtue and now I again give you the same exhortation. Let us put aside our hatred for one another.[102] Let no one be an enemy to his neighbor for even a single day. He must rid himself of anger before nightfall. If he does not do this but rather goes off by himself, in his hatred, he will compile a list of all that was said and done. And this will make it harder to end the quarrel and more difficult to effect a reconciliation.[103]

(59) Sometimes the bones of our body become dislocated. If they are reset without delay, they again take their proper place without much pain and trouble. But if they stay out of joint for a long time, it is difficult for them to return again and go back to the place where they belong. And after they have been reset, they require many days to knit exactly, to become properly seated, and to stay in place.[104]

(60) In the same way, if we are reconciled with our enemies and fit together the dislocated parts without delay, it takes no great trouble for us to return to our former friendship. But if we have let our hatred blind us and a long time intervenes, then our shame makes us blush and we require the help of

---

100 Although some Arian Anomoeans were probably present to hear his homily, many were no doubt absent. These, too, must be instructed. Chrysostom now speaks to the orthodox in his congregation and suggests that they have a ministry of instructing the heretics and bringing them back from their error to the truth. In this way they will join good works to their faith and will come to salvation.

101 Perhaps an echo of Hom.VIII.24–25.

102 The remainder of this homily is devoted to an exhortation to lay aside enmities, and on the importance of being reconciled without delay. At first Chrysostom seems to mean that the heretics are the enemies with whom his congregation must be reconciled and to whom they must be gentle and kind. Such were the exhortations he gave in Homilies I.40–48; II.51–55. But now Chrysostom makes his exhortation more general to include all enemies.

103 Chrysostom shows a keen insight into the psychology of anger and the danger of letting it fester in the soul. Quarrels must be settled the day they start since the difficulty of reconciliation increases each day the quarrel remains unresolved.

104 Chrysostom is fond of metaphors drawn from the physician's art. Cf., e.g., his *Baptismal Instructions* (ACW 31) 38, 100, 105–8, 272; *Against Judaizing Christians* (FOTC 68) 4, 35, 53, 89, 94–95, 214, 239. See also Hom.XII.28.

others to bring us back together again and to reset what has become dislocated. And even after we have gone back into place again, we still need the help of others to see to it that we stay exactly in place and begin to knit together until we regain the old frankness and confidence between us.[105]

(61) Let me say nothing now about the ridicule and the shame. Let me only ask you how great is the blame which we would deserve if we need the help of others to bring us together with our own limbs and members? Yet this is not the only terrible thing which happens when we delay and put off reconciliation. What else happens? Because of the delay, we take to be offenses against us things which are not really offenses at all. Whatever our enemy may say, we take it all with suspicion, not only his words but his outward bearing, the way he looks at us, the way he walks.

(62) When we lay eyes on him, the sight inflames our hate-hardened hearts. And even when we do not see him, it again causes us like pain and distress. For, as a rule, not only the sight of those who have hurt us but even the recollection of the harm they have done causes us constant pain. Even when we hear someone else talking about our enemy, we, too, again start to talk about him in the same hostile way as before. In fact, we simply spend our whole life in sadness and distress. Because, while we keep up this constant warfare in our soul, we are doing greater harm to ourselves than to our enemies.

(63) Beloved, you know all this and realize it well. Therefore, let us be especially eager to make no man our enemy. If any hatred for another ever arises, let us be reconciled on that very same day. If our anger reaches a second or a third day, quickly the third becomes a fourth, the fourth a fifth, and that will give rise in us to many more days of hatred. The longer we put it off, the more will we blush with shame. Are you still ashamed to go up to the one who has hurt you and to offer him a gesture of peace?

(64) Such an act of reconciliation wins everyone's approval,

---

105 The comparison of setting a dislocated bone without delay is particularly telling because fractured friendships dislocate the members of Christ's mystical body.

deserves a crown and a hymn of praise. It gains profit for us and a treasure house filled with countless blessings. Your enemy himself will gladly receive you, everyone standing nearby will commend you. But even if men should censure and blame you, God will without doubt award you a crown.[106]

(65) But if you wait for your enemy to come to you first and ask your pardon, you will not gain so great a profit. He will get there ahead of you, take the reward before you do, and transfer the whole blessing to himself. But how can you hurt yourself or be made worse off if you anticipate him and get there first? Instead, you have overcome your anger, you have shown yourself superior to your passion, you have given a good example of the life of virtue. By being obedient to God you have made the rest of your life more desirable and you have freed yourself from your troubles and confusion.[107]

(66) Not only in the sight of God but also in the judgment of men it is a risky and dangerous thing to have a host of enemies. But why do I say a host? It is dangerous to have even one enemy, just as it assures our safety if we have all men as our friends. No revenues, no weapons, no walls, no moats, nor any number of other devices for sieges and battle can, by their nature, make us so secure as true friendship.

(67) Friendship is a bulwark, it is security, it is abundance and wealth, it is luxury. It makes us lead our present life in cheerfulness and it grants us the grace of the life to come. Therefore, let us think on all these matters, let us consider how great a profit we will gain from it if we do everything and make ready every means to reconcile our enemies to ourselves. Furthermore, let us do all we can to prevent hatred between

---

106 All these benefits will come to him who takes the initiative in reconciliation. Wherever the original blame for the quarrel may lie, the one who makes the first move toward reconciliation is following Christ's instructions given in Mt 5.23–24, where even worship must be postponed for reconciliation. As J. McKenzie notes (JBC 43:36), this establishes the primacy of fraternal relations over cultic duties.

107 Certainly no harm can come to him who initiates the reconciliation. Indeed, by healing the rift, he has proved his return to a life of virtue by obeying the two great commandments, loving God above all and his neighbor as himself (Mk 12.30–31).

ourselves and those who would be our foes. Finally, let us work as hard as we can to make the friends we have more secure in their love for us.

(68) Surely, love is the beginning and the end of every virtue.[108] May it come to pass that we enjoy a true and constant love for others and that we come to the kingdom of heaven through the grace and loving-kindness of our Lord Jesus Christ, to whom be glory and power forever and ever. Amen.

---

108 Indeed, love is the greatest of virtues and encompasses them all. It upbuilds (1 Cor 8.1) and never fails (ibid. 13.8). It is greater than faith and hope (ibid. 13.13). We must put on love over all the other virtues, because love binds those other virtues together and makes them perfect (Col 3.14). And above all love for one another must be constant, because love covers a multitude of sins (1 Pt 4.8).

HOMILY XI

HAVE TALKED WITH YOU[1] for but a single day,[2] and, after that day, I have come to love you as if I had been reared and brought up with you from the very start and from my first day on earth. The bonds of this love have united me to you just as strongly as if I had enjoyed the great pleasure of your society for time beyond telling. Nor was it my own friendly and affectionate nature which brought this about. It is because I have found you desirable and lovable beyond all others. Who could fail to admire and marvel at your burning zeal, your sincere love, your kindness and good will toward those who teach you,[3] your oneness of mind and concord with one another.

(2) Are not all these reasons enough to draw even a heart of stone to you? This is why I love you no less than I love that Church in which I was born, nurtured, and reared.[4] This Church of yours is a sister Church of that one, and you have proved by your deed that this kinship exists. If the Church of Antioch is older in terms of time,[5] this Church of Con-

---

1 The following homily is concerned with the glory of the only begotten, the equality of the Son's power with that of the Father, and the consubstantiality of the Father and the Son. See Introduction, paragraphs 78–91 and Montfaucon, *Notice* IV.

2 This is a certain proof that the present homily was only the second Chrysostom had delivered at Constantinople, where he had been consecrated bishop on December 15, 397 (See *Acta sanctorum novum propylaeum*, ed. H. Delehaye [Brussels 1902] 312–13). Chrysostom's first homily, which unfortunately has not come down to us, was quite possibly also against the Anomoean Arians (who were still strong in Constantinople), and may have dealt with the incomprehensibility of God.

3 Chrysostom's first homily given in Constantinople (the one which has not come down to us) must have elicited a most favorable response from his new congregation.

4 I.e., the Church of Antioch.

5 The Church of Antioch dated back to apostolic times. It was there that those who followed the teachings of Jesus were first called Christians (cf. Acts 11.26).

stantinople is more fervent in its faith. The congregation[6] at Antioch is larger and its theater more famous, but your patience and endurance are greater. And this is a more cogent proof of your strength of spirit.

(3) On every side[7] wolves surround you, but your flock is not destroyed. A surging sea, storms, and waves have constantly encircled this sacred ship, but those who sail on it are not engulfed by the waters. The fires of heresy threaten with their encircling flames on every side,[8] but those who are in the midst of the furnace enjoy the blessing of a heavenly dew.[9] In like fashion, it is an unexpected and wonderful thing to see how this church has been planted in this section of the city.[10] To see

---

6 *Syllogos* might mean a congregation (and Baur 2.14 translates it so in his version of the present passage), but then it makes a strange bedfellow with the theater, which Chrysostom often criticizes (cf., e.g., ACW 31.40, 321; FOTC 68.9, 10, 44, 92, 102, 177) and calls a pomp of Satan (ACW ibid. 189, 240, 306). Nonetheless, the oldest theater in Constantinople stood near the cathedral (cf. A. Vogt, "Le Théâtre à Byzance", *Revue des questions historiques* 115 [1931] 259). Hence, we have followed Baur in translating *syllogos* as "congregation."

7 The wolves, no doubt, are the Arian Anomoeans. From 339 to 379 Arianism had been supreme in Constantinople, and orthodox Christians did not possess a single church. In 379 the emperor Theodosius took away both the churches and the political power of the Arians, who were no longer permitted to have churches within the walls of the city; these churches, including the cathedral, were turned over to the orthodox Christians. Even these Christians, after the long tenure of Arianism, probably still needed instruction in the orthodox faith. Besides, a moderately small group of Arians still lived in Constantinople and obstinately held to their heretical beliefs. See Baur 2.47–48.

8 The cathedral stood in a central area which contained also the theater, the baths, the imperial palace, the senate, and the circus, but the residences surrounding these structures may well have constituted an Arian neighborhood. See Baur 2.25.

9 Cf. Dn 3.50. The church and its congregation are compared to the fiery furnace into which King Nebuchadnezzar had had Shadrach, Meshach, and Abednego thrown. But they suffered no harm because an angel of the Lord made the inside of the furnace as though a dew-laden breeze were blowing through it.

10 Emperor Constantius had built his new "Great Church" to replace Constantine's Church of Peace, which had become too small. The new "Great Church" had been consecrated in 360 (during the Arian ascendancy) to Hagia Sophia. After it was turned over to the orthodox Christians by Theodosius, it became Constantinople's Cathedral. In it Chrysostom was consecrated bishop and he preached most of his homilies there. The second ecumenical council was also held there in 381. See Baur 2.51–52. See also Montfaucon's *Notice* IV.4–5.

it here is like seeing an olive tree in bloom, weighted down with fruit, yet standing in the middle of a furnace.

(4) Since you are so kindhearted and considerate, since you deserve countless blessings, come now, and let me, with all love, make payment on the promise I made to you recently[11] when I discussed with you the weapons of David and Goliath. In my discourse I showed that Goliath was protected by the power of his weapons and the strength of a full set of armor, whereas David had none of that panoply. But he was fortified by his faith.[12]

(5) Goliath had the external protection of his glittering breastplate and shield; David shone from within with the grace of the Spirit. This is why a boy prevailed over a man, this is why the one wearing no armor conquered the one fully armed, this is why the shepherd struck down the soldier, this is why a stone in a shepherd's hand crushed and destroyed the bronze weapons of war.

(6) Therefore, let us take in our hands that stone, I mean the cornerstone, the spiritual rock.[13] If Paul could think in these terms of the rock in the desert, no one will in any way feel resentment against me if I understand David's stone in the same sense. In the case of the Jews in the desert, it was not the nature of the visible stone but the power of the spiritual stone which sent forth those streams of water. So, too, in David's case, it was not the visible stone but the spiritual stone which sank into the barbarian's head.[14] This is why, at that time, I

---

11 Again "recently" translates the Greek word *prōēn*. Cf. above Hom.IV.note 1. Chrysostom states what the promise was in paragraph 6 below.

12 Cf. 1 Sm (1 Kgs) 17.4–7, 40. The story recounted in 1 Sm 17 presents problems inasmuch as it seems to spring from more than one tradition. In an effort to harmonize the traditions, LXX omits verses 12–31. J. Turro (JBC 9:29) points out that the theological implication of the event is that it is the Lord and not material advantage that prevails for Israel. What development of the incident Chrysostom made in the lost homily cannot be surmised, except that the Lord triumphed over Israel's foes because of David's faith.

13 The allusion is to the Israelites in the desert who "All drank the same spiritual drink (they drank from the spiritual rock that was following them, and the rock was Christ)," as Paul says in 1 Cor 10.4.

14 As the spiritual rock slaked the thirst of the Israelites in the desert, so it is the spiritual stone (the Lord) which slays Goliath and avenges his insults to the people of the Lord.

promised that I would say nothing based on reasoned arguments.[15] "Our weapons are not merely carnal but spiritual,
demolishing sophistries and reasoning and every proud height
that raises itself against the knowledge of God."[16]

(7) Therefore, we are commanded to demolish reasonings
and not to exalt them; we are ordered to destroy sophistries
and not to arm ourselves with them. "For the reasonings of
mortals are timid,"[17] the inspired writer says. Why does he say
"timid?" Even if the timid man walks in a safe place, he feels no
boldness but trembles with fear. So, too, even if something
which is proved by reasoned arguments is true, these arguments do not provide an assurance which is full enough nor a
faith which is sufficient for the soul. Since reasoned arguments
are so weak, come, let us join battle with our opponents with
arguments from the Scriptures as our weapons.

(8) From what source am I to begin my discourse? From
whichever source you wish, either from the New Testament or
from the Old. We can see that the glory of the only begotten
shines forth with a great abundance of light not only in the
words of the evangelists and apostles but also in what the
prophets said and in the entire Old Testament. I think it is best
to fight my adversaries with weapons taken from the Old
Testament because, if I draw my arguments from that source,
I can strike down not only those enemies but many other
heretics as well. I mean Marcion, Manichaeus, Valentinus, and
all Jewish communities.[18] When Goliath fell at the hand of

---

15 Here is Chrysostom's promise mentioned above in paragraph 4. He will not
use against the heretics any arguments which depend on human reason
but, rather, he will use spiritual weapons which rely on God's revealed
word.

16 Cf. 2 Cor 10.4–5. See also Homilies I.39, VIII.1. Hom.I definitely attacked
the pretensions of knowledge of the Anomoeans, knowledge which en-
abled them, they said, to know God in his essence. Hom.VII (to which
VIII.1 refers), however, stresses the "glory of the only begotten," the
consubstantiality of the Son with the Father.

17 Wis 9.14. *Timid* means "uncertain" according to A. Wright, JBC 34:29.
Chrysostom applies this uncertainty to reasoned arguments. Hence, he will
use the spiritual arguments of Scripture.

18 For Marcion, Manichaeus, and Valentinus see Hom.VII.17 and notes. All
were Docetists and, hence, denied the plan of redemption. The Jews, who
rejected Christ as the Messiah, would join with these heretics in this denial.

David, the whole army fled. One head was struck and one man died, but the whole army shared in the cowardly rout. So, too, when a single heresy has been struck down and falls, there will be a rout in which all those I mentioned will share.

(9) The Manichaeans and those who are sick with their disease seem to accept the Christ who was foretold but they dishonor the prophets and patriarchs who foretold him.[19] On the other hand, we see that the Jews accept and revere those who foretold Christ, I mean the prophets and the lawgiver, but they dishonor him whom they foretold.[20]

(10) Therefore, when we shall prove, with God's grace, that the great glory of the only begotten was foretold in the Old Testament, we will be able to put to shame all those mouths which fight against God and we can curb their blasphemous tongues. When it will be clear that the Old Testament did foretell Christ,[21] what defense will there be for the Manichaeans and those who join them in dishonoring the Scripture since it has foretold the coming of the common Master of us all? And what excuse or pardon will there be for the Jews if they refuse to accept him whom the prophets have foretold?

(11) Since our wealth of weapons for winning a victory is so abundant, let us turn our discourse to the older books and to the one which is more ancient than all the rest, I mean the book of Genesis. And let us go to its very beginning. So that you may know that Moses had much to say about Christ, listen to Christ himself when he says: "If you believed Moses, you would believe me, for he wrote about me."[22] Where did Moses write about him? I shall now try to show this.

(12) The whole creation was readied, the heavens were crowned with a varied throng of stars, and the earth below shone forth with every sort of flower. The peaks of the mountains reached their full height, the fields and valleys and, indeed, the whole face of the earth were filled with plants and trees and grasses. The flocks and herds leaped and frolicked,

---

19 The Manichaeans rejected the OT.
20 The Jews rejected the NT because they rejected Jesus as the Messiah.
21 These OT prophecies are recounted at length in Chrysostom's *Demonstration on the Divinity of Christ* (PG 48.815–17).
22 Jn 5.46. See Hom.VII.5 and cf. Dt 18.15.

the choirs of singing birds showed their proper nature and filled the whole sky with song. The sea teemed with creatures of the deep, the pools and fountains and rivers were filled with the fish which are native to them.[23] When everything was readied and nothing was left incomplete, then the body sought after its head, the city searched for its ruler, and creation for its king. By this, of course, I mean man.

(13) When God was about to mold him, he said: "Let us make man in our image and likeness."[24] To whom did he say this? It is quite clear that he was speaking to his only begotten. God did not say, "Make." He would not have you think that what he said was a command given to a slave or servant. He said, "Let us make," so that, from the character of the consultation indicated by his words, he might reveal the equality of honor which belonged to him to whom he spoke. For God is sometimes said to have a counsellor and sometimes he is said not to have one.

(14) This is not because the Scripture contradicts itself but because it is revealing to us ineffable teachings by both these modes of expression. When Scripture wishes to show that God needs no one, it says that he has no counsellor.[25] When it wishes to show the equal honor of the only begotten, it calls the Son of God his counsellor.[26]

(15) The Scripture wishes you to learn both these teachings. It wishes you to learn that the prophets call the Son his counsellor not because the Father needs the Son's counsel but so that you may know the honor of the only begotten. Listen to Paul so that you may know that the Father needs no counsellor.

23 Chrysostom here summarizes the first five days of creation as recounted in Gn 1.1–25.
24 Gn 1.26 and NAB note ad loc., which suggests that man resembles God primarily because of the dominion God gives him over the rest of creation. E. Maly (JBC 2:20) notes a distinction between "image," which ordinarily means an exact copy or reproduction, and "likeness," which ordinarily means a resemblance or similarity. Ps 8 is an inspired commentary on man's creation. Verses 2–5 of this Psalm contrast man's finite nature with God's infinite majesty; verses 6–10 extol the dignity and power to which God has raised man. Chrysostom's purpose here, of course, is to establish the equality of power of the Father and the Son, as it was above in Hom.IX.15.
25 Cf. Is 40.13.
26 Cf. ibid. 9.5.

Paul says: "O the depth of the riches and wisdom and knowledge of God! How incomprehensible are his judgments and how unsearchable his ways! For, 'who has known the mind of the Lord, or who has been his counsellor?' "[27] Here, then, Paul has shown that the Father needed no one to counsel him.

(16) Again, it was Isaiah who was speaking of the only begotten when he had this to say: "And they shall be willing even if they were burned with fire. For a child is born to us and a son is given to us, and his name is called the messenger of great counsel, wonderful counsellor."[28] If he is a wonderful counsellor, how is it that Paul said: "For who has known the mind of the Lord, or who has been his counsellor?"[29]

(17) The reason, as I have already said, is because Paul wishes to show that the Father needs no counsellor. But the prophet wishes to show the equal honor of the only begotten. And this is why, in the text from Genesis, the Father did not say, "Make this" or "Do this," but rather, "Let us make."[30] For to say, "Make this" is to use words proper to a command given to a servant. What I shall now tell you makes this clear.

(18) Once a centurion came up to Jesus and said: "Lord, my servant is at home sick of the palsy and is grievously tormented."[31] What, then, did Christ say? "I will come and cure him."[32] However, the centurion did not have the boldness to

---

27 Rom 11.33–34 and cf. Is 40.13; Wis 9.13.

28 Cf. Is 9.5–6. Chrysostom omits "whose government is on his shoulders" of LXX, and LXX omits "wonderful counsellor" of Chrysostom, but the title is found in the Vulgate. Either "wonderful counsellor" was found in Chrysostom's version of the LXX or he has conflated Is 9.6 and 40.13. "Wonderful Counsellor" is listed in the critical apparatus of the LXX as a variant reading.

29 Cf. Rom 11.34.

30 Cf. Gn 1.26.

31 Mt 8.6. This event is also recounted (with variations) in Lk 7.1–10. A centurion was an officer in a Roman legion in charge of a cadre of 100 men which may well have constituted the Roman garrison at Capernaum. The cure of his servant, as J. McKenzie points out (JBC 43:57), is the occasion by which the faith of the gentile centurion is manifested and contrasts the unbelief of the Jews with the faith of the uninstructed gentile (Mt 8.10).

32 Mt 8.7. Jesus will go to the centurion's house even though, for a Jew, entering the house of a gentile incurred uncleanness. But Jesus is the lawgiver, and charity is paramount.

drag the physician into his home. But, because of his concern and loving-kindness, Christ promised of his own free will that he would go to the centurion's house. He did this so as to give the centurion a reason and an opportunity to show his virtuous character. Christ knew what the centurion was going to say but still he promised that he would come. Why? So that you might learn how pious and godly a man the centurion was.

(19) What did the centurion say? "Lord, I am not worthy that you come under my roof."[33] The pain of his servant's sickness and the demands made by illness in his own house did not make the centurion forget his godly disposition. Even in the midst of disaster, he recognized the superiority of the Master. This is why he said: "Only say the word and my servant will be healed. For I, too, have soldiers subject to me; and I say to this one, 'Go,' and he goes, and to another, 'Come,' and he comes, and to my servant, 'Do this,' and he does it."[34]

(20) Do you see that the words, "Do this" are the words of command spoken by a master to his servant? Therefore, "Let us make this" are the words spoken by one who is equal in honor with him to whom he speaks them. When a master speaks to his servant, he says, "Make this." But when the Father speaks to the Son, he says, "Let us make."[35]

(21) The heretics will say: "Suppose the centurion suspected this, but what he suspected was not the fact? The centurion is not an apostle, is he? He is not a disciple, is he, so that we should accept what he says? It is likely that he was wrong." Very good. But what then? Let us look at what follows. Did Christ correct this? Did he chide the centurion for being wrong and bringing forward corrupt teachings? Did Christ say to him: "My friend, why are you doing this? The opinion you have of me is greater than what belongs to me. You are showing me more favor than I deserve. You think that I give orders

---

33 Mt 8.8.

34 Cf. Ibid. 8–9. The centurion's faith knows that personal contact is unnecessary and that Jesus need only speak to achieve the servant's cure. His word will produce work as a superior's command produces obedience in an inferior.

35 Gn 1.26. Chrysostom's point is that the Father's words are spoken to an equal.

because I have authority, but I have no authority." Christ did not say anything like that, did he? Of course not.

(22) Rather, Christ confirmed what the centurion thought of him and said to those who were following him: "Amen, I say to you, I have not found such great faith in Israel."[36] Therefore, the master's praise ratified what the centurion had said. No longer are they words spoken by the centurion; they now express a declaration from the master. For when Christ praises what has been said and reckons the words as well spoken, I take these words as a solemn response from God. For they have received a confirmation from above because of what Christ said in reply.

(23) Do you see how the New Testament agrees with the Old and how both of them show that Christ does have authority? But what about this? Suppose Christ did make man but, in making him, he acted only as a subordinate.[37] Enough of this quarrelsome dispute! For when God said: "Let us make man," he did not add: "According to your image which is less than mine." Nor did he say: "According to my image which is greater than yours."

(24) What did God say? "According to our image and likeness."[38] And by speaking in this way, he showed that there is a single image of the Father and the Son. For he did not say "images" but "our image." There are not two unequal images but one and the same equal image of the Son and the Father. This is why the Son is said to sit at the right hand of the Father[39]—that you may learn that they are the same in honor

36 Cf. Mt 8.10. Cf. McKenzie's observation in note 31 above. Christ's failure to correct the centurion's affirmation that a word was sufficient to effect the cure is proof both of Jesus' power and the centurion's faith.

37 See Introduction, paragraph 27, where it is pointed out that such Subordinationism was an Arian tenet.

38 Cf. Gn 1.26.

39 The texts which speak of the Messiah as seated at the right hand of God are fairly numerous and come from both the OT and NT. They refer sometimes to the ascension (e.g., Mk 16.19) or the exaltation (e.g., Heb 1.3) or the enthronement (e.g., Heb 1.5–14) of Jesus. Chrysostom is more interested in showing that the image of sitting at the right hand is a proof that the risen Christ possesses the same honor and power as the Father because they are one in Godhead. To sit at the right hand signifies their perfect equality. To stand at the throne of God is the sign of a servant or subordinate.

and exactly alike in power. For a subordinate does not sit with his superior but stands alongside him.

(25) To sit on the throne in the same honor and in exactly the same way is a mark of the power of a master. To stand alongside is the mark of the power of a subordinate who does what he is ordered to do. That you may know that this is true, listen to what Daniel said: "I watched until the thrones were set and the Ancient of Days sat down. Thousands upon thousands were ministering to him and myriads upon myriads stood alongside and attended him."[40]

(26) And, again, Isaiah said: "I saw the Lord sitting on a high and exalted throne and the Seraphim stood round about him and attended him."[41] And Micah said: "I saw the Lord God of Israel seated on his throne with the whole host of heaven standing by and attending on his right hand and on his left."[42] Do you see that in all these texts the powers above are standing alongside and attending while the Lord is seated? Therefore, when you see that the Son, too, is seated at the Father's right hand, do not think that his is the dignity of one who ministers and is subordinate. You must realize that his dignity is that of a master possessing authority.

(27) Paul understood both these things, namely, that to stand alongside and attend is proper to those who minister and serve, but to sit down is the mark of those who give orders and commands. See how he distinguishes between these two when he says: "Of the angels he says, 'He makes his angels spirits, and his ministers flaming fire;'[43] but of the Son, 'Your throne,

---

40 Cf. Dn 7.9–10 and NAB note ad loc. Of course, in this and the following two theophanies God is seen by condescension and accommodation. See Hom.IV.18–19.

41 Is 6.1–2 and cf. Homilies III.16 and IV.18–19.

42 Cf. 1 Kgs (3 Kgs) 22.19 and Hom.IV.18, 19.

43 Heb 1.7. These words are quoted from Ps 103(104).4 (LXX) and, as M. Bourke says (JBC 61:11), their meaning probably is that God changes his angels into wind and fire since they are mutable transitory beings, unlike the Son, whose rule is everlasting.

O God, is forever and ever.' "[44] By means of the throne he is showing us the Son's kingly power.

(28) Therefore, since our discourse has proved by all these texts that the Son is not valued as one who ministers but has the dignity of a master, let us worship him as our master because he is equal in honor to the Father. He himself commanded us to do this when he said: "So that all men may honor the Son just as they honor the Father."[45] Let us join the rightness of our way of life and the deeds we do to the correctness of the teachings we embrace so that what pertains to our salvation may not be divided in two.

(29) But nothing can set your lives straight and make them exactly right so much as can your constant attendance at church and your eager attention in listening to what is said here. What food is to the body, the teaching of God's word is to the soul. "For not by bread alone will man live, but by every word which comes forth from the mouth of God."[46] He therefore knew that failure to share in this table[47] produces famine.

(30) Listen, then, to God when he makes this promise, which he also holds out as a threat of punishment and vengeance. For he said: "I shall give them not a famine of bread, or thirst for

---

44 Cf. Heb 1.7–8. These words are quoted from Ps 44(45).6 (LXX). M. Bourke (ibid.) suggests that what the author of Heb envisages is the Son's everlasting rule, which is consequent upon his messianic enthronement. This is quite in keeping with Chrysostom's interpretation.

45 Jn 5.23. In the previous verse Jn points out that the Father has given all judgment to the Son. Man will receive the judgment he merits on the basis of his acceptance or rejection of Christ. Since Jesus is equal in honor to the Father, one cannot accept the Father and reject the Son. If one accepts by faith the teachings of Christ but rejects them by his actions, he rejects both the Father and the Son and runs the risk of eternal condemnation on the day of Judgment.

46 These words from Mt 4.4 are a quotation from Dt 8.3 spoken by Jesus when Satan tempted him in the desert to turn stones into bread. As J. McKenzie notes (JBC 43:25) Jesus' answer subordinates even basic physical necessities to the revealed word of God. Jesus does not fulfill his mission by providing for basic physical necessities but by proclaiming the word that is life.

47 The table is the table of instruction at which we are fed with God's word. Chrysostom uses this metaphor in his *Baptismal Instructions* (ACW 31) 119, 266 note 31, 282 note 5.

water, but a famine for hearing the word of the Lord."[48] How foolish is it, then, to busy ourselves and do everything to drive off bodily hunger but, of our own accord, to take on ourselves a famine of the soul? Will we do this even though famine of the soul is much more difficult and dangerous inasmuch as the loss and damage we suffer involve things which are more important?

(31) I beg and entreat you, let us not take such poor care of ourselves; let us prefer the time we spend here in church to any occupation and concern. Tell me this. What profit do you gain which can outweigh the loss you bring on yourself and your whole household when you stay away from the religious service? Suppose you find a whole treasure house filled with gold, and this discovery is your reason for staying away. You have lost more than you found, and your loss is as much greater as things of the spirit are better than the things we see.

(32) Even if those earthly blessings be many in number and come flowing to us from every side, they do not go with us to the life hereafter. They do not change earth into heaven for us nor do they stand by our side at the dread tribunal. Often enough, even before the end of life, they slip away and abandon us. And even if they stay with us to the end, they are completely cut off when our life is over. But a treasure of the spirit is a possession which cannot be taken away.[49] It follows us everywhere we go, wherever we travel. It gives us great confidence as we stand before the tribunal of judgment.

(33) If the profit from other gatherings is so great, the benefit we gain from the assemblies here in church is twofold.

---

48 Cf. Am 8.11. P. King (JBC 14:26) understands this as meaning that the Israelites will search in vain for a prophet to proclaim to them the word of God. The punishment will be visited on them because of their greed to get back to material transactions after the inactivity imposed by the Sabbath and other holy days. Chrysostom applies the text to those who absent themselves from the assemblies in church and, hence, miss out on the spiritual food which comes from the instruction and from hearing God's word.

49 Spiritual blessings must always be preferred to material goods since the latter, even if still in our possession up to death, cannot follow us into the life hereafter. But treasures of the spirit cannot be taken away from us.

Surely, we reap benefit because we refresh our souls with the word of God. But this is not the only gain. We also benefit because we are scattering great shame over our enemies[50] and because we offer much comfort and encouragement to our brothers. For this is the kind of benefit which comes to an army drawn up for battle when we hurry to the part of the line which is in distress and filled with danger.

(34) That is why we must all come together here in church and drive back the onslaught of our foes. Do you say that you cannot preach a long discourse, that you have no instruction to give? Merely be present here in the church, and you have done everything you have to do.[51] The presence of your person is an addition to the flock. If you are here, it makes your brothers ready and willing to fight the foe. And at the same time, you cover your enemies with the disgrace of defeat.

(35) Suppose a man comes through these holy doors and sees that the congregation is small. He came ready and willing to join the battle, but the few people he sees here quench his desire. He grows numb, he shrinks back, he feels more hesitant and less ready to fight. So he goes away. And then, little by little, in this way our whole congregation will grow weaker and more indifferent. But suppose this man sees people running together with earnestness and zeal, suppose he sees them streaming in from every side. The readiness of these others serves as a basis to make him eager and willing, even if his heart has grown very sluggish and slack.

(36) If one stone is rubbed against another, does this not often make sparks leap forth? And is this not true even if there is nothing colder than a stone and nothing hotter than a fire? Nonetheless, continuous rubbing overcomes the cold nature of the stones. If this happens to stones, it will happen all the

---

50 The "enemies," no doubt, would be the Arian Anomoeans and the other heretics mentioned above in paragraphs 8 and 9. Chrysostom is not preaching hatred for one's enemies. Rather, he is expressing the hope that the united front of the orthodox (as evidenced by their attendance at the church assemblies) will shame the heretics into admitting their errors.

51 The Christians are not expected to instruct but to be instructed. But their presence in church makes it clear that they are eager to learn and be supportive of their fellow Christians.

more to souls which are rubbed together and which then become inflamed with the fire of the Spirit.[52]

(37) Did you not hear that, in the time of our forebears, the number of those who believed was one hundred and twenty?[53] Rather, before the one hundred and twenty believed, there were only twelve. And not all of the twelve persevered, but one of them, Judas, perished.[54] And then eleven were all that were left.[55] Still, from the eleven came the one hundred and twenty and from the one hundred and twenty came three thousand,[56] and then five thousand.[57] And then they filled the whole world with the knowledge of God.[58] The reason for this growth was that they never left their gathering. They were constantly with one another, spending the whole day in the temple, and turning their attention to prayers and sacred readings.[59] This is why they kindled a great fire, this is why their strength never waned, this is why they drew the whole world to them. We, too, must imitate them.[60]

---

52 A small and sluggish congregation discourages growth; an eager and growing congregation will attract new members who will make it stronger. Each Christian has an apostolic mission to arouse the fervor of the Spirit in his brothers and sisters.

53 Cf. Acts 1.15.

54 Two different accounts of Judas' end are given in Mt 27.3–10 and Acts 1.16–19.

55 In the first chapter of his *Demonstration* (PG 48.714), Chrysostom says: "He [Christ] had only eleven men to start with, men who were undistinguished, without learning, ill-informed, destitute, poorly clad, without weapons or sandals, men who had but a single tunic to wear." In the *Demonstration* Chrysostom is proving that Christ is divine because, from such lowly beginnings, his Church enjoyed such a miraculous growth.

56 Cf. Acts 2.41. Actually Luke says that, after the descent of the Holy Spirit and Peter's discourse, three thousand were baptized and added to the Christian community.

57 Cf. Acts 4.4.

58 Chrysostom recounts the miraculous spread of the Church over the known world in his *Demonstration*, chapters 12–13 (PG 829–32).

59 Cf. Acts 2.42–47 and NAB note ad loc.

60 Here Chrysostom attributes the growth of the early Church to the fervor of the first Christians, because his purpose is to increase the fervor and number of his congregation in Constantinople. In his earlier work, the *Demonstration*, his purpose was to prove the divinity of Christ. Therefore, in that work, he saw the Church spreading over the world because of the power of Christ, who was no "mere man."

(38) Suppose we fail to show as much thought and concern for our brothers in the Church as women show for other women who are their neighbors. Would this not be absurd? Yet, when women see some young girl who is poor and has no one to protect her, they all take the place of the girl's relatives and contribute to her from their own resources. And you would see a large and noisy crowd there on the day of the young girl's betrothal. Some of the women—and this often happens—make contributions of money; others lend their presence in person. And this is no small thing. The eagerness of these women hides their frugality and, in this way, they cover over their poverty by showing themselves ready and willing to help. You must do this for the Church of Constantinople.

(39) Let us come running from every side and let us cover over her poverty. Rather, let us free it from poverty by coming here constantly. "The husband is the head of the wife."[61] The wife is the aide of the husband. Therefore, do not let the head be allowed to set foot in this sacred place without its body, let not the body be seen without its head, but let whole human beings come in, head and body, bringing their children with them.

(40) It is pleasant to look upon a tree with a new plant rising up from its roots. But it is much more pleasant to see a man—a man who is more delightful than any olive tree—with the child sprung from his roots standing next to him like a new plant.[62] For, as I said before, there will be from this child a greater recompense for the congregation.[63]

---

61 Cf. Eph 5.23. The text continues: "just as Christ is head of his body the Church . . ." Therefore, the wife is the body as the husband is the head and, together, they form a whole person. It is whole persons, heads and bodies, who must attend the assemblies in church, bringing their children with them.

62 "Like a new plant (*neophytos*)" here means newly planted in the Christian Church. Offspring, like new plants, must be brought to the assemblies to be nurtured by the instruction, to be fed on God's word, and to swell the ranks of the congregation.

63 Cf. above paragraphs 34–36.

(41) We do not marvel at a farmer when he takes care of land which has been farmed many times before. We marvel at him when he takes places which have never been plowed or sown and considers them deserving of much work and care. This is what Paul used to do when he was eager to spread the gospel in places where Christ's name was not known, in fact, in places where the name of Christ had never been heard. Let us imitate Paul so that we may both advance the Church and help ourselves.[64]

(42) Let us run here to be present at each assembly. If lustful desire burns in your heart, the mere sight of this house of prayer will easily enable you to quench the flames. If you are in a fit of rage, you will have no trouble in laying that wild beast to rest. If some other passion besets you, you will be able to quell the storm and bring much calm and peace to your soul.[65] May it come to pass that we all enjoy this peace by the grace and loving-kindness of our Lord Jesus Christ, with whom be glory to the Father together with the Holy Spirit, now and forever, world without end. Amen.

---

64 Parents must see to it that their children, like newly planted fields, receive the proper care. They must also imitate St. Paul by bringing new converts to the church as well as Christians who may have become indifferent to their faith.

65 Attendance at the assemblies and the eucharistic liturgy will be a strong weapon against lust, anger, and every passion which would destroy peace of soul.

HOMILY XII

LESSED BE GOD![1] At each assembly[2] I see that the produce of our fields has grown, our crops are in full bloom, our threshing floor has been filled, our sheaves are multiplying. Even if we count how few were the days since we sowed this seed,[3] look how rich a crop has sprouted up because of your obedience. This makes it clear that it is not the power of any man but God's grace which is cultivating and tending this Church. For this is the nature of a spiritual sowing. It does not wait for time or a number of days, or cycles of months, or the right seasons, or the fullness of years. In a single day, it is possible for the sower of this spiritual seed to harvest his crop. He can do it in so short a span because that brief time was full and complete enough for the task.[4]

(2) However, those who cultivate this earth which we see and feel must work with great diligence and must put up with long delays. These farmers must yoke the oxen which draw the plow, they must cut a deep furrow, they must plant the seeds in abundance, they must smooth out the surface of the earth and cover over all the seeds they have sown. Then, they must wait for the rains to fall in amounts suited to the seeds, they must

---

1 "Blessed be God" is a favorite opening of Chrysostom. Not only does he use it in his Easter homily to the newly-baptized (cf. *Baptismal Instructions*, ACW 31.56) but it begins at least twenty other authentic homilies dating both to Antioch and Constantinople.

2 This translates the Greek *synaxis*, frequently used by Chrysostom at Antioch to denote the assemblies both for the instruction and for the Eucharistic Liturgy.

3 In Hom.XI.29–42, delivered only a few days before, Chrysostom had made an eloquent plea for the faithful to take upon themselves the ministry of increasing the congregation. Thanks to God's grace, the crop has been a rich one.

4 The sowing of spiritual seed does not depend on season or weather, since it is for God to give the increase.

work hard at many other tasks, and wait a long time, and then, finally, they attain the end for which they have labored.

(3) Here, in the Church, we can sow and reap winter and summer. It often happens that we do both on the same day, especially when the souls we are cultivating happen to be rich and fertile. Indeed, we can see that this is so in your case, and this is why we come hurrying to you all the more eagerly. Why? Because a farmer works hardest to make ready for cultivation that field from which he has often filled his threshing floor.

(4) Therefore, since you, too, provide me with rich returns after little labor on my part, I take up my task of cultivation and give it my full attention. I have come to provide you with the conclusion to what I said earlier.[5] At that time, I wove my discourse on the glory of the only begotten Son of God from Old Testament texts. Now I shall continue to do the same thing and will take my start from the same Testament.

(5) In my earlier discourse, I mentioned that Christ had said: "If you believed Moses, you would believe me."[6] Now I am telling you that what Moses said was this: "The Lord your God shall raise up for you a prophet from among your brethren as he raised up me; to him shall you listen."[7] Christ sent the Jews back to Moses so that, through Moses, he might draw them to himself. In the same way, Moses hands over his disciples to his teacher and commands them to believe him in all things.

(6) Therefore, let us believe in whatever Christ does or says, both in all other things and also in that miracle which you heard in today's reading. And what was that miracle? Scripture says: "There was a feast of the Jews, and Jesus went up to Jerusalem. Now there is in Jerusalem by the Sheepgate a pool called in Hebrew Bethesda which has five porticoes."[8] The gospel narrative then has it that, when an angel arrived at certain times, he used to go down into the pool, and his

---

5 This homily will end Chrysostom's series on the "glory of the only begotten."

6 Cf. Jn 5.46 and see Hom.XI.11.

7 Cf. Dt 18.15, but Chrysostom cites the text as quoted in Acts 3.22.

8 Jn 5.1–2 and NAB notes ad loc. The cure of the paralytic on the Sabbath was the gospel reading assigned for that day's liturgy. This explains Chrysostom's choice of this miracle to prove the divine power of Christ's word.

presence was known because the water was stirred up. The first one to go down into the pool after the surging of the water was cured, no matter what sickness he had.[9] And in those porticoes there lay a great multitude of the sick, the blind, the lame, and those with shrivelled limbs, waiting for the stirring of the water.[10]

(7) Why, then, does Christ continually choose Jerusalem and why is he in the habit of coming to the Jews on the feast days?[11] Since those were the days when crowds gathered together, Christ used to observe closely that place and that time so as to come upon those who were sick. For the sick were not so eager to be freed from their illness as the physician was anxious to free them from their ailment. Therefore, when a large crowd gathered and the audience was ready, then he used to come into their midst and show them the truths that bring salvation to their souls.

(8) And so it was that a multitude of the sick was found lying there, waiting for the stirring of the water.[12] And the first one

---

9 NAB omits Jn 5.4, which contains the details mentioned by Chrysostom in this sentence. B. Vawter explains this omission (JBC 63:82) when he tells us that in verse 3 the authentic text merely states that the porticoes were crowded with the sick. The Vulgate adds to verse 3 ". . . waiting for the moving of the water." Verse 4, which was known to the Western Church in the second century and to the fourth-century Greek Fathers, must have appeared in the Greek NT used by Chrysostom. This verse reads (with variations): "For the angel of the Lord went down into the pool from time to time and stirred up the water; and whoever was first to step in after the stirring of the water became healed, no matter what disease he had." These added words are missing in the oldest and most reliable MSS and the language is not Johannine. Although they represent a very old tradition, they must have been a later addition devised to explain Jn 5.7.

10 Cf. Jn 5.3.

11 Chrysostom says in his *Commentary on John* (FOTC 33.352) that the feast day mentioned in Jn 5.1 was the Jewish Pentecost. But later in this present homily, the emphasis is less on which feast it was and more on the fact that Christ cured on the Sabbath. Jesus and his disciples came to Jerusalem at least three times a year to observe the feasts of Passover, Pentecost, and Tabernacles as enjoined by Dt 16.16. Cf. FOTC 33.352 and FOTC 68.179 n.

12 The stirring of the water was probably due to an underground spring which fed the pool and which became intermittently more active. As NAB note on Jn 5.4 says: The appearance of the angel is probably a popular explanation of the turbulence and the healing power attribu~~~~ water. See JBC 63:82.

to go down into the pool after the stirring of the water was cured; the second was not. The medicine was used up, the healing power of that grace was spent. Thereafter, the waters remained deserted just as if curing the sickness of the first one to go down into the pool had wiped out all its power to heal. And this was quite within reason because the grace came through a servant.[13]

(9) But this was not the case after the master had come.[14] The first man to go down into the pool of the waters of baptism was not the only one to be cured. The first, the second, the third, the tenth, the twentieth—all were cured. Even if you speak of ten thousand or twice or three times that many, if you speak of numbers without limit, if you put the whole world in the pool of waters, its grace is not made less, it stays just as strong as it washes all those people clean. That is the great difference between the power of a servant and the authority of a master. The servant cured a single person; the master cures the whole world. The servant cured a single person once a year;[15] if you wish to put ten thousand in the pool every day, the master returns them all to you sound and healthy.

(10) The servant[16] cured by going down into the pool and stirring up the water. The master does not do this. It is enough merely to invoke his name over the waters and so to bestow on them the entire cause of their power to cure. The servant

---

13 The servant, of course, was the angel, whose power was limited to curing only the first one to descend into the pool.

14 Chrysostom will now contrast the limited power of the servant with the infinite power of Christ in baptism. The pool of Bethesda was a symbol; the pool of baptism is the reality. Chrysostom makes the same contrast in his *Commentary on John* (FOTC 33.353): "Just as here it was not merely the nature of the water that healed . . . but water supplemented by the power of the angel, so in our case: it is not merely the water that acts, but, when it has received the grace of the Spirit, then it frees us from every sin." Again we see the vast difference between the type and the reality.

15 Since the Scriptural account specifies no set time between "stirrings of the water," Chrysostom's statement of "once a year" may be merely rhetorical. It is not impossible, however, that the cures at the pool did occur at yearly intervals during one of the fixed feasts which brought pilgrims to Jerusalem. At least, the pool's porticoes were crowded with sick people on this particular feast day (Jn 5.3).

16 Again the servant is the angel.

healed imperfections and mutilations of the body; the master cures the wickedness of the soul. Do you see how clear in every way it becomes that there is a great and immeasurable difference between the servant and the master?[17]

(11) And so a multitude of the sick was lying there, waiting for the movement of the water.[18] Indeed, the place was a spiritual clinic. In a clinic you can see many blind men, many maimed in leg or ailing in some other limb. They are lying there in the sight of all as they wait for the physician. So, too, at the pool, you could see the multitude of those who had gathered there. "In the porticoes was one man who had been sick for thirty-eight years. When Jesus saw him lying there and knew that he had been sick for a long time, he said to him: 'Do you wish to get well?' The sick man answered him and said: 'Yes, Lord. But I have no one to put me into the pool when the water is stirred; while I am coming, another steps down before me.' "[19]

(12) Why did Jesus pass by all the others and come to this man?[20] He did it so that he might show his power and his loving-kindness. His action showed his power because the man's disease had already become incurable, and his weakness had come to the point where he was beyond help. It showed his loving-kindness because, in his care and concern, he saw that this man, more than the others, was the most deserving of his mercy and benefaction.

---

17 The difference between servant and master is immeasurable because the power of the master is infinite.
18 Cf. Jn 5.3.
19 Cf. ibid. 5–8 quoted rather loosely. The evangelist's account does not imply that the man who had been so long infirm spent all thirty-eight years at the pool; however, verse 7 seems to presuppose that he had been there for some time or, at least, had returned there many times in hope of a cure.
20 The evangelist gives no reason why Jesus singled out this man. As B. Vawter sees it (JBC 63:82), John was interested only in the miracle as a sign of Jesus' power. Chrysostom also sees Jesus' choice as an opportunity to manifest his divine power by curing an incurable. But Chrysostom sees it further as an act of Christ's loving-kindness toward one whose patience and perseverance deserved his mercy and concern.

(13) Let us not lightly pass over either the place or the thirty-eight years the man had been in the grip of his infirmity.[21] Let all men listen carefully, all those who have grown old in unending poverty, all who live with the weakness of their infirmity, all who endure the crises of worldly affairs, all who have lived with the surging storms of unexpected troubles. This paralytic[22] lies before us as a haven open to all, as a safe port from human disasters.

(14) No one is so foolish, no one is so miserable and distressed that, if he looks at this man he would not generously and willingly endure whatever troubles may befall himself. If he were sick for twenty years or ten or only five, would not these years have been enough to destroy his strength of soul? Yet this man did not leave the pool but stayed there for thirty-eight years and proved his great patience. Perhaps you think the length of time he stayed there is a marvellous thing. But if you listen to what he said, then especially will you come to know the virtue and discipline of his whole way of life and to know all the patience with which he endured his lot.[23]

(15) Christ stood there and asked him: "Do you wish to get well?"[24] And who would not have known that he wished to get well? Why, then, did Christ ask him? Surely, it was not because he did not know how the man would answer. He who knows the unspoken thoughts in our minds more surely knew what was clear and obvious to all. Why, then, did he ask the question? It was for the same reason as when, at another time,

---

21 Jn 5.5 specifies the thirty-eight years. The place, of course, was the pool where the waters, when stirred, effected a single cure.

22 The evangelist merely states that the man was sick but does not name his infirmity. Chrysostom refers to the sick man as paralyzed or a paralytic eleven times here and in the following paragraphs. As an incurable paralytic who was actually cured after so many years, he serves as a beacon of hope to all who are suffering disasters.

23 His faith gave him the hope and perseverance to endure his lot.

24 Jn 5.6. In his *Commentary on John* (FOTC 33.354), Chrysostom states as the reason why Jesus asked the question: "It was not that he might get this information (that was unnecessary), but that he might show the perseverance of such a person as this, and that we might learn that it was because of his perseverance that he passed by the rest and came to this man."

he said to the centurion: "I will come and cure him."[25] It was not that he did not know what the centurion was going to say but because he knew this beforehand and understood it very exactly. But he also wished to give the centurion a reason and opportunity to speak so that all might see his godly spirit, which had been veiled in shadow, and so that he might say: "No, Lord, for I am not worthy that you should come under my roof."[26]

(16) So, too, in the case of this paralytic, Christ knew what the man was going to say but he still asked him if he wished to be cured. Christ did not ask him because he did not know the answer but he did it so as to give the paralytic an opportunity and a reason to tell of his personal disaster in tragic terms and so to teach us a lesson in patience. For if Christ had cured the man without asking the question, we would have suffered the greatest loss. Why? Because then we would not have learned from the paralytic this lesson in patience and endurance of soul.

(17) Christ did cure and correct the ailment from which the paralytic was suffering at that moment. But he also was considering the future ills of others which were also deserving of his concern. Therefore, he showed forth this man who would teach all who dwell in this world a lesson in patience and endurance. How did Christ do this? He did it by putting the paralytic in a position where he had to answer the question: "Do you wish to get well?"[27]

(18) What, then, did the paralytic say? He did not take the question in bad grace, he did not become angry, he did not say in reply: "You see that I am paralyzed and you know how long I have been sick. Do you still ask me if I wish to get well? Did

---

25 Mt 8.7. Chrysostom may have brought in the centurion's story at this point for two related reasons: first, the centurion's servant was also paralyzed (Mt ibid. 6) and second, Jesus wished to elicit a reply from the centurion as he did from the paralytic. The centurion's reply proved his faith and godly spirit; the paralytic's answer proved his faith and perseverance. Of course, in both cases Jesus knew what the reply would be; he also knew that both answers would benefit us. Cf. Hom.XI.18–22.
26 Cf. Mt 8.8.
27 Cf. Jn 5.6.

you come to make fun of my misfortune and to ridicule
another's troubles?" And you can be sure that sick men are
sullen and surly even if they have been confined to bed for only
a year. But when your illness has been your constant com-
panion for thirty-eight years, how likely could it be that your
virtuous way of life and your self-discipline would not have
been spent and used up in so long a span of time?

(19) Nonetheless, the paralytic neither said nor thought any
such thing. With great reasonableness he made his reply and
said: "Yes, Lord, but I have no one to put me into the pool
when the water is stirred."[28] See how many troubles gathered
together to besiege him. He was sick, he was poor, he had no
one to stand by his side. "While I am coming, another steps
down before me."[29]

(20) This disappointment is more pitiful than all the others.
By itself, it is enough to bend and move a heart of stone. I can
imagine seeing the man, each single year, crawling along and
coming to the mouth of the pool. I can imagine him, each
single year, hanging at the very brink of having his hope come
to a happy fulfillment. And what is worse, he endured this not
for two or three or ten years but for thirty-eight years. He
showed every effort but failed to reach the reward. The race
was run, but the prize went to another over these many years.
And still more difficult was the fact that he saw others freed
from their disease. For you certainly know that we get a keener
perception of our own troubles when we see that others have
fallen into the same dreadful ills but then are freed from them.

(21) This is why a poor man feels his own poverty all the
more when he sees another man who is rich. The sick man feels
more pain when he sees that many of those who were afflicted
have rid themselves of their ailments, while he has no hope of
such a happy end. We get a clearer perception of our own
misfortunes in the well-being of others. This is what happened
to the paralytic at that time. It is true that he was struggling
against sickness, poverty, and loneliness for so long a time. It is

---

28 Cf. ibid. 7.
29 Cf. ibid.

true that he saw others freed from their ills, while he was always trying but never had the strength to succeed. It is true that he had no expectation for the future of again being rid of his suffering. Nonetheless, he did not leave the pool and go away. Each year he hurried to the waters as fast as his ailment allowed.[30]

(22) As for ourselves, after we pray once to God for some favor or other and fail to get it, we become troubled and fall into the utmost indifference and deepest grief. We withdraw from prayer and put an end to all earnest effort. Can we praise the paralytic as he deserves? Can we condemn ourselves enough for our negligence? What defense or pardon would we deserve when we slacken our efforts and lose heart so quickly, whereas he stood steadfast and patient for thirty-eight years?

(23) What, then, did Christ do? When the paralytic showed that he deserved to be cured, in all justice Christ came to him before the others and said to him: "Rise, pick up your mattress, and walk!"[31] Do you see how the thirty-eight years did him no harm because he had endured everything with patience? His soul had become more virtuous and disciplined in that long span of time.[32] It had been tested by his misfortune as in a smelting furnace and, therefore, he received his cure with greater glory. For it was not an angel but the master of the angels himself who cured him.

(24) Why did Christ command him to take up his mattress?[33]

---

30 His pitiable condition and constant failure to be cured never destroyed his hope and perseverance. In his *Commentary on John* (FOTC 33.360) Chrysostom says: ". . . what more pathetic than his plight? Do you perceive that his spirit had been chastened by his long illness? Do you see that all spleen had been checked? He did not utter any blasphemy, as we hear many doing in the midst of troubles. He did not curse the day he was born; he did not rant at his questioner, nor did he say: 'It is to ridicule and make fun of my condition that you ask whether I want to get well,' But gently and very mildly: 'I do, Lord.' "

31. Jn 5.8.

32 As had been the case with the man born blind and with Elizabeth, mother of the Baptist. Cf. Hom.X.35.

33 Another reason is given by Chrysostom in his *Commentary on John* (FOTC 33.361) where he says: "He also bade him take up his pallet, so that the miracle which had taken place was believed, and no one thought the incident an illusion or a deceit. For he would not have been able to carry his pallet if his limbs had not been made very strong and sturdy."

Particularly for this reason which was his first and foremost purpose. He did it so that he might free the Jews for the future from observing the Law.³⁴ When the sun is shining, there is no longer any need to sit next to a lamp.³⁵ After they had been shown the reality, no longer did the Jews have to cling to the type. Still, if Christ ever broke the Law of the Sabbath, he did so by working a very great miracle on that day.³⁶ Why did he do this? He did it so that the surpassing magnitude of the marvel he wrought, might astound those who witnessed it, undermine the observance of rest on the Sabbath and, little by little, bring it to an end.³⁷

(25) His second reason was to block up their shameless mouths. The judgments they were making about his miracles were grossly malicious. By their slander, they were trying to hide the glory of what he was doing. This is why he ordered the paralytic to make a public display of carrying his bed, as if he were exhibiting a monument to the defeat of his disease and an indisputable proof of his return to health.³⁸ Christ also gave this order to keep the Jews from saying what they had said in the case of the man born blind. What had they said about him?

---

34 In the present homily the stress is on Jesus' equal power with the Father as giver of the Law. He who gave the Law can also amend it. But when Christ amends the Law, he does not annul it; rather, he brings it to perfection. Cf. Hom.X.25–29; 36–43.

35 Chrysostom uses the same figure in *Against Judaizing Christians* (FOTC 68.69) in contrasting the Old Law with the New Covenant, when he asks: "Why, then, do you sit beside a lamp after the sun has appeared?"

36 Such as the cure at the pool of Bethesda and restoring his sight to the man born blind (cf. Jn 9.14 and Hom X.30–32). Jesus, as master of the Law and Lord of the Sabbath (cf. Mk 2.28), stated his position on the Sabbath, when he said to the Pharisees that the Sabbath was made for man, not man for the Sabbath (ibid. 27). Rabbinic casuistry listed 39 types of work prohibited on the Sabbath, but many were petty and overly rigorous. Jesus did not wholly reject the Sabbath; he laid down no particular precepts for its observance but left it to prudent and humane judgment to determine when the Sabbath should yield to matters of greater importance such as healing. See J. McKenzie, DB 751–52.

37 J. McKenzie (DB 752) says that the Sabbath is profaned when one makes it an excuse to evade one's own duty of providing for one's own essential needs or of doing good to another. Jesus did not intend that it should not be kept holy or that it should be done away with; it should be observed according to reasonable standards and not by man-made restrictions.

38 Cf. Jn 5.10 and NAB note ad loc.

"This is the man. This is not the man. This is he."[39] To prevent them from expressing any such doubt as to the paralytic's identity, Christ ordered him to take up his mattress, and the bed held high was a denunciation of their impudence and an accusation of their shameless conduct.[40]

(26) Furthermore, I can bring up a third reason, a reason just as strong as the two which I discussed. Christ commanded the paralytic to carry his bed so that you might know that the entire marvel was wrought not by human skill but by divine power. In this way Christ offers the strongest and clearest proof that the paralytic was truly and absolutely restored to health. He did this so that none of those blasphemers might say that the paralytic was acting as Christ's accomplice in feigning a cure and, as a favor to Christ, pretended to walk without help.[41]

(27) This is why Christ ordered the paralytic to carry a load on his shoulders.[42] Unless his limbs had been made solid and his joints held fast, he would not have been able to support the weight on his shoulders. In addition to all this, he also showed that, when Christ gave the command, everything happened in a single moment—he was both free from his disease and returned to health.

(28) Even if physicians free their patients from diseases, they cannot bring a sick man back to health in a single moment. They still need another long period of time for the patient to recuperate, so that traces of the disease may, little by little, be driven out and cast forth from the body. But Christ does not cure in this way. In a single moment of time he both frees from disease and restores to health; there is no interval between the

---

39 Cf. Jn 9.8,9.
40 The paralytic had been miraculously and genuinely cured; he was not an imposter, an accomplice of Jesus pretending a cure. The shameless conduct of the Pharisees was that they ignored the miracle but railed against the violation of the Sabbath. Cf. paragraph 31 below.
41 The third reason Chrysostom gives is that, in ignoring the miracle, the Pharisees are ignoring the divine power of Jesus who worked the miracle. If the cure had been feigned, Jesus would be no more than a charlatan. If the cure was genuine, to deny it would be blasphemous.
42 To carry a burden on the Sabbath was a capital crime. Cf. Nm 15.32–36 and paragraph 42 below. But Jesus commands the paralytic to carry his bed to prove he had been cured by divine power.

cure and the recovery. As soon as the sacred word was uttered by his holy tongue, the sickness fled, the word became deed, and the whole illness was completely cured.[43]

(29) When a maidservant is rebelling but then sees her master coming, she grows humble and returns to her good behavior. So, too, the paralytic's body had revolted like the maidservant, and this caused the paralysis. But when the body saw its Master coming near, it returned to its good behavior and resumed its proper discipline. And the word of Christ accomplished all this. Yet the words were not mere words but the words of God, of which the prophet said: "The works of his words are mighty."[44] For if God's words made man when man did not exist, much more will they make him whole again and restore him to health even though he has grown feeble and weak with disease.

(30) At this point, I would be glad to question those busybodies who are inquisitive about God's essence.[45] How did the paralytic's limbs come back to normal? How were his bones made solid? How did his muscles, so long destroyed, become strong again? How did his sinews, so long relaxed, grow taut and stretch? How was his long-damaged strength restored and roused from slumber? But they could not tell me how. Therefore, marvel only at what was done. Do not be inquisitive about the way it was done.

(31) When the paralytic did as he was ordered and took up his couch, the Jews saw him and said: "It is the Sabbath; you are not allowed to take up your mattress on the Sabbath."[46] They

---

43 The fact that the cure was instantaneous proves that Jesus' act was a miracle and beyond any natural powers.

44 Jl 2.11 (LXX).

45 "Meddlesome busybodies" are watchwords by which Chrysostom describes the pretensions to knowledge of the Anomoeans, e.g., in Homilies I.36; II.8, 16, 19, 31, 32, 39; IV.3; V.29. All of these places are dealing with the incomprehensibility of God's nature. Here, the question is the divine power of the Son, the "glory of the only begotten." Some of the Anomoeans may have been present to hear Chrysostom's questions, but the tone of both Homilies XI and XII is far more instructive than polemic.

46 Cf. Jn 5.10–11 and see note 36 above. B. Vawter (JBC 63:83) notes that a specific rabbinic law prohibited the carrying of one's bed on the Sabbath.

should have adored the one who wrought the wonder, they should have marvelled at the miracle he performed, but they kept talking about the Sabbath. Why? Because in all truth "they were straining out the gnat but swallowing the camel."[47]

(32) What, then, did the cured man say? "He who made me well said to me, 'take up your mattress and walk.' "[48] Do you see the man's courtesy and gratitude? He acknowledged who the physician was and said that the lawgiver who commanded him was worthy of his trust. Just as the man born blind summed it up for them so, too, did the cured paralytic. How did the blind man argue? They said to him: "This man is not from God because he does not observe the Sabbath."[49] And what did he say? "We know that God does not hear sinners. But this man opened my eyes."[50] So his argument goes something like this: "If he transgressed the law, he sinned. But if he sinned, he would not have so much power. Where there is sin, there can be no manifestation of power. But he did show his power. Therefore, he did not transgress the law and did not sin."[51]

(33) The paralytic argued in the same way. When he said: "He who made me well,"[52] this is what he was hinting at. "If this

---

47 Cf. Mt 23.24. This obvious hyperbole points out how ludicrous were the Scribes and Pharisees, who so carefully observed the externals of the Law while neglecting its weightier matters—justice and mercy and good faith (ibid. 23). J. McKenzie (JBC 43:159) clarifies the straining out of tiny gnats while swallowing the camel (the largest animal known to Palestinians) by explaining that, in the ancient world, strainers were attached to the mouths of decanters because any liquid might contain foreign matter. Pharisaic observance used the strainer also to strain out any ritually unclean substance which one might inadvertently consume. Casuistry can get so lost in details that it neglects to question justice, mercy, and fidelity in an action.
48 Jn 5.11.
49 Cf. ibid. 9.16. In the same verse other Pharisees also objected: "If a man is a sinner, how can he perform signs like these?" The blind man answers both sets of objectors even though Chrysostom cites only the first.
50 Cf. ibid. verses 30 and 31. When Chrysostom discusses the cure of the blind man in Hom.X.30–35, his purpose was to prove that Jesus is the master of the Law. Hence, he does not debate with the Pharisees in that homily.
51 The argument Chrysostom puts in the mouth of the man cured of his blindness is the power of Jesus. Such power (as in Hom.X.30–35) can belong only to the lawgiver. Hence, Jesus did not transgress the Law nor is he a sinner.
52 Jn 5.11.

is a man who has proved his power, he would not be obliged to answer charges of breaking the law."[53] And what did the Jews say? "Where is the man who said to you, 'Take up your mattress and walk?'"[54] See how lacking in judgment and perception they are! Look how their souls are swollen with arrogance!

(34) The eyes of envious men see nothing whole and entire. As a result they can only find an opportunity for argument. This was the case with those who questioned the paralytic. When he had been cured and confessed that Christ had both cured him and ordered him to take up his bed, they failed to see the one thing but spoke of the other. They closed their eyes to the miracle but denounced the breaking of the Sabbath.[55] They did not say: "Where is he who made you well?" They remained silent about the cure but they did say: "Where is the man who said to you: 'Take up your mattress and go away!'"[56] But how could the cured man answer them? For, as the evangelist says: "But he did not know, for Jesus had quietly gone away because there was a crowd in the place."[57] And this action provided both a very strong defense for the man and the greatest proof of Christ's concern for him.

(35) When Christ stood beside him, the paralytic did not greet him as the centurion did nor did he say: "Only say the

---

53 Again, the cured paralytic's argument is based on the power of Jesus, who would not be obliged to answer charges of breaking the Law because he is the lawgiver.

54 Cf. Jn 5.12.

55 See above paragraph 25 and note 40.

56 Cf. Jn 5.12.

57 Ibid. 13. In his *Commentary on John*, (FOTC 33.364) Chrysostom gives as the reasons why Jesus slipped away in the crowd: first, that if he were not there, the cured man's testimony might be above suspicion; second, so as not to cause the Pharisees' ill feeling to flare up more strongly, because he knew that the sight of the object of envy kindles no small spark in the envious; finally, so that the discussion would be between the healed man and his accusers. Thus, Jesus would not have to speak about himself and inflame their hatred further. In the present homily, Chrysostom sees Jesus as slipping off because of his concern for the man he had healed. If the cured paralytic did not know the identity of his physician, he could more easily defend himself against the Pharisees.

word and my servant will be healed."[58] When you hear this, do not accuse the cured paralytic of lack of faith for failing to recognize him. He did not even know who Christ was. How could he have known him since he had never seen him? This is why he said: "I have no one to put me into the pool."[59] If he had known Christ, he would never have mentioned the pool or going down into the waters. He would have expected to be cured just in the way he was cured. But he thought Christ was one of the crowd, a mere man, and this is why he mentioned the others who got there before him and were cured.[60]

(36) And it is a proof of Christ's care and concern that he left the man cured but did not reveal himself to him. He kept his identity secret to prevent the Jews from suspecting that the paralytic was a counterfeit witness. For the Jews would have thought that the paralytic said this because Christ was present and urging him to say it. But the fact that Christ was not there and that the man did not know him removed this chance of suspicion. For the evangelist said: "He did not know who he was."[61]

(37) This is why Christ sent the cured man off alone and by himself. Now the Jews might take him aside and question him to their heart's content on what had happened. And after they had gotten sufficient evidence on what had really occurred, they might put a stop to their ill-timed madness. This is why Christ said nothing himself but provided the Jews with proof by his very deeds. And these deeds spoke more distinctly in every way and in tones clearer than any clarion's call.

(38) For, in this way, all suspicion was now removed from the testimony given by the paralytic. "He who made me well said to me, 'Take up your mattress and go away.' "[62] The paralytic becomes an evangelist, a teacher of those unbelievers, a physician and a herald to put them to shame and condemn them. He was a physician not by his words alone but by his

---

58 Cf. Mt 8.8 and See Hom.XI.19, where Chrysostom says that even in the midst of disaster, the centurion recognized the superiority of the master.
59 Cf. Jn 5.7.
60 Cf. ibid.
61 Cf. ibid. 13.
62 Ibid. 11.

actions. He did not heal by what he said but by what he did. What did he do? He carried about with him a clear and indisputable proof; by his cured body he established the truth of the testimony he gave.

(39) "Afterwards Jesus found him and said to him: 'See, you are cured. Sin no more, so that nothing worse may happen to you.' "[63] Did you see the physician's wisdom? Did you see his concern? Not only did he free the man from his ailment at the time he was cured but he also made him safe against disease for the future. And this was a very opportune time to do so.

(40) When the man was lying on his couch, Jesus said nothing like this to him; he did not then remind him of his sins. For the souls of those who are sick are distressed and somewhat morose. So first he drove out the disease, first he restored the man to health. Then, after he proved by his deed his power and his concern for him, he gave his timely exhortation and advice. Why? Because Christ had already shown by the very things he did that he now deserved to be believed.

(41) Why did the cured man go off and show himself to the Jews?[64] It was because he wished them to share in the true teaching of Christ. But this was why, as the evangelist says, they hated and persecuted Christ. Pay careful attention to me here because here is the crux of the whole struggle. "This is why they kept persecuting him, because he did these things on the Sabbath."[65] Let us see, therefore, how Christ defends himself. For the way he presents his case shows us whether he is a free

---

63 Ibid. 14 and see NAB note ad loc.

64 Cf. ibid. 15. B. Vawter (JBC 63:83) says that the healed paralytic was probably acting in good faith and answering the question put to him by the Pharisees in verse 12. Chrysostom sees him as fulfilling an apostolic mission.

65 Ibid. 16. As B. Vawter says (JBC 63:84), the attitude of Jesus toward the fulfillment of the Sabbath obligation was the initial cause of the Jewish leaders' hostility. Jesus' defense in verse 17 (cf. NAB note ad loc.) is: "My Father works even until now, and I work." Verse 18 shows the Jews reaction to Jesus' words. They were more determined to kill him because he was not only breaking the Sabbath, but, worse still, was speaking of God as his Father, thereby making himself equal to God. Chrysostom will now prove that Jesus is equal in power to the Father and is one with the Father in divine nature.

man or a servant, whether he is one who serves or one who commands.

(42) What he had done seemed to be a most serious violation of the law. In fact, there was a time when a man who had gathered wood on the Sabbath was stoned to death because he had carried burdens on the Sabbath.[66] Christ was accused of this serious sin because he had violated the Sabbath. Let us see, therefore. Does he first ask for pardon as would a servant and a man subject to orders? Or does he show himself as a man with power and authority, like a master who presides over the law and who has himself given the commands? How, then, does he make his defense? He said: "My Father works even until now, and I work."[67]

(43) Did you see his authority? However, if he were inferior to and less than the Father, what he said is no defense. Rather, it is a greater charge and a more grievous accusation. Suppose a man does something which only one superior to him may do. Suppose he is then caught and accused. Suppose he says: "I did it because one superior to me has done it." Not only does this kind of defense fail to free him from the charges but it makes him subject to greater blame and more grievous accusation. For it is a mark of haughtiness and arrogance to attempt things which transcend one's dignity and true worth.

(44) Therefore, if Christ, too, was inferior to the Father, what he said was no defense but, rather, grounds for a more serious charge. But because Christ was equal to the Father, it constituted no grounds for any charge at all. If you wish, I shall clarify what I am saying by an example. Only a king or the emperor is permitted to wear a purple robe and a crown on his head. No one else is allowed to do so. Suppose, then, some man from the crowd is seen wearing this adornment and is then

---

66 Cf. Nm 15.32–36 and see paragraph 27 above.
67 Jn 5.17. B. Vawter's commentary on this verse (JBC 63:84) notes that God's "resting" on the Sabbath cannot be taken to mean a literal cessation of God's creative action, without which the world would cease to exist. What Jesus is saying is that just as the Father is not inhibited by the Sabbath, neither is Jesus, who is his Son and equal. This statement corresponds to Mark's declaration that the Son of Man is also Lord of the Sabbath (Mk 2.28). See also Hom.VII.12.

dragged into the courtroom. Suppose he says: "I am wearing this adornment because this is what the emperor wears." This kind of defense does not free him from the charge but even makes him subject to more serious punishment and vengeance.

(45) Again, if we think of the worst sorts of men—murderers, highwaymen, grave robbers, and those who have dared to commit other crimes like these—to free such criminals from punishment can only be an act of imperial generosity. Now suppose that some judge lets such a condemned man go without the emperor's approval and is himself then prosecuted for this. Suppose he, too, says: "I let him go because the emperor lets condemned criminals go." This kind of defense does not set the judge free but kindles a stronger fire of anger against him. And this is very reasonable.

(46) For inferiors have no right to transgress the law,[68] attack the authority of their superiors, and then to offer the actions of these superiors in defense of their own misconduct. For this is still greater outrage against those who put the power in their inferiors' hands. Therefore, no one who is an inferior and a subject will ever defend himself with such arguments. But if a man is himself an emperor or one who has the same dignity, he will feel quite confident in saying that he is only doing what the emperor does. Just as their preeminence is one and the same, so, too, their power would naturally be one and the same.[69] Therefore, if we see someone offering this argument in his own defense, he must in every way be a person of the same dignity as the one whose power he puts forward in his own defense.

---

68 Since neither PG's reprint of Montfaucon's edition nor the texts of Savile and Morel make very good sense here, I have ventured a conjecture of my own. PG reads *en paroiniais* (in fits of drunken violence). Savile and Morel have *en paroimiais* (by dark sayings). I have conjectured *en paranomiais* (by transgressions of the law), which I have translated freely as a verb (to transgress the law).

69 In the year 363 the Roman emperor, Valentinian, chose his brother Valens as his colleague in ruling the empire. The two emperors decided to divide the empire; Valentinian took the West and ruled from Rome, while Valens ruled the East from Constantinople.

(47) Therefore, when Christ used this argument to justify to the Jews what he had done, he gave us an indisputable proof that he is of the same dignity as the Father. If you wish, let us compare my example to the words of Christ and to the work he did. And so, let his use of power to violate the Sabbath be the same as wearing the purple robe and crown, the same as letting the condemned criminals go.

(48) The emperor alone is allowed to do those things. None of his subjects is permitted to do them. But if someone is seen doing them, and doing them in all justice, he too must be an emperor. So, too, we here see Christ doing these things with authority. If he is then accused and puts forward his Father as his defense when he says: "My Father works even until now,"[70] it is altogether necessary that Christ be equal to the Father, who also acts with authority.

(49) If Christ were not equal to the Father, he would not have used this kind of plea to defend himself. So that you may understand more clearly what I am saying, recall that once the disciples violated the Sabbath by plucking ears of grain and eating them on the Sabbath.[71] In the case of the paralytic, Christ, too, violated the Sabbath. The Jews accused the disciples and they accused Christ. Let us see how he defended the disciples and how he defended himself. From the difference between the two you may understand the superiority and dignity of his argument in his own defense.

(50) What argument, then, did he offer in defense of what the disciples did? "Have you not read what David did when he was hungry?"[72] When he is pleading in defense of those who are servants, he appeals to David, their fellow servant. But

---

70 Jn 5.17.
71 Cf. Mt 12.1. J. McKenzie (JBC 43:79) explains that the disciples plucked ears of wheat and rubbed the grains in their hands to make a rough meal. The preparation of food was listed by the rabbis as one of the 39 forms of work forbidden on the Sabbath even though the plucking of stray ears in a field was permitted in Dt 23.26.
72 Mt 12.3. Jesus defends his disciples by citing the example of David (1 Sm [1 Kgs] 21.2–7) when he and his men ate the showbread (Lv 24.5–9) in the Tabernacle of the temple because they had no other food.

when he is defending himself, he refers the argument to his Father. "My Father works, and I work."[73]

(51) What kind of work is it to which he refers? Perhaps someone might say: "After six days God rested from all his work."[74] So the work to which Christ refers is God's daily providence.[75] For God not only produced the creation but he holds together what he produced. Whether you are speaking about the angels, the archangels, the powers above, or simply every creature both visible and invisible, they all enjoy the benefit of his providence. And if they are ever deprived of that providential action, they waste away, they perish, they are gone.

(52) Therefore, Christ wished to show that holding creation together is the work of persons who exercise providence and care rather than of things which benefit from this providence and care. He wished to show that this is the work of those who sustain by their activity rather than of things which are sustained by it. That is why he said: "My Father works, and I work."[76] He wishes to prove that he is equal to the Father.

(53) Keep this in your mind and guard it with all possible care. Make your way of life a robe which is woven together from good moral conduct and correct doctrine. This was my exhortation to you just recently;[77] it is my exhortation to you today. And I will never stop exhorting you to this. Nothing contributes to a virtuous and moral way of life as does the time you spend here in church. Barren land, which has no one to water it, is soon filled with thorns and thistles. But land which enjoys the labor of the farmer's hands produces in abundance, flourishes, and teems with fruit.[78]

---

73 Jn 5.17; see Hom.VII.12 and paragraphs 41–42 above.
74 Cf. Gn 2.2 (LXX).
75 Divine providence is God's plan for guiding every creature to its proper end. He has supreme dominion over his creation and has ordained its ends in his infinite wisdom. By his care and providence, he sustains every creature in being, conserves it in existence, and concurs with it in its every activity.
76 Cf. Jn 5.17.
77 See Hom.XI.28–42.
78 Cf. Heb 6.7–8. Thistles and thorns are signs of a neglected field.

(54) It is the same with the soul. The soul which enjoys the watering that comes from the words of God produces in abundance, flourishes, and teems with the fruit of the Spirit. But when a soul has become dry, is left uncared for, and needs such watering, it becomes desert, its vines grow wild and run to wood, it produces an abundance of thorns. And these thorns have the natural characteristics of sin. For where there are thorns, there will you find snakes, serpents, scorpions, and every power of the devil.[79]

(55) If you do not believe what I am saying, come now and let us compare our souls to those which have been left untended. Then you will see how great the difference is. Rather, let us examine what kind of souls we are when we enjoy God's teaching and what kind of souls we are when it happens that we are deprived of this help for a long time. When we have such a great source of profit, we must not waste it. The time we spend here in church is the basis of every blessing.[80]

(56) When a man goes home from church, his wife sees him as a more worthy husband. When a woman goes home from here, her husband sees her as a more desirable wife. For physical beauty does not make a wife more lovable, but the virtue of her soul does.[81] Cosmetics, eye shadow, gold ornaments, and expensive clothes cannot do this. But chastity and sobriety, goodness and virtue, and a firm fear of God can win and keep her husband's love.

(57) Spiritual beauty cannot be developed perfectly anywhere else except in this marvellous and divine stronghold of

---

79 Snakes, serpents, and scorpions are all seen here as powers of the devil. The snake (*drakōn*) (Rv 12.3 and 9) and the serpent (*ophis*) mean the devil figuratively (Rv 12.9) or actually (2 Cor 11.3); the scorpion (*skorpios*) is feared much for its sting (Rv 9.3, 5, 10) and is used figuratively for an extremely harmful person or type (Ez 2.6). In Lk 10.19 snakes and scorpions are "powers of the enemy," i.e., Satan.

80 See Hom.XI.33–36. But the benefits derived from that time in church will accompany us home and into our family life.

81 Chrysostom speaks of the true adornment of women in his *Baptismal Instructions* (ACW 31.36–39). In his homily *In Matt.* 30 (PG 57.369), speaking to the husband, he says: "If you mold the face of her soul so that it is beautiful, you will not see her bodily face ugly with blood red lips, with a mouth like the blood-smeared mouth of a bear, with eyebrows covered with soot as if from a pot, and with cheeks powdered like the walls of a tomb."

the church. Here the apostles and prophets wipe clean and beautify the face, they strip away the marks of senility left by sin, they apply the bloom of youth, they get rid of every wrinkle, stain, and blemish from our souls.[82] Therefore, let us all, men and women, be eager to implant this beauty in ourselves.

(58) Sickness withers physical beauty, length of years destroys it, old age drains it dry, death comes and takes it all away. But beauty of the soul cannot be marred by time, disease, old age, death, or any other such thing. It stays constantly in bloom. But many a time physical beauty provokes to licentious deeds those who look upon it. When the beauty is beauty of the soul, it draws God himself to love it. It is just as the prophet said when he was addressing the Church: "Hear, O daughter, and see; turn your ear, forget your people and your father's house, and the King shall desire your beauty."[83]

(59) Therefore, beloved, let us develop this beauty every day and so become dear to God. Let us wipe away every stain by reading the Scriptures, by prayer and almsgiving, by peace and concord with one another. Let us do this so that the King may come to love the beauty in our souls and deem us worthy of the kingdom of heaven. May it come to pass that we all gain this through the grace and loving-kindness of our Lord Jesus Christ, with whom be glory to the Father together with the Holy Spirit, now and forever, world without end. Amen.

---

82 Cf. Eph 5.27.
83 Cf. Ps 44 (45).11–12 (LXX).

INDICES

INDEX

and n., 79 and n., 80, 81 and n., 83, 85 and n., 86 and n., 87, 88, 90 and n., 95, 96 and n., 97 and n., 98 and n., 99 and n., 100, 101, 102 and n., 103 and n., 105, 106, 107, 108, 110, 111, 112 and n., 113, 114, 116, 117 and n., 120 and n., 121 and n., 122 and n., 123 and n., 124, 125 and n., 126, 127, 131, 132 and n., 133, 135 and n., 137, 138, 140, 141, 142 and n., 143 and n., 145 and n., 146 and n., 148, 150, 153 and n., 154, 155 and n., 156, 158, 160, 161n., 162, 163, 165n., 166, 167, 168n., 169 and n., 170, 171 and n., 176, 177n., 179, 180, 183, 186n., 188, 189 and n., 191n., 195, 197, 201, 203, 204, 205, 206, 207 and n., 208, 209, 212 and n., 214 and n., 215, 217n., 218, 219n., 221, 222, 224, 228 and n., 231 and n., 234, 235, 236, 237, 238 and n., 239 and n., 245, 250, 251, 253, 254, 256, 262n., 268 and n., 274, 275 and n., 278, 279n., 280 and n., 286 and n., 294, 298, 301n., 302n., 305, 307 and passim.; essence, *see* s.v., Father, son, Spirit; gift of, 5, 53 and n., 64n.; glory of, 5, 93, 123n.; 133, 204n., 287; form of, 5, 189, 263, 264; Son of living, 5, 203n., 224; revelation of, 5, 74, 75, 76, 84n.; equal with, 5, 78n., 263 and n., 264, 301n.; true, 6, 7, 15, 28, 190; right hand of, 6, 124, 146n., 278n.; perfect, 7; wisdom of, 8, 60, 62, 74n. 99, 120, 144n., 175n., 176n., 305n.; Son of, 10, 15, 35, 46, 88n., 139, 147, 275, 287; unity of, 11, 14; incomprehensible, 12, 23, 27, 98n., 108, 115, 124, 188n., 214; image of, 12; substance of, 13, 62n., 189; Word is, 13, 145; power of, 13, 81, 82n., 84n.; nature of, 23, 27, 29, 32, 33, 117, 154n., 164n., 187n., 214, 215; creative act of, 24; knowledge of, 24, 25, 32, 33, 34, 59n., 63, 65 and n., 67, 74n., 77, 127, 149n., 153n., 212 and n., 273, 276, 283; exists, 26, 65, 91n., 154; incomprehensibility of, 32, 33, 35, 40, 102, 137n.,

138 and n., 188; made flesh, 34; Christ is, 40, 47; word(s) of, 51n., 74, 188n., 206, 273n., 280 and n., 281n., 282, 284n., 297, 306; servant(s) of, 52; fear of, 54, and n., 306; omnipresence of, 58n., 61; command of, 59n., 183; mystery of, 60n., 221; presence of, 60n., 61n., 66, 156; providence of, 62 and n., 63 and n., 305; peace of, 64n., 69; glory to, 66, 84 and n., 96 and n.; Lamb of, 75, 202 and n.; promise of, 76, 84; wrath of, 78n., 178; changeless, 79; will of, 83, 93n., 156n., 201n., 228n.; freedom of, 83n., 85n.; dishonor, 84, 96 and n.; help of, 90n., 98n.; name of, 98, 141, 142, 143, 145, 146; condescension of, 102, 103 and n., 107, 108, 122; throne of, 106 and n., 131n., 278n.; of mercy, 114, 163, 180n.; accommodation, 118, 122; depths of, 140, 148; Spirit of, 140, 148, 175n.; one, 140, 141, 142, 147, 186n.; freedom to speak to, 158 and n.; dignity of, 169; grace of, 170, 173 and n., 221, 274, 286 and n.; has no form, 190; dear to, 307

god(s), 125 and n., 146, 147, 159n., 186n., 188 and n., 190 and n.

Godet, P., 28n.

Godhead, 14, 28, 141 and n., 262n., 265n., 278n.

godlessness, 68, 73, 78, 92, 93, 109, 226

Godman, S., 8n.

Goggin, Sr. Thomas Aquinas, 8n., 21n.

gold, 40, 103, 104n., 167, 177 and n., 182, 185, 210, 228, 281, 306

Goliath, 33, 272 and n., 273

Gomorrah, 78n., 235

Gonzaga, Sr. M., 21n.

gospel(s), 44, 47, 120, 136n., 175n., 231n., 233n., 285, 287 and n.; of John, 193; synoptic, 204n.; preaching of, 212n.

governance, 64, 65, 86 and n.

grace(s), 53, 61, 62, 73n., 98n., 99n., 114, 120, 135, 144n., 169n., 289; of Spirit, 95, 169, 272, 289n.; God's, 170, 173 and n., 185, 221, 274, 286 and n.; of Christ, 187; life

326

risen, 88n.; Christ, 278n.
ritual, 93n., 168, 250n., 256n.
ritually unclean, 298n.
river, 57n., 72, 173, 175, 275
rob, 210, 231n., 254
robber, 26, 134, 159
robbery, 5, 263 and n., 264 and n., 265
robe, 208, 239, 305; purple, 302, 304
rock, 203n., 272; spiritual, 272
Rolfe, J., 112n.
Roman, 14, 16, 37, 86 and n., 170n., 303n.
Rome, 4, 21, 303n.
roof, 238, 277, 292
room, 74n., 156n., 205, 250
root, 52, 71n., 76, 77, 95 and n., 96n., 98, 99n., 115, 116, 156, 162, 173, 220, 252n., 284; evil, 96
royal, 89, 231
rule, 98, 107, 172, 223n., 225, 230, 253, 279n., 280n., 303n.
ruler, 98n., 113, 121 and n., 230, 249, 275

Sabbath, 35, 281n., 287n., 288n., 295 and n., 296n., 297 and n., 298, 299, 301 and n., 302 and n., 304n.; resting on, 302n.; violate, 304
Sabellian, 10, 261n.
Sabellianism, 11n., 13, 142n.
Sabellius (the Libyan), 11, 142; and n., 197 and n.
sacred, 74n., 132, 165, 179, 235; writer, 100n., 101n., 143, 148; moment, 113, 129 and n., 133; Pasch, 175 and n.; table, 178; essence, 201; ship, 271; readings, 283; word, 297
sacrifice, 39, 74n., 113, 147, 254, 262n.; eucharistic, 113n.; spiritual, 178
sacrificial, 181
Salaville, S., 19n.
salvation, 9, 16, 51n., 63n., 80, 93n., 96, 113, 156n., 172 and n., 178, 192n., 216, 224, 228n., 265, 266n., 280, 288; through Christ, 99n.; plan of, 9, 63n., 119n., 144 and n., 176n., 191n.
Samaritan, woman, 154n.
sanctuary, 74, 75, 168
Sarah, 78n., 84

Satan, 135n., 155, 158, 171 and n., 192n., 203, 206, 224, 280n.; hands of, 171 and n.; pomp of, 271n.; devil in Job, 134n.
save, 53, 81n., 93 and n., 155, 156, 172, 180, 228, 229, 237
Savile, H., 29, 43, 226n., 233n., 303n.
Savior, 9, 145 and n., 156, 222, 231n., 234, 236, 237, 238
Saydon, P., 145n.
Schoeps, H.-J., 6n.
scorn, 80, 188, 211, 232; brothers, 131
Scribes, 260, 298n.
Scripture(s), 18, 24, 25, 26, 56, 95 and n., 98n., 109n., 143, 145, 146, 185n., 187, 191, 253, 261n., 275, 307; allegorical interpretation of, 12, 214n.; arguments from, 24, 33, 150, 262n., 273 and n.; proof from, 74, 188, 193, 235, 262; divine, 91, 153, 155, 186, 199, 214; holy, 91, 185; no contradicton in, 140n., 275; dishonor the, 274; reading the, 307
Scriptural, 37, 218n., 236, 289n.
sea, 72, 79, 80, 82, 100, 118, 180, 185, 186, 220, 252, 271, 275; Red, 79n.; Euxine, 82; depth of, 60, 61n., 63
season, 286 and n.
seat, 119, 124, 126, 128, 152, 225, 226, 278n., 279
secret, 61, 62, 120, 300
sect, 6, 174
Sellars, R., 19n.
semi-Arian, 16, 18
sense, 105, 116, 126, 137, 141n., 145n., 181n., 220; biblical, 154n., 171n.
senseless, 218
Seraphim, 66, 80, 97, 101 and n., 102, 106, 108, 115, 124, 132, 133n., 208, 279
sermon, 27n., 35, 38, 39, 40, 41, 42, 43, 44, 45, 46, 47
serpent, 57n., 59n., 97n., 306 and n.
servant(s), 60, 68, 69, 74, 106, 119, 134, 144, 156, 161, 202, 209, 219, 230, 249, 253 and n., 263 and n., 264, 275, 276 and n., 277 and n., 278 and n., 279, 289 and n., 290 and n., 292n., 300, 302, 304; fellow, 75, 105 and n., 110, 111, 160, 182, 183, 304; of Lord, 202n.; of father,

breath of, 186; Helper, 224n.; life-giving, 243; fire of, 283; fervor of, 283n.; descent of, 283n.; fruit of, 306
spirit(s), 12, 26, 28, 30, 34, 51, 54n., 139, 148, 151n., 155, 181, 205, 248n., 271, 279, 281, 294n.; lowly, 28; weapons of, 34; distinction of, 54n.; of piety, 110; evil, 121n., 252n.; powers above are, 124; pure, 124n.; God is, 154, 155; pray with, 155n.; parents in, 164n., 165; of just men, 167; of faith, 177; virtuous, 177; of good will, 194; of almsgiving, 218; poor in, 254; contrite, 254; steadfast, 254; of humility, 261
spiritual, 13, 24, 33, 39, 54n., 72 and n., 83, 92n., 98, 103 and n., 151, 192n., 214, 244; fathers, 24, 39, 72 and n., 110, 128; teaching, 138; wisdom, 143; vines, 173; sacrifice, 178; fire, 182 and n.; wealth, 245; discourse, 246; gift, 246; rock, 272 and n.; stone, 272 and n.; drink, 272n.; weapon, 273 and n.; argument, 273n.; food, 281n.; blessings, 281n.; sowing, 286; seed, 286 and n.; beautify, 306
stand, 60n., 75, 101, 102, 105, 106 and n., 114, 117, 122, 129, 131 and, n., 132 and n., 133, 146, 156, 159, 162, 163, 206, 251, 253, 272, 278n., 279, 281, 284, 291, 293, 299; aloof, 179; nearby, 240 and n., 251, 257, 268
star, 80, 121n., 185, 186, 228, 274
steal, 168n., 179, 264, 265
Stein, L., 40n.
Stephenson, A.A., 192n.
sterile, 75, 77n., 257
sterility, 75, 78n.
Stoic, 8, 12
stone, 33, 96, 118, 189n., 193 and n., 259, 270, 272, 280n., 282; precious, 104n., 182, 228; sapphire, 107; spiritual, 272; heart of, 293; to death, 302
storm, 161, 186, 209, 271, 285, 291; calming of, 252n.
strength, 75, 81, 93, 104, 105, 111, 132, 135n., 138n., 159, 192, 252, 271, 272, 283, 294, 297; of soul, 291

strengthen, 172 and n.
strong, 76, 197n., 289, 294n.; God the, 143
Stuhlmueller, C., 74n., 78n., 81n., 130n., 171n., 172n., 175n., 178n., 186n.
sublime, 193, 195, 196, 198
sublimity, 198
subordinate, 9, 12, 278, and n., 279, 280n.
Subordinationism, 4n., 13, 278n.
substance, 3n., 8, 9, 10, 11, 16, 18, 19, 23, 24, 42, 85 and n., 148n., 187, 188, 189, 191, 197, 298n.; of Father, 8; one in, 28; of God, 13, 62n.; Word and Father same, 13; Three Persons are of same, 141n.
suffer, 10, 96n., 112, 135n., 165n., 180, 185, 192n., 202, 203n., 214n., 231, 258, 271n., 281, 291n., 292
suffering, 86, 88 and n., 162, 166, 214n., 228, 294
sun, 63, 112n., 144n., 170, 186n., 209, 228, 258, 295 and n.
Sun of Justice, 144n., 186 and n., 258 and n.
supernatural, 54n.; angel, 7
superior, 12, 69, 97n., 100, 106n., 123n., 148, 263, 268, 277n., 279, 302, 303
superiority, 104n., 110n., 146n., 150, 159, 277, 300n., 304
supper, 178n., 199, 201; Last, 175n., 189n., 199n., 234n., 250n.
supreme, 38; power, 112, 278; dominion, 305n.
suspect, 100, 198, 300
suspicion, 299n., 300
swaddling clothes, 176, 205
sword, 96, 212, 227; flaming, 239 and n.
symbol, 16, 186n., 231n., 239n., 256n., 289n.
synod, 14, 15, 20; of Antioch, 109n.

Tabernacle, 74n., 304n.
Tabernacles, feast of, 288n.
Tabitha, 89n., 238 and n.
table, 180, 181, 182, 249, 251; of altar, 177; sacred, 178; of instruction, 280 and n.
talent, 169, 219, 246n.

INDEX OF HOLY SCRIPTURE

(Books of the Old Testament)

CPSIA information can be obtained
at www.ICGtesting.com
Printed in the USA
BVHW080148090119
537376BV00001B/14/P

9 780813 210278